WORKS ISSUED BY
THE HAKLUYT SOCIETY

———

THE ICELAND JOURNAL OF
HENRY HOLLAND, 1810

SECOND SERIES
NO. 168

THE
ICELAND JOURNAL OF
HENRY HOLLAND
1810

EDITED BY
ANDREW WAWN

THE HAKLUYT SOCIETY
LONDON
1987

ISBN 0 904180 22 0
ISSN 0072–9396

Printed in Great Britain at the
University Press, Cambridge

Published by the Hakluyt Society
c/o The Map Library
British Library Reference Division
London WC1B 3DG

FOR KRIS

veiztu, ef þú vin átt,   þannz þú vel trúir,
farðu at finna opt;
þvíat hrísi vex   oc hávo grasi
vegr, er vætki trøðr.

(*Hávamál*, v.119)

CONTENTS

ILLUSTRATIONS AND MAPS

Henry Holland's field drawings and maps:

PREFACE

On 18 April 1810, Sir George Mackenzie (1780–1848), accompanied by a party of young Edinburgh scientists, set sail for Iceland, the first significant British expedition to travel to the island since the celebrated visit of John Thomas Stanley (1766–1850) in 1789. Amongst Sir George's companions were two young physicians, friends since their Bristol schooldays – Richard Bright (1789–1858), subsequently famed for his research into renal disease, and Henry Holland (1788–1873), who was later to make his professional name as a London society physician, numbering Queen Victoria amongst his eminent clientele. The principal object of this new enterprise was the field investigation of several of Iceland's most singular volcanic regions, in the hope of making observations which could contribute decisively to the increasingly controversial European mineralogical debate in the early nineteenth century. The party undertook three journeys within Iceland – to Gullbringusýsla, to the Snæfellsnes peninsula, and to Rangárvallasýsla. Throughout their stay, whether in Reykjavík or in the countryside, the explorers found that the investigation of eternal geological verities was not immune to the periodic intrusion of immediate political miseries, as the disastrous effects of the Napoleonic wars pressed in upon a vulnerable and isolated nation.

On their return to Britain in September 1810, two members of the expedition prepared a written record of their journey. Henry Holland produced a fair copy of the journal he had kept throughout his period in Iceland; whilst 1811 saw the publication of the first edition of *Travels in the Island of Iceland during the summer of the year 1810*, a volume bearing Sir George Mackenzie's name on the title-page, and the first book length treatment of Iceland to appear in English for nearly forty years. Mackenzie's book, and with it Mackenzie's name, came to enjoy, and still enjoys, a widespread celebrity amongst those with any interest in nineteenth century British responses to Iceland. By contrast, Holland's manuscript journal, and with it its author's association with Iceland, sank almost at once into near oblivion. Yet, as this edition of the journal seeks to suggest, without Henry Holland's manuscript, there may never have been any published volume on Iceland by Sir George Mackenzie. It can be shown that Sir George's book is massively, though clumsily, dependent on Holland's scrupulously prepared and long neglected text. The present edition of the manuscript is the first in English; the journal's only previous appearance in print was through Steindór Steindórsson's admirable Icelandic translation of much, though not all, of the text.

THE MANUSCRIPT

The journal survives in a neatly written manuscript, bound in two volumes (iv+135 pp. and 151 pp.), of quarto size (22.9×18.6 cm.), now owned by Landsbókasafn Íslands in Reykjavík (Lbs MSS 3875–6 4to), the gift of David Holland Esq., the great grandson of Sir Henry (as he later became). The entire first volume (its weather register apart) and pp. 1–99 of the second volume record the daily sequence of events, with narrative material on each right hand page, and authorial annotation, including maps and field sketches, on the facing left hand pages. The remainder of the second volume consists, firstly, of supplementary documents and analysis, material heavily drawn upon by the concluding sections of the two editions of Sir George Mackenzie's Iceland book; secondly, the end of the second volume has a scatter of blank pages (pp. 114–15, 119–27, 141–3, 145).

EDITORIAL POLICY

This edition includes all the manuscript's narrative material, all the annotation (marked HH to distinguish it from editorial annotation), all Holland's maps and sketches (marked in the text by superscript capital letters), and all the documentary material with the single exception of a brief section (II, pp. 100–11) of answers supplied in Latin by (perhaps) Bishop Geir Vídalín, to questions submitted relating to the legal and administrative structure and practices of Icelandic society in 1810. A digest of this material is provided by Holland in Mackenzie (1811, pp. 312–23), and contains little that is not addressed in the journal's main narrative and annotation.

Throughout the edition, Henry Holland's eccentricities and

inconsistencies of word division, of spelling of English and, in particular, of Icelandic words and names, and his uncertain and erratic command of Icelandic accentuation have been retained. So, for the most part, have his habits of punctuation. Words supplied editorially are marked by square brackets; all emendations to the text are footnoted; the principal contractions are silently expanded; occasional gaps in the text, left by Holland for subsequent completion, or the result of an errant memory or the unavailability of documents, are left blank.

ACKNOWLEDGEMENTS

I would like, firstly, to record my thanks to David Holland for his help and encouragement at various stages of my work on his distinguished ancestor. I am grateful to both Mr. Holland and to Landsbókasafn Íslands for permission to publish the text of the Holland Iceland journal; I am also grateful to the Council of the Viking Society for Northern Research for permission to incorporate in the Introduction to this edition material from my essay on Sir Henry Holland published in Saga-Book XXI (Parts 1–2) (1982–3). A number of factors have facilitated the preparation of this edition: firstly, a research grant from the British Academy; secondly, the good offices of librarians and archivists at many libraries and record offices – I would particularly mention the National Library of Scotland, the Bodleian Library, the British Museum of Natural History where David Moore was of the greatest assistance to me, the Brotherton Library at the University of Leeds, the excellence of whose Melsteð collection of Icelandic books has made sometimes difficult editorial work not only possible but pleasurable, and above all, Landsbókasafn Íslands, where I have been the grateful beneficiary of many kindnesses and courtesies from Grímur Helgason and his colleagues in the Handritadeild, and from Gísli Ragnarsson; thirdly, the capacity of Lena Covermacker expertly to decipher and type the frequently indecipherable and untypable; fourthly, the practical help of academic colleagues – Dr. Anthony Faulkes and Dr. Ben Benedikz of Birmingham University; Miss Barbara Raw and Dr. Hugh Torrens of Keele University; Dr. Jim Binns of York University; Professor Vincent di Marco of the University of Massachusetts; Professor Geoffrey Arnott, Professor Gordon Leedale, Professor Derek Wood, Dr. Peter Dowd, Mr. Ken Rowe and Dr. David Fairer of Leeds University and Mrs. Elsie Duncan-Jones of Cambridge, whose characteristically learned and generous intervention at the eleventh hour unravelled one especially intractable textual crux. I owe a particular debt to Professor Tom Shippey and Dr. Rory McTurk, my colleagues in the School of English at the University of Leeds, whose sceptical gaze and energetic commitment to Icelandic studies have created a most stimulating atmosphere in which to pursue Sir Henry Holland around Iceland.

One further academic indebtedness deserves particular prominence. Any English editor working on Henry Holland and Iceland soon learns to tread gratefully in the magisterial footsteps of Steindór Steindórsson whose Icelandic translation of much of the Holland journal reveals a remarkable sensitivity to the artful complexities and eccentricities of the language of Jane Austen's England, along with, it need scarcely be added, an unsurpassed knowledge of the regions through which the Britons trekked. It is a happy chance that the dedicatee of this edition is one of Steindór's former students at Menntaskólinn á Akureyri.

Throughout Henry Holland's Icelandic travels in 1810, he was the grateful and often humbled recipient of the endless good food, good fellowship and good humour of his frequently baffled and bewildered Icelandic hosts and friends. His modern editor can confirm that Icelandic hospitality has changed little over the intervening two centuries. For many clearly remembered acts of kindness, I would particularly like to thank Dr. Guðmundur Stefánsson and Sigríður Guðmundsdóttir and their parents; Jóhannes Sigurðsson and Soffía Kristjánsdóttir and their family; Heimir Bergsson; and Vilborg Kristjánsdóttir, a wonderfully tolerant hostess over several years.

Henry Holland's principal Icelandic philosopher, guide and adviser was the deplorable Ólafur Loptsson: I have been a great deal luckier. Of the dedicatee of this volume, Kristján Pálmar Arnarsson, I would like simply to say that without his help and that of his family, it is doubtful whether this edition could have been started; it is certain that it would not have been completed. From Staffordshire to Stóra-Laxá, from the Hawthorns to Hótel Saga, from the Sneyd Arms to Snæfellsnes, he has remained the most loyal and generous of friends.

ANDREW WAWN

Leeds and Reykjavík
September 1986

ABBREVIATIONS

ÁHÍF	Árbók Hins íslenska fornleifafélags
BJHS	British Journal of the History of Science
BL	British Library
FÍÁ	Ferðafélags Íslands: Árbók
HH	Henry Holland
JRL	John Rylands Library, Manchester
Lbs	Landsbókasafn Íslands, Reykjavík
Linn.	Linnæus
ME	Letters from Henry Holland to Maria Edgeworth, in the possession of David Holland Esq.
MÍ	Manntal á Íslandi (Icelandic census returns)
Mod.Ice.	Modern Icelandic
MS, MSS	Manuscript, manuscripts
NLS	National Library of Scotland
NLS 7515	National Library of Scotland, MS Accession 7515
Suð	Suðuramt (Southern area of census returns)
TRSE	Transactions of the Royal Society of Edinburgh
Vest.	Vesturamt (Western area of census returns)

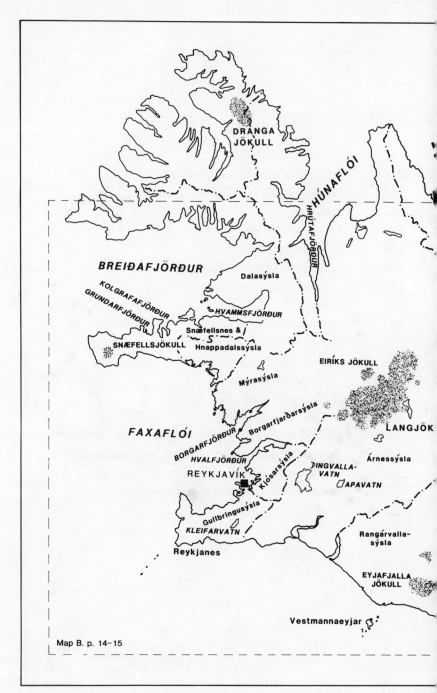

Map B. p. 14–15

Map

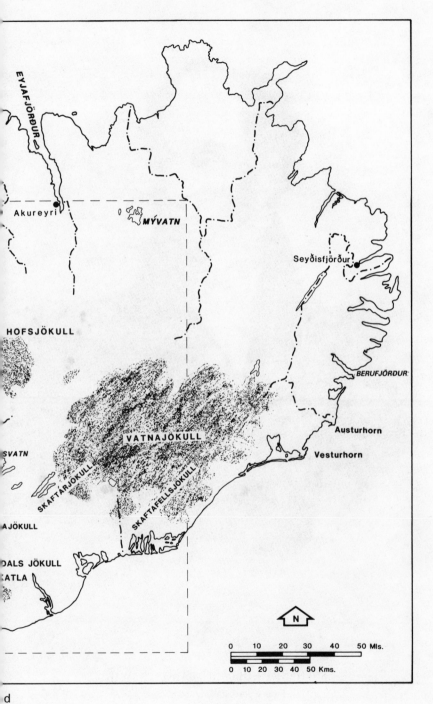

EYJAFJÖRDUR

Akureyri

MÝVATN

Seyðisfjörður

HOFSJÖKULL

BERUFJÖRDUR

SVATN

VATNAJÖKULL

Austurhorn

Vesturhorn

SKAFTÁRJÖKULL

SKAFTAFELLSJÖKULL

AJÖKULL

DALS JÖKULL

KATLA

N

0	10	20	30	40	50 Mls.

0	10	20	30	40	50 Kms.

d

SIR HENRY HOLLAND, BARONET, M.D.

From a portrait made about 1840

INTRODUCTION

On a stormy August day in 1871, two of Victorian England's most celebrated Icelandophiles met, probably for the first and almost certainly for the last time, in a small house in the middle of, appropriately, Reykjavík.[1] Their hostess for the evening was María Einarsdóttir, sister-in-law of the Icelandic bibliophile Eiríkur Magnússon, and the two travellers were William Morris, literary collaborator and friend of Eiríkur, and Sir Henry Holland (1788–1873), by then best known as physician to Queen Victoria, tireless world traveller and cousin of Mrs. Elizabeth Gaskell, the novelist.[2] Morris, accompanied by Eiríkur, was near the end of a six-week visit, his first, to the 'grey minster of lands'[3] whose hold over his increasingly harassed spirit had become profound, and whose saga literature had fascinated him since his days as a student in Oxford.[4] Eiríkur Magnússon and he had, by 1871, produced translations of several saga narratives, and the 1871 expedition at last enabled Morris to go 'as pilgrim to the holy places of Iceland'[5]; that is, to the fells and farms associated with such sagas. Indeed on August 22, when Sir Henry Holland's ship berthed at Reykjavík, Morris himself was trekking up the fertile valley of the Hvítá in Borgarfjarðarsýsla in search of Gilsbakki,[6] the homestead at the heart of *Gunnlaugs saga ormstungu*, a

[1] William Morris, *Journals of travel in Iceland 1871, 1873* (London, 1911), p. 178: Vol. 8 in *The collected works of William Morris*, 24 vols. (London, 1910–15).

[2] The fullest published discussion of Holland's life is autobiographical: Henry Holland, *Recollections of past life* (London, 1872); its contents are summarised briefly in Brian Hill, '"More fashionable than scientific": Sir Henry Holland Bt., M.D., F.R.C.P., F.R.S.', *The Practitioner*, CCXL (1973), 548–54. There is an urbane and amusing obituary in *The Times*, 31 October 1873.

[3] William Morris, *Poems by the way* (London, [1891]), p. 109, 'Gunnar's howe above the house at Lithend', l.2.

[4] Richard L. Harris, 'William Morris, Eiríkur Magnússon and Iceland: a survey of correspondence', *Victorian Poetry*, 13 (1975), 119–30; Roderick Marshall, *William Morris and his earthly paradise* (London, 1979), pp. 168–96.

[5] Morris, 1911, p. 67.   [6] Morris, 1911, pp. 157–9.

translation of which he and Eiríkur had published in the *Fortnightly Review* in January 1869.

Whether, as Morris claims in his Icelandic journal, it was because of an exhaustion induced by extended exposure to

> the sight of this desolate strand
> And the mountain-waste voiceless as death
> but for winds that may sleep not nor tire[1]

or whether, equally likely, it was because of the apparent absence of any reciprocal visionary gleam in Sir Henry Holland's venerable and urbane countenance, the meeting seems not to have proved an especially joyous one. Morris's journal records the confrontation:

to Mrs Maria's house again, where was dinner, and the courtly old carle, Sir Henry Holland, whose age (eighty-four) I thought was the most interesting thing about him. I was rather low, after all, and cowed by the company, and a sense of stiffness after our joyous rough life just ended. So to bed.[2]

Morris's saddle-sore insensitivity towards the 'courtly old carle' from Britain seems less surprising in the context of the account, also recorded in his 1871 journal, of a visit to the great Geysir in Haukadalur, some weeks before. Morris makes no attempt to hide his impatience and disgust at the 'stinking steam' of the 'beastly place':

'Let's go home to Haukadal, quoth I, 'we can't camp in this beastly place.'
'What is he saying,' said Eyvindr to Gisli [the guides]:
'Why, I'm not going to camp here,' said I:
'You must,' said Eyvindr, 'all Englishmen do.'
'Blast all Englishmen!,' said I in the Icelandic tongue.[3]

Beneath the discomforts of the moment, this scene, and indeed the subsequent uncomfortable meeting in Reykjavík, hints at a significant contrast of sympathies between two generations of British Icelando-philes. Whilst Morris was repelled by hot springs, but stirred by the romantic wildness of saga with its haunting echoes of his personal agonies, 'all Englishmen' of an earlier generation, motivated by the more forensic severities of experimental science, had made straight for Geysir, then regarded as one of the wonders of the world, and had been relatively little touched by Iceland's great literary past. The most prominent figures of this earlier generation had been Sir Joseph Banks

---

[1] 'Iceland first seen', 11.18–20 in Morris [1891], p. 40.
[2] Morris, 1911, p. 178.   [3] Morris, 1911, pp. 67–8.

(1743–1820),[1] John Thomas Stanley of Alderley (1766–1850),[2] and Sir George Mackenzie (1780–1848).[3]

The young Henry Holland was in a sense a transitional figure, for whilst it was unquestionably science, medical and mineralogical, which had first drawn him to Iceland, he was also, through his authorship of the learned 'Dissertation on the history of Iceland' which prefaced Sir George Mackenzie's *Travels in the island of Iceland during the summer of the year 1810* (Edinburgh, 1811),[4] responsible for what is arguably the best informed and most influential analytic discussion of Icelandic literary culture written in Britain in the early nineteenth century. It is a bizarre irony, therefore, that it should have been Holland of all the early enthusiasts for Iceland, who was exposed to the loftiness of Morris's fractious disdain, for it was Holland's Dissertation which had helped to promote and develop interest in some of the great saga texts, not least *Gunnlaugs saga ormstungu*, which were later so to intoxicate Morris. Henry Holland's was a major contribution to British understanding of and engagement with Icelandic life and letters over the period ranging back from his 1871 meeting with Morris to his membership of Sir George Mackenzie's notable expedition to Iceland, an extraordinary sixty-one years earlier.

The full extent of this contribution has not, however, generally been recognised. The widely circulated published account of the 1810 expedition has always been popularly associated with Sir George Mackenzie alone, not least because the title-page bears his name alone. In fact, quite apart from the lengthy Dissertation, and the several further sections identified in the table of contents as the work of 'Dr. Holland' – 'Present state of education and literature' (Mackenzie, 1811, pp. 285–311), 'On the government, laws and religion' (pp. 312–33), 'On the diseases of Icelanders' (pp. 405–16), and a miscellaneous

---

[1] The earliest published account of observations from Sir Joseph Banks's 1772 visit to Iceland is Uno von Troil, *Bref rörande en rese til Island MDCCLXXII* (Uppsala, 1777); English translation, *Letters on Iceland* (Dublin, 1780); see also Roy Rauschenberg, 'The journals of Sir Joseph Banks's voyage up Great Britain's west coast to Iceland and to the Orkney Isles, July to October, 1772', *Proceedings of the American Philosophical Society*, CXVII (1973), 186–226; and Halldór Hermannsson, *Sir Joseph Banks and Iceland, Islandica* XVIII (1928).

[2] See Andrew Wawn, 'John Thomas Stanley and Iceland: the sense and sensibility of an eighteenth-century explorer', *Scandinavian Studies* 53 (1981), 52–76; John F. West (ed.) *The journals of the Stanley expedition to the Faroe islands and Iceland in 1789*, 3 vols. (Tórshavn, 1970–6).

[3] Andrew Wawn, '*Gunnlaugs saga ormstungu* and the Theatre Royal Edinburgh: melodrama, mineralogy and Sir George Mackenzie', *Scandinavica* 21 (1982), 139–51.

[4] A revised second edition was published in 1812.

section[1] – Mackenzie's three central narratives of the principal journeys undertaken within Iceland by the British travellers were each massively though erratically dependent on an unpublished manuscript journal[2] which Henry Holland had kept devotedly through the summer of 1810. Detailed comparison of this journal with Sir George Mackenzie's narratives certainly highlights this slavish dependence, but also reveals sharp differences of descriptive priority and temperament between the young Cestrian medical student and his Scottish baronial leader. It was indeed the differences rather than the dependence which, as 'Mackenzie's *Iceland*' took its uncertain shape, were a source of grievous exasperation and indignation to the scrupulous Holland. Published now for the first time in its original English version, the extant fair copy of Holland's journal represents the account of the 1810 Iceland expedition which could and, Holland might be forgiven for having thought, should have been published on their return from the North.

BRITAIN AND ICELAND: CONTACTS AND CONTEXTS 1400–1800

The eighteenth-century Britain into which Henry Holland was born in 1788 offers significant witness to the powerful imaginative hold which matters relating to Iceland had come to exercise on many an educated and impressionable British consciousness. There had long been commercial interest in Iceland.[3] The Elizabethan lyricist Thomas Weelkes could speak in bookish awe of distant Thule as the 'period of cosmographie',[4] whilst earlier in the century, a distracted Henry VIII, his mind soon to be absorbed as much with marriage as with mercantilism, could choose to ignore such benefits as might have accrued to England from accommodating the Danish king's desire to place

---

[1] Mackenzie, 1811, pp. 457–68. First identified as Holland's work in the 1812 edition. The section includes material on berserks, prayers for times of volcanic eruptions, the structure of Icelandic verse, sections from Finnur Magnússon's poem on the 1809 events in Reykjavík, lines from Jón Þorláksson's *Essay on Man* translation, a list of publications from the Leirárgarðar press, a note on the Icelandic alphabet and numerals, a short glossary of common Icelandic words, and a letter from Rasmus Frydensberg, the *landfógeti*, to Sir George Mackenzie.

[2] Lbs MSS 3875–6 4to. For previous discussion of the journal, see Steindór Steindórsson, *Dagbók í Íslandsferð eftir Henry Holland* (Reykjavík, 1960), pp. 9–22; and Ian Grimble, 'Holland's Iceland journal', *The Norseman*, IX (1951), 163–71.

[3] See E. M. Carus-Wilson, *Medieval merchant venturers* (London, 1954; second edition, 1967), pp. 98–142; also Björn Þorsteinsson, *Enska öldin í sögu Íslendinga* (Reykjavík, 1970).

[4] E. H. Fallowes, F. W. Sternfield and David Greer (eds.), *English madrigal verse 1588–1632* (Oxford, 1920; revised third edition, 1967), p. 293, VII–VIII, l.1.

Iceland in pawn,[1] as if to confirm the tartly dismissive medieval judgement that 'Of Yseland to wryte is lytill nede / Save of stokfische'.[2] Yet those same fish had for centuries ensured that 'Out of Bristowe and costis many one/ Men have practised by nedle and by stone / Thiderwardes' to Iceland,[3] in order to harvest the teeming coastal waters of an island whose two episcopal sees, at Hólar and Skálholt, were occupied for periods during the early fifteenth-century by English clerics.[4] These priests were no doubt aware of, if not particularly enamoured with, the proximity of their northern cures of soul to Mount Hekla, the *mons perpetuo ardens* of sixteenth-century cartographers,[5] which, if it fell short of Weelkes's claim that its 'sulphurious fire /Doth melt the frozen clime and thaw the sky' (ll.2–3), did indeed frequently vomit forth terrifying streams of molten lava from vast cavities, then widely believed to be the earthly portals to the infernal regions of the *perpetuis damnata*.[6]

Succeeding generations of British ecclesiastics and scholars started to correspond with learned Icelanders, whose works began to appear in English translation, and hence to serve as timely correctives to popular Elizabethan cartoon-like images of the Icelanders as 'beastly creatures, unmanered and untaughte',[7] living in a 'dull, Lenten, Northren clyme', nearly poisoned by 'sulphureous stinking smoak', with lakes capable of turning men into marble, and of freezing birds to death; 'one of the chiefe kingdomes of the night', containing only 'stock-fish, whetstones, and cods-heads'; a land in which the natives' only solace was frozen ale 'that they carry in their pockets lyke glue, and ever when they would drinke, they set it on the fire and melt it',[8] like some prototypical 'drink on a stick'.

[1] Björn Þorsteinsson, 'Henry VIII and Iceland', *Saga-Book of the Viking Society*, XV (1957–61), 67–101, especially 75–80.

[2] *Libelle of Englyshe polycyce* [1436], ed. Sir G. Warner (Oxford, 1926), p. 41, ll.798–9.

[3] *Libelle*, ll.802–4.

[4] Björn Þorsteinsson, 1970, pp. 136–54 discusses the career of John Craxton, who served at both Hólar and Skálholt.

[5] Hekla as described on the Iceland map in Gerald Mercator, *Atlas sive cosmographicæ meditationes de fabrica mundi et fabricati figura* (Duisburg, 1595), reproduced in Haraldur Sigurðsson, *Kortasaga Íslands*, 2 vols., (Reykjavík, 1971–8), I, facing p. 24.

[6] A phrase from the description of Hekla in Abraham Ortelius's map of Iceland in *Additantum IV: Theatri orbis terrarum* (Antwerp, 1590); reproduced in Haraldur Sigurðsson, 1971–8, II, p. 15, and facing p. 16.

[7] Andrew Boorde, *The fyrst boke of the introduction* (1542), ed. F. J. Furnivall, *Early English Text Society*, Extra series 10 (1870), p. 141; more generally, see Ethel Seaton, *Literary relations of England and Scandinavia in the seventeenth century* (Oxford, 1935), pp. 5–56.

[8] All phrases from *The terrors of the night* (1594), in *The works of Thomas Nashe*, ed. Ronald B. McKerrow (revised F. P. Wilson), 5 vols. (London, 1904–10; revised edition, Oxford, 1958), I, 360.

To counter such 'vain phantasies', Arngrímur Jónsson's *A briefe commentarie on Island*[1] reveals its intentions in its sub-title:

wherin the errors of such as have written concerning this Island, are detected, and the slanders, and reproches of certaine strangers, which they have used over-boldly against the people of *Island*, are confuted. (p. 550)

The British reader is reassured that whoredom *is* considered a sin in Iceland (pp. 585–6), that guests at a feast do not 'wash their hands and their faces in pisse' (p. 586), and that, more apocalyptically, Iceland suffers little from ice 'making a miserable kind of mone' round its shores (pp. 562–3), and in so far as such a feature is to be encountered, the groaning is not that of lost souls being dragged into Hell through nearby Hekla; moreover, the heat of Hekla is comfortingly identified as volcanic rather than diabolic (pp. 559–61). A similar disdain for 'fables more trifling than old wives tales' (p. 552) was also to inform a parallel work of demystification offered to eighteenth-century readers in Britain: *The natural history of Iceland* (London, 1758), a truncated English version of Niels Horrebow's refutation[2] of an earlier 'crude, indigested'[3] treatise on Iceland, written by Johann Anderson,[4] a credulous Hamburg burgomaster, largely on the basis of ill-informed quay-side gossip garnered from sailors. Dr. Samuel Johnson was amongst the taciturn Horrebow's keen readers, delighting to boast that he could repeat the book's seventy-second chapter by heart, a feat of memory not unduly daunting, it transpired, for the entire content of the chapter reads 'There are no snakes to be met with throughout the whole island'.[5]

The demystification process to which Arngrímur Jónsson and Horrebow contributed in print, was further augmented by the ready co-operation of Icelandic scholars, especially those to be found visiting Britain, who patiently furnished replies to the detailed and systematic enquiries about the 'natural philosophy' of their land which the founding of the Royal Society in 1662 had helped to instigate and

[1] Arngrímur Jónsson, *Brevis commentarius de Islandia* (1593), in Richard Hakluyt, *The principal navigations, voiages, traffiques and discoveries of the English nation*, 3 vols. (London, 1598–1600), I, 515–50 (Latin text); I, 550–91 (English translation).

[2] Niels Horrebow, *Tilforladelige efterretninger om Island* ([Copenhagen], 1752).

[3] Niels Horrebow, *The natural history of Iceland* (London, 1758), p. iv.

[4] Johann Anderson, *Nachrichten von Island, Grönland, und der Strasse Davis* (Hamburg, 1746).

[5] G. B. Hill and L. F. Powell (eds.), *Boswell's Life of Johnson*, 6 vols. (Oxford, 1934), III, 279.

coordinate.[1] As, in turn, philologists such as Francis Junius,[2] Thomas Marshall[3] and, crucially, George Hickes (1642–1715)[4] came to address the study of the Icelandic language and its early runic orthography, the texts cited (often from newly available and scholarly European editions),[5] played a seminal part in establishing the increasingly familiar image of the bloodstained, vengeful, death-scorning Viking, long on heroic virtue and short on fuse. A crucial misunderstanding of a single complex Icelandic poetic expression could contribute quite disproportionately to this habitual process of distortion, as when the notion that Vikings drank wine from the skulls of their slain enemies proved to be based on a Latin mistranslation by Magnús Ólafson of the Icelandic kenning *ór bjúgviðum hausa* 'from the curved branches of skulls', that is, from drinking horns made from antlers.[6]

This picture of the Viking, whether newly distilled and defined in English by Sir William Temple's essay 'Of heroick virtue' (published in 1690),[7] or exhaustively documented in Latin by Ole

---

[1] See Sir Thomas Browne, 'An account of Island, alias Ice-land in the yeare 1662', in Sir Thomas Browne, *Works*, ed. Geoffrey Keynes (London, 1928–31; revised edition, 4 vols., 1964), III, 345–6. The work, dated 15 January 1663, declares itself prepared for 'the noble Societie' (the Royal Society) and represents a digest of information supplied to Browne by Theodore Jónsson, a pastor in Hítardalur in Iceland, 'who comes Yearly into England' and 'is readie to performe for mee what I shall desire in his Country'.

[2] Two manuscripts exemplify his Icelandic interests: Bodléian MS Junius 36, a long extract from Runólfur Jónsson's *Grammaticæ Islandicæ rudimenta* (Copenhagen, 1651); and Bodleian MS Junius 120, a copied text of Guðmundur Andrésson's *Lexicon Islandicum* (Copenhagen, 1683).

[3] See, for example, Bodleian MS Marshall 80, a commonplace book containing a table of runic letters, and Danish, Swedish and Icelandic literary extracts. See also Paul Morgan, 'Bundið fyrir Íslending: Guðbrandsbiblía í Hafnarbandi', *Landsbókasafn Íslands: Árbók* (1974), 113–17.

[4] George Hickes, *Linguarum veterum septentrionalium thesaurus grammatico-criticus et archæologicus* 2 vols. (Oxford, 1703–5); popularised through [Maurice Shelton, trans.] *Wotton's short view of G. Hickes's grammatico-critical and archæological treasure of the ancient northern languages* (London, 1735), a translation of William Wotton's 1708 Latin digest of the Hickes *Thesaurus*. On Hickes, see J. A. W. Bennett, 'Hickes's *Thesaurus*: a study in Oxford book-production', *English Studies*, New Series 1 (1948), 28–45; also Richard L. Harris, 'George Hickes, White Kennett, and the inception of the *Thesaurus linguarum septentrionalium*', *Bodleian Library Record*, XI (1983), 169–86, and David Fairer, 'Anglo-Saxon studies', in *The History of the University of Oxford* – Vol. 5 *The Eighteenth Century*, ed. L. S. Sutherland and L. G. Mitchell (Oxford, 1986), pp. 807–29.

[5] Particularly influential in Britain were Olaus Verelius (ed.), *Hervarer saga* (Uppsala, 1672) and Peder Resen (Resenius) (ed.), *Edda Islandorum* (Copenhagen, 1665).

[6] Conveniently discussed by E. V. Gordon, *An Introduction to Old Norse* (Oxford 1927; revised edition, 1957), pp. lxix–lxx.

[7] William Temple, 'Of heroick virtue' in *Miscellanea: the second part* (London, 1690), Essay 3: 'such an alacrity or pleasure in dying was never expressed in any other Writing, nor imagined among any other People' (p. 93).

Worm[1] and Thomas Bartholin[2] amongst others, washed over into the eighteenth century there to be picked up by an age increasingly prepared to regard the ancient Northern world as an appropriate source of 'rational amusement'.[3] 'The waking of Angantýr', the poem which marks a climactic moment in *Hervarar saga*[4] illustrates this process clearly enough. It dramatises an eery confrontation between Hervor, an implacably defiant daughter, and her long deceased father Angantýr, in which the dead warrior reluctantly agrees to yield up from the tomb the fateful sword Tyrfing, distraught in the knowledge that many deaths within her family will result. First known in Britain through Verelius's 1672 edition of the saga, the poem was quoted in full by Hickes in his *Thesaurus*,[5] and furnished with an English translation, the first complete Old Norse poem to be thus provided. This English version soon reached a wider audience through its inclusion in John Dryden's sixth poetic *Miscellany* (1716),[6] and circulating in these ways, the poem was inevitably one of those selected for inclusion in Bishop Thomas Percy's *Five pieces of runic poetry* (London, 1763).[7] This small collection, Percy having been prevented from including five further pieces which survive amongst his manuscripts, effectively established the canon of Old Norse texts (each one presented in a new English prose translation with Latin and Icelandic texts included as appendices) from which, particularly after the publication of Thomas Gray's 'The fatal sisters' and 'The descent of Odin' in 1768,[8] an enthusiastic though less accomplished group of poets was able to choose items on which to focus their sometimes crude but always committed efforts at adaptation, paraphrase and modernisation. With 'The waking of Angantýr', these

[1] Ole Worm, *Antiquitates Danicæ* (Copenhagen, 1651) incorporating amongst other works his influential *Literatura runica* (1636).

[2] Thomas Bartholinus, *Antiquitatem Danicarum de causis contemptæ a Danis adhuc gentilibus mortis* (Copenhagen, 1689).

[3] [John Campbell], *The polite correspondence, or rational amusement* ([1741]; revised edition, 1754), a series of letters exchanged between 'Phaon', 'Celadon' and 'Leander', reflecting considerable knowledge of and enthusiasm for ancient English and Scandinavian literature. See Alan D. McKillop, 'A critic of 1741 on early poetry', *Studies in Philology*, 30 (1933), 504–21.

[4] The poem and the saga became known in Britain through Olaus Verelius's 1672 text.

[5] Hickes, 1703–5, Part 1, pp. 193–5.

[6] John Dryden and Jacob Tonson (eds.), *The sixth part of poetical miscellanies*, 6 vols. (London, 1716), VI, 387–91.

[7] I hope to discuss the genesis of Thomas Percy's volume in a forthcoming article.

[8] *Poems by Mr. Gray* (London, 1768). The poems were written no later than May 1761: see Roger Lonsdale (ed.) *The poems of Gray, Collins and Goldsmith* (London, 1969), pp. 210–12.

efforts are constantly in evidence. William Bagshaw Stevens, whilst still a student at Magdalen College in Oxford, included in his *Poems, consisting of Indian odes and miscellaneous pieces* (Oxford, 1775) a piece entitled 'Hervor and Angantyr. An Ode, Imitated from an antient scald, author of a book intitled Hervarer Saga, Published by Olaus Verelius';[1] T. J. Mathias's *Runic odes imitated from the Norse tongue in the manner of Mr. Gray* (London, 1781) offers a 'Dialogue at the Tomb of Argantyr [sic]',[2] with new editions appearing in 1790, 1798 and 1806, the latter published in New York; 1790 also saw the publication in Britain of 'The Hervarer Saga, a Gothic Ode, From the Septentrionalium Thesaurus of Dr Hickes', attributed to one W. Williams of Pembroke in the September issue of the *Gentleman's Magazine*;[3] two years later Richard Polwhele's collection *Poems, chiefly by Gentlemen of Devonshire and Cornwall* (Bath, 1792) finds the poem bearing yet another title as 'The Incantation of Herva', with a footnoted acknowledgement to Thomas Percy's *Five pieces of runic poetry*;[4] eventually Hervor's track came very close to Henry Holland through Anna Seward, the 'Swan of Lichfield' and friend of John Thomas Stanley, who wrote around 1788–9 and published in 1796 'Herva, at the tomb of Argantyr: a Runic dialogue',[5] with George Hickes's translation appended for comparison.

The extent of interest in anything and everything 'from the Icelandic' at the time of Henry Holland's birth, on 27 October 1788, can be strikingly charted. A two year period from his birthday saw the publication of 'The message of Skirner', of 'A song of Hymir' and of 'The descent of Odin' (paraphrastic versions of Eddic poems) in the November and December 1788 issues of the *Analytical Review*;[6] of Richard Hole's *The tomb of Gunnar* in the October 1789 *Gentleman's Magazine*;[7] the re-publication of Joseph Sterling's *Odes from the Icelandic*,

---

[1] See Georgina Galbraith (ed.), *Collected poems of the Reverend William Bagshaw Stevens* (London, 1971), pp. 93–7; discussed briefly in Georgina Galbraith (ed.) *The journal of the Rev. William Bagshaw Stevens* (Oxford, 1965), pp. 67–8.

[2] See Frank E. Farley, *Scandinavian influences in the English romantic movement* (Cambridge, Mass., 1903), p. 50, note 1. Mathias, 1781, p. 2 cites Bartholinus, 1689, and Percy's *Northern antiquities*, 1770, as sources for the four Norse-associated odes in the collection.

[3] *Gentleman's Magazine*, LX, 1790, 844.

[4] Farley, 1903, p. 52.

[5] Anna Seward, *Poetical works*, ed. Sir Walter Scott, 3 vols. (Edinburgh, 1810), III, 90–103.

[6] Farley, 1903, pp. 108–9. These poems reappeared in the wake of the 1787 Copenhagen *Edda* first volume.

[7] *Gentleman's Magazine*, LIX (1789), 937.

first printed in Dublin in 1782;[1] the first appearance of Frank Sayers' ambitious *Dramatic sketches of Northern mythology* (Norwich, 1790); the composition of Anna Seward's 'Harold's complaint' (not published until 1810);[2] and there was, of course, in the background her friend John Thomas Stanley's major expedition to Iceland in the summer of 1789.

The quality of many of these pieces was dismal. The eddic voice often seduced but rarely inspired its British imitators. Verse after verse is awash with shields, spears and wounds drenched (or sometimes anointed) with blood, and with jet black ravens wading up to their beaks through the gore of the slain.[3] The poetic price to be paid in the pursuit of 'a species of savage greatness, a fierce and wild kind of sublimity, and a noble contempt of danger and death'[4] was a substantial one. Nevertheless, there were many whose enthusiasm for northern antiquity in its rediscovered form could accommodate a less than accomplished manner in the service of an ideologically bracing cause. There had grown up during the late eighteenth century a widely perceived Whiggish association between the Norsemen and the early cultivation of European liberty. Prefatory matter to Joseph Sterling's 1782 Icelandic Odes makes the point clearly:

To them we are indebted for laying the foundation of that liberty which we now enjoy: they were the heroes who broke the splendid shackles with which domineering Rome had fettered mankind for so many ages.[5]

Iceland, of all the countries of Europe, had been least shackled and fettered by tyranny:

liberty and peace, with learning and the arts in their train, took refuge in this inhospitable clime; and found on the confines of the polar circle, an asylum which the plains of France or Italy could not have afforded them.[6]

---

[1] Joseph Sterling, *Poems* (Dublin, 1782). The two poems are 'The Scalder: an ode' (1782 edition, pp. 36–41), and 'The twilight of the gods: An ode' (pp. 42–6).

[2] *Works*, ed. Scott, 1810, pp. 29–33.

[3] See, for example, *Poems by Hugh Downman M.D.* (Second edition, Exeter, 1790), pp. 148, 151. On other poets in this group, and on eighteenth-century interest in Scandinavian literary material, see Farley, 1903, and Margaret Omberg, *Scandinavian themes in English poetry* (Uppsala, 1976).

[4] Downman, 1790, pp. 145–6.

[5] Sterling, 1782, p. 31. On the Whig-Gothic connection, see Samuel Kliger, 'The "Goths" in England: an introduction to the Gothic vogue in eighteenth-century aesthetic discourse', *Modern Philology*, 43 (1945), 107–17; also John L. Greenway, *The golden horns: mythic imagination and the Nordic past* (Athens, Georgia, 1977), pp. 83–98.

[6] Anonymous review of Mackenzie, 1811 in *Edinburgh Review*, 19 (1811–12), 416.

Thus the world into which Henry Holland was born already recognised Iceland as a source of legitimate fascination, whether through the scholarly study of Northern antiquity, or through the translations and original compositions of contemporary poets, or through the indefaatigable eighteenth-century traveller's hunger for geographic novelty, or through the genteel cultivation of armchair primitivism, or through the pull of the emergent science of mineralogy, or through the island's potential for commercial exploitation.[1]

THE GENESIS OF AN ICELANDOPHILE: HENRY HOLLAND 1788–1810

Henry Holland was born at Knutsford, in the south-east of Cheshire, in 1788, and so, indirectly, was his interest in Iceland. More than one Cestrian had shown an active interest in Iceland towards the end of the eighteenth century. Thomas Falconer (1736–92), the Recorder of Chester, had corresponded enthusiastically with Sir Joseph Banks about the possibility of a further expedition there: 'the truth is I revolved in my mind very frequently the topic of a Northern Voyage, but alas to very little purpose'.[2] Though this projected enterprise came to nothing, Falconer's curiosity about volcanoes and hot springs continued, nourished no doubt by Banks's full and informative letters about his experiences in the North: 'The periodical rising of steam at Geiser hath so puzzled my little philosophy that after several attempts I have given up the point & shall wait impatiently for your further answer'.[3] Falconer lived long enough to read the learned and influential scientific papers from the Banks voyage, which were published in English translation in 1780,[4] and then to learn of the visit to and analysis of the hot springs at Geysir by another Cestrian, John Thomas Stanley from Alderley Edge, a neighbour of the Holland family. In 1789 the young Stanley undertook a brief but remarkable voyage to Iceland, chiefly in order to examine the hot springs at Reykir and Haukadalur. Though he published only two scientific papers relating to those phenomena,[5] in

[1] As, for example, John Thomas Stanley's interest in kelp: letter to Grímur Thorkelín, 28 May 1790 (Sorøe Akademis Bibliotek).
[2] Banks correspondence, Royal Botanical Gardens, Kew, I, 35.
[3] Banks correspondence, Kew, I, 34; see also Warren R. Dawson, *The Banks letters: a calendar of the manuscript correspondence of Sir Joseph Banks* (London, 1958), pp. 318–19.
[4] von Troil, 1780.
[5] 'An account of the hot springs near Rykum in Iceland' and 'An account of the hot springs near Haukadal in Iceland', *Transactions of the Royal Society of Edinburgh*, 3 (1794), 127–37, 138–53.

spite of the persistent urgings of his friends to do more and sooner, Stanley's was a lifetime's absorption. He maintained to the end of his long life an unobtrusive, practical and supportive interest in the voyagings of others,[1] as well as a persistent inclination to annotate and reflect upon material in the unpublished (during his lifetime) journals written by his colleagues during their 1789 Iceland venture.[2]

It is likely that Stanley, already a friend of Dr. Peter Holland, Henry's father, soon took an interest in the doctor's young son. Certainly it was eventually through Stanley's influence[3] that Henry was invited to prepare an important commissioned report on the agriculture of Cheshire for the Board of Agriculture, which was published in 1808.[4] The extraordinarily accomplished way in which Holland discharged this taxing assignment before his twentieth birthday unquestionably played its part in helping to establish for him a limited but discernible national reputation, which was to serve him well in easing him into intellectual and society circles in Edinburgh, after his arrival there to commence his medical studies in October 1806. Henry Holland had previously investigated the possibility of a commercial career, working for two summers as an articled clerk in the hectic mercantile atmosphere of Liverpool, across the Mersey from Stanley's favourite seaside retreat at Hoylake: Holland spent the intervening couple of winters as a private student at Glasgow University, supported by his employers.[5] The risks and pressures of merchant adventuring proved more akin to aversion therapy than to profitable stimulation for Holland; medical studies in Edinburgh came to seem an altogether more fulfilling and less worrisome prospect. He discovered no reason to regret the decision to return to Scotland as a student, and it was as a young scholar of significant achievement and greater promise that he was approached by Sir George Mackenzie[6] as a potential member of his forthcoming Icelandic expedition. Holland's 1810 journal makes frequent reference to his Cestrian mentor Stanley, both to his observations from 1789, and to the affection with which he was still regarded by Icelanders who recalled their meetings with him over thirty years earlier.[7] Moreover, Holland, in preparing the journal, certainly had access, no doubt at

[1] See Lbs MS 604 fol., a letter written forty-five years after his own expedition, to help the 1834 explorer John Barrow.

[2] Wawn, 1981, pp. 69–71. [3] Holland, 1872, p. 21.

[4] General view of the agriculture of Cheshire (London, 1808).

[5] Holland, 1872, pp. 16–17. [6] Mackenzie, 1811, p. xiii.

[7] See below, pp. 91, 135, 245.

Stanley's bidding, to diaries and sketchbooks from the 1789 voyage; two journal entries, for example,[1] refer to the diary of one of Stanley's companions, John Baine.[2] Holland's Cheshire background and connections, then, unquestionably provided him from the outset with at least one important and influential Icelandophile friend, known in and knowledgeable about both the Edinburgh where Henry was to study and the Iceland to which he would sail and through which he would trek.

There were, however, two other influences of Henry Holland's youth which may well have prepared the way for the subsequent focussing of his imagination on the 'costes colde'[3] of Iceland. Firstly, in 1803–4, he went at the age of sixteen to the Reverend J. P. Estlin's school on St. Michael's Hill in Bristol, where he joined his future Iceland companion Richard Bright (1789–1858),[4] 'my most intimate friend'[5] of the time, and later to become a physician famed for his study of what came to be known as Bright's Disease. Estlin's education had been at the dissenting academy in Warrington, 'the seat where science learnt to dwell,/Where liberty her ardent spirit breathed',[6] and it is apparent that the same atmosphere of broad and humane learning later prevailed at Estlin's own school. Estlin's circle of friends, the Bright family, Coleridge, Southey, Priestley and Joseph Cottle amongst them, make it certain that young Henry Holland's formative years were spent in a notably stimulating intellectual environment.

The surviving records of borrowings from the holdings of the Bristol Library Society[7] provide a glimpse at least of this enlightened community. Though neither Holland nor his friend Richard Bright junior were enrolled as members of the Library Society, Estlin and Richard Bright senior were members of the organising committee which ordered new books, and both men were regular borrowers of the books they bought. Indeed the borrowings of the Bright family over the period of Holland's stay in Bristol can be taken as representative of the kinds of literary and cultural influences which could have irrigated the

---

[1] See below, p. 187; note 2, p. 256.   [2] West (1970–6), III.

[3] *Libelle*, l.805.

[4] See Pamela Bright, *Dr. Richard Bright 1789–1858* (London, 1983); also Robert M. Kark and David Moore, 'The life, work and geological collection of Richard Bright, M.D. (1789–1858)', *Archives for Natural History*, X (1981), 119–51.

[5] Holland, 1872, p. 11.

[6] Quoted in Kark and Moore, 1981, p. 120.

[7] The following discussion is based on my examination of Bristol City Library MSS B 7473–6, for the years 1803–6.

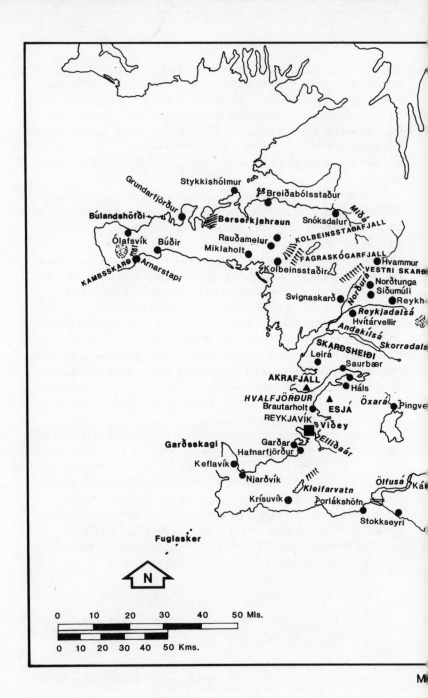

Grundarfjörður   Stykkishólmur   Breiðabólsstaður
                                                        Miðá
Búlandshöfði   Berserkjahraun   Snóksdalur   GAFJALL
        Ólafsvík   Búðir   Rauðamelur   KOLBEINSSTAÐ
                            Miklaholt   FAGRASKÓGARFJALL
KAMBSSKARÐ   Arnarstapi   Kolbeinsstaðir   VESTRI SKARÐ   Hvammur
                                                        Norðtunga
                                                        Siðumúli
                                  Svignaskarð   Reykh
                                          Norðurá
                                          Reykjadalsá
                                          Hvítárvellir
                                       Andakílsá   Skorradals
                                  SKARÐSHEIÐI
                                  Leirá   Saurbær
                         AKRAFJALL   Háls
                         HVALFJÖRÐUR   Öxará
                         Brautarholt   ESJÁ   Þingve
                         REYKJAVÍK   Viðey
               Garðsskagi   Garðar   Elliðaár
                         Hafnarfjörður
                  Keflavík
                         Njarðvík
                                     Kleifarvatn   Ölfusá   Ká
                  Krísuvík   Þorlákshöfn
                                                Stokkseyri

        Fuglasker

              N

0   10   20   30   40   50 Mls.

0   10   20   30   40   50 Kms.

M

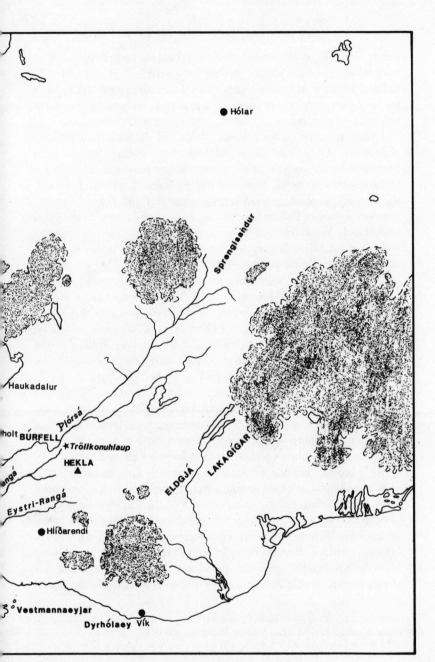

● Hólar

Sprengisandur

Haukadalur

Þjórsá

holt BÚRFELL

★Tröllkonuhlaup

HEKLA ▲

angá

Eystri-Rangá

ELDGJÁ LAKAGÍGAR

● Hlíðarendi

3° Vestmannaeyjar

Dyrhólaey Vík

stern Iceland

15

minds of able young men such as Holland and Bright. These borrowings reveal some of the characteristic tastes of the Enlightenment – an earnest and voracious curiosity about and appetite for books on travel and antiquities; a persistent enthusiasm for works reflecting developments in exciting new sciences such as mineralogy, and keen attention paid to works of dogged domestic and agrarian practicality. Only two items catalogued as 'belles lettres' were borrowed by any of the Bright family in the period around 1804 – William Godwin's newly published *Life of Chaucer* (London, 1803), and, significantly, a volume entered in the register as 'Runic Poetry' – almost certainly a copy of Bishop Percy's *Five pieces of runic poetry*. In the years immediately before Holland's arrival in Bristol, this had not been the only work of Norse literary and antiquarian interest which had been available to and borrowed by members of the Estlin-Bright circle, as British interest in Scandinavian antiquities blossomed.[1] Robert Southey, Coleridge and Joseph Cottle had been frequent and therefore presumably enthusiastic borrowers of the first volume (1787) of the great three volume Copenhagen edition of *Edda Sæmundar hinns froda* [sic] (1787–1828), and of Percy's *Five pieces of runic poetry*. Coleridge was also amongst those who borrowed Amos Cottle's *Icelandic poetry; or the Edda of Sæmund, translated into English verse* (Bristol, 1797), a version whose 'rhapsodical effusions' and 'ludicrous bombast'[2] offended contemporary reviewers and Victorian critics alike, all of whom were conscious of the distortions of the Copenhagen *Edda*, both of spirit and letter, which jostled one another for attention in the volume. The work, complete with Southey's prefatory poem, had been printed in Bristol by Cottle's brother Joseph, whose own lumbering epic *Alfred* (London, 1800), in the course of substantially outstaying its welcome, exhibits a certain arthritic imaginative engagement with the 'ensanguined'[3] world of Scandinavian antiquity. Other influential works relating to the North which were available to borrowing members of the Bristol Library Society included Bishop Percy's 1770 translation[4] of Paul Henri Mallet's immensely influential *Introduction á l'histoire de Dannemarc* (Copenhagen, 1755), William Coxe's *Travels in Poland, Russia, Sweden*

---

[1] Farley 1903, Omberg 1976, and Edward J. Cowan, *Icelandic Studies in eighteenth and nineteenth century Scotland, Studia Islandica*, 31 (1972), 109–51.

[2] Thomas Percy (revised I. A. Blackwell) *Northern antiquities* (London, 1847), p. 374.

[3] The adjective, deriving from Milton, particularly favoured by eighteenth-century poets when describing Viking battlefields: see Wawn, 1981, pp. 56–62.

[4] *Northern antiquities*, 2 vols. (London, 1770).

and Denmark (London, 1784), and James Johnstone's *Antiquitates Celto-Scandicæ* (Copenhagen, 1786). There was, additionally, much to be gleaned from reviews in the periodical literature of the time.[1]

Thus with travel, mineralogy, antiquities and Norse literature among the enthusiasms of those in whose company and under whose direct or indirect influence Holland spent his time in Bristol, it is not difficult to imagine his sharing their fascination with such areas of interest. Such influences will have extended over the school holidays, too. These were spent away from Bristol, with Dr. Aikin,[2] an old friend of Henry Holland's father, who lived at Stoke Newington and in London. Dr. Aikin senior, a friend of Southey, had been afflicted by a paralysing stroke in 1789 and no doubt therefore it was the Aikin children who had more contact with and influence over their young guest. The elder son Arthur was a founder editor of the *Annual Review*, a short-lived periodical to which Southey and William Taylor, another enthusiast of the 'gothick', the 'eddick' and the 'runick' gave support.[3] Arthur Aikin's other particular interest was mineralogy and, as well as publishing several works on the subject, he played a leading role in the founding of the Geological Society of London in 1807,[4] a society with which Holland was to have significant dealings after his return from Iceland.[5] The younger son Charles had trained as a doctor and took over his paralysed father's London practice. His published work included a collaborative (with his brother) work on geology and also in 1800 a treatise on cow pox.

It may thus be appropriate at this point to set the list of identifiable Bristol and London influences on the adolescent Holland – Norse antiquities, geology, medicine in general and cow pox in particular – alongside what can be discovered of his subsequent career: the passionate interest in geology whilst he was studying in Edinburgh; his decision to train as a doctor in Edinburgh; and the demonstrable fact that his journey to Iceland in 1810 had three impulses behind it – first,

[1] Susie I. Tucker, 'Scandinavica for the eighteenth-century reader', *Saga-Book of the Viking Society*, XVI (1962–5), 233–47.
[2] Betsy Rodgers, *Georgian chronicle: Mrs Barbauld and her family* (London, 1958); also Holland, 1872, p. 12.
[3] Farley, 1903, pp. 137–43.
[4] M. J. S. Rudwick, 'The foundations of the Geological Society in London', *BJHS*, 1 (1962–3), 325–55; see also H. S. Torrens, 'Arthur Aikin's mineralogical survey of Shropshire 1796–1816 and the contemporary audience for geology', *BJHS* 15–16 (1982–3), 111–53.
[5] Kark and Moore, 1981, pp. 128–30; also NLS MS Acc. 7515, a letter from Henry Holland to his father in Knutsford, 3 June 1811.

the search for geological specimens; second, to investigate diseases in Iceland for his M.D. dissertation, with a particular interest in cow pox, a scourge he sought to eradicate by re-introducing vaccine crusts into Iceland;[1] third, curiosity about Icelandic learning and literature, the fruits of that curiosity appearing in the form of his scholarly, discriminating and influential account of Icelandic cultural history which prefaced Sir George Mackenzie's *Travels in the island of Iceland during the summer of the year 1810.*

Yet if Holland's brief period of formal schooling in Bristol had sown the seeds of a potential interest in travelling in general and travel in the North in particular, it was the exuberance of intellectual life in Enlightenment Edinburgh which, from the time of his arrival at the University late in 1806, fostered such interests, as had previously been the case with his mentor John Thomas Stanley. Holland had spent the winters of 1804–5 and 1805–6 studying in Glasgow, a period about which his *Recollections of past life* (1872) is characteristically and frustratingly vague (pp. 19–20), but it was Edinburgh which was to provide the specific impulse through which Holland and Iceland were brought together. An important collection of unpublished letters[2] from Henry to his father in Knutsford, covering the years 1810–11, offers many a vivid and representative glimpse of the social and intellectual ferment and bustle of a great city with a spring in its cultural stride.[3] During this eighteen month, documented period, so many things clamoured for Holland's eager attention, as revealed in the letters – a Handel concert (NLS 7515, 10 March 1811); a new tragedy by Joanna Baillie (NLS 7515, 6 February 1810; 25 January 1811); a new poem by Sir Walter Scott (NLS 7515, 3 June 1811); visits to the fashionable picturesquenesses of Stirling Castle (NLS 7515, 11 August 1811); gossip about politics and assorted professorial amatory entanglements; new issues of important journals (NLS 7515, 4 March 1810); the latest books, from 'Wilson on Febrile Diseases' to 'Mrs Leadbeater's *Cottage Dialogues*' (NLS 7515, 25 January 1811; 26 January 1811); uproar at the Medical Society (NLS 7515, 4 March 1811); the health of French prisoners-of-war (NLS 7515, 31 March 1811); patent remedies for chest colds (NLS 7515, 24 March 1811); and, seemingly, every breakfast, tea and dinner passed in the company of this learned or that noble

[1] Mackenzie, 1811, p. 410.

[2] NLS MS Acc. 7515; there is one stray letter from the sequence in Lbs MS 4925 4to. Subsequent references will be marked NLS 7515 or Lbs 4925.

[3] See Anand C. Chitnis, *The Scottish enlightenment: a social history* (London, 1976).

companion. Amidst this invigorating whirl of cultural and social ephemora scattered through the letters, two themes assume a central importance – mineralogy and Iceland. Indeed, as the early letters in the sequence make clear, the one was to lead directly to the other.

It was in February 1810, at a meeting of the Royal Society of Edinburgh, appropriately, that the suggestion was first put to Holland by Sir George Mackenzie that he might care to join a forthcoming venture to Iceland (NLS 7515, 6 February 1810). In the stimulating if frequently acrimonious atmosphere of the Wernerian-Huttonian mineralogical debate on the possible origin of rocks,[1] the Royal Society had played a leading role in favouring the Huttonian proposition that rocks were igneous in origin, formed by subterranean heat acting under pressure on debris previously weathered and eroded from the earth's surface. The consolidation of this debris, argued the Huttonians, could take place beneath the floor of the ocean where the immense heat could combine with the great pressure to bind together the constantly deposited fine silt of sandstone, limestone, clay, pebbles and other such materials. Huttonian theory was essentially cyclical rather than progressive – denudation of matter from the earth's surface, transportation by wind of the denuded matter, sedimentation at the bottom of the sea, consolidation through pressure and heat, elevation and subsequent exposure to the winds and weather, through which agencies the denudation process could start anew. The supporters of the Wernerian position argued that all rock formations, with their complex stratifications were the products of chemical or mechanical precipitation from aqueous solution and suspension: they claimed (with demonstrable biblical support) that the waters had once covered the earth, and that the surface features of the earth were deposited during that period, finally to be revealed as those same waters subsided. The crucial battleground between the two theoretical positions and their sometimes excessively committed supporters was how to account for strange geological features such as bent or tilted strata, the form and variety of veins in rocks, the crystalline state of many rocks, and the columnar structure of such so-called trap formation rocks as basalt. Huttonians earnestly believed that the twin notions of rocks solidifying

[1] See Gordon L. Davies, *The earth in decay: a history of British geomorphology, 1758–1878* (London, [1969], pp. 145–96; also Roy Porter, *The making of geology: earth science in Britain, 1660–1815* (Cambridge, 1977), pp. 157–215; M. J. S. Rudwick, 'Hutton and Werner compared: George Greenhough's geological tour of Scotland', *BJHS*, 1 (1962–3), 117–35; and Mott T. Greene, *Geology in the nineteenth century* (Ithaca, New York, 1982), pp. 19–68.

from molten state and of forcible intrusion of matter from below were of particular value in helping to explain such phenomena.

Sir George Mackenzie was a prominent supporter of the Huttonian position and it was in the hope of finding specimens and other contextual evidence which might confirm the thesis that he was drawn towards Iceland. Even those whose defiant and studied empiricism led them to look sceptically on any all-embracing geological theory, could scarcely fail to be excited by the prospect of Iceland as an environment in which the precepts of John Walker, until 1804 the Professor of Natural History at Edinburgh University, could be followed and fulfilled:

The objects of nature themselves must be sedulously examined in their native state, the fields and mountains must be traversed, the woods and waters must be explored, the ocean must be fathomed and its shores scrutinized by everyone that would become proficient in natural knowledge.[1]

Henry Holland, already by this time revealed in his letters as an empiricist with Huttonian leanings, certainly needed little persuasion to undertake the 'sedulous examination' of Iceland's geological 'objects of nature'. Letters to his father in the days after Mackenzie's initial invitation reveal an inquisitive and anxious involvement with mineralogical debate, and an ambitious sense of what a successful expedition to Iceland could accomplish for science and signify for himself. It would, he claimed:

be productive at once of pleasure & advantage. The pleasure seems to me to be secured by – agreeableness of associates, novelty of scene, & the many objects of interest which would occur to us – The profit ... would be derived partly from the opportunity of cultivating some desirable branches of knowledge, as mineralogy ... partly perhaps from the sort of notoriety, which might possibly be connected with the accomplishment of the scheme. (NLS 7515, 17 February 1810.)

The invitation accepted, Holland's energies were thereafter appropriately directed. There were drawing lessons (NLS 7515, 17 February 1810); studies of relevant rock collections; 'geological walks' undertaken with due impartiality in the company of the Wernerian Robert Jameson,[2] Keeper of the University's Natural History Museum,

[1] Quoted in Anand C. Chitnis, 'The University of Edinburgh's natural history museum and the Huttonian-Wernerian debate', *Annals of Science* 26 (1970), 88; the quotation taken from a lecture of Walker's delivered in 1781.
[2] See Chitnis, 1970.

and John Walker's professorial successor, and the Huttonian Sir James Hall; lengthy and impulsive letters to his friend Maria Edgeworth,[1] informing her of his plans; mining the rich veins of malicious gossip deposited by Lord Brougham's farcically unsuccessful expedition to Iceland in 1799,[2] an under-motivated (to put it mildly) venture which staggered to a wine-soaked halt at Ullapool, all alcoholic provisions having been improvidently squandered in riotous wassailing with highland laird after highland laird. More colourfully still, the period before Holland set sail enabled him to cultivate the acquaintance of Ólafur Loptsson, an Icelandic medical student, who was to be the mercurial, unreliable and disreputable guide for Sir George's party in Iceland, spreading misinformation amongst the visitors and venereal disease amongst the natives.[3] His dismal performance as guide in Iceland was to contrast vividly with the tale told to Holland of Ólafur's exotic arrival in Scotland and his introduction to Mackenzie, events which, as Holland remarks in a letter to Knutsford (NLS 7515, 17 February 1810), 'might well serve as the basis of a romance'.

Ólafur had studied medicine in Reykjavík for five years, a pupil of the island's chief physician Tómas Klog. He then set course for Copenhagen to study cow pox, at that time a grievous affliction throughout Iceland. Foundering in a violent, wintry storm, Ólafur's ship was wrecked and the young Icelander was washed ashore, an improbable Prospero, on the island of Lewis, where he was taken prisoner, penniless and unable to speak English. Limited though his medical prowess was at that time, it was sufficient soon to endear him to the lonely island crofters, and his fame spread sufficiently for him to be summoned for consultation by 'some Baronet on the western coast of Ross-shire'. In due course he met Sir George Mackenzie, spent a highland summer with him, before making his way to Edinburgh, by now a figure of some celebrity, to pursue his medical studies under Sir George's benevolent patronage. In this same letter, Henry Holland delights in reporting Ólafur's fulsome tribute to his new-found mentor

---

[1] Some of these letters survive, in the possession of David Holland Esq., who has kindly supplied me with transcripts. Further references to these letters will be marked with the abbreviation ME, followed by the date of the letter.

[2] See Henry Brougham, *The life and times of Henry Lord Brougham*, 3 vols. (London, 1871), I, 110–12; Warren R. Dawson, 'Supplementary letters of Sir Joseph Banks', *Bulletin of the British Museum (Natural History)*, Historical Series III (1971), 73–93 – letter dated 21 July 1799; also NLS 7515, letter dated 17 February 1810.

[3] Jón Espólín, *Íslands árbækur í sögu-formi*, 13 parts in 3 vols. (Copenhagen, 1821–55), XII, 49.

and to Lady Mackenzie: 'I would be drowned – twice, tree times drowned for dose two people – I cannot say to you all dey have done and do feel for one'. Mackenzie's enchantment with Ólafur did not long survive the return from Iceland in the autumn of 1810. Ólafur is said by Holland to have secured Mackenzie's promise that he could accompany them to Britain again after the expedition. The promise seems not to have been kept, however. Certainly, in the battle for the young Icelander's soul, Caliban seems too often to have triumphed over Prospero. Even the story of Ólafur's shipwreck is banished by Sir George from the Preface to his revised edition of his Iceland book.[1] Ólafur himself proved harder to banish from Sir George's life. Abandoned women and illegitimate children beat a path to Mackenzie's Edinburgh door where they had to take their turn behind indignant letters from furious fathers of humiliated Icelandic daughters all seduced by Ólafur's claims for his glittering prospects as a physician in the British army, a position allegedly procured for him by Sir George. Mackenzie's verdict is crisp: 'He is one of the most unworthy objects on whom charity was ever bestowed',[2] and in due course he seems to have passed into unfulfilled obscurity.

ICELAND 1809: TALLOW AND TURMOIL

If the time spent with Ólafur Loptsson recalled for Holland and Mackenzie the heady world of high literary romance, the time spent before their departure in correspondence (NLS 7515, 17 February 1810) with Sir Joseph Banks, with the Danish governor of Iceland Count Frederick Trampe, and with W. J. Hooker (1785–1865), newly returned from an engrossing but ultimately calamitous expedition to Iceland the previous summer, must have brought them much closer to the bleak and granite face of real tragedy. Banks, Trampe and Hooker would have lost no time in making it plain that any projected voyage to Iceland in 1810 was a voyage to a land whose turbulence was not confined to the geysers and volcanoes: by 1810 Iceland had become an anxious, enfeebled and, to an extent, strife-riven land.[3] The anxiety and

---

[1] The story appears briefly in Mackenzie, 1811, pp. viii–ix; omitted from 1812 Preface.
[2] BL MS Addit. 33982, ff. 94–5.
[3] In this section I have drawn on a variety of primary and secondary sources and discussions: William Jackson Hooker, *Journal of a tour in Iceland in the summer of 1809* (Yarmouth: privately printed 1811; revised edition, 2 vols. 1813), II, 3–102; Mackenzie, 1812, pp. 474–81; Samuel Phelps, *A treatise on the importance of extending the British fisheries*

enfeeblement stemmed in part from a succession of wretched winters and subsequently disappointing harvests. But it was helplessness in the face of the trade and travel restrictions deriving from the Napoleonic conflicts still gripping Europe that lay much closer to the heart of Icelandic distress. At the time of the 1807 Treaty of Tilsit, the French strategy of attempting to isolate Britain and to force strategically important countries such as Denmark, already briefly a member of the essentially anti-British League of Armed Neutrality as early as 1801, to side with the Napoleonic axis intensified. Canning, the British foreign secretary, instructed the ambassador in Copenhagen to submit to the Danish government a demand that they accept a defensive alliance with Britain, the Danish fleet to be placed under British control until the cessation of hostilities. Denmark, judging not unreasonably that an alliance with an apparently invincible France represented a more realistic strategy, rejected the British diplomatic overtures and the British fleet in turn unceremoniously bombarded Copenhagen, with native Danes, visiting Icelanders and priceless antiquarian libraries proving as memorably (for the victims) vulnerable as military targets.[1] Britain further instituted a trade blockade of Scandinavian ports, with disastrous results for the Icelanders, crucially dependent on the trading vessels of Danish merchants. These unprotected and isolated ships represented an all too easy prey for the vigilant Royal Navy patrols in the North Atlantic.

A number of ways in which the hardship caused to Iceland might be mitigated suggested themselves: Danish shipping which sought to trade

---

(London, 1817); a summary of the no longer extant account of the 1809 events by Andrew Mitchell, a Scottish merchant resident in Reykjavík since 1803 – Historical Manuscripts Commission, *Report on the manuscripts of Earl Bathurst preserved at Cirencester Park* (London, 1923), pp. 84–6; Jón Þorkelsson, *Saga Jörundar hundadagakóngs* (Copenhagen, 1892); Helgi P. Briem, *Byltingin 1809* (Reykjavík, 1936); Halldór Hermannsson, 1928; Knut Gjerset, *A history of Iceland* (London, [1923?]) pp. 344–67; A. N. Ryan, 'The causes of the British attack on Copenhagen in 1807', *English Historical Review*, LXVIII (1953), 37–55; Derek McKay, 'Great Britain and Iceland in 1809', *Mariner's Mirror*, LIX (1973), 85–95; Anna Agnarsdóttir, 'Ráðagerðir um innlimun Íslands í Bretaveldi á árunum 1785–1815', *Saga: tímarit sögufélags*, XVII (1979), 5–58; Trausti Ólafsson (trans.), *Íslandskóngur: sjálfsævisaga Jörundar hundadagakonungs* (Reykjavík, 1974).

' Grímur Thorkelín refers in anguish to the incident in a letter to Lord Buchan, dated 21 April 1812: NLS MS 3278, ff. 47–52. The attack was 'wicked, treacherous and flint-hearted' and the bombing led directly to 'the cries of suckling babes, torn from the bosom of their mothers, murdered with Congreve's fiery darts and bursting shells; the groans of half-burnt parents, moaning their children, butchered with wanton cruelty'. Bodleian MS Douce d.23, letter dated 23 May 1819, contains a less indignant reference to the same events.

between Iceland and mainland Scandinavia could be provided with special licenses to operate unmolested; British merchants might seek to fill the vacuum left by the banished Danes, with the breeze of Adam Smith in their sails, eager at least to investigate the call of entrepreneurial opportunity, even when it hailed from 66° North; or Britain might effect the annexation of Iceland, on either a temporary or permanent basis, with such little force as would be necessary to achieve this change of sovereignty. Mackenzie, doubtless influenced amongst other factors by harrowing tales of Icelandic hardship told to him by Ólafur Loptsson, favoured the option of annexation,[1] as did others who viewed the plight of the Icelanders through the glinting eye of commercial opportunism as well as through the moistened eye of human compassion.

In no eye was the glint brighter than in that of Samuel Phelps, an enterprising and uncomplicated soap manufacturer from London.[2] It was around his 1809 commercial venture to Iceland in search of tallow that many of the potentially inflammable diplomatic and commercial tensions of the time finally ignited, the effects of which were still smouldering by the time Sir George Mackenzie's party arrived the following summer. The complex sequence of events can be traced back to 29 November 1808, when Phelps first received government permission to sail a single ship to Iceland to trade for tallow. By the beginning of January 1809, Phelps arrived at Hafnarfjörður with his companions, including James Savignac, who was to be his resident commercial agent in Iceland, and Jörgen Jörgensen, a former Danish naval captain, now a paroled prisoner-of-war, and who had first drawn the attention of Phelps to the abundant supplies of tallow available in Iceland. The authorities' initial reluctance overcome, an agreement granting freedom to trade for the British party was signed on 19 January. The British traders decided to warehouse their cargo which they had brought to Iceland, pending more favourable market conditions in Reykjavík in June. Phelps and Jörgensen returned to England, leaving Savignac in charge of the as yet untraded merchandise. Phelps returned to Iceland with Jörgensen towards the end of May in the *Margaret and Anne*, which, through the good offices of Sir Joseph Banks, had been granted letter of marque. Arriving in Reykjavík on 21 June, they found that their way had been prepared by

[1] Mackenzie, 1811, p. 271; Dawson, 1958, p. 564.
[2] See Phelps, 1817.

Captain Francis Nott in the *Rover*, a British warship, from Leith. Nott had arrived at Hafnarfjörður on 11 June to discover that Governor Trampe, himself returning to Reykjavík from a prolonged stay in Denmark, had torn up the 19 January free trade agreement. Nott pressurised Tampe into a further agreement, signed on 16 June, after which Nott returned to Britain. Trampe, freed from the intimidating presence of a hostile warship, could hardly have been less vigorous in the implementation of the new agreement. Thus Phelps and his colleagues, arriving on 21 June, were confronted with proclamations posted to the effect that any attempt to trade with foreign merchants was punishable by death. These were, in fact, the proclamations relating to Trampe's earlier abrogation of the January free trade agreement. Noting the distance between Reykjavík and the one operational printing press at Leirárgarðar, more than a day's journey away, Trampe may well have convinced himself that innocent delays in the printing and transportation of new proclamations for the 16 June agreement lay behind the continued prominence in public places of the previous and more threatening ones, but he certainly convinced few others. The whiff of gubernatorial prevarication and duplicity was in the air.

Samuel Phelps was quite clear about his own position. He had been granted British government permission to trade in Iceland; Captain Nott's arrival and negotiations with Trampe had underlined Phelps's case; if, in the face of these two factors, Phelps's trading plans were now to be impeded by the Danish authorities in Reykjavík, he felt entitled to use all measures necessary in order to secure satisfactory trading conditions. Accordingly, Trampe was unceremoniously arrested on 25 June and imprisoned on board the *Margaret and Anne*, sharing the doubtful victuals and company of its inevitably rough-hewn crew. A decision had then to be taken about the governance of Iceland, with Trampe now unavailable. Phelps, though aware of the much canvassed policy option of British governmental annexation of Iceland, was equally well aware that the British government had not agreed to implement such a policy and seemed unlikely ever to agree to do so. He was, thus, in no position to annex Iceland in the name of that government. On the other hand, some government was urgently needed, and Phelps and Jörgensen were able to persuade themselves that it would be more appropriate were authority to pass into Jörgensen's hands. He was not a British subject, and his actions would not therefore be seen to implicate or embarrass the British government. So it was that

Jörgensen, on 26 June, proclaimed not the annexation of Iceland to Britain, but merely the independence of Iceland from all foreign authority. Thus, with the new national flag – three white codfish on a blue field – soon fluttering from government house, 'His Excellency' Jörgen's brief and quixotic 'reign' began, despised by the prosperous Danish traders, some of whose money he swiftly confiscated; egged on by the unscrupulous Savignac; variously viewed by the influential members of the indigenous Icelandic community – from overt hostility to covert acquiescence; whilst the support of the bewildered commonalty fell, at best, some way short of the romantic revolutionary fervour ascribed to the citizenry by Jörgensen's twentieth-century stage chronicler, Indriði Einarsson, in his play *Síðasti Víkingurinn* (Reykjavík, 1936), a work which has as many echoes of the Spanish Civil War as it does of Reykjavík 1809.

The final act of the real life drama began on 14 August with the unexpected arrival of the British warship *Talbot* at Reykjavík, under the command of Captain Alexander Jones. Within days, articles of agreement[1] were signed by Phelps, Jones and two ambitious native Icelanders, Magnús and Stefán Stephensen, loyal to each other rather than to Trampe, and aware that the Danish Governor's ill wind seemed likely to blow them, at least, some good. According to the agreement, Jörgensen's seizure of authority was declared null and void; government was to devolve, at least temporarily, onto the Stephensens; all Danish property and monies were to be restored to their rightful owners; and, happily for the Icelanders, the 16 June trading agreement was to be published and implemented throughout the country.

Whilst the outline and sequence of these hectic events is well documented and not in dispute, the interpretation of what happened was much less clear at the time. There are extant accounts written by many of the active participants, amongst them Phelps, Jörgensen, and Trampe, not to mention the accounts of those less directly but still significantly involved – W. J. Hooker, Sir Joseph Banks and Sir George Mackenzie and a Scottish merchant resident in Reykjavík, Andrew Mitchell. Banks is ultimately very hostile to Phelps and Jörgensen; Hooker is suspicious of Trampe and very sympathetic to Jörgensen, not least because the Dane saved him from drowning when the *Margaret and Anne* was destroyed by fire not long into its return voyage to Britain; Sir George Mackenzie is very supportive of Trampe and hostile

---

[1] Detailed in Phelps, 1817, pp. 63–5.

to Jörgensen; Phelps is very sympathetic to Phelps and the estimated £40,000 which the expedition had cost him; Jörgensen is very sympathetic to Jörgensen and the lifetime's banishment in Australia which his actions were ultimately to cost him.[1] Diverse folk, diversely they spoke. On one point, however, they could all agree – the dust of controversy would take some time to settle.

ICELAND 1810: JOURNEYING AND THE JOURNAL

When Sir George Mackenzie and his colleagues arrived in Iceland the following summer of 1810, the aftermath of the previous year's turmoil was everywhere in evidence. Their introduction to Reykjavík involved a succession of tragi-comic scenes of personal jealousy and commercial intrigue. There was, for instance, Magnús Stephensen's studied reluctance to drink the health of the absent Governor Trampe at a welcoming dinner for the British travellers (Journal, p. 99). It was a reluctance which proved soundly based, for his brief and uneasy tenure of political office, which had begun the previous summer, was brought to an abrupt end when the rare arrival of a Danish vessel from Liverpool brought letters from Trampe authorising the removal of Magnús Stephensen from office and dividing his responsibilities between three other officials (Journal, pp. 140–1). Of no less moment, Samuel Phelps's new commercial agent, the conscientious Michael Fell, clashed inevitably with Phelps's previous and still resident agent, the irascible and lecherous Savignac over the custody of the London merchant's warehoused goods. Whilst the tallow trading cat had been away, the fraudulent mouse had been at play. As matters came to a head, muskets and blunderbusses were brandished, even the *Elbe*'s cannons came briefly into action, and Sir George and his party were no more than appropriately prudent to sleep with loaded pistols in their bedrooms (Journal, p. 102).

The more generally baleful influence of the war on Iceland was everywhere in evidence, from the earliest stages of Mackenzie's voyage: companies of veterans, optimistically posted in the Orkneys to deter French privateers (Journal, p.71); banquets in Iceland at which toasts to the British and Danish monarchs were uneasily celebrated, with

[1] Jörgensen and Hooker corresponded long after 1810: see, for example, Hooker Correspondence, Kew, Australian letters 1834–51, letter dated 28 October 1836; Australian and New Zealand letters 1835–43, letter dated 4 October 1840.

Holland well able to discern a censorious chill beneath the surface glow of Danish civility (Journal, pp. 273–4); prominent traders throughout Iceland sorely harassed by the restrictions of war – Holger Clausen at Ólafsvík (Journal, p. 191) and Christian Jacobæus at Keflavík, the latter still waiting for restoration of funds confiscated by Jörgensen were two such (Journal, p. 135), whilst Hans Hjaltalín, less fortunate still, could only wait abroad in frustrated exile, his commercial enterprises at Arnarstapi faltering in his prolonged absence (Journal, p. 186); the war had brought harmful constraints on the important summer markets in Reykjavík (Journal, pp. 224–5); it caused damaging delays in the construction of the new printing house at Leirárgarðar (Journal, p. 164) and the much needed new school premises at Bessastaðir (Journal, pp. 118–19); tallow, eagerly sought by Phelps for soap, was even more eagerly sought by the natives as a dismally unappetising substitute for butter (Journal, p. 225); Mackenzie's party experienced difficulty in bartering for items of national costume at Eyvindarmúli, the natives reluctant to part with articles for which replacements were no longer readily available (Journal, p. 266); the visitors endured the embarrassment of a confrontation with the venerable former Governor Ólafur Stephensen, still indignant at the attack by Captain Gilpin and his band of British freebooters on his home on Viðey island in 1808 (Journal, pp. 106–8); even a shattered umbrella, the property of Oddur Hjaltalín, physician at Stykkishólmur, had a tale to tell – Oddur, a resident in Copenhagen during the 1807 British bombardment, was fortunate not to have shared the fate of his umbrella, having been sitting under it as the guns found their range and took their toll (Journal, p. 204).

The variously manifested effects of war's turmoil cast a persistent shadow over each of the three lengthy and sometimes hazardous journeys undertaken by the travellers within Iceland – to the Reykjanes peninsula, to Snæfellsnes and to the hot springs of Haukadalur in the south. They could not, however, permanently distract the travellers from the geological turmoil of the Icelandic landscape which they anxiously sought to observe and record, spurred on by the remarkable growth of speculative curiosity and knowledge which had been generated by the late eighteenth-century 'heroic age' of European geological and mineralogical science. As Holland crouched nightly in buffeted tent or dank church recording the rough notes of his day's observations, from which the fair copy of his journal could later be prepared, the fastidiousness and scholarly coolness of the narrative style cannot completely obscure the excitement of a young geologist let loose in the land of his mineralogical dreams. The responsibilities of a geological chronicler to the broader scientific community at this time were potentially burdensome. The extraordinary assemblage of geysers, glaciers, newly formed islets, and recent and ancient volcanic devastations to be found within Iceland or off its shores offered a unique and in its way awesome opportunity for a young scientist to be exposed to the geological drama of the earth's surface in its apparently endless process of reduction and renewal, being and becoming.[1] Wherever else in the world *terra* was *firma*, it certainly was not Iceland: rather, its surface was seethingly alive, maintaining the ceaseless volcanic and geothermal upheaval of the centuries. The close observations and theoretical acuity of the mineralogist could serve to penetrate the apparently chaotic results of such upheavals and find, in the astonishing shapes of caves and columns and chasms, not so much evidence of chance and the aberrant grotesqueness of an unfathomable Nature, but rather evidence of discernible pattern and predictability, if only the underlying rules of matter's shaping and structuring energies could be deciphered. Such understandings depended on the painstaking collection, annotation and subsequent analysis of rock samples, each one a kind of abbreviated and intensified expression of the larger processes of Nature. They were, in Professor Stafford's phrase, 'natural hieroglyphs',[2] metonyms of geological change.

The rock samples could return with the travellers, so could the sketches and diagrams. But faced with the scientific importance, not to mention the considerable emotional impact of these strange and beautiful rockscapes, the journalist's task was daunting as well as enviable. No-one doubted that the land was significant enough for the writer; but was the writer articulate enough for the land? The density and scrupulousness of Holland's own geological annotations in his journal leave the reader in little doubt that the chronicler's mineralogical responsibilities have been fully and responsibly discharged. At the same time, Holland, who during the trip encountered, at the Leirárgarðar printing-house, copies of Jón Þorláksson's 1798 Icelandic translation of Alexander Pope's *Essay on Man* (Journal, p. 164), reveals himself sensitive enough to be able

---

[1] In preparing this section, I have derived much stimulus from Barbara M. Stafford's brilliant study *Voyage into substance: art, science and the illustrated travel account 1760–1840* (Cambridge, Mass., 1984).

[2] Stafford, 1984, pp. 305–19.

to share that poet's sense of awe and humility in the face of the infinite mysteries of nature's 'one stupendous whole':[1]

In the present state of philosophical research, the conceptions of man are scarcely adequate to that vast scale of operation, which exists in the phenomena of the mineral world. We can trace with scientific calmness the gradual development of an insect or a flower; but shrink back, almost with terror, from those great and sublime workings of nature, which seem to bring us a step nearer to the greatness & sublimity of the Deity himself.[2]

Holland, like Pope, needed no reminder that the proper study of mankind was man as much as it was minerals. Thus, throughout the journal there are many prominent or at least singular characters and incidents arrestingly depicted. In a letter to Maria Edgeworth, Holland expresses the fear that 'I am not blessed with the faculty of condensation in a suitable degree',[3] yet the journal provides many moments when a keen sensibility, a concentrated gaze, an urbane wit and a discreet fascination with the grotesque severally serve him well. Many an individual encountered along the Icelandic way is thus brought briefly but memorably to life: the wretched old sailor who fell to his death whilst the *Elbe* struggled through a North Atlantic squall (Journal, p. 76); the unquenchable spirit of the octogenerian Ólafur Stephensen, all port and *politesse*; the loathed James Savignac, the nectar of his disposition long ago soured irretrievably, locked in a 'disgraceful, but ridiculous *fracas*' with a hapless native fisherman (Journal, p. 226); the irrepressible and contagious good humour of the wondrously obese Bishop Geir Vídalín, a jester without a court; the vulnerable Guðrún Johnsen, former affinine of Jörgensen, and a young woman whose subsequent story is as much the stuff of romantic melodrama as anything associated with Ólafur Loptsson; the learned and dedicated Steingrímur Jónsson of Bessastaðir, finding prosperity and fulfilment at Oddi; the unlearned and undedicated Jónas Scheving, *sýslumaður* of Borgarfjörður, red of hair and thick of head; the unnamed wife of Christian Jacobæus from Keflavík, sixteen years in Iceland and never having ventured outside the village (Journal, p. 136); Sæmundur Hálfdanarson, the snuff-stained whisky-priest of Eyvindarmúli, spirit submissively willing, flesh subversively weak (Journal, pp. 266–7); the

---

[1] 'An Essay on Man', in *The Twickenham edition of the poems of Alexander Pope*, 11 vols. in 12 (London and New Haven, 1939–69), III, ed. Maynard Mack, p. 47 – Book 5, l.267. See Journal, note 4, p. 116.
[2] Lbs MS 4275 4to, p. 12.   [3] ME letters 2 August 1811.

dismissed Magnús Stephensen, condemned by Trampe's letter to wrestle with private resentments and public feignings of elaborate unconcern, his fall from power leaving Holland to reflect on 'the precariousness of all human grandeur' (Journal, p. 141); and, constantly, the ubiquitous presence of nameless natives, gazing in mute incomprehension as the Britons painstakingly collect and record numerous fragmented specimens of what the natives, in Holland's words, 'deem so little valuable' (Journal, p. 182).

It would be easy but quite wrong occasionally to discern in Holland's comments and judgements on such people an element of heedless aristocratic disdain for a remote and primitive society. In his M.D. Dissertation *De morbis Islandiæ* (Edinburgh, 1811), he remarks 'Natura terræ et cœli non ratione vel mentis cultura, Island sunt barbari' (p. 6). When contemplating the chill desolation of Iceland and its inhabitants, admiration and respect are never far from the surface of his remarks. Thus, in his 'Memoir on the Mineralogy of the Island of Iceland', delivered in Lisbon in July 1812, Holland notes:

Whilst their condition with respect to all the comforts or necessities of life is scarcely superior to the savage state, their moral & intellectual qualities raise them to a level even with the most civilized communities of Europe – and amidst the desarts which surround them, they still keep alive much of that spirit of literary pursuit, which in the 10th, 11th, & 12th centuries gave to their ancestors so much celebrity among the northern nations.[1]

It is not that occasions did not arise designed to test to the full Holland's reserves of phlegm and cultural relativism, as at Snóksdalur (Journal, pp. 208–10), on the southern shores of Breiðafjörður, when a biting North-East wind, and a 'dreary and repulsive' countryside, mineralogically barren and scenically featureless for 'the lover of picturesque beauty', would have proved sufficiently dispiriting without the subsequent domestic trials of a draughty church billet with a damp and rotten floor on which to sleep, and the hospitality of neighbours whose warmth of spirit and intention could not entirely compensate for their habitual method of cleaning the eating utensils – 'by the simple process of passing them through the mouth, and afterwards wiping them upon a dirty wadmal'.

The resilience of Holland's humble and tolerant admiration for the Icelanders and their country was, however, rarely compromised. A

---

[1] Lbs MS 4275 4to, p. 1.

letter to Maria Edgeworth catches the more characteristic tone well enough:

The toils of a day's travel over lava & cinders, without sight of a human habitation or human face – the hasty repose of a few minutes sleep, either on the rude & rocky flooring of a cave, or beneath the open face of a cold & tempestuous sky – the evening's scanty meal of stock fish, rye bread & curds – & the nightly abode in a small damp & gloomy church . . . all these events of almost daily occurrence were in the first instance recommended by novelty – afterwards rendered tolerable by habit. Occasionally indeed a sort of desolation of thought arose amidst the dreariness of surrounding nature; but it was akin to the feeling of the sublime, and its presence might almost have been solicited by the mind . . . The spectacles presented . . . are probably as magnificent as any on the surface of the globe . . . There is a singular disparity between their physical & moral condition; such as probably is found in no other community. They have little good turf & no good potatoes – they live amidst all the asperities of soil & climate, the face of nature is to them everywhere dreary & desolate – they are deprived not merely of all the luxuries, but even of what are deemed the essential comforts of life – yet these people have good temper & cheerfulness of mind – they have warm domestic & social affections, they have a high sense of moral rectitude, and an admirable observance of moral restraints – they have an excellent system of education throughout all the classes of the community . . . I have heard Latin spoken with Ciceronian elegance, & have known poetry composed on the purest models by men who earn a part of their subsistence fishing upon the stormy sea which surrounds their native island.[1]

Holland's absorption with the results of the 'excellent system of education' is, along with the war, the rocks and the people, a constant reference point throughout his journal. He might allow himself, in the same letter just quoted, the rhetorical extravagance of claiming that during his stay in Iceland:

no other books than those of external nature & of human character were open to me, yet I would not exchange the results of this reading for those of any studies which might have engaged me, had I remained within the quiet pale of domestic occupation;

but in fact books and bookishness invariably catch his eye. Holland is careful to note the presence of foreign (especially English) books in Icelandic households and other institutions – Bishop Geir Vídalín's ownership of Rollin's *Histoire Ancienne* (Journal, p. 87); Danish translations of Samuel Richardson's *Sir Charles Grandison* and of Joseph

[1] ME Letters 30 January 1811.

Addison's *Cato* in the possession of Pétur Ottesen at Síðumúli (Journal, p. 214); the Jón Þorláksson translation of the *Essay on Man* on the shelves of the printing press at Leirárgarðar (Journal, p. 164) and amongst Markús Magnússon's books at Garðar (Journal, p. 116); at the Latin school at Bessastaðir, the shelves were packed with works by eighteenth-century German theologians (Journal, p. 116); an English text of Tobias Smollett's *Roderick Random* had found its way into the possession of Holger Clausen of Ólafsvík (Journal, p. 198), a merchant who was almost as much an itinerant as Roderick himself; and, not least, as a result of Henry Holland's gift, Magnús Stephensen came to own James Thomson's *The Seasons* (Journal, p. 99).

Holland's journal also indicates the interest of Holland and his companions in Icelandic books. His friend Richard Bright purchased at Oddi a magnificently bound composite text bible printed at Hólar in 1637 (Old Testament) and 1644 (New Testament) (Journal, p. 270); he was also the dedicatee of a fine manuscript copy of part of Bishop Hannes Finnsson's *Lexicon Islandico-Latinum*,[1] and also acquired manuscripts of a fifteenth-century prayer book,[2] and of the lawbook of King Magnús Hákonarson, from Guðmundur Jónsson at Staðarholt;[3] Holland himself was loaned a copy of Runólfur Jónsson's *Grammaticæ Islandicæ rudimenta* (Copenhagen, 1651) (Journal, p. 95), by Finnur Magnússon, whose subsequent efforts to supplement his income led to the sale of countless valuable Icelandic manuscripts to collectors in Britain and further afield. Holland visited Leirárgarðar, site of what had become the only printing house operating in Iceland, autocratically controlled by Magnús Stephensen who, the generosity of his family's hospitality to the Britons and his manifest breadth of intellectual sympathies notwithstanding, seems not to have impressed Henry Holland. Amongst the Leirárgarðar publications acquired by Holland were an Icelandic cookbook, Jón Þorláksson's *Essay on Man* translation, and fourteen volumes of works issued by the *Lærdómslistafélag* (Icelandic Educational Society), these latter books purchased at Oddi, along with the Hólar bible and other unnamed titles (Journal, p. 270), from the library of Gísli Þórarinsson, who had been priest there until his death in 1807.

It is conceivable that amongst those unnamed titles was a copy of the 1786 Copenhagen edition of *Víga-Glúms saga* and certainly, whether

---

[1] Bodleian MS Icel. e. 3.   [2] Bodleian MS Icel. g. 1
[3] Bodleian MS Icel. e. 2.

purchased in Reykjavík or back home in Britain, Holland's ownership was to provide a striking focal point for a rather pathetic (as it turned out) meeting back in Scotland in the Spring of 1811. Holland had been asked whether he knew about an Icelander who was stranded and destitute in Leith and longed to return to his wife and ten children in Iceland. The man, he was told, was intending to publish in England a Latin-Icelandic lexicon 'with a view to making a little money', only to be confronted by his physician at Leith who had 'represented to him the impossibility in this country of deriving any profit from such a work' (NLS 7515, 17 March 1811). On visiting the man, Holland discovered him to be a 'Mr Peterson' and it is possible to identify that this was in fact Guðmundur Pétursson (1748–1811), the brother of the popular playwright and poet Sigurður Pétursson (1759–1827), well known to Holland through visits to his lodgings in Reykjavík at Bishop Geir Vídalín's house.[1] Holland learnt that Guðmundur intended to go to London (NLS 7515, 24 March 1811):

He has the idea that by the assistance of Sir Jos. Banks, to whom he has an introduction from Prof. Thorkelin, he shall be enabled to publish his Icelandic Lexicon . . . a supposition which the poor man will find (I hope not too late) to be entirely erroneous. I shewed him some of my specimens & sketches, with which he was highly delighted.

In the same letter to his father, Holland continues:

I wish, however you could have seen his still more vehement rapture, when he accidentally took up a work of his own, published at Copenhagen about 20 years ago, which I happened to have lying upon the table. He was almost ready to hug me upon the discovery – an effect which not even my frequent experience of such things in Iceland would have enabled me to relish.

Guðmundur Pétursson was, Holland would then have realised the editor of the 1786 *Víga-Glúms saga*, one of the important group of Icelandic texts edited and published in Copenhagen towards the end of the eighteenth century, texts which were to become eagerly sought after in Britain early in the nineteenth century, not least in the Edinburgh to which Holland had returned at the end of the 1810 expedition.

[1] Bogi Benediktsson, *Sýslumannaæfir*, 5 vols. (Reykjavík, 1881–1932), IV, 787–91; Stefán Einarsson, *A history of Icelandic literature* (Baltimore, 1957), pp. 217–18.

In the months following his return to Edinburgh there was for Henry
Holland the welcome inevitability that his experiences in Iceland would
generate numerous opportunities for both wistful recollection and
intellectual advancement. The periodic arrival of letters from Iceland
kept Holland in touch with many of his concerns and curiosities: the
beneficial impact of his prescribed remedies on Benedikt Gröndal's
depression (NLS 7515, 7 September 1811), the unpredictable impact of
John Parke, the new British consul in Iceland on commercial activity in
Reykjavík (Lbs 4925, 2 August 1811); and the inevitable impact of
Ólafur Loptsson's latest 'infamous acts' (Lbs 4925, 2 August 1811) on
the manners and morality of the island's capital. The periodic arrival of
his Icelandic specimen boxes at Leith enabled Holland enthusiastically
to fulfil his obligations and respond to requests made before his
departure, as with the rock samples directed to 'the Mineralogical
cabinet at the Dublin college' (NLS 7515, [12?] April 1810), and the
bottles of sea-water drawn from different depths at different latitudes,
to be distributed amongst colleagues in Edinburgh and further afield.
The periodic arrival of Icelanders at Leith, still a sadly common
occurrence as the Anglo-Danish hostilities bound up with the
Napoleonic conflict spluttered damagingly on, afforded Holland eagerly
seized opportunities to repay vividly remembered kindnesses. Thus on
one occasion he was able to welcome four Icelandic friends *en route* to
Copenhagen (Lbs 4925, 2 August 1811) – there was Christian
Jacobæus, the Keflavík merchant with whom he had stayed for three
storm beaten days; there was Bjarni Sívertsen of Hafnarfjörður, whose
wife and family had, in the absence of Bjarni, welcomed Holland and his
companions with unforgettable generosity – hashed mutton, currant
pancakes, London porter, Windsor soap and Eider down mattresses
(Journal, p. 115) and whose presence and diplomatic activity in Britain
at this time presaged the return to Iceland of the ill-gotten gains of the
1808 Gilpin raid on Reykjavík and its environs;[1] there was Halldór
Guðmundsson Thorgrímsen, stepson of Holland's learned friend
Bishop Geir Vídalín, the young man's unheralded arrival enabling
Holland to take pleasure in his guest's wide-eyed and disbelieving
delight in all that was revealed to him of the lush picturesqueness of

[1] Halldór Hermannsson, 1928, p. 53, note 1.

lowland Scotland; and, as has been noted, there was the sad figure of Guðmundur Pétursson.

To more distant friends, amongst them Bishop Geir, Finnur Magnússon, and Ólafur, the promising twenty year old son of Magnús Stephensen, Holland sent gifts of books accompanied by letters in Latin (NLS 7515, 7 April 1811); to Tómas Klog, Iceland's chief physician, there were medical texts for his practice and seeds for his garden (NLS 7515, 7 April 1811); whilst, to the silken-clothed Guðrún Johnsen,[1] 'a pocket book and some other little things' were to act as 'witness of my tender affections' (NLS 7515, 7 April 1811). An equivalent *tendresse* is discernible in the ardent letters recalling his trip which Holland sent to Maria Edgeworth in Ireland.

The recollections with which Holland favoured the scholarly community nearer home were exclusively geological, keenly awaited, and anxiously prepared. He was as aware of the Huttonian-Wernerian controversy as Sir George Mackenzie, and a good deal more sensitive towards it. In preparing a paper for the Geological Society of London, he consulted widely, avoided polemics and offered support for his conclusions with a discriminating selection from the crates of carefully labelled rock specimens, before forwarding the manuscript text which was to be read at a Society meeting in May 1811 by Richard Bright, his Iceland travelling companion. A shorter version of this paper,[2] again cautious in tone, was to reach a learned audience in Lisbon the following summer.

Ultimately, however, if, as he had assured his father, 'advantage' and beneficial 'notoriety' were to accrue from the Mackenzie expedition, a full-length travel book, anticipated and pre-empted before they set sail (NLS 7515, [12?] April 1810) by the Edinburgh publisher Archibald Constable would have to be written. The auguries for such a publication were surprisingly unpromising. Dr. Syntax could claim in 1812 that 'I'll make a tour – and then I'll write it',[3] the habit having by then become familiar to the point of parody, and Holland, in a letter to Maria Edgeworth, clearly recognises the fashion: 'nobody, you know, travels now a days without writing a quarto to tell the world where he

[1] See Andrew Wawn, 'Hundadagadrottningin. Bréf frá Íslandi: Guðrún Johnsen og Stanleyfjölskyldan frá Cheshire, 1814–16', *Saga: tímarit sögufélags*, 23 (1985), 97–133.

[2] Lbs MS 4275 4to. The longer version is amongst the Richard Bright manuscripts in the British Museum (Natural History), Department of Mineralogy Library.

[3] William Combe, *The tour of Dr. Syntax in search of the picturesque* (1812), quoted in Charles L. Batten, *Pleasurable instruction: form and convention in eighteenth-century travel literature* (Berkeley, 1978), p. 9.

has been, & what he has beheld' (ME, 30 January 1811). However, the fact was that previous British explorers of Iceland had not by any means been seized by this apparently uncontrollable compulsion. Dr. Johnson had once contemplated a voyage to Iceland, and, had he gone, would no doubt have written memorably of it;[1] but from those who did go, the publications were few in number and modest in length. Sir Joseph Banks' own manuscript journals from his 1772 voyage remained unpublished until 1973,[2] though some scientific papers by von Troil and his other colleagues were first published in 1777; none of the journals of John Thomas Stanley's companions on his 1789 expedition was published until 1970,[3] whilst Stanley himself, after producing two brief essays on the hot springs of Reykir and Haukadalur for publication in 1794, subsequently turned a deaf ear to the persistent urgings of his friend Dr. Charles Scot, himself a frustrated sentimental traveller, who had been forbidden from accompanying Stanley by an over-possessive mother. Expressing a wish that Stanley would produce a published Iceland journal, Scot asserts:

I know it will do you much credit – but you need not hurry yourself – many Travellers have been much longer before they communicated their Observations & discoveries than you probably will.[4]

adding subsequently:

You have the power to make the history of your Expedition to Iceland very interesting. With facts & observations for the Philosopher, social incidents, & delineation of character, with sentiment & moral reflections, for the more elegant part of mankind what would be wanting to gain you a preference above all those who have given any account of the countries you visited? Indeed my friend I shall be really sorry to hear that you have given up all thoughts of this design.[5]

Even twenty years later, as the preparations for Sir George Mackenzie's 1811 volume went ahead, Holland expressed to his father (Lbs 4925, 2 August 1811) the concern that material in his own Preliminary Dissertation might interfere with any future publication plans which Stanley might be entertaining. He need not have worried.

The reluctance to publish which seized both Banks and Stanley even

---

[1] Hill and Powell, 1934, I, 242; III, 455.
[2] Rauschenberg, 1973.　　　　　　　　[3] West, 1970–6.
[4] Cheshire County Record Office, MS DSA 7/3, letter dated 'January 1790'.
[5] Cheshire County Record Office, MS DSA 7/3, letter dated 28 February 1790.

touched W. J. Hooker briefly and partially. By March 1811 only 100 copies of Hooker's two volume privately printed account of his 1809 visit to Iceland were in very limited circulation, and it was not until late July in the same year (Lbs 4925, 2 August 1811) that Hooker indicated almost apologetically to Richard Bright that it was now his intention to publish his account more widely, having previously indicated to Mackenzie his intention not to do so. The possibility of its formal publication at this or some future stage represented a stimulus rather than a threat to Constable, Mackenzie and Holland, for it helped to ensure that their own volume would be ready in sufficient time to catch the new autumn bookselling season in 1811. Certainly the contents of Hooker's book complemented rather than duplicated the Mackenzie-Holland volume: Reykjavík 1809 was a very different town from Reykjavík 1810; Hooker's account[1] of the Jörgensen 'insurrection' was staunchly supportive of the Dane, whereas Mackenzie was to dedicate his volume to Count Trampe, and to include in the revised edition,[2] an account of the same events hostile to Jörgensen and favourably inclined to the volume's dedicatee; Hooker's interests were avowedly botanical and he does not hesitate to refer those of his readers with mineralogical interests to the Mackenzie volume, the chief mineralogical interest of his own volume lying in a lengthy account of the Skaftáreldar eruptions of 1783, translated from Magnús Stephensen's published account of these events by none other than Jörgen Jörgensen.[3] Holland notes with understandable if uncharitable satisfaction (NLS 7515, 7 April 1811) that Hooker's introduction 'interferes scarcely at all' with his own Dissertation, that several of Hooker's prints and illustrations are 'miserable' and 'wretched', that Hooker's text is written in a 'careless' and 'somewhat inelegant' manner, that Hooker offers no account of 'the wonderful phenomenon of the alternating geyser', having indeed neither seen nor heard it in spite of his having been within half a mile of Geysir and Strokkur during his southern Iceland travels. Holland's concluding tribute to the Hooker narrative falls some way short of complete graciousness: he claims it is 'touched with a sort of naivete of description which would I think render it interesting to the reader, who

---

[1] Hooker, 1813, II, 3–63.

[2] Mackenzie, 1812, pp. 474–81. Mackenzie's dedication to Trampe is a 'testimony of respect for his public character, and of gratitude for his kind exertions to render the journey through Iceland agreeable and successful'.

[3] Hooker, 1813, II, 124–261. Magnús Stephensen's work was *Kort beskrivelse over den nye vulcans ildsprudning i Vester-Skaptefields-Syssel paa Island i aaret 1783* (Copenhagen, 1785).

has none of the local associations, which I bring to its perusal', thus striking a note of polite condescension similar to that which was later to characterise the reaction of John Thomas Stanley's wife to the Mackenzie-Holland volume.

Lady Stanley did at least find words of praise for Henry Holland's major contribution to the volume. Holland had prepared a brief section on the commerce and trade of Iceland, drawing extensively on a then recent survey of eighteenth century Iceland which the prolific Magnús Stephensen had written and a copy of which the Britons had acquired in Reykjavík.[1] Holland also wrote a section on the laws and government of contemporary Iceland, apparently basing it on information which is included as a rather indigestible Latin appendix to his manuscript journal. Of his main contribution, Lady Stanley comments: 'The introductory chapter by H. Holland on the "History of Iceland" is well done',[2] and the tribute, however sparing, is well deserved, as is confirmed by material from the essay being extensively extracted in the *Annual Register* 1811[3] and warmly commended in the *Edinburgh Review* 1811–12.[4]

Essentially a work of synthesis and distillation, the Preliminary Dissertation is a major achievement, formidable in the range of authorities cited, and impressive in the confidence with which they are deployed. Holland claims in the preparation of the Dissertation:

I have bestowed much minute attention upon all the more important records of the histories & antiquities of the north, and have held my patient course through page after page of wearisome, monotonous detail. (ME, 30 January 1811).

The text certainly confirms the effort expended if not the tedium experienced. The extensive and fastidious footnotes reveal a remarkable breadth of reading, both ancient and modern – from Saxo Grammaticus to Snorri Sturluson, from Ari Þorgilsson to Arngrímur Jónsson, from

[1] *Island i det attende aarhundrede: historisk-politisk skildret* (Copenhagen, 1808). Holland copies two tables of trading figures from the book (Stephensen, 1808, facing pp. 270, 432) into his account of Icelandic trade, introducing four small errors as he does so; these tables, with additional errors, are printed in Mackenzie, 1811, facing pp. 281, 285. See below, Appendix E; also note 1, p. 274.

[2] Jane H. Adeane, *The early married life of Maria Josepha, Lady Stanley* (London, 1900), p. 336.

[3] There are two extracts from Holland's material: on Icelandic literature and education (pp. 426–38) and on the religious practice of the Icelanders (pp. 438–9); Mackenzie's section on Icelandic 'rural affairs' is also extracted (pp. 439–45).

[4] Pp. 416–35, especially pp. 416–18.

Björn of Skarðsá to Þormóður Torfason, from Hakluyt to Hálfdan Einarsson, from Ole Worm, Grímur Thorkelín and 'of greatest value',[1] Finnur Jónsson, right down to the hapless Amos Cottle. The works of several of these writers had been known in England fifty years earlier as Thomas Gray prepared his Norse odes for publication in 1768, but latterly the task facing writers who shared Gray's Northern enthusiasms was lightened by the publication in Copenhagen of major editions of Icelandic prose and verse texts, with generous annotation and with facing-page Latin translations. This latter provision was of particular benefit to Holland who knew little Icelandic. We know that Holland owned the 1786 edition of *Víga-Glúms saga* (as did John Thomas Stanley)[2] – other Copenhagen texts available included *Kristni saga* (1773), *Landnámabók* (1774), *Sagan af Gunnlaugi Ormstungu og Skalld-Rafni* [sic] (1775), *Hervarar saga* (1785), *Eyrbyggja saga* (1787), and most notably the first volume of the great *Sæmundar Edda* (1787). Use was also made of texts printed during the eighteenth century in Iceland itself – at Leirárgarðar, Hólar, and Hrappsey, as well as of newly published English translations of seminal reference works such as Eggert Ólafsson and Bjarni Pálsson, *Reise igiennem Island* (Sorøe, 1772), which had become available in a somewhat truncated English version – *Travels in Iceland* (London, 1805).[3] This doggedly utilitarian version of *Reise igiennem Island* would have taught Holland much about Iceland if little about its literature – the equal length of sections entitled 'Of steeped and macerated fish' (p. 16) and 'Of their sagas and historical recitations' (pp. 25–6) was indicative of the work's priorities! Another publication often cited in Holland, less specifically Icelandic, more determinedly literary, and immensely influential, was Bishop Thomas Percy's *Northern antiquities* (London, 1770), a translation (albeit sometimes an amplified and realigned one) of Paul Henri Mallet's authoritative *Introduction á l'Histoire de Dannemarc* (Copenhagen, 1755). Percy's translation, which absorbed his 1763 *Five pieces of runic poetry*, was published in a new edition in Edinburgh in 1809. Holland also makes occasional use of William Herbert's *Select Icelandic poetry* (London, 1804–6), a two-volume collection of texts, translations and extensive and learned footnotes by another leading English scholar of Northern antiquities.

[1] Holland, 1872, p. 82, note.
[2] The present editor owns this copy, with Stanley's name-plate on the inside cover.
[3] Also newly available was a revised edition of von Troil's *Letters on Iceland* in John Pinkerton, *A general collection of the best and most interesting voyages and travels in all parts of the world* 17 vols. (London, 1808–14), I, 621–734.

'Wearisome and monotonous' as the process of assimilating these diverse source materials may have been the resulting essay, perceptive, engaged and ambitious, is impressive. Holland identifies three stages of Icelandic cultural development – the golden age after the Settlement period; the decline into lethargy until the end of the sixteenth century; and the subsequent revival of learning, of which the Copenhagen texts cited above were both symptom and cause. In some respects the essay reveals Holland to be a man of his time. The period of the great Eddic poems and of the great historical writing (which for Holland meant sagas as much as it meant Ari) was set against a characteristically romantic and Whiggish backcloth – brave Norwegian exiles from the 'despotic sway' (Mackenzie, 1811, p. 17; all further references are to this edition) of tyrannical royalty at home had settled a desolate land and made it fertile, bringing with them their mythology 'propitious to poetic fiction and ornament' (p. 17), which was then Icelandicised, poeticised and, along with the sagas, written down in circumstances the contemplation of which stirs and steers Holland's imagination in recognisably Wordsworthian directions:

The summer sun saw them indeed laboriously occupied in seeking their provision from a stormy ocean and a barren soil; but the long seclusion of the winter gave them the leisure, as well as the desire, to cultivate talents, which were at once so fertile in occupation and delight. During the darkness of their year, and beneath the rude covering of wood and turf, they recited to their assembled families the deeds and descent of their forefathers; from whom they had received that inheritance of liberty, which they now dwelt among deserts to preserve. (p. 18)

Holland was, however, only too aware that for those hungering for the 'native woodnotes wild', Old Icelandic literature returned a blank stare. With the Eddic poetry 'it is difficult now to appreciate the beauty or propriety of these alliterations' (p. 22), whilst, with the prose, there is frequently 'minute and wearisome description of events' (p. 29) in overgenerous profusion. Yet sometimes the poetry can yield, amidst its artful and jagged complexity, and even if only by accident, a 'homeliness and simplicity of style' (p. 22) attractive to Holland, whilst the sagas at their best offer:

pictures of manners and feelings, in which simplicity itself is the charm, and where the imagination is insensibly led back to the times, the people, and the scenes [of Iceland] (p. 29).

There is no doubt that Holland's imagination was particularly engaged by *Gunnlaugs saga ormstungu*. In this he was not alone amongst his contemporaries – the same saga inspired (if that isn't too generous a term) a forgettable poem by Landor;[1] an unforgettable play by Sir George Mackenzie, the unintentionally ludicrous *Helga*;[2] and an extended plot summary by William Herbert.[3] Holland knew of Herbert's account of the story:

Were it less interesting, as a specimen of the manners and literature of the ancient Icelanders, the repetition of what he has so ably done, would not have been attempted (p. 32).

Holland's own summary in the Preliminary Dissertation transcends mere repetition, however. Behind the placid decorousness of the prose, there are hints of a vivid imaginative response to the narrative, far removed from the blandness of Herbert's account. Thus the tensions and the pathos of Gunnlaugr's arrival at the uneasy wedding celebrations for Helga and Hrafn, a scene completely ignored by Herbert, are strikingly characterised:

Gunnlaug shewed himself on a sudden among the assembled guests, eminent above all from the beauty of his person and the richness of his apparel. The eyes of the lovers hung upon each other in mute and melancholy sorrow; and the bitterest pangs went to the heart of the gentle Helga. The nuptial feast was gloomy and without joy. A contest between the rivals was prevented by the interference of their friends, but they parted with increased animosity and hatred (p. 31).

The decline of a literature of such precocious achievement exercised Holland a good deal in the Preliminary Dissertation. Mallet's explanations for the rise of Icelandic literature were well known and often cited,[4] but the decline had been little considered. Holland offers three reasons. First, as native European literature burgeoned, there was no further need for the services of the itinerant Icelandic skalds who previously had been feted in the courts of Scandinavia and further afield – skalds such as Gunnlaugr and Hrafn themselves. An impetus to poetic creativity, Holland argues, had been removed (p. 54). Second, Holland, a Unitarian, required little encouragement to associate himself with that

---

[1] Walter Savage Landor, *The complete works*, ed. T. E. Welby and Stephen Wheeler, 16 vols. (London, 1927–36), XIII, 91–102.

[2] Wawn, 1982.

[3] Herbert, 1804–6, I, 65–70.

[4] For instance, by Coxe, 1802, V, 153.

group of romantic critics who believed unswervingly that the Catholic church had exercised a baleful influence on medieval literature. Holland argues that, in the Icelandic context, its corrupting wealth, the unhappy influence of its crude miracle stories and hagiographic traditions, and the decay in secular jurisprudence occasioned by overmuch attention to the rites and formalities of the church, had collectively sapped the native literary spirit (p. 55). Third, he offers an interesting variant on the thesis favoured by late romantic critics well into the present century – namely that the surrender of Icelandic independence to the tyranny of the Norwegian throne in 1262 crushed the native individualism of the Icelanders' creativity. Holland suggests that 1262 represented 'rather an alliance than a timid surrender of rights' (p. 48) and that the subsequent Norwegian and Danish royal rule was 'lenient and forbearing' (p. 51). That, Holland felt, had been the problem:

Had the foreign yoke been a tyrannical one, the primeval spirit of the Icelanders might possibly have been maintained by the persecution which laboured to suppress it (p. 50).

As things turned out:

Repose and security, succeeding to internal broils, produced a state of comparative apathy and indolence. The same call was not made for individual exertion, nor the same rewards proposed to its successful exercise. Rank and property became more nearly equalized among the inhabitants; and, all looking up to a superior power, the spirit of independence declined, and they expected from others the support and protection which they had once afforded to themselves (p. 51).

It is worth remarking in the context of their single unhappy encounter that, amongst those who might have been expected to share Holland's view that external hostility had caused early Icelandic cultural creativity to be leaner and fitter, was William Morris, who came to recognise in Iceland an irresistible icon for his belief in creativity energised by hardship:

'. . . amid waning of realms and their riches
and death of things worshipped and sure,
I [Iceland] abide here the spouse of a God,
and I made and I make and I endure.'[1]

The final stage of Iceland's cultural development, the halting of the

---

[1] 'Iceland first seen', ll.53–6, in Morris [1891], pp. 41–2.

late medieval decline, was activated, argues Holland, by the Reformation spiritually (p. 58), and by the printing press technically (p. 57). Hence his chivalrous, in the context of the then active Anglo-Danish conflict, praise for the Danish efforts to publish some of the great monuments of Iceland's literary past (pp. 68–9). In the analysis which Holland offers of this stage, and of both the earlier stages, it is not the sometimes uncertain nature of the claims and explanations offered which is important so much as the fact that explanations were attempted at all. The evidence suggests that this section did not come easily. In the documentary appendices to Holland's manuscript journal, an account of Icelandic literature is announced, but the subsequent pages were left blank.[1] It seems that belatedly the Preliminary Dissertation served to provide this missing section. Holland's essay could have turned into a leaden-footed trudge through the lifeless contents of half-read books. It was his ambition, learning and sympathy which prevented this.

'WRITING A QUARTO' (2): COLLABORATION AND FRUSTRATION

The Dissertation and his own other contributions to the forthcoming book completed, Holland might reasonably have expected to be able to put his concern with the volume to one side, and to be able instead to give renewed attention to other pressing priorities – his studies, for instance. His summer final examinations in medicine, which had 'lately become much more strict than formerly' (NLS 7515, 31 March 1811) were already casting their shadow, and his M.D. dissertation had still to be completed and Latinized (NLS 7515, 31 March 1811): this latter work was an account of the diseases of Iceland distilled partly from his own observations – scurvy (p. 11), psoriasis (p. 13) and hypochondria (p. 24) for example – and partly from the knowledge of Tómas Klog, the *landphysicus*, who had recent first-hand knowledge of Tetanus in the Vestmannaeyjar (p. 25). Holland might also have hoped for the opportunity to devote some time to the many enticing demands made by Edinburgh society and by the diversity of its and his intellectual sympathies during the last few months he was to spend in the northern capital. If ever entertained, these were to prove forlorn expectations. The week ending 24 March 1811 is entirely representative of his problems (NLS 7515, 24 March 1811). His diary was packed with

[1] Lbs MS 3876 4to, pp. 118–27.

engagements, his mind more than fully occupied. There was 'the labour of the three Latin epistles which I am about to write to Iceland'; there was the preparation of his paper for the Geological Society of London which was delaying his writing yet another lengthy letter to Maria Edgeworth; there were willingly undertaken but time consuming visits to locally imprisoned French troops stricken by pneumonia and in constant need, he believed, of therapeutic bleeding; more of the Iceland boxes had arrived, the state of whose contents – cheese, Eider duck eggs, butter and Geysir water – can, six months after their dispatch, only be imagined; there was the luckless Guðmundur Pétursson to interview again; on the Monday evening, Sir George Mackenzie was delivering a paper 'on the more theoretical parts of the mineralogy of Iceland' at the Edinburgh Royal Society, an event from which Holland could hardly absent himself, whatever his misgivings about the lecturer and his material; there were geological walks to undertake with different sets of companions; Wednesday evening offered the prospect of a large gathering at a Mrs. Grant's house for music and dancing; Thursday brought a drearily unavoidable dinner engagement with a young Mr. Miller 'who carried with him as strong a character of idiotcy as any individual I ever saw', and with Miller's equally tiresome mother, anxiously engaged on the forlorn task of trying to 'introduce him [her son] into the society of Edinburgh' – by the end of a dismal evening, Holland might have been forgiven had he envied the fate of young Miller's brother, 'who shot himself in Oxford last summer'. At the end of such a week, if Holland was unable to claim that there had never been a dull moment, he could assuredly have claimed that there had never been a quiet one. Yet the principal drain on his energies during this week had been none of these activities but rather the progress of the Iceland book. Sir George's Monday evening lecture, in the event, went surprisingly well: Sir George's book was going unsurprisingly badly.

That it was going badly was certainly not the fault of Constable, the publisher, as Holland's 24 March letter makes clear. He had returned from London buoyant with accounts of the eager expectations which the announcement of the volume had already aroused. Holland was pleased with the choice of a 'particularly good paper, the same as was employed in the 8vo edition of the Lady of the Lake'; several of the engravings and vignettes for the volume, brought back from London by Constable, were judged 'very excellent and praiseworthy', with particular enthusiasm directed towards the four aqua-tinted prints; the presses were ready, able to proceed at a rate of twenty pages a week; and Holland was much impressed with the intelligence of the printing shop supervisor. Holland calculated that his Preliminary Dissertation could be run off in three weeks, after which would come 'Sir G. with *his* composition'. Therein lay the problem, or problems.

Mackenzie was responsible for writing the narrative accounts of the Reykjanes, Snæfellsnes and Geysir journeys of the previous summer. Holland had sensed the troubles ahead as early as January, but, glowing from initial praise for his own Dissertation (Mrs. Hamilton's 'own expression was . . . it was delightful' (NLS 7515, 26 January 1811)), and believing it to be 'the most successful composition in which I have yet been engaged' the young scholar had allowed himself a note of cautious optimism about the enterprise as a whole:

I confess to you I begin to entertain better hopes of this Icelandic work. Sir G's paper of last Monday was so greatly superior to anything else I have seen of his composition, that if we can but approach the rest of his writing to the same level, all will go very well . . . the terms on which I stand with Sir G are such, that as respects the arrangement and conduct of the work, I believe I can effect any alteration I chuse. A style is not so easy to change. (NLS 7515, 26 January 1811.)

How prophetic his final remark proved to be. Sir George had enjoyed access not only to his own notes and journals, such as they were, but also to those of Richard Bright and, most importantly, to those of Henry Holland. The results, as they gradually emerged, however, were a frustrating and largely irretrievable disappointment, even after Mackenzie had been 'compelled' by Holland to expand his mineralogical section by five or six pages, 'that the number 400 may be seen at the top – a circumstance which may perhaps be of some little advantage to the sale of the book – with those at least who judge from the general aspect of contents' (Lbs 4925, 2 August 1811). If the quality was becoming a lost cause, Sir George could at least get the width right.

Holland's growing disappointment with the pallid quality of the narrative found frequent expression in his letters: 'the narrative part of the volume must remain a very common place performance – common place equally in matter and style' (NLS 7515, 31 March 1811); 'the plain truth is that he has no powers of description, and no taste in matters of style' (NLS 7515, 6 June 1811); or, more witheringly, 'the last Chapter is now printed, and a very poor and paltry one it is – inconsiderable in length, and miserably ill-written' (NLS 7515, 22 July 1811). Sir

George's inability to achieve an appropriate amplitude in his material even led Holland to lament the high speed with which the printing seemed to be proceeding (NLS 7515, 13 June 1811). He wished it could take a good deal longer – or rather, he wished that there was more of Sir George's material to print.

Of what there was to print, its indebtedness to Holland's own Journal is constantly apparent, with whole sections lifted verbatim from Holland's manuscript at every stage of Mackenzie's narratives. The main problems, indeed, arose when Sir George chose to deviate from his primary source. A midnight visit to a hot spring by Leirá provides a first glimpse of these problems. Comparison of the accounts by Holland and Mackenzie of this brief incident reveals the extent of Sir George's indebtedness. First Holland's account:

Before supper, Sir G. Mackenzie observed in a causeway leading to the house, a singular fragment of stone, resembling much an incrustation, & containing numerous vegetable impressions & petrefactions – Upon enquiry we found that there is a hot spring near Leira, in the vicinity of which we are told that a large assemblage of these stones appear – After supper, we set off by the light of an Icelandic midnight, to visit this spring, under the guidance of the Atatsrood – We found it on an open part of the plain about a mile to the NW of Leira. The hot water issues in small quantity from two holes in the rock, & runs down to a stream which flows just below. A considerable cavity in the rock, close to one of the springs, through which the hot water runs, has been used as a bath. About a hundred years ago, a magistrate of the district suddenly died, while bathing in this place. We found an incrustation in a state of incipient formation on the rock below the springs – A hundred yards further to the NW, a large bed appeared of fragments exactly resembling that we had found at Leira, evidently the incrustations derived from some spring or springs formerly existing on this spot. No other vestige, however, of such springs is to be seen at the present period – On our way back to Leira, we observed another similar assemblage of fragments, about ½ a mile from the Sysselman's house – This walk was finished exactly at 12 o'clock at night, on the 21st of June – Though the sky was covered with thick & lowering clouds, the light was sufficient for the perusal of the smallest type without difficulty or inconvenience (Journal, pp. 162–3).

Then Mackenzie's version:

On our arrival at Leira, I had observed, in a causeway leading to the house, a fragment of stone, appearing to be an incrustation, or deposit from water, and containing numerous vegetable petrefactions. Upon inquiry, we found that there was a hot spring at the distance of about a mile from the Sysselman's house. After supper, we set off, by the light of an Icelandic midnight, to visit this spring, being guided to it by Mr. Stephenson and his nephew. We found the water, which had a temperature of 138°, issuing from two or three small holes in the rock, and running into a stream which flows near the spot. A small cavity which has been formed so as to receive the hot water, is occasionally employed as a bath. Near the springs, we observed a considerable extent of surface covered with curious petrefactions, evidently formed by deposition from some more ancient hot springs, which have now disappeared. Our walk was finished a little before 12 o'clock at night. Though the sky was cloudy and lowering, and a high range of mountains limited the horizon towards the north, yet the light was such as, even within the house, to be sufficient for the perusal of the smallest type, without difficulty or inconvenience. (Mackenzie, 1811, pp. 152–3.)

The extent of the verbal parellelism cannot, however, hide completely the changes which Mackenzie has seen fit to make. On the one hand he does add the detail of the water temperature, but, against that, precision as to direction and distance, 'a hundred yards to the NW', becomes merely 'near the springs'; the 'similar assemblage of fragments' encountered half a mile from the house on the return journey is omitted; the certainty of 'two holes in the rock' gives way to the less decisive 'two or three small holes in the rock'; and the vivid anecdotal reference to the drowning magistrate finds no favour with Mackenzie.

The next day the travellers were shown round the important printing house at Leirárgarðar. This is Holland's version:

At the distance of a few hundred yards from the Sysselman's House, we stopped some time to examine the interior of the Leira printing office – the only establishment of this nature in the whole island. Formerly there were two – one at Hrappsey – the other at Hoolum – These were given up – and the office at Leira established in the year 1794 – The establishment is at present supported by the Icelandic Society (for an account of which see Vol. 2^d). Two men are employed in the office, and have a pretty constant occupation – They have eight founts of types – 6 of the German or Gothic, 2 of the Roman character – Also a few types of the Greek character – The press is constructed much in the usual way – the printer's ink is made on the spot of lamp black, & oil. The building is altogether a miserable one – situated on a piece of swampy ground, & greatly inferior in appearance to an English cottage. It has latterly been much injured by the winter floods, & it is now in projection to construct a new building on the same spot – the execution of which is only delayed from the scarcity of timber in Iceland during the period of war – In one room of the Printing office, are kept some of the books which have been published by the Society – These are sold on the spot by Mr Schagfiord, the head-printer. We purchased a few of them – among others, as a literary curiosity, a translation of Pope's Essay on Man into Icelandic verse – They are at present engaged here in printing a work of the Atastrood's on the Polity of Iceland (Journal, p. 164).

Mackenzie's version of the same scene reads:

We left Leira next morning; and the Sysselman attended us for some miles. We visited in our way the only printing-office now in Iceland, which is close to Leira, in a small and miserable wooden building, situated in the midst of a bog. This establishment is at present kept up by the literary society, of which Mr. Stephenson is at the head. He has the sole management of the press; and is so fond of his own compositions, that few other people now give it employment; none liking to submit their works to so severe a censor. This state of the press is extremely injurious to the literature of Iceland. Two men are engaged in the printing-office: they have a press of the common construction, and make their own ink of oil and lamp-black. There are eight founts of type; six Gothic, and two Roman; with a few Greek characters. We found a small collection of books, which had been printed within the last few years, and remained here for sale. We purchased several of these, among which was Pope's Essay on Man, translated into Icelandic verse. During the last winter, the printing-office, with all its contents, was very nearly swept away by a flood; and, at the present time, the building is in a state of wretched repair. (Mackenzie, 1811, p. 153.)

Again, behind the closely parallel passages, there is Mackenzie's willingness to sacrifice Holland's fondness for telling detail – the date of the press at Leirárgarðar, the name of the chief printer, the venues of the two former printing houses, the title of the work currently being seen through the press, the reference to the war, the comparison with an English cottage – in favour of inserting censorious comment, toned down in the revised edition, on Magnús Stephensen's rather tyrannical reputation as head of the printing-house.

An earlier visit to Bishop Geir Vidalín's house in Reykjavík provides a third slightly different kind of example. First Holland:

We called this morning upon the Bishop – His house is in no wise distinguished externally from those around it, and as regards the interior, it is considerably inferior to many others we saw in the town. We were ushered into a room, which appears to serve at once as a library, parlour, and levee-chamber – Its cleanliness could not be applauded – it was clear that a long period had elapsed since either water or broom had visited the flooring & walls – The Bishop's Library appears to consist of 4 or 500 volumes – the greater number Icelandic or Danish – a considerable number of classics – We noticed Rollin's Ancient History on one of the shelves. A large map of Europe, published in London in 1804, was hanging in the room. The Bishop's reception of us was very friendly, but the necessity of employing an interpreter threw considerable difficulty upon the conversation. He has four sons, – some of whom were present in the room. They gazed upon us intently, but did not speak during our stay in the house (Journal, pp. 86–7).

And then Mackenzie:

The first visit we paid, after landing on the 8th of May, was to the bishop, Geir Vidalin, who received us with great kindness. He is a good looking man, above the ordinary stature; corpulent, but not unwieldy; with an open countenance, which seems to declare his feelings without disguise. He is an excellent classical scholar, and speaks Latin fluently; and his general knowledge is equal, if not superior, to that of any person in Iceland. (Mackenzie, 1811, pp. 83–4.)

Mackenzie's eye never really gets past the houseowner, his appearance, personality, and intellectual attainment; Holland's eye is caught more by the books in the library, the map on the wall, the dirt on the floor, the dumbstruck sons in the room. Moreover, whilst Mackenzie is quite correct to state that Bishop Geir spoke Latin fluently, Holland's journal entry makes it reasonably clear that Latin was not the language spoken on this occasion. He and the bishop subsequently conversed freely in Latin whenever they met, but Holland's reference to the services of an interpreter on this first meeting, suggests that the language in use by Bishop Geir was Icelandic. Mackenzie's is generalised recollection in tranquillity: Holland's is particularised observation recorded at the time (or at least the same day) and lending a characteristic immediacy to his chronicle of the Icelandic expedition which frequently eludes Sir George.

The additions which Mackenzie makes to Holland's journal material are as revealing as his omissions, realignments and modifications. A visit to Ólafur Stephensen on Viðey, the island just offshore from and to the east of the Reykjavík town centre, illustrates this strikingly. On the day before the visit, the British party lunched with James Savignac and then explored a 'boiling spring, about 3 miles from the town' (Journal, p. 89). Holland details their findings – Mackenzie mentions neither the lunch nor the springs. Much material is common to both accounts of the Viðey expedition, but whilst Holland dutifully records the type and condition of Ólafur's livestock, Mackenzie introduces into the 1812 revised edition of the text, a snuff-box exchange:

While awaiting the hour of dinner, one of the party happened to take a little snuff from a box of no great value; but as it attracted the notice of our host, and he seemed to admire the snuff no less than the box, he was entreated to accept of both. The present was received with the highest marks of satisfaction; and the good old gentleman instantaneously drew from his pocket a curious box, ornamented with silver, which had been made in Iceland, and insisted on being permitted to return the compliment. This mark of politeness, and the beauty of the box, produced very warm expressions of admiration from the whole party; when our host suddenly left the room, and returning with a silver box of far greater value, snatched the first from the person who held it, and insisted on an exchange with so good a grace, and with so much earnestness, that this heavy balance against the trifle he had got could not be refused. We afterwards found that the box belonged to his father, whose initials were wrought on the cover. We were very much struck with the refined, at the same time heartfelt politeness which accompanied this little transaction (Mackenzie, 1812, pp. 83–4).

In Holland's Journal at this point there is not a snuff box to be seen or scented. For all its much ado about very little, the scene is a pleasing and revealing one, much more likely to catch the attention of Sir George Mackenzie, with his erratic but strong taste for 'human interest' stories, than it was to appeal to the rather sterner gaze of Henry Holland; yet it is an incident given excessively generous coverage by Mackenzie and it was, no doubt, with such scenes in mind that a contemporary reviewer of the volume, perhaps Francis Jeffrey, notes the occasional presence of detail 'more minute than was quite necessary' and the occasional concern with events which 'though they might affect the comfort of the traveller at the time, do not throw much light either upon the natural or moral history of the country'.[1] The same indiscriminate profligacy of detail is in evidence when Mackenzie then turns to the description of the native Icelandic costume on show at Ólafur Stephensen's house. Two laborious pages are devoted to such description, most of it being promptly rendered redundant by a facing page full-colour engraving of all the outfits described, accompanied by Sir George's disarming observation that 'the different dresses are better explained [by the engraving] than by words' (Mackenzie, 1811, p. 87; in 1812 the picture was moved to the front of the volume). Small wonder that Holland was very enthusiastic about all the engravings: any one of them promised to be worth at least a thousand of Sir George's maladroitly chosen words.

So it was that Mackenzie's contributions rarely did justice to the attention lavished on their journal source by Henry Holland. Too often, the 'simplicity' (1811, p. xiv) identified by Sir George as the governing principle of his narrative style proves to be mere dilution, as brisk and

[1] *Edinburgh Review* (1811–12), p. 418.

sharp-eyed observation is compromised by eccentric narrative priorities and a pervasive imprecision. The scrupulous chronology of events is irrecoverably misted over; the mass of hard won geological data in Holland's facing page notes in his journal is reduced to a relatively brief appendix (1811, pp. 435–56); yet, perversely, each opportunity to mention, for instance, any sort of passing horse in the narrative is lovingly lingered over by Mackenzie, irrespective of the importance (invariably none) of the animal. Sir George shows little interest in Icelandic ancient lore and legend, yet equally little interest in its current political instability or, a brief but powerful section on Icelandic annexation apart (Mackenzie, 1811, p. 271), the politics of Europe and their effects on Iceland. He shows more concern for the possible commercial exploitation of the natural phenomena encountered than he does in the forensic observation and description of them.

There is one further stylistic feature much in evidence which distinguishes Holland's journal from Mackenzie's narrative: the nature of the descriptive vocabulary. In a letter of Maria Edgeworth, Holland identifies the problems associated with descriptive writing about Iceland. So striking are the natural features encountered, that both imagination and memory are taxed to the limit adequately to generate verbal pictures of the succession of extraordinary landscapes experienced:

It would require power of no common kind, to place before the mental eye of the reader the strange & uncommon objects which form the scenery of Iceland: and those discordances of nature which rivet the mind more than her fair proportions and harmonies. In truth, I have no great faith, from my own experience, in the efficacy of descriptive writing – and I am glad to be able to say that our book will be well furnished with plates, illustrative of the most striking features of the country.

The problem was a familiar one for eighteenth-century travel writers, as they sought to exhibit truthfully the teeming plenitude of the external world.[1] A fondness for masses of quantitative detail had given way to some impatience with the indigestible forms such material often took and, secondly, with the limited opportunities for originality which such descriptive priorities gave to any two travel writers visiting the same celebrated spot. The ever-improving quality of illustrations with which texts could now be furnished liberated the travel writer, in the eyes of some, from the responsibility of conveying massive quantities of

---

[1] Discussed by Batten, 1978, pp. 82–101.

indigestible raw fact. The writer could trust the illustrations to offer specificity of descriptive detail, leaving him to concentrate more on the effects which individual scenes might have had on his mind, and also to ponder on the philosophical conclusions which might be drawn about the general frailties of the human condition from particular observations of life in individual countries. The writer could feel as well as measure, reflect as well as observe; there was room for sensibility as well as sense.

Set in this context, Mackenzie's fondness for the descriptive vocabulary of the fashionable picturesque traveller, dusted over with a certain graveyard pallor drawn from the world of Edward Young's *Night thoughts* (1742–5), accorded well with current tastes and is much in evidence in his narratives – 'dreadful marks of fire' (1811, p. 100), 'all sorts of fantastic forms' (1811, p. 101), 'mingled awe and astonishment' (1811, p. 118), 'the "random ruin" it so awfully displays' (1811, p. 108), lava scenes 'rendered more gloomy by floating mist and a perfect stillness, contributed to excite strong feelings of horror' (1811, p. 111–12) and much else that is 'terrific', 'hideous' and 'rugged'. Indeed Mackenzie's fondness is more strongly exhibited in the 1812 edition of the Iceland book, as when the bleak lava fields beyond Hafnarfjörður inspire him to augment his earlier account with the following additional atmospheric detail:

we chose the most convenient spot for our tent, and settled ourselves for the night. It would be difficult to imagine a country more wild and dreary than that which now surrounded us. The melancholy whistling of a few solitary plovers, and our horses moving slowly with their fettered limbs in search of withered herbage, contributed to the horror of the scene (1812, p. 107).

The mood thus created is heightened by occasional decorative quotations[1] in the book from James Thomson and from Oliver Goldsmith, the following of whose lines appear on the title-page:

> The shuddering tenant of the frigid zone,
> Boldly proclaims that happiest spot his own;
> Extols the treasures of his stormy seas,
> And his long nights of revelry and ease . . .
> Such is the Patriot's boast, where'er we roam,
> His first best country ever is – at home.

[1] Mackenzie, 1811, cites Oliver Goldsmith, *The Traveller, or a prospect of society*, ll.63–8, 73–4 (facing title page), ll. 175–84 (p. 270); James Thomson, *The Seasons*, 'Winter', ll.904–9 (p. 77).

This comforting (for the sentimental traveller) view of primitive society finds fuller expression at the end of Mackenzie's narrative, in another Goldsmith passage:

> Yet still, e'en here, content can spread a charm,
> Redress the clime, and all its rage disarm.
> Tho' poor the peasant's hut, his feasts tho' small,
> He sees his little lot, the lot of all;
> Sees no contiguous palace rear its head,
> To shame the meanness of his humble shed;
> No costly lord the sumptuous banquet deal
> To make him loathe his *hard-earn'd* meal;
> But calm, and bred in ignorance and toil,
> Each wish contracting, fits him to the soil.

It can only have been Mackenzie's sense of the stylistic propriety of including verses to, in the words of Chaucer's Pardoner, 'saffron' his 'predicacioun', that led him to include lines so grotesquely at odds with the aching and unsentimental realities of Iceland with which his travels had insistently brought him face to face.

Holland was no armchair primitive. He notes at the end of his life with no sense of guilt that he had never been 'seduced into the paths of poetry'[1] and it is doubtful whether Mackenzie's selection of verses, or the values which they insinuated would have met with his warmest response. Nor was Mackenzie's own descriptive vocabulary likely to find resounding favour. There is a strong sense that Holland, the young medical student, was suspicious of the associative and transfiguring power of the 'affrighted imagination',[2] and though his journal is very occasionally touched with moments of fashionable 'gloom' and 'horror', the sacrifice of fact to fancy was ultimately unappealing to him. Amongst travellers and their readers at the end of the eighteenth century, familiarity may have bred a weary contempt for a quantitative descriptive style applied to the well-known antiquities encountered on the standard grand tour of Europe. But Iceland was not part of the standard grand tour of Europe. For romantic Icelandophiles it might have been hallowed ground, but it certainly was not familiar ground. There may have been a clash of temperaments between Holland and Mackenzie – the younger, earnest, doggedly dedicated and tidy-minded

[1] Holland, 1872, p. 20.
[2] The phrase is Defoe's: *The life and strange surprizing adventures of Robinson Crusoe, of York, mariner*, ed. J. Donald Crowley (Oxford, 1972), p. 154.

Cestrian, and the warmer, more expansive, impatient highlander. But at the heart of their differences, and the single most distinctive feature of Holland's journal when compared with Mackenzie's writings, stands Holland's faith in narrative and descriptive priorities closer in spirit to those of the founding fathers of the Royal Society than to the sentimental traveller, especially though not exclusively when applied to lands little explored.

Mackenzie ought surely to have understood this. He knew and had commended Holland's *General view of the agriculture of Cheshire* (1808). Knowledge of this remarkably precocious work could have alerted Sir George to the way Holland's mind worked. The book is framed by two quotations, the selection of which immediately suggests high-minded youthful rectitude. The prefatory quotation on the title-page is from Rousseau, a favourite author of Holland's mentor John Thomas Stanley.[1] In it, the perceptive traveller who is anxious to comprehend 'la puissance publique' of any society, is urged to leave to 'le bel-esprit' all 'les palais du prince, ses ports, ses troupes, ses arsenaux, ses villes' and turn instead to 'la chaumière du laboureur'. The book's concluding section (pp. 345–7) asserts that a community's prosperity must be soundly based in agricultural efficiency bolstered by constant revitalising 'improvements' and must seek to avoid the condition of appearing, like the palace of ice in William Cowper's *The Task* (1785) as then quoted, 'a scene/Of evanescent glory . . ./As transient in its nature, as in show/'Twas durable. As worthless as it seemed/ Intrinsically precious. To the foot/Treach'rous and false, it smiled and was cold'.[2] Between these quotations, the book bristles with dates, times, yields, acreages, and suggestions for improvement of every aspect of the rural economy – buildings, implements, enclosures, forests, orchards, pasture land, arable areas, waste land, fertilizers, stock, nutrition, and much else. A 'general view' of one medium sized English county generates 375 pages, seventeen carefully ordered and documented chapters, three appendices and a conclusion. The heavy freight of information carried by the book no doubt suited, and may well have been the obligatory house-style for a commissioned work for the London Board of Agriculture, but so many of the same characteristics can also be found in Holland's first major published work after the appearance of the revised Iceland book.

[1] See JRL MS 722, John Thomas Stanley's 1813 journal, full of Rousseauiana.
[2] Holland, 1808, p. 347. Full quotation can be found in William Cowper, *Poetic works*, ed. H. S. Milford and Norma Russell (revised fourth edition, Oxford, 1967), p. 203, ll.166–74.

At first sight, *Travels in the Ionian Isles, Albania, Thessaly, Macedonia etc. during the years 1812 and 1813* (London, 1815) could not be more different from the Cheshire work: the one commissioned, the other volunteered; one strongly quantitative and analytic, the other primarily narrative; the crumbling peasant cottage at Alderley Edge set against the scented luxuriance of Ali Pasha's Albanian court. Holland, writing with a more relaxed confidence and authority than he sometimes achieves in the Iceland Journal, allows himself plentiful space for diverting anecdote, reflection and occasional whimsy, and clearly 'les palais du prince' are no longer out of bounds. But the book's 552 pages are densely packed in the same copious and systematic way as the Cheshire report with scrupulously detailed footnotes, documentation and quantification of observations, the same meticulous clarity of organisation, the same infinite capacity for taking descriptive and narrative pains – and this in spite of the loss of many of his maps, papers and journals, which were stolen at Carbonara in the spring of 1812, on the express order of the devious and suspicious Ali Pasha, convinced that the Englishman had discovered and committed to paper the whereabouts of some vast source of hidden treasure.[1] Holland's 1808 and 1815 publications may thus be taken to represent gentle but insistent rebukes to what Mackenzie's Icelandic book actually did become, and modest reminders of what it could and should have become.

Having tried the patience of his ambitious young collaborators by the inadequacies of his narrative style and his misuse of sources, Mackenzie drew further on their tolerance by the way in which he chose to indicate, or, rather, chose not to indicate his heavy indebtedness to their source materials. Holland and Bright came to realise that the material Sir George had liberally harvested from their records appeared to be going largely unacknowledged by the harvester. There was, it is true, a general statement in Mackenzie's prefatory remarks of his use of Bright's 'many valuable remarks, and much useful information'[2] and of the 'materials of Dr. Holland's journal, and my own', but the only specific attribution of source material within the narratives themselves was to Bright's account of the Snæfellsjökull ascent, and to Stanley's much earlier account of Geysir. Sir George exhibited a marked preference for 'I' rather than 'we' in '*his*' composition, as he would have

[1] Holland, 1815, p. 505; confirmed by Holland, 1872, pp. 60–2, who returned to the area in 1861 to find the robbery still recalled by local people.
[2] Mackenzie, 1811, p. xii.

it called and considered' (NLS 7515, 24 March 1811), and maintained an 'invincible silence' (NLS 7515, 31 March 1811) in the face of polite invitations to change. As Holland indicates to his indignant father, he was determined to achieve acknowledgement without contamination. Holland insisted upon 'the *nous*, wherever observations are concerned', whilst leaving 'the *je* to Sir G in all matters of speculation' (Lbs 4925, 2 August 1811), notably in the potentially important, but sadly undernourished and imprudently polemical mineralogical section prepared by Mackenzie. As a further cosmetic improvement, Holland became increasingly attracted to his publisher's suggestion that his own Dissertation should have 'Preliminary' added to its running title, and should have that title stand on a separate blank page, as well as above the text (NLS 7515, 24 March 1811). The Dissertation was, in effect, to be quarantined from Mackenzie's material. Holland was not slow to agree. As he laconically remarks in the same 24 March letter, 'I could not myself object to any plan which more distinctly separated my part of the work from Sir G's'.

'WRITING A QUARTO' (3): REVISION AND RECEPTION

Whatever running repairs may have been possible in respect of layout, pronouns, and small-scale amplification of material, there was insufficient time and (as far as Mackenzie was concerned) not overmuch inclination to address, before the Iceland volume's first edition appeared, its broader inadequacies of content and style. The unexpected and welcome prospect of a second edition, raised by Constable even before the publication of the first, provided a clearer opportunity for amendment. Holland needed no prompting to grasp it, attending first to his Preliminary Dissertation. For the revised edition, he frequently corrected punctuation, capitalisation, and word division; metaphor was trimmed and an excessive fondness for doublet adjectival phrases was restrained;[1] vocabulary was sharpened and periodic awkwardnesses of

---

[1] On metaphor, see for instance, 'the philosopher or moralist, while they glean over the fields of history for the materials for their study, will find a harvest provided even in the annals of this remote and desolate island' (1811, p. 4) becomes 'the philosopher or moralist, while he gleans over the fields of history for the materials for his study, will find his researches successful even in ...'; on doublets, see for instance 'quickness and promptitude of talent', 'dignities and honours', and 'rights and independence' (1811, pp. 18, 48, 7) become 'quickness of talent' 'dignities' and 'independence' (1812, pp. 18, 48, 7).

syntax and slovenliness of expression were resolved.[1] The content also benefitted from revision. Material from Holland's later sections of the first edition was recast within the Dissertation,[2] whilst a better informed and hence more confident sense of historical perspective was allowed to play over Holland's account of the early governance and religion in Iceland and crucial narrative details were added.[3] The process of revision as undertaken by Holland reveals that he shared with many an eighteenth-century writer a proper sense of self-distrust in respect of his own writings. It had led him frequently to seek the judgement of others during the composition of his sections; it now enabled him to regard the business of revision as an ethical imperative as well as a stylistic convenience.[4]

The necessity for some revision was borne in upon Mackenzie under rather more humiliating circumstances. Inspired, if that is the word, by Holland's affecting account of the story of *Gunnlaugs saga ormstungu* in the Preliminary Dissertation, Mackenzie seized the opportunity afforded by a delay in the printing of the Iceland volume's first edition during the summer of 1811 to compose *Helga, or the Rival Minstrels*, conceived as a tragic melodrama, received as a ludicrous farce. Based on the saga's central tragic feud between Gunnlaugr and Hrafn for the love of the beautiful Helga, the play was staged at the Theatre Royal in Edinburgh on 22 January 1812 where, in the words of Sir Walter Scott, a member of the convulsed first night audience, it was '"damned to everlasting redemption", as Elbow says, and that after a tolerable hearing'.[5] The briefest glance at Mackenzie's flatulent tragedy reveals all too cruelly why any audience would have thought ill of it. However,

---

[1] See, for instance, 'A pirate of much celebrity in those times, Floke by name, was . . .' (1811, p. 6) becomes 'Floke, a pirate of much celebrity in those times, was . . .' (1812, p. 6); 'this art he had early cultivated' (1811, p. 30, note) becomes 'an art which he had early cultivated' (1812, p. 31, note).

[2] Material on trial by jury, for instance, is incorporated in 1812, p. 15 from 1811, p. 317, note.

[3] Additional details include, in describing the effects of the 1783 eruptions: a cloud of lava dust 'covered the whole of Iceland, obscuring almost entirely the light of the sun, and extending its effects even to the northern parts of continental Europe' (1812, p. 64), whilst 1811, p. 64 lacks 'obscuring . . . and'; two further instances, from the plot summary of *Gunnlaugs saga ormstungu*: 'Gunnlaug shewed himself on a sudden' (1811, p. 31) becomes 'Gunnlaug, having hastened forwards from his father's house, shewed himself on a sudden' (1812, p. 31); and 'Gunnlaug here sees his beloved Helga for a few moments, and for the last time' (1812, p. 32), whereas 1811, p. 31, does not include 'for a few moments, and'.

[4] Paul Fussell, *The rhetorical world of Augustan humanism* (Oxford, 1965), p. 79.

[5] Sir Walter Scott, *Letters*, ed. Sir Herbert Grierson, 12 vols. (London, 1932–7), III, 101. See *The Scots Magazine* (February, 1812), pp. 134–5, 153–4; also Wawn, 1982.

Mackenzie was able to console himself with a not wholly implausible conspiracy theory. The theatre had certainly been packed with Wernerian geologists, all of whom were baying (only just metaphorically) for Mackenzie's blood in the wake of his tendentious account of the mineralogy of Iceland in the 1811 volume, in which he too often struck an ironic and provocative note at their expense. Thus the first and last night of *Helga* gave the Wernerians their opportunity for revenge. Small wonder that Mackenzie lost no time in removing some at least of the offending provocation from his revised mineralogical section.

The need for other revisions may have been less woundingly brought to Sir George's attention, but need there certainly was. There is some evidence (a bad tempered letter from Mackenzie to Constable)[1] that Sir George's willingness to make substantial additions to his narrative sections may in part have been frustrated by the publisher. It is certain, moreover, that Mackenzie was not able personally to supervise the printing and checking of the revised edition, his restless spirit having taken him off on yet another mineralogical expedition, this time to the Faroe Islands.[2] The Advertisement for the 1812 volume claims that the author has 'revised the work carefully'[3] and Mackenzie's 17 January 1812 letter to Constable states that he has 'taken considerable pains to improve the work'. Though comparison of the 1811 and 1812 texts reveals that for lengthy sections of the narrative chapters, not so much as a comma has been changed, there is some evidence of the reviser's efforts scattered through the volume. 'I' has become 'we' far more generally than it had by 1811; there is some attempt at greater precision in botanical references,[4] in the measurement of the height of mountains,[5] and in latitude and longitude citations;[6] occasionally, new and learned footnotes are appended;[7] an

---

[1] NLS MS 673, a copy of a letter dated 17 January 1812.

[2] NLS MS 673, letter dated 27 April 1812.

[3] Dated April 1812.

[4] For instance 'Lichen Islandicus' (1811, p. 152) becomes 'Iceland Lichen (*Cetraria Islandica*)' (1812, p. 150).

[5] For instance, compare the waffling 1811, pp. 249–50 attempt to describe the height of Hekla, with the more authoritative statement in 1812, p. 247, albeit that the authority appears to derive from consultation with John Thomas Stanley rather than from observations by Mackenzie and his colleagues.

[6] For instance, the latitude of Snóksdalur is cited as 'about' 65° 10' in 1811, p. 192, and changed to the less inaccurate 'about' 65° 5' in 1812, p. 190.

[7] 1812, p. 181, note relating to theories for the calculation of altitudes at different latitudes.

instinctive tendency to ironic condescension is better controlled.[1] Holland was no doubt frustrated to find that the overall effect of the revisions was still further to shorten the already under-written narrative sections. Small-scale stylistic changes apart, and these are far less extensive than in Holland's material, the main priorities of the Mackenzie revisions lay, firstly, in curbing a slightly oppressive readiness to encourage horticultural advancement in both the Orkneys and Iceland by relentless assertions of the value of an enterprise culture and by laborious suggestions for agrarian 'improvements', as with the leaden paragraph (1811, p. 278) omitted in 1812 in which the 'erroneous notion ... entertained even by the higher classes' about producing better grass is earnestly corrected. A second priority was the removal of a brief but prominent section at the end of the final narrative in which Mackenzie touchingly advocates British annexation of Iceland, underlining his case by repeating 'an ancient prophesy' which, he claims, was often cited by Icelanders in his presence – 'when the Danes have stripped off our shirts, the English will clothe us anew'.[2] The prolonged disinclination of the British government to undertake this course of action, not to mention concern for the feelings of Count Trampe, the Iceland volume's dedicatee, may have led Mackenzie temporarily at least to suspend advocacy of the cause,[3] though his feelings for the plight of Iceland are clear:

In these pages enough will probably be found to excite compassion in every British heart, for the calamitous situation of an innocent and amiable people, at that critical period when oppression or neglect may overwhelm them in misery. The distracted state of Europe will not, we trust, be considered as a reason that Britain should disregard their wants, or withhold relief; for Iceland requires no sacrifice of blood or treasure (1812, p. 268).

[1] For instance, 'the manners of Madam Hialtalin were those of a lady, and appeared to us, who had seen no one in Iceland entitled to this appellation, to the greatest advantage' (1811, p. 173) – 'who had seen ... appellation' omitted in 1812, p. 171; 'she took each of us by the hand, but we dexterously evaded the usual proffered salute [a kiss]' (1811, p. 119), omitted in 1812.

[2] Mackenzie argues: 'The possession of Iceland would not be burdensome to England. An exuberant and inexhaustible supply of fish from the sea, and the rivers, would alone repay the charitable action of restoring freedom to the inhabitants, who, under the fostering care of a benevolent government, might soon improve their soil and their own condition' (1811, p. 271; omitted 1812, p. 268).

[3] For Mackenzie's renewed diplomatic activity in 1813 urging the merits of annexation, see Rigsarkivet, Copenhagen, Korres. Litr. I: Island and Færoerne 1758–1846, a correspondence between Mackenzie, Holger Clausen and the Danish foreign minister: Mackenzie to Clausen, 2 July 1813; Clausen to Rosenkranz, 25 September 1813. See also Anna Agnarsdóttir, 1979, pp. 49–52.

A third priority in Mackenzie's revisions is the removal or modification of irrelevant observation about Icelandic manners and censorious observation about Icelandic morals. Banished, for instance, is his appalled account of the immorality at the heart of Reykjavík society, as revealed at an early Ball organised by the British party for their Icelandic hosts. The material has no parallel in Holland's journal. The excision, a substantial one, may in fact have been in deference to Holland, whose friend Bishop Geir emerges in a singularly unfavourable light from Mackenzie's vigorous 1811 edition denunciation, which bristles with crusty autocratic disapproval:

Several ladies, whose virtue could not bear a very strict scrutiny, were pointed out to us. One was present, who, since her husband had gone to Copenhagen on business, had lived with another merchant by whom she had had two children. Another, thinking her husband too old, had placed herself under the protection of a more youthful admirer, and left the good easy man to brood over his misfortune, or to find a partner more suited to his age. These ladies . . . were received into company, and treated with as much complaisance and familiarity as the most virtuous. This total disregard to moral character, and the rules of decorum, may, without breach of candour, be regarded as impeaching the virtue even of those who maintain the appearance of greater strictness in their behaviour . . . Where no guardian of morals is present; or where there is one, if he winks at such indecorum; if he converses with those who have broken the dearest ties of affection; there may, indeed, be some excuse. Here we saw the bishop himself countenancing vice in its worst shape, and appearing perfectly familiar with the persons who, he must have known, bore the worst characters. I was informed, that when a couple are dissatisfied with each other, or when a lady chuses to change her helpmate, the separation is sanctioned without inquiry into the case, and new bands solemnly unite those who have most openly slighted their former engagements. Such are the morals of the people of Reykjavik (p. 95).

Yet despite excisions and modifications, the overall process of revision of the 1811 volume could not avoid remaining fundamentally an exercise in damage limitation, with the initial problems caused by Mackenzie's failure, as Holland regarded it, to make adequate use of Holland's own manuscript journals, and the guidance they could have given Sir George, whether at the primary level of selection and arrangement of material, or even in the subsequent processes of correction and revision.

Holland's revisions in his own journal manuscript reveal clearly how his mind worked. There is an anxious care exercised in correcting matters of fact or nomenclature. Thus, 'Mark Valley' becomes '*Markar-Fliot*'; 'the great valley of the Borgar fiord' becomes 'the great valley of the Hvitaá'; '*Atastrood*, as his title stands in Iceland' becomes 'Etatsraad, a Danish title equivalent to Counsellor of State'; 'Mr Frydensberg, a *Sysselman* or Magistrate' becomes 'Mr Frydensberg, the Landfogd or Treasurer of the Island'; 'the last eruption of Mt Hekla' is corrected to 'the last eruption of Skapte Fells'[1] and 'iron ring', 'wood' and 'yellowish green substance' become, respectively, 'copper ring', 'whale's rib', and 'a quantity of olivine'.[2] There is an equally anxious care displayed in small-scale stylistic changes. Henry Holland was not immune from the mildly self-indulgent verbal fondnesses of literary society in the heyday of Jane Austen, notably a taste for attention-seeking French locutions (such as *sang froid*, *annoncement*, *tout-ensemble* and *petit-maitre*).[3] Most of his observable stylistic corrections in the manuscript, however, reveal an unswerving though not obsessional concern for literary punctilious-ness and rectitude. To examine his fair copy of the journal manuscript is to observe a work which has gradually achieved its proper stylistic decorum, as when, for example, 'country priest', 'displays', and 'head of the school' are elevated to 'Icelandic divine', 'bespeaks' and 'Rector of the school',[4] whilst 'proffered', 'prospect', and 'offered to our eyes' are simplified to 'given', 'view' and 'offered to us', and the hyperbole of 'prodigiously great', 'excellent common sense' and 'magically pleasing' is tempered to 'very great', 'good common sense', and 'at once extraordinary and pleasing'.[5] It was just these qualities of fastidiousness and exactitude which Holland too often sought in vain in the narrative prose of Sir George Mackenzie.

Whatever the tensions and frustrations associated with its publication, and whatever the shortcomings of its finally published form, *Travels in the island of Iceland during the summer of the year 1810*, having enjoyed considerable exposure in the *Annual Register* (1811) and the *Edinburgh Review* (1811–12), came to be widely known amongst educated readers. The Bristol Library Society records again offer illuminating and representative detail as to its popularity and influence.[6] The volume was ordered for the Society on 29 January 1812, and first borrowed on February 17. Over the next two years it was taken out by

[1] Journal, pp. 261, 171, 98, 88, 82.
[2] Journal, pp. 179, 207, 96 (95, n.5).
[3] Journal, pp. 86, 103, 128, 263.   [4] Journal, pp. 175, 160, 117.
[5] Journal, pp. 100, 223, 208; 89, 100, 260.
[6] Bristol City Library MSS B 7480-5.

some twenty-eight subscribers, often being returned and borrowed again the same day. It is likely that Holland's association with the volume did much to commend it to the Bristol readership, for his earlier survey of Cheshire agriculture was regularly borrowed during the period 1808–11. The popularity of the Iceland volume, when set against the borrowings of other available volumes of obvious Northern interest, is striking. In the same period, the von Troil account of Sir Joseph Banks's 1772 expedition, published in 1780, was borrowed three times; Bishop Percy's translation of Mallet's *Northern Antiquities* was borrowed twice; the 1787 Copenhagen *Edda* volume three times; Amos Cottle's Icelandic translations twice; William Herbert's translations twice; Saxo Grammaticus and Johnstone's *Antiquitates Celto-Scandicæ* once each. In the nine-month period from the 1813 publication of W. J. Hooker's account of his 1809 expedition to Iceland, the Hooker volumes were borrowed six times whilst the Mackenzie-Holland Iceland book was borrowed seven times.

There is moreover, the strong suggestion from the borrowing records that the popularity of the Mackenzie-Holland volume not only reflected a taste for travel literature, but created or, more accurately, recreated a taste for things Icelandic amongst the Bristol readership. In 1808–9, von Troil's Iceland book was not borrowed. In 1810, the year of the Mackenzie-Bright expedition it was borrowed three times – first by the father of the young Richard Bright, no doubt in order to learn more of the distant land to which his son was to travel later that summer; thereafter it was borrowed a good deal more frequently. Again, over the two-year period up to November 1810, the 1787 Copenhagen *Edda* was not borrowed. Thereafter a steady trickle of borrowings re-occurs. Further, before the publication of the 1811 Mackenzie volume, there were no borrowings of either the Amos Cottle translations or the William Herbert volumes, or of Percy's Mallet. In 1812 each text finds at least one Bristol borrower. The cumulative evidence suggests that local Bristol interest in the 1810 expedition, due to the participation of Richard Bright and his youthful friend Henry Holland, together with the publication of the Mackenzie volume with identifiable contributions by Holland, already a writer of established repute, was responsible for renewed Bristolian interest in Icelandic literature and antiquities.

SIR HENRY HOLLAND AND ICELAND: THE LATER YEARS

Holland's subsequent associations with Iceland took their place within a dauntingly hectic life of high society medical practice in London and exhausting foreign travel. His appetite for travel, whetted by the first experiences of it in Iceland, developed almost insatiably.[1] In the fifty and more years between his first entering professional life in London in January 1816 and his death in Rome in 1873, there were only two autumns when he did not turn aside from his clinical responsibilities in order to journey abroad, usually on his own, for up to two months. He left behind him, over the years, a remarkable list of patients including, at one time or another, six British prime ministers, at least one American president, Prince Louis Napoleon, King Leopold of Belgium, Talleyrand, Wordsworth, Sir Walter Scott, the Prince Consort, on whose dying days he attended at Windsor, and most notably, Queen Victoria herself, whose Physician in Ordinary he became at the close of 1852, following an earlier appointment as one of her Physicians Extraordinary from 1837.

His foreign travelling virtually put a girdle round the earth. He went eight times to the United States, visited every capital in Europe, many of them on several occasions, travelled in Asia Minor, the Middle East, North Africa; explored islands as far apart as the Faroes, the Canaries and the West Indies; he stood at the top of Hekla, Vesuvius and Etna, at the bottom of salt mines in Poland and at the foot of windmills in La Mancha; he nearly froze to death in Thessaly, nearly fell victim of pirates off the Greek islands, and nearly perished at the hands of Moorish tribesmen on the Barbary coast; he visited the ancient battle fields of Greece as well as the more melancholy modern ones of the Peninsula Wars and the American Civil War; he was feted and honoured in Harvard and arrested in Cracow. Even on his sea-born passage to such places, time was put to earnest good use in the composition of many essays and reviews on a bewildering range of subjects and interests, papers which subsequently appeared first in journals and then in collected volumes assembled by their author.[2] Sir Henry, as he became in April 1853, wrote on sleep and on Shakespeare;

---

[1] The following paragraphs draw extensively on Holland, 1872.

[2] *Essays on scientific and other subjects* (London, 1862), a collection of his reviews published previously in the *Edinburgh Review* and the *Quarterly Review*; F. J. Holland (ed.), *Fragmentary papers* (London, 1875); *Chapters on mental physiology* (London, 1858), whose back page advertises a new edition of his *Medical notes and reflections*.

on Australian coral reefs and Atomic theory; on insanity and on instincts and habits; on the perfectibility of the soul and the pathology of the colon; and, when he could write no more, he claimed to enjoy gazing at the sea and studying the waves. There was not a moment wasted!

Inevitably in such a frenetic life, Iceland was unlikely regularly to attract Holland's attention in such a way as to register prominently in surviving documentary evidence, but sporadic instances make their point. In 1814 Holland found time to present a set of geological specimens from Iceland to the Geological Society in London, seven of which still survive. Holland was clear that his celebrity as an Iceland explorer was amongst the factors instrumental in securing his election to a Fellowship of the Royal Society in 1816.[1] Later in 1817 a copy of the Iceland book was forwarded to the Danish king; Mackenzie received a polite note of thanks and a copy of *Flora Danica* for his pains.[2] Henry Holland may well have played no part in this transaction. Later in 1834, John Barrow's *A Visit to Iceland ... in the summer of 1834* (London, 1835) warmly acknowledges the help which Holland had afforded him by allowing him access to the 1810 expedition journal.[3] Then, in 1842, the publication of a revised (by Mackenzie) and less expensive edition of the 1812 edition of the Iceland book ensured that Holland's writings reached a new and wider audience, including those potential Iceland travellers whose ardour had not been dampened by Sir George's new Preface which stressed, deadeningly, that any voyage to Iceland involved 'resigning everything connected with what is so highly prized in Britain – comfort'. One such undaunted traveller, the American Pliny Miles, knew the 'distinguished' Dr. Holland's 'learned dissertation' well, and in preparing his own Iceland journal was happy to acknowledge Holland as 'one of the most intelligent travellers that ever visited Iceland'.[4] There is evidence too, that towards the end of his life, it was the turn of Icelanders visiting London to seek out the by now venerable 'old carle'. Guðbrandur Vigfússon was one such visitor in March 1865. He writes to Bjarni Þorsteinsson:

---

[1] Holland, 1872, p. 211.

[2] Rigsarkivet, Copenhagen, Ges. Ark. London III, Indkomme skrivelser fra D.f.u.A. 1814–17, letter in French dated 17 September 1817.

[3] Pp. xx, 184, 222, 309. Barrow notes Mackenzie's 'great indebtedness' to Holland, 'an able and intelligent writer', Lbs MS 604 fol., p. 4`.

[4] *Norðurfari, or rambles in Iceland* (London, 1854), p. 225.

Eg var hissa að sjá mann, sem eg hélt að væri kominn undir græna torfu ... Eg hlakka til að sjá Sir Holland aptr og tala við hann.[1]

Guðbrandur had no doubt that Banks, Mackenzie, Holland and Ebenezer Henderson were the 'bestu ferðamenn sem á Islandi hafa verið fyrir utan Rask og Maurer'.[2]

Moreover, as a *ferðamaður* elsewhere in the world, Holland found memories of Iceland suddenly reviving to provide reference points against which to set newly encountered phenomena, as when many years after visiting Þingvellir, its great volcanic lake came to his mind whilst scanning the expanse of the Dead Sea.[3] Holland recognised, too, that his lifelong fascination with the investigation of volcanic features all over the world had been initially sharpened by the volcanoes of Iceland.[4] And again, if specific instances of Holland's association with Iceland after 1810 are relatively few, his *Recollections of past life* (1872) makes it apparent that at the age of eighty-four, his mind had retained over sixty years vivid memories of his first foreign visit – memories, for instance, of Geysir, magnificent as a spectacle' (p. 77), and of 'my friend' Bishop Geir Vídalín:

coming home to a small and rude timber-frame house from his day of sea-fishing in the Faxe-Fiord, and sitting down to Latin conversation with an English stranger! If his Latinity did not reach the level of Erasmus's 'Colloquies', it certainly was better than any I could reciprocate with him; impeded as I was by that perverse fashion of English pronunciation, which even Edinburgh teaching had only partially removed (p. 93).

In a book of forgiveable vagueness of recall, the recollection of Bishop Geir is an unusually sharp one, freshened no doubt by the quite astonishing return visit to Iceland undertaken by Sir Henry at the age of eighty-three in the company of his second son. It was during this trip that Holland became acquainted with William Morris's travelling companion Eiríkur Magnússon and, on his return to England, was amongst Eiríkur's supporters when the Icelander sought a post in the

[1] Lbs MS 342c fol., letter dated 6 March 1855. Translation: 'I was eager to see the man who I believed to have been laid under the green turf long ago ... I look forward to seeing Sir [Henry] Holland again and talking with him'.
[2] Translation: 'The best travellers who have been in Iceland apart from [Rasmus] Rask and [Konrad] Maurer'.
[3] Holland, 1872, pp. 71–2.
[4] Holland, 1872, p. 69.

University Library in Cambridge.' Much had changed over sixty years
in the Reykjavík to which Holland returned – a restored cathedral, a
new college, more people, better trade, finer houses, more productive
domestic cultivation. But memory provided some continuities. Bishop
Geir's house was now occupied by 'my excellent friend Dr. Hyaltalin –
a child of three years old when I slept in his father's church [at Saurbær]
on the shores of the Hual-fiord'.² Moreover, the children and grand-
children of former friends showed much kindness and warmth to an old
man whose recollections, he was convinced, had been 'matured rather
than enfeebled by a long intervening life'.³

The romance of travel had begun for Holland sixty-one years earlier
amidst the lava and lyme grass of Iceland; and now his life as a traveller
was almost at an end as he revisited 'that wonderful island'.⁴ Another
celebrated English Icelandophile, W. H. Auden, also returning to
Iceland after a long absence, wrote:

To me Iceland is sacred soil. Its memory is a constant background to what I am
doing. No matter that I don't make frequent references to the country; it is an
equally important part of my life for all that ... It is a permanent part of my
existence ... Iceland is the sun colouring the mountains without being
anywhere in sight.⁵

Sir Henry Holland would surely have understood.

' Stefán Einarsson, 'Eiríkur Magnússon – the forgotten pioneer', in Benedikt Benedikz
(ed.), *Studia centenalia in honorem memoriæ Benedikt S. þórarinsson* (Reykjavík, 1961), p. 50,
note 9.
² Holland, 1872, p. 32. ³ Holland, 1872, p. 31.
⁴ NLS MS 2630, f. 88.
⁵ Quoted in Sigurður Magnússon, *Northern sphinx* (Reykjavík, 1977), p. ix.

JOURNAL OF A VOYAGE &c
TO ICELAND
IN THE SUMMER OF 1810

VOL. I

On Wednesday, the 18th of April, 1810, we sailed from Leith in the Sloop Fingal and after a favourable passage of two days, landed on Friday Morning at Stromness, where we had an appointment to meet the Elbe, a London Vessel, in which a passage was engaged for us to Iceland. The non-arrival of this Vessel at the time appointed detained us a week at Stromness – a period which we occuped in surveying the features of the surrounding country.

Stromness is situated at the south-western angle of Pomona, or the Mainland, the largest of the Orkney Islands.[1][A] It consists of a single, irregular street, stretching along the shore of a small bay – This bay furnishes an excellent harbour for shipping, and is much resorted to by vessels going round the north of Scotland – Most of the Greenland Ships put in here on their passage northwards; and at some periods of the years 30 or 40 large vessels may frequently at once be seen in the harbour. The population of Stromness is 13, or 1400; – Two companies of veterans are kept here by Government, to defend this part of the Orkneys, from the aggression of privateers etc.[2]

The country in the neighbourhood of Stromness is well inhabited, and the land in some places brought into a state of tolerable cultivation – The farms, however, are invariably very small. Oats & barley are the grain exclusively grown. The plough[3][B] of the country is peculiar, & has many disadvantages of construction: the English plough, however, is now coming gradually into use – Kelp[4] is much used as a manure for potatoes

[1] This and all subsequent superscript capital letters in the Journal text refer to Holland's field sketches and maps which are reproduced in this edition.

[2] The Ninth Royal Veteran Battalion was stationed at Kirkwall until 1813. See W. R. Mackintosh, *Glimpses of Kirkwall and its people in the olden times* (Kirkwall, 1887), p. 238.

[3] An Orkney plough had a single stilt or handle and was ineffective and awkward to use. See H. Marwick, '"A Description of Orkney (1773)": An account of an unpublished manuscript of Rev. George Low, Minister of Birsay, 1774–1795', *Proceedings of the Orkney Antiquarian Society*, II (1923–4), picture facing p. 52.

[4] There was much interest among Iceland explorers in the commercial exploitation of kelp as a fertilizer. See Wawn, 1981, pp. 65, 75 (note 51).

POMONA or the MAINLAND
with some
of the Adjacent Islands

ST. RONSA

COPINSHA

Auskerry

Reinsholm Head

Greenholms

EGILSHA

Wire

Gousa

ROWSA

Sauchal

Westness

Steel

Eva

THE

Sandwick

Mause

Black Craig

STROM NESS

Hoy Sound

HOY

SHAPINSHA

Elwick

Cliffdale

Carness

Salt

Rendal

Burness

DAMSA

Stenhouse

Stenhold Loch

Harray Loch

Firth

Sandside

Mull Head

Deer Sound

KIRKWALL

Scapa

Saba

Grenshall

Clestron

Houton

Barrel of Butter

Tapmar

Grimsholm

CAVA

Roteness

BURRA

GRENSA

72

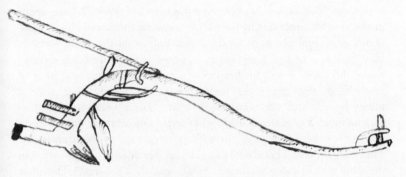

B. An Orkney plough

and barley – The horses of the country are small. – The cottages in the Orkneys are of a miserable description, both as regards exterior appearance & internal comforts.

Some of the views in the vicinity of Stromness are striking; those especially which include the neighbouring island of Hoy; the hills on the northern side of which have a greater elevation than any other land in the Orkneys. One of them is 1250 feet in height.[1] The channel which separates Hoy from the Mainland, called Hoy Sound, is very narrow; the tide flows through it with great impetuosity. The Mainland is considerably varied in its general surface; but affords little variety in the objects dispersed over its extent. Not a tree or shrub is to be seen upon the island. To the north of Stromness, two extensive pieces of water, the Lochs of Stenhouse & Harrow, spread themselves over the country. On an isthmus intervening between these lakes, are situated a number of large stones or pillars, some of them 20 feet in height[2] – their history not accurately known; whether they are to be considered as places of burial, as memorials of warfare, or, as some have supposed, the situations where justice was administered.

The country around Stromness is interesting in a mineralogical point of view. It is the only *primitive district*[3] in the Orkneys. The hills immediately behind the town are composed of *Gneiss*[4] – probably also

[1] Probably either Ward Hill or the Cuilags.
[2] The stones of Stenness. See John Thomas Stanley's speculations in John F. West (ed.) *Journals of the Stanley expedition*, I, 17; II, 26–9; III, 28; and in Lbs MS 3886 4to, pp. 40f.
[3] An area thought to belong to the earliest geological period.
[4] For explanations of important geological terms cited in the journal text, see Appendix G.

with some *Mica Slate*, as we observed fragments of this rock lying about in the neighbourhood. On the shore, close to the town, the Granite seems in several places to be disclosed. Following the shore towards Hoy Sound, a bed of *Conglomerate* appears, – probably lying directly above the *Gneiss* – Still further in the same direction, inclined beds of *sandstone* & *slate clay* make their appearance, penetrated in several places by veins of the same *conglomerate.*[1] These veins we found to contain much *lead glance* & *sulphate* of *barytes.* One of them was formerly worked for the former ore, but without advantage to the proprietors. They contain also a good deal of *calcareous spar* & some *iron pyrites.* – In the same tract of shore we found a small vein of *red hæmatite* – The other parts of the Mainland which we visited, appear to be composed entirely of sandstone, sandstone slag, & slate clay. We understand that all the other islands of the Orkneys have a similar structure.

During our stay at Stromness we visited the minister of the church there, Mr *Cluston,*[2] – The Manse is about a mile from the town – Before tea, glasses of brandy & cinnamon water were handed about to all the party – and the same process was repeated after tea – Mr C. was formerly minister of Sanda,[3] one of the most northerly of the Orkneys – well known from the frequency of shipwrecks upon its shores.

The Elbe did not make her appearance at Stromness until the evening of Wednesday the 25th – Friday Morning was fixed for the recommencement of her voyage northwards, and we went on board at this time; but owing to the prevalence of a strong south-easterly wind, and some untoward accidents in the harbour, we did not finally set sail until 1 o'clock on Saturday. The wind continued from S.E until evening, when it completely died away – During the night it was a perfect calm, & the ship made very little progress on her way.

Sunday 29th [4] During the greater part of the day, a continuance of the

[1]^{HH} It is probable that these strata would be considered as belonging to the *Independent Coal Formation* of the German school, though we did not observe any actual appearances of coal amongst them. (See Jameson's Geognosy p. 179) |Ed: Robert Jameson, *Elements of Geognosy*, 3 vols. (Edinburgh 1804–08), III, 179|. This formation is stated to contain 'three rocks which are nearly peculiar to it', viz. a *conglomerate*, a *micaceous sandstone* & *slate clay.* – It is stated also that the *Slate Clay* in this formation passes into a fossil much resembling *Lydian Stone* – This circumstance we very distinctly observed in the *Slate Clay* on the shores near Stromness.

[2] Rev. William Clouston (1747–1832), minister of Sandey from 1794.   [3] Sandey.

[4]^{HH} *Sunday* At 12 o'clock Lat. 59° 15', by observation
Long. 4° 13' W. by account
At 1 o'clock took a bottle of Sea Water from the Surface – temperature 50°
— Do — at depth of 28 fathoms – temp. 45°

calm – All the wind we have from the N. – Towards evening, a slight breeze from the N.N.E.

The Elbe is a vessel of 350 tons register, coppered and armed with 12 Guns. The Cabin accommodations particularly good. Captain Liston, who commands her, is an active intelligent man. He went out to Iceland last year in the Margaret & Anne letter of marque,[1] the vessel by which the Danish Government in Iceland was for some time deposed.[2] On the voyage homewards, when about 150 miles from land, the ship was entirely consumed by fire: the crew saved by the vicinity of another ship.[3] Mr Hooker was on board at the time, with the collection he had made during his summer's residence in Iceland. This was almost wholly lost[4] – The Elbe is going to Reikaviik, on account of Messrs Phelps & Co[5] of London, the owners of the Margaret and Anne. Her cargo is of a miscellaneous description. Mr Fell[6] is going out as agent for the house.

Monday 30th April. Early this morning the breeze freshened from the NNE. It increased till 5 or 6 in the afternoon, & got more towards the eastward – The ship's rate during the day has varied from 4 to 7 knots in the hour. At 12 o'clock we got a good observation of the sun.[7] Towards evening the breeze declined.

Tuesday May 1st During the night we have made a progress of from 5 to 7 knots per hour. At 8 o'clock this morning we were called upon deck to see a whale, 15 or 20 yards ahead of the ship. It was of the kind called the *Finner Whale,* from a fin on the top of the back – Its length was apparently 30 or 40 feet.[8] The vessel passed close to it, and it was afterwards seen a-stern, throwing up water into the air – Scarcely any

---

[1] Vessels granted 'letter of marque' were entitled to be armed during hostilities and to engage enemy merchant shipping. On Anglo-Danish tension at this time, see Ryan, 1953, pp. 35–53.

[2] See introduction pp. 24–5.

[3] Hooker, 1813, I, 360–7.

[4] Hooker was rescued by Jörgen Jörgensen, leader of the 1809 Reykjavík insurrection, and remained permanently grateful for the fact, corresponding with the Dane long after Jörgensen had been exiled in Australasia. See Hooker Correspondence, Royal Botanical Gardens, Kew: Australian Letters 1834–51, letter dated 28 October 1836; and also Australian and New Zealand Letters 1835–43, letter dated 4 October 1840.

[5] Phelps, Troward and Bracebridge, London soap manufacturers, who wished to import Icelandic tallow in an arrangement suggested by Jörgensen's friend James Savignac. See Phelps, 1817, pp. 51–77.

[6] Michael Edward Fell [n.d.].

[7] HH *30th April* At 12 o'clock, Lat. 59° 17′ 17″ by observation
Long. 4° 42′ W

[8] *Balænoptera musculus* (Linn.), Mod.Ice. *Langreyður.*

HH: This species of whale yields only a very small quantity of Blubber – A *Finner* 40 or 50 feet in length, yields only 7 or 8 Butts.

wind during the morning, & the ship making little progress – At 12 o'clock got an observation of the sun[1] – At this time we are about 58 miles south of the Faroe Islands. A perfect calm in the afternoon & evening – and the ship making no progress.

Wednesday May 2[d2] – Very little way during the night – The wind NW by N – The ships course during the morning SW by W. In the afternoon made a long tack N & by E.

Thursday. May 3[d]. Early this morning a violent squall of wind came on from the N.E. The previous north westerly wind had produced so much swell from that quarter, that the ship pitched excessively, when turned into her course. Owing to this circumstance, one of the seamen, an elderly man, was thrown from the mizen-top-sail, and fell upon the deck – a height probably of nearly 40 feet. The poor fellow was sensible, when taken up – he was carried to his berth, bled and examined as carefully as circumstances would admit of – There was no external injury, not did there appear to be any dislocation or fracture. In the course of the morning he had some sleep, apparently natural – About 2 o'clock, however, coldness of the extremities came on, and two or three hours afterwards, he went off without pain or struggle.[3]

During the whole of the day it blew a hard gale from the N.E. The rate of the ship's course from 6 to 9 knots in the hour. A good deal of snow and hail in the course of the day.[4]

Friday May 4[th][5] The rolling of the ship very heavy during the whole of the night. At 9 o'clock a large shoal of porpoises about the vessel – The wind entirely subsided in the course of the morning, but the heavy swell consequent upon the preceding gale from the N.E., rendered the motion of the ship exceedingly unpleasant – Sir G.M, and M[r] B[6] continued in bed during the whole of the day – both very unwell. In the afternoon a breeze got up from the S. About 8 o'clock, the wind came

---

[1][HH] *May 1st* At 12 o'clock Lat. 60° 30'
　　　　　　Long. 7° 30' W
　　　　At 11 o'clock took a bottle of water from the depth of 40 fathoms – another from 20 fathoms – a 3[d] from the surface. Thermometer in the shade at 12 o'clock 56°

[2][HH] *May 2*[d] At 12 o'clock Lat. 60° 35'
　　　　　　Long. 8° 21' W

[3] The incident haunted Bright throughout his life. See Pamela Bright, 1983, pp. 54–5.

[4][HH] *May 3*[d] At 12. Lat. 60°55'
　　　　　　Long. 10° 17' W　　Therm. at 12 o'clock 34°

[5][HH] *May 4*[th] At 12 Lat. 61° 23'
　　　　　　Long. 14° 43' W　　Therm. at 12 o'clock 38°

[6] Richard Bright.

C. Klausturhöfði viewed from the sea

suddenly round to the north east, and at 10 it blew a violent gale from this quarter, accompanied with much snow and hail. The ship for a considerable part of the night ran under bare poles, her rate varying from 7 to 10 knots in the hour.

Saturday May 5th [1] The dawn of this morning disclosed the first view of the coast of Iceland. At 3 o'clock two mountains, covered with snow, appeared in the northern horizon, at the distance probably of 18 or 20 leagues – We had some difficulty in ascertaining the correspondence of this high land with the maps of the island in our possession. By referring to Capt[n] Liston's charts, & to the *Lat[e]*. & *Long[e]*., as ascertained at 12 o'clock, it would appear that the promontory here formed, is that called *Cape Closter*,[2] [C] and that a small island off the eastern extremity of the Cape, is the *Isle of Portland*[3] of the charts. The delineation, however, of this coast in the different maps is exceedingly varied & apparently very incorrect in all. In a Dutch chart[4] in Captain L's possession, this headland is called *Cape Hecla*.[5]

At 1 o'clock, (having steered since we came in sight of land nearly a northern course) we were within a few leagues of the headland. The mountains which form this promontory have a great elevation, probably not less than 3 or 4000 feet;[6] though this is merely conjectural

---

[1][HH] *May 5th* At 12 o'clock. Lat. 62° 57′ } Thermometer at 12 o'clock – 36°
　　　　　　　　Long. 17° } In the morning the shrouds coated with ice

[2] Klausturhöfði.

[3] Dyrhólaey. This headland was frequently marked as an island named Portland on early maps. See Haraldur Sigurðsson, *Kortasaga Íslands*, 2 vols. (Reykjavík, 1971–8), II, 107. The Jan de Vos 1761 map (p. 112) names the same location 'Klooster Eyland'.

[4] Probably one of the Van Keulen charts: Gerard van Keulen's 1728 map, for instance. See Haraldur Sigurðsson, 1971–8, II, 105–13, especially the map facing pp. 104–5.

[5] Hekluhöfði.

[6][HH] I afterwards found that I had under-rated the height of these two mountains, in stating it only at 3 or 4000 feet. The observations of the Danish lieutenants [Ed: see Haraldur Sigurðsson (1971–8, II, pp. 212–19], engaged in the survey of the Icelandic coasts, make the elevation of Eyafialla Jokull, which forms one part of this high land, to be not less than 5526 feet – that of Cape Hecla or Cape Closter to be 4962 feet.

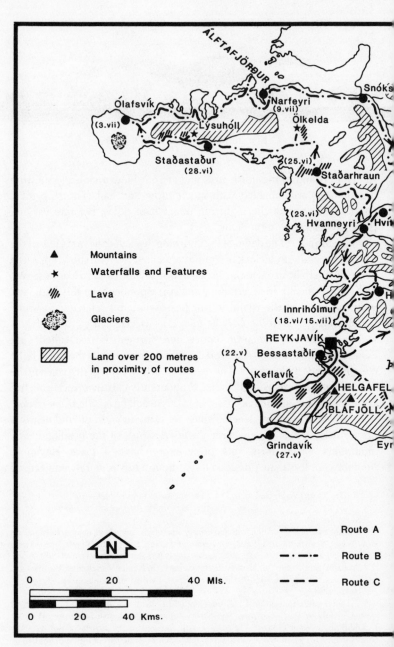

Map C. Routes

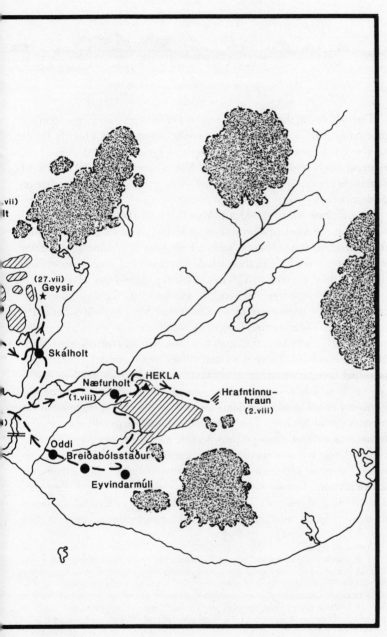

enry Holland

The Westmann Islands, seen from the SSE, distant 3 or 4 Leagues — Vestmannar Eyar.

D. Vestmannaeyjar viewed from the sea

– The whole of their surface was covered with snow, excepting a precipitous cliff, which along their whole extent, forms a barrier to the waves of the ocean. Several steep clefts or ravines shewed themselves, running back into the mountains. Not a single sign of animal or vegetable life appeared upon the land – every thing was gloomy, barren & desolate.

At 2 o'clock we obtained a distinct view of the *Westmann Islands*,[1] situated at the most southern point of Iceland, and distant a few miles from the mainland – These islands are singular & picturesque[2] in their appearance. Stretching in their whole extent several leagues from N.E. to S.W., they present to the eye, viewing them from a distance, a grotesque assemblage of rocky masses, of various size and configuration – some perfectly conical in their form – others pillar-like – others again, of larger size, formed by a collection of irregular rounded eminences[D] – The largest of these islands, that of *Heimaklettur*,[3] is the only one inhabited. There is a small village, with a church upon it. The principal occupation of the inhabitants is to collect the feathers of the sea-fowl, which resort to these islands in prodigious numbers – Formerly two Danish merchants resided on the island, engaged in the exportation of feathers. The *Westmann Islands* are usually inaccessible from the Mainland, during a considerable part of the year. The island of Heimaklettur has one small harbour, the approach to which, however, is very difficult. Sheep are kept on many of the smaller islands; on which account they are visited once or twice in the course of the year – The catching of sea-fowl, and the taking of their eggs form also a means of support to the inhabitants of Heimaklettur. In this occupation they

[1] Vestmannaeyjar.

[2] The search for 'picturesque' scenery, in which the order and symmetry of nature matches that of art was very much in vogue at this time and a frequent reference point in the journal. The vision of the 'picturesque traveller' is an essentially idealizing one as he seeks to convey scenic impression through description of feelings evoked as much as through forensic survey. See, for example, Thomas Gilpin, 'On picturesque travel' in *Three Essays* (London, 1792), pp. 41–58; more generally, see Batten, 1978, pp. 95–110.

[3] Holland's error. The island is Heimaey. Heimaklettur is one of its several prominent hills.

80

pursue the same adventurous methods as are practised by the people of Faroe, and some of the Scotch isles. The *Fulmar*, *Sea parrot*, the *Shear Water*, the *Solan Goose*, the *Guillemot* &c[1] frequent the Westmann Islands in prodigious numbers. The Solan Goose & Fulmar are salted & used by the inhabitants as winter food – The population of the Westmann Islands in the year 1804 was 157 souls.[2]

Several storms of hail & snow occurred in the afternoon of this day. Upon the whole, however, the weather has been clear and serene – At 8 in the evening we were abreast of the Westmann Islands,[3] the vessel taking a course to the south of the whole groupe – A continued range of mountainous coast seems to extend from Cape Closter to these islands, and there is every reason to believe that the delineation in the maps of Iceland, of large arms of the sea, running up into the country from this line of coast, is inaccurate, and devoid of foundation.

Sunday. May 6[th4] The winds irregular and varying during the night. At 3 or 4 in the morning, a smart breeze came on from the N.E. – the cold very severe – At 8 o'clock we were abreast of *Thorlaks Hafn*,[5] an inlet of the sea which receives some large rivers from the interior of the island. During the next six hours, our attention was much engaged by the very interesting coast of the *Guldbringe Syssel*,[6] or Guldbringe District, along which the vessel pursued her course, at the distance of six or eight miles from the shore. The day was peculiarly favourable for such observations – perfectly cloudless and serene. The appearances presented along the coast were altogether singular and novel, & greatly elevated our expectations of the objects which were to engage our attention when surveying in detail the features of the country. Every thing indicated the volcanic nature of this district – The rude & abrupt rocky masses, rising into every variety of form, and in many places *fringed* upon their summits & sides, so as to afford the appearance of *scoriæ* – the occurrence here & there of jets of smoke or vapour – and still more the bursting forth of a thick mass of sulphureous vapour from a cleft in the rocks, all afforded the strongest testimonies to this fact –

[1] The birds, in order, are *Fulmarus glacialis* (Linn.), Mod.Ice. *Fýll*; *Fratercula Arctica* (Linn.), Mod.Ice. *Lundi*; *Puffinus major* (Faber), Mod.Ice. *Skrófa*; *Sula bassana* (Linn.), Mod.Ice. *Súla*; *Uria troile* (Linn.), Mod.Ice. *Langvía*.

[2] Confirmed by *Manntal á Íslandi 1801: Suðuramt* (Reykjavík, 1978), pp. 183–7.

[3]HH The variation of the compass at the Westmann Islands is 3¼ points West.

[4]HH At 12 o'clock Lat. 63° 58′

Long. [Ed: omitted]   } Therm. at 12 o'clock – 36°

[5] Þorlákshöfn.

[6] Gullbringusýsla.

Nothing of vegetation was seen upon the surface – every thing wore the appearance of the most extreme desolation and barrenness.

The inaccuracy of the maps & charts occasioned considerable perplexity to Captn L. in steering his course for Cape Reikianes.[1] Off this Cape are four[2] small rocky islands, stretching out to sea nearly in the same line with the projection of the Cape itself. Beyond the outermost or most southern of these islands, a reef of rocks extends 10 or 12 leagues further towards the S.W, terminated by a rock, called *Fugle Skiœr*,[3] which appears above the surface. This rock is said to have been formerly a considerable island, the greater part of which disappeared during the last eruption[4] of Skapte Fells[5] – None of the maps notice this extended reef of rocks[6] – a deficiency of much importance in relation to the navigation round Cape Reikianes. The *Margaret & Anne* very nearly got upon it in her voyage to Iceland last summer. The passage round the Cape, when the wind is favourable, is made between the point of the Mainland & the first of the islands, a distance of 5 or 6 miles, – but when there happens to be little wind, there is considerable difficulty in this, owing to the direction of the

[1] Reykjanes.

[2] MS superscript erasure reads 'three'.

[3] Fuglasker.

[4]HH *May 30th. Kieblavík* – We obtained from Mr Jacobæus, a more accurate & detailed report of the appearance near Cape Reikianes, connected with the eruption in the *Skapte Fells* A.D. 1783 – For three or four months previously to this eruption, flames were observed rising out of the sea, a few leagues to the W. of Cape Reikianes – giving an appearance which resembled the burning of two or three large ships at this distance – M[r] J himself was a frequent witness of this phenomenon – Connected with the bursting out of these flames, occasional noises were heard, and there was an appearance of small islands or rocks rising from the sea – No such rocks, however, were afterwards found – but during this period, vast quantities of *pumice stone* were floated on the surface of the sea into the *Faxe-Fiordr*, and large banks of this substance formed upon different parts of the shore – This was especially the case with a southerly wind. – After these phenomena had continued for 3 or 4 months, they suddenly ceased – & immediately afterwards the great volcanic eruption commenced at *Skapte Fells*, covering with lava and scoriæ a district of great extent. The cessation of the flames at Cape Reikianes was also followed by frequent earth-quakes, which affected the whole island – The flames were first seen about the latter end of January – & the volcanic eruption took place at the beginning of June.

The name of *Reikianes* signifies in its literal translation, the *promontory of smoke*; so called from some hot springs appearing upon the Cape.

[5] Skaftáreldar at Lakargígar. MS superscript erasure reads 'Mt Hekla'.

[6] Haraldur Sigurðsson, 1971–8, II, 196–209, prints several maps which clearly mark the visible rocks; notably those of Hans Erik Minor, 1788, and Aaron Arrowsmith, 1808, the latter known to Hooker and printed as a frontispiece to his *Journal*, 1813. Hooker (II, 258–9, 261–9) does confirm Holland's story of 'Blinde Fugle Skiœr', rocks first appearing during the 1783 eruptions and subsequently representing a grave hazard to shipping, after they had sunk just beneath the surface of the sea within a year.

E. Snæfellsjökull

tides, which run in the course of the islands & the reef – Such a difficulty occurred to us in rounding the Cape – When entering between the island and the Mainland, a calm came on, which detained the vessel in the passage for several hours, & afforded some anxiety to Captn Liston, – who apprehended the falling back of the ship upon the islands. By degrees, however, we got round the Cape, (which is formed by a low ridge of rocks, gradually descending into the sea), and at 10 o'clock in the evening were off the point, called *Skagen*,[1] which forms the north-western extremity of the *Guldbringe Syssel* – At this time, a gun was fired for a pilot, but none came on board.

Monday May 7th During the night we made no progress, the vessel beating up and down at the opening of the *Faxe-Fiordr*.[2] The morning disclosed to us a singularly interesting view of the mountainous shores which surround this bay. – On the preceding afternoon we had obtained a first glance of *Snæfield's Jokull*,[3] considered to be the loftiest mountain in the island. It was then seen across the mouth of the bay, at a distance of 80 miles. We now viewed it with much more distinctness, though still more than 60 miles distant;[E] and were enabled to follow with the eye, the whole range of rugged mountains which stretch, in a semi circular form from *Snæfields Jokull* to the *Guldbringe Syssel* – The day was even finer than the preceding one – the objects in the most distant parts of the horizon perfectly clear and distinct – all the mountains covered with snow –

Early in the morning another gun was fired for a pilot – At this time we were off the village of *Kieblevüg*,[4] where there is a small harbour – We here for the first time saw the natives of Iceland. Eight or ten small fishing boats appeared about the ship, each containing four or five

[1] Garðsskagi.   [2] Faxaflói.
[3] Snæfellsjökull; HH: Thermometer at 12 o'clock 38°.
[4] Keflavík.

83

people, busily occupied in the various departments of fishing. One of these boats came up to the Elbe; – We took the men on board, and purchased her cargo of fish; giving four shillings for 16 or 18 cod of very large size. The appearance of these fishermen was novel & striking – Most of them were stout, well made men, with long, light-coloured hair & blue eyes – their dress well suited to their occupation, being composed of sheep & seal skins, cloth of the thickest and coarsest kind, with woollen stockings & gloves of native manufacture. They each received a glass of spirits & some biscuits, & left us much satisfied – Another boat at the same time came up, with a pilot from *Kieblevüg*; a tall, lank-haired man, who seemed as little fitted for this occupation, as he would have been to officiate in a perfumery shop in Bond Street. He took his stuff every two or three minutes, gazed vacantly upon the sails & made errors in his directions respecting the ship, which threw us back several hours in our course. His companions, meanwhile, who were taken on board, were amusing themselves with beef & biscuit, of which they consumed by mouth & pocket an enormous quantity.

The wind being off the shore, we were obliged to make long tacks in the Bay during the whole of the morning – A compensation for this delay was derived from the opportunity of examining the various features of the very singular country which now spread itself before us – We were interested also by a sight of one or two whales, and by the numerous flocks of sea-fowl coming about the ship. About noon, another pilot from Reikiavik[1] made his appearance – a man clad in sheep-skins from head to foot, but having a good physiognomy & displaying more activity & intelligence than his predecessor in the office – At 3 o'clock we entered the bay of Reikiavik; and at 5, (after much detention & some risk from the occurrence of a calm, while among the rocky islands in the bay) we cast anchor off the town of Reikiavik, at the distance of ½ a mile from the shore.

Our voyage was, upon the whole, a favourable one, though the singular state of the weather exposed us to many of the peculiar evils of the sea. Either complete calms, or squalls & gales of wind prevailed during the whole passage, and had it not been for the excellent accommodations of the Elbe, our discomfort from various sources must have been extreme. In this respect, however, we were peculiarly fortunate. Every thing was done both by M[r]. Fell & Captn Liston for

[1] Reykjavík.

the promotion of our convenience, & we had nothing to complain of but evils unavoidable in themselves.

The approach by sea to the metropolis of Iceland, for such is Reikiavik, by no means prepossessed us in its favour. A few habitations, constructed of wood, and scattered along the beach, with an awkward edifice, called a cathedral in the back ground, were the only objects in the first instance presented to our eyes.[1] The country around the town wore the appearance of complete barrenness – a rude, irregular surface, covered every where with moss or fragments of rock. Such was the first impression of the place – Some time before we cast anchor, Mr Savignac,[2] an agent of Messrs Phelps & Co,[3] came on board. He had been resident in Iceland since the spring of 1809 – Shortly after coming to the anchorage, we took the boat, and were landed on the beach of Reikiavik – happy to set our feet again on shore, and still more happy that that shore should be Iceland. A large assemblage of the inhabitants crowded to the beach to witness our disembarkation – Among others, we were honoured by the presence of the Bishop of Iceland[4] – a personage, from whom the first impression received regarded only a prodigious rotundity of features and form. We were introduced to him in our progress along the town, & received individually many external marks of civility – The principal medical man in the island, Dr Klog,[5] was likewise one of the assemblage who greeted us upon our landing. Our fellow traveller & interpreter, Mr Loptson,[6]

[1] A double-page engraving from Mackenzie's sketch of Reykjavík appears in Mackenzie 1812, facing p. 80.

[2] James Savignac [n.d.], Samuel Phelps' commercial agent in Reykjavík and a leading figure in the Jörgensen insurrection: see introduction, pp. 24, 30.

[3] Phelps, 1817, pp. 51–77 reveals himself as a spirited entrepreneur, with no love for the Danes in Iceland, and with vivid memories of his turbulent Icelandic summer of 1809.

[4] Geir Jónsson Vídalín (1761–1823), Bishop of Skálholt from July 1797; moved to Reykjavík in 1806, having become Bishop of all Iceland in October 1801, after the unification of the sees of Skálholt and Hólar. A learned and popular man, of ample girth, he became known as 'Geir Góði' (Geir the good). See Finnur Sigmundsson, *Geir Biskup góði í vinarbréfum* (Reykjavík, 1966), pp. 5–10.

[5] Tómas Klog (1768–1824), Iceland's chief physician 1804–15. Holland's M.D. dissertation *De Morbis Islandiæ* (Edinburgh, 1811) is dedicated to Geir Vídalín and to Klog, 'Landphysicus Islandiæ, ingeniose et perite in patria medicinam faciennti'. Hooker, 1813, I, 16, nottes that Klog's name was 'pronounced Clo'.

[6] Ólafur Looptsson (b. 1783) had been a pupil of Tómas Klog. His ship foundered on its way from Iceland to Denmark; he was subsequently brought to Edinburgh, and hired as guide on the 1810 expedition. See Jón Espolín, 1821–55, XII (Part 10), 49; Mackenzie, 1811, pp. viii–ix; also see introduction, pp. 21–2.

had been his pupil for some years, when formerly in Iceland, & he was received by his old master with every symptom of cordiality & pleasure. We had before observed in the fishermen, who came to the ship, the custom of *salutation by the lips* among individuals of the male sex; – and we now had the most ample opportunity of witnessing the repetition of this practice. Loptson was kissed by his old master, & by many of the men who crowded about the landing place – and a boy who had been taken to England the summer before, & placed at school there by Mr Phelps, was abundantly greeted in the same way. In despite, however, of a custom, which to a stranger seems to shew so much overflowing of heart, we could not but be struck with a sort of *sang froid* which marked the reception by words & countenance. Loptson had been absent from Iceland nearly three years – it was scarcely known whether he was alive or dead – his return was unexpected – yet many of his old friends merely addressed him with a quick, *how do you do?* ( )[1] & proceeded without further notice –

We drank coffee this evening at Mr Savignac's house, and returned in the evening to the vessel, where we passed the night.

Tuesday May 8th [2] Early this morning we again came on shore. In passing through the town, we met Dr Klog, who took me with him to see one or two of his patients in the immediate neighbourhood – Dr K. has been twice in England; & by mixing his broken English with some scraps of Latin, we contrived to keep up conversation with tolerable facility. His practice appeared, upon the whole, to be judicious, and he evinced considerable information in Anatomy & Physiology. He promised to afford me all the assistance in his power in examining the diseases &c of Iceland – These visits with Dr.K. enabled me to examine into some circumstances connected with the interior economy of an Iceland cottage. We had been struck with the wretchedness of the cottages in Orkney; but one which we visited this morning wore all the characters of rudeness in a much higher degree. The people seemed superior to their habitation – there was an expression of features & manner about them, which could not have been looked for under a hovel so miserable.

We called this morning upon the Bishop – His house is in no wise distinguished externally from those around it, and as regards the interior, it is considerably inferior to many others we saw in the town. We were ushered into a room, which appears to serve at once as a

---

[1] The omitted Icelandic expression was never supplied.

[2] HH The weather to day fine, though more cloudy than on the preceding days. No observation of the Thermometer.

library, parlour, and levee-chamber[1] – Its cleanliness could not be applauded – it was clear that a long period had elapsed since either water or broom had visited the flooring & walls – The Bishop's Library appears to consist of 4 or 500 volumes – the greater number Icelandic or Danish – a considerable number of classics – We noticed Rollin's Ancient History[2] on one of the shelves. A large map of Europe, published in London in 1804,[3] was hanging in the room. The Bishop's reception of us was very friendly, but the necessity of employing an interpreter threw considerable difficulty upon the conversation. He has four sons,[4] – some of whom were present in the room. They gazed upon us intently, but did not speak during our stay in the house.

The remainder of the morning was chiefly occupied in the attempt to procure for ourselves a habitation on shore. In this attempt we succeeded infinitely beyond our expectations, owing to a peculiar combination of circumstances. During the preceding summer, Count Trompe,[5] the Danish Governor of Iceland, had been taken a prisoner, & carried on board the *Margaret & Anne*, while she lay at Reikiavik. His authority was for a while assumed by a Dane of the name of Jergenson,[6] – who adopting all the forms of Government, took possession of the Governor's house, created a guard for his person, & endeavoured to establish himself securely in his new situation – After enjoying his borrowed splendour for a short time, he was taken prisoner by the Talbot sloop of war,[7] carried to England; and in consequence of Count Trampe's representations, confined in the hulks at Chatham, where he still remains – Count T. went over to England last summer, & passed the winter in London. During the spring Sir George Mackenzie had much correspondence with him, relative to our expedition; & we were much gratified by the friendly manner in which he gave his assistance in the promotion of the scheme, & by his professions of future service to us, when on the island – Being unexpectedly, however, called over to Copenhagen, his own voyage to

---

[1] A reception room.

[2] Charles Rollin, *Histoire ancienne des Égyptiens, des Carthaginois, des Assyriens, des Babyloniens, des Mèdes et des Perces, des Macédoniens, des Grecs* (Paris, 1730–8).

[3] Probably the large map of Europe published by William Fadden in April 1804: *British Library catalogue of printed maps*, V (London, 1967), p. 709 (Map S.T.E.1).

[4] Only one son, Árni, survived into adulthood.

[5] Frederik Trampe (1779–1832). See introduction, pp. 22–7.

[6] Jörgen Jörgensen (1780–1844). See introduction, pp. 24–7.

[7] The chance arrival of the *Talbot*, commanded by Captain Alexander Jones, at Hafnarfjörður led directly to the failure of the insurrection. See Phelps, 1817, pp. 60–6; McKay, 1973, pp. 92–3.

Iceland was delayed, and upon our arrival at Reikaviik,[1] we found his house wholly unoccupied. – Being unable to procure any lodgings in the town, we adopted the advice of Mr Savignac, & resolved to apply to some of Count T's confidential friends, to learn whether we might not avail ourselves of two or three rooms in the Government house for our temporary accommodation – In pursuance of this plan, we called upon M[r] Simonson,[2] a very respectable inhabitant of Reikiavik, who is Count T's agent, & keeps the keys of his house. We were gratified by our reception. M[r] S. has a countenance expressive of honesty & kindness, and we found a most ready acquiescence in our plans & wishes – While we were with him, M[r] Frydensberg,[3] the Landfogd or Treasurer[4] of the Island & the principal inhabitant of Reikiavik, entered the room. We spoke to him (every thing being done by interpretation) on the same subject, and received an equally ready assent – The keys were put into our hands, with a license to avail ourselves of all the accommodations of the house; excepting only a single room, where the Government papers are kept. We immediately proceeded to examine our proposed habitation, & were abundantly satisfied with the prospect of accommodation which it held out to us for our residence at Reikaviik.

These circumstances were the more fortunate, as we now discovered that our stay at Reikiavik must necessarily be much longer than we had originally calculated upon. – Owing to a complaint which, during the

---

[1] HH *Description of Reikiaviik.* Reikiaviik, the metropolis & most considerable town in Iceland, is situated on the southern shore of a broad bay, stretching into the interior of the country from the *Faxe Fiord* or *Faxe Bugten* – The harbour is somewhat difficult of access, owing to some small islands in the Bay, which in foggy weather render the navigation dangerous & uncertain. Half a mile west of the town, a muscle bed extends from the shore to the nearest island; forming a reef nearly dry at low water. The best place of anchorage is directly opposite to the town, & ½ a mile or a mile from the shore.

The Latitude of Reikiaviik, as ascertained with exactness (May 15) is 64° 8′ 46″ – Its Longitude, by Minor's Chart, [Ed: see note 6, p. 82] about 21° 50′ W of the meridian of Greenwich – The town consists of about 35 habitations & warehouses, constructed of timber, and of 40 or 50 cottages, scattered irregularly around the others. These last are principally the habitations of fishermen, and are rudely constructed of stones, mud and turf. The wooden buildings are arranged with some degree of regularity.

[2] Gísli Símonarson (1774–1837).

[3] Rasmus Frydensberg (1778–1840), a Dane who came to Iceland in 1803; from 1806 he held the office of *landfógeti*, with responsibilities for collection of taxes, auditing public expenditure, and overseeing the enforcement of trade laws; served through the difficult summers of 1809–10 before returning permanently to Denmark.

[4] MS superscript erasure reads 'a *sysselman* or Magistrate'. Holland's correction is appropriate, for Frydensberg had been a *sýslumaður* (prefect or sheriff of a county-sized area) of Kjósarsýsla (the administrative area across the bay to the North East from Reykjavík) from 1803–6.

winter, had prevailed among the horses in the country, we found that there would be an extreme difficulty in procuring a sufficient number of these animals for our expeditions into the interior of the country. The number lost in this part of the island was very great; and many of those left were for the present unfit to be used. We were assured too that before the beginning or middle of June, it would be wholly impossible to traverse the country, partly from the snow, partly from the difficulty of procuring forage for the horses. Under these circumstances, we were compelled to consider ourselves as stationary residents in Reikiavik for some time.

We dined this day at Mr Savignac's – In the afternoon a walking party was made to a boiling spring,[1] about 3 miles from the town – This little excursion formed our first introduction to the natural wonders of Iceland – The spring occurs in the course of a small stream, which empties itself into Reikiavik Bay, at its upper extremity – At the edge of this stream, in two or three places close to each other, a quantity of water gushes from the ground, of a very high temperature – at the time when we visited it, 188 of Fah^t – there is no very evident fissure from which the water arises, nor does it form any jet from the surface – occasionally air bubbles are thrown up in considerable abundance – The more minute examination of the spring we deferred until a second visit – The walk to this spot presents nothing very interesting. Our route led us over an extensive tract of boggy ground, covered here & there with vast assemblages of fragments of lava. The whole of the country in the immediate vicinity of Reikiavik is of a similar character –[2]

We slept this night on board the Elbe, our arrangements not yet being made for a residence on shore.

Wednesday May 9th On the preceding day we had sent a note to Mr Steffensen,[3] a gentleman of very large property, & formerly Governor of Iceland, to inform him of our plans with respect to Count Trampe's house, & to express our intention of paying our respects to him to day – To this note we received a very polite answer – and accordingly preparations were made this morning for paying the visit – M^r. Steffensen lives at *Vüdoe*,[4] an island in the Bay of Reikiavik, about 4

[1] Probably in the area now known as Laugardalsvöllur.

[2] Hooker, 1813, I, 22 likens it to 'the summit of Ben Nevis'.

[3] Ólafur Stephensen (1731–1812), served in important legal and administrative capacities, including eventually Governor-General, from 1756–1806; a pioneering figure in the Icelandic 'enlightenment' period. See þorkell Jóhannesson, 'Magnús Stephensen', *Skírnir*, CVII (1933), 180–4.

[4] Viðey.

miles from the town – This island is entirely the property of Mr S., and though small in extent, derives a very high value from being a great resort of the *Eider Duck*[1] – The *down* of this bird, well known as an article of luxurious convenience, is obtained here every year in great quantity. The number of the Eider ducks upon the rocky shores of *Viidoe* and upon other insulated rocks in this part of the Bay is truly astonishing.

Our party to Viidoe was a large one, comprizing Sir G. Mackenzie, Mr Bright, Mr Fell, Captn Liston, Mr Savignac & our interpreter, Loptson. We went thither in the boat belonging to the Elbe. In passing along the coast, we observed the appearance of Basaltic columns, which we marked as an object of subsequent examination. The old governor's habitation is situated upon the island, about 50 yards from the shore. It is probably the largest house in Iceland[2] – certainly much more considerable than any in Reikiavik. – comparing it with English habitations, it very much resembles a good farm-house – We were met at the door by Mr Steffensen – an old, grey-headed man, having much that is venerable in his appearance. He was dressed in the full uniform of a Colonel of the Danish guards – a cock & pinched hat[3] – scarlet coat with epaulets & numerous other ornaments, blue pantaloons – and boots with silver spurs – This uniform, to which he is entitled from his former situation as Governor, is introduced on all occasions of form; – As such, our arrival was considered – and on entering the house, we found every arrangement made for our reception which hospitality, aided by a little vanity, could dictate. On entering the house, we passed into a large wainscoated room, the walls hung round with sundry old pictures of Danish kings &c. Through this apartment, we passed into a smaller room, well-heated by a stove, & containing a large bed, the *swelling* mattress of which shewed that the old Governor had availed himself of the luxurious stuffing which his Eider Ducks afford him. Brandy & rusk biscuits were upon the table, & of these we partook previously to sitting down. – All conversation with Mr Steffensen was carried on by interpretation, as he is not acquainted with the English language. He enquired with much affection & interest after Sir Joseph

---

[1] *Somateria mollissima* (Linn.), Mod.Ice. *Æður*.

[2] Viðeyjarstofa. Built for Skúli Magnússon between 1752–5 and regarded at that time as unique amongst Icelandic houses for its size and style; delapidated remains survive to the present day; Mackenzie, 1812, p. 83, notes the onset of decay, the house seeming as if it 'would not long survive its venerable inhabitant'.

[3] Apparently a pleonastic expression, standing for 'cock[ed] and pinched'. To cock a hat was to pinch it into shape, making an original round shape into a two or three cornered one.

Banks, of whom, though 37 years have elapsed since Sir Joseph was in Iceland, he retains the most lively recollection.[1] He shewed us a letter which he received from him last year by Mr Hooker – His remembrance of Sir John Stanley[2] was equally perfect, & he enquired much relatively to his present residence & circumstances – Mr Steffensen is now more than 80 years of age. His character we were enabled without difficulty to comprehend. Vanity is the predominating ingredient – & but for the respectability which his years & other dispositions communicate, would afford considerable annoyance to those around him. Scarcely had we been ten minutes in the house, before a box was brought forth, containing various honorary medals and titles which he has received. From a survey of these we found that he is a Fellow of the Antiquarian Society of London – of the Genealogical Society of Copenhagen &c. Shortly afterwards, a young lady,[3] a relation of the Governor, & a sort of housekeeper to him, entered the room, evidently for the sole purpose of exhibition. She was dressed in the height of the Icelandic fashionable costume – a black cap, formed by the careful folding of a broad ribband about the head, with a conical termination of white cotton, the extremity turned downwards, somewhat like the *fool's cap* of our English schools – the upper part of the dress made of dark green cloth with a long waist, and an open lacing in front – under the lacing, a longitudinal band of scarlet cloth – the tag of the lacing silver, and other silver ornaments about this part of the dress – a belt round the waist, with a clasp richly adorned – the lower part of the dress composed of a green stuff much lighter than the copper. After this dress had been duly examined & admired, the young lady left the room.

Dinner was soon afterwards announced. This we had not calculated upon; but the entreaties of the old Governor were of such a nature as not to be resisted. We were again ushered into the large outer room & seated round the table. The first dish which made its appearance was a large tureen of Sago Soup,[4] to which we were all most liberally helped.

[1] Ólafur Stephensen is mentioned briefly in von Troil, 1780, p. 71.

[2] Stanley's meeting with Ólafur Stephensen is recorded in West, 1970–6, I, 76–7; more generally, Wawn, 1981, 52–76.

[3] Ingibjörg Jónsdóttir (b. 1784). See Finnur Sigmundsson (ed.) *Sendibréf frá íslenskum konum 1784–1900* (Reykjavík, 1952), pp. 27–39, a letter from Ingibjörg to her brother with cynical references (p. 28) to 'Doktor og prófessor O. Loppesen' (Ólafur Loptsson).

[4] Magnús Stephensen's sister-in-law Marta María published a cookbook, *Einfaldt matreiðslu vasa-quer* (Leirárgarðar, 1800), which includes (p. 80) a sago soup recipe, requiring ingredients available only in the wealthier households – sago, red wine, cherries, raisins, cinnamon and lemon.

A sirloin of beef baked was then put upon the table, & this was succeeded by a dish of fritters made with flour, & sugared over – A ceremony of some importance next came on – A large silver goblet was brought upon the table, ornamented around with little medallions, on which were imprinted the names of the Governor, his wife, & each one of their children. This was filled to the brim by the old man with a wine resembling claret, or thin port – Sir G.M. was at the top of the table & I sat next to him on his left hand – The cup was held out to me, & I was desired to take off the lid. Mr Steffensen then drank Sir George's health, & took off the contents of the goblet. I was next directed to fill the cup, and to present it to the person immediately opposite me, to have the lid taken off. This being done, I drank his health, & transferred the goblet to his hands for the performance of a similar ceremony – Any deviation from this form of proceeding was punished by a repetition of the bumper – and the old man derived infinite delight from the opportunity of enforcing the fine. Sir G. Mackenzie was the last person to whom the goblet was given – He drank the Governor's health, and was allowed, as part of the regular procedure, to put the cup to his lips, without a previous examination of its contents by another person's taking off the lid – This ceremony gone through, two large dishes were brought in, containing cakes of sago jelly, swimming in cream – a piece of cookery which certainly did much credit to the economy of the Governor's kitchen. Here the dinner concluded. After taking a little more wine, we walked out upon the island – visited M^r S's farmyard, and examined his cows, which had just been brought into the fold – This breed appears to be a valuable one – the animals well formed & the udders large – They have a considerable resemblance to the Highland breed of cattle. – While walking about the house, we were joined by a young man, who has just taken orders as a minister.[1] I had a good deal of conversation with him in Latin. He seemed to be intelligent and well-informed; & promised us a detailed account of the agricultural economy of the Icelanders –

Upon our return to the house, coffee was served out to us, by an elderly lady,[2] the mother of the young woman we had before seen. The service was one of Saxon porcelain, tolerably handsome. Here we conceived that the eating & drinking of the day had its termination; but

---

[1] Perhaps Þorlákur Loptsson (1779–1842), served Ólafur Stephensen on Viðey 1807–12; removed in disgrace from the priesthood in 1815; rehabilitated in 1817 and reconsecrated in 1820.

[2] Kristín Eiríksdóttir (b. 1749), mother of Ingibjörg Jónsdóttir.

to our astonishment & dismay, the coffee was succeeded by a prodigious tureen of hot punch, which we were not allowed to quit, till the last drop was exhausted. Toasts were given to each glass, the Kings of England & Denmark, prosperity to Iceland, &c – This being over, we bade adieu to the old man, who accompanied us to the boat, gave us all sort of good wishes, & expressed his earnest desire to see us speedily again. We were much struck with his manner & stile of conversation – There was a degree of *politesse*, of courtliness & compliment in his speeches, which little accorded with our preconceived ideas of a country-gentleman in Iceland – His health of late has been very indifferent – and I was honoured by a formal consultation upon his case. His extreme age, however, considered, his constitution is wonderfully robust, and he may yet see many years of life. His cordial & friendly reception of us, engaged all our warmest wishes in his behalf.

We slept on board the Elbe this night, our preparations on shore not yet being complete.

Thursday May 10th – We came to the town early this morning, & brought most of our luggage with us – The greater part of the morning was occupied in making the arrangements at our place of residence, with which we continued to be exceedingly well satisfied. We had originally planned to occupy only two rooms & the kitchen on the ground floor; but the addition of Mr Fell to our domestic party led to an extension of this scheme; & we now took two or three rooms on the upper story for our better accommodation – Count Trampe's house is certainly the best in Reikiavik, yet the name of *Government house* might lead to the expectation of something much more splendid than the reality would fulfil – The edifice, which is only two stories in height, is constructed of timber, upon a base of fragments of lava, rudely put together – There are only six small windows in front – three on each side of the door. On the ground floor are three or four rooms, with a small place called the kitchen, & a pantry – The largest of these apartments, which we made our sitting room, is not more than 17 or 18 feet in length by 12 in width – On the upper story are four small rooms; one of them, which was Count Trampe's room, containing a stove. The rooms below are all warmed by large stoves of cast iron – this being the case in all the better houses in Iceland. In the kitchen there is no grate; but a hearth raised two or three feet above the ground supplies all the purposes of cooking &c – A tolerably good stable & yard are connected with the house – and a small garden lies behind it; at present, however, wholly uncultivated.

We had made an engagement with Dr Klog to meet him this morning at the Bishop's, to inoculate some children with the Cowpock. We brought with us from Leith two cow-pock crusts, from an idea that there might possibly be of some utility in this. The supposition was well founded. The Cow-pock[1] had been introduced into Iceland from Denmark, but owing probably to the small number of children requiring inoculation, the matter was entirely lost – The Icelanders have an excessive dread of the small pox – and not without sufficient reason, as the island has, at different periods, suffered dreadfully from its ravages – We inoculated this morning five children – one of them a daughter of the Sysselmann Frydensbergs.

We slept this night in the Government house – We were not yet able to procure a servant or house keeper, but the washerwoman of the town, *Madame Krag*[2] (for even washerwomen have here the title of Madame as an adjunct to their names) officiated *pro tempore* in our little kitchen. This good woman, in every respect very much resembling a housekeeper in an English family, has the reputation of being the best cook in Reikiavik.

Friday May 11th This morning the poor fellow who was killed during our passage from Britain, was buried – The burial place is within the town. The minister at Reikiavik,[3] to whom we had before been introduced at the Bishop's, officiated on this occasion. The ceremony is a simple one – As soon as the procession enters the burial ground, the priest & precentor commence together a chaunt which is continued without intermission for a considerable time. – The coffin is then committed to the ground – the priest says a few words, & throws three shovel-full of soil into the grave. The filling of the grave then commences & this being done, the procession leaves the ground –

We called this morning upon Mr Frydensberg, & were introduced to his lady, a pleasing, good-humoured woman.[4] M^r F is a Dane – He has resided in Iceland 7 years; and holds a high office in the government of the island; all legal matters coming under his cognizance before they pass into the court of law. His title, corresponding to this office is *Landfoged*.[5] He is likewise the magistrate or *Sysselman* of a particular

---

[1] See D. J. Guthrie, *A history of medicine* (London, 1945), pp. 246–9.

[2] Unidentified. No obvious candidate in *MÍ 1801: Suð.* or *MÍ 1816* (Akureyri, 1947–74), p. 380, entry for Keflavík.

[3] Brynjólfur Sigurðsson Sívertsen (1767–1837), consecrated as priest in 1797 and served until 1813 in Reykjavík.

[4] Unidentified.   [5] *landfógeti* (see note 3, p. 88).

district; – an office distinct from the former. His house is one of the best in Reikiavik, and the domestic arrangements appear to be better than in most of the Icelandic habitations – Mr Frydensberg in his official capacity has a clerk of the name of Magnuson,[1] a young [man][2] who was educated at Copenhagen, and has the reputation of being a good scholar. – To him we were indebted for the loan of an Icelandic Grammar,[3] published at Copenhagen in 1651 by Ranolphus Jonas, a native of Iceland. The book is a very rare one.

We dined this day on board the Elbe, with a large party – Englishmen, Icelanders, Danes, and Americans.[4] In the evening came again on shore.[5]

[1] Finnur Magnússon (1781–1847), studied in Copenhagen 1798–9; an official in Rasmus Frydensberg's office after 1803; refused to support Jörgensen in 1809; returned to Copenhagen 1812. His association with books, whether as antiquarian, author, scholar, administrator, or, less happily, occasional importunate hawker, continued until the end of his life. See Jón Helgason, 'Finnur Magnússon', in *Ritgerðakorn og Ræðustúfar* (Reykjavík, 1959), pp. 171–96; also Sveinbjörn Rafnsson, *Frásögur um fornaldarleifar 1817–23*, 2 vols. (Reykjavík, 1983), pp. iv–xxxv. Sections of a poem by Finnur, including hostile verses about Jörgensen, are included in Mackenzie, 1812, pp. 453–5.

[2] MS has 'man' added in pencil by later, different hand.

[3] Runólfur Jónsson, *Grammaticæ Islandicæ rudimenta* (Copenhagen, 1651), the first printed Icelandic grammar book; reprinted in Oxford in 1688, the first Icelandic book printed in England.

[4] The presence of Americans in Reykjavík at this time is not surprising. American trading vessels arrived there in both 1809 and 1810. Samuel Phelps hoped to by-pass wartime trading restrictions by shipping British goods to Iceland, trading with the Americans the Icelandic goods obtained in exchange for the British provisions, and receiving in turn from them valuable produce for the British market. There were also allegations that Count Trampe and other Reykjavík residents sought, during Phelps's absence in the Spring of 1810, to annex his goods from their Reykjavík warehouses and ship them profitably to America. See Halldór Hermannsson, 1928, pp. 66–8; Phelps, 1817, pp. 61–7; Gjerset, [1923], pp. 359–60.

[5]^{HH} The vicinity of Reikiaviik presents much uniformity of mineralogical character. It may best be studied by pursuing the course of the shores in the neighbourhood of the town – These shores exhibit appearances in the rocks, decidedly indicating their having been acted upon by heat at some former period. It is somewhat doubtful, however, whether the beds which they compose have ever actually flowed under the form of lava – It is a probable circumstance that the changes which appear in the structure of the rock may have been effected simply by the application of heat from below.

On the shore to the NW of the town, there are the appearances of three distinct beds of this rock (Specimens A 1.2.3) presenting some differences of internal structure. – These appearances, however, are not observable with the same distinctness on other parts of the shore – A3 is most characteristic & uniform in its appearances – The surface of these beds of rock along the shore afford in numerous places a decidedly scoriated appearance – Columnar appearances, tolerably regular, likewise occur in several places. – On the shore to the east of the town, the same general characters of the rock present themselves. – the columnar appearances more perfect. – The substance of which A5 is a specimen, occurs in the rock ½ a mile from the town – also A6.

Saturday May 12th An invitation from Dr Klog led us to adopt for this morning's occupation, a walk to his house, which is situated about 2 miles from Reikiavik on a point of land called the *Næs*,[1] which projects into the sea to the north west of the town. We took our hammers, and walked along the shore for the purpose of examining the termination of the lava towards the sea. (See page 26). On our way we called at Mr Severtsen's, the minister of Reikiavik. His house[2] is in every respect inferior to a common cottage in England. An entrance, scarcely passable from the smallness of all its dimensions, conducted us to a dark and gloomy apartment, in which there was just space enough for a bed, a desk, & two or three chairs. Here the minister introduced us to Madame Severtsen[3] & his family.[4] We were presented with a large bowl of milk, the produce of M^r S's own cows. His salary as a clergyman is equivalent only to about £20 per annum; – though in this respect he is greatly better off than the majority of his brethren. The opportunity, from his situation, of constantly providing himself with fish, is a circumstance of much importance to him. In the entrance to the house we observed a large quantity of fish curing for the winters consumption – We saw here too a hand-mill for crushing grain, composed simply of one circular block of stone revolving upon another – A similar implement is much used in the Highlands of Scotland – & the name in the Gaelic & Iceland is almost precisely the same – *kuerne or cuarne.*[5]

Dr Klog's house is about a mile beyond Mr Severtsen's – His situation here is not merely that of a private individual – He is appointed by the Danish government with a considerable salary[6] and connected with the establishment is an Apothecary's shop managed also by a person officially appointed. This shop & the Apothecary's

---

Much of the rock along these shores in the vicinity of Reikiaviik contains a quantity of olivine – appearing especially in the more compact parts of the rock, & often in considerable quantity.

The rising grounds on each side of the fresh water lake behind Reikiaviik are covered with fragments of the same rock which appears on the shores – In some places the bare rock itself appears on the surface, in small rounded eminences, as if heaved up by some force from below – These eminences present numerous fissures.[F]

[1] Nes (on Seltjarnarnes).
[2] Situated at Sel.
[3] Steinunn Helgadóttir (1770–1857).
[4] Five children survived into adulthood.
[5] Mod.Ice. *handkvörn*; Scot. *quern* (various spellings).
[6] MS superscript in Holland's hand, '500 dollars per annum'.

house are situated close to Dr Klog's – The object of the whole

F. Lava columns on the shore at Reykjavík

establishment is to provide medical assistance for the poor of the island, and particular regulations exist for this purpose. These regulations, however, do not preclude the profits of private practice among the wealthier people in the neighbourhood – Dr Klog's house is a tolerably good one & fitted up with some neatness. Madame K.,[1] who is a Danish lady, gave us some excellent chocolate, & exhibited, at our request, some more novel articles of Icelandic diet – butter, two years old – stock fish, &c &c – To the butter we could not with any sincerity give our applause. Its external appearance, which was of various tints of colour, did not prepossess us in its favour, and the taste justified all these predictions. Butter thus kept is called by the Icelanders   .[2] It is made without salt, & may in many places be seen of three or four years standing.

Before leaving D^r K's I went with him to an adjoining house to see a patient, formerly a sort of assistant Governor of the island.[3] The

[1] Magdalene Sofie Jensen [n.d.].
[2] Blank in MS.
[3] Benedikt Jónsson Gröndal (1762–1825), a noteworthy poet who held judicial office 1800–17; supported Jörgensen in 1809 and was injured during the insurrection. See Hannes Þorsteinsson, 'Benedikt Jónsson Gröndal: yfirdómari og skáld, 1760–1825', *Skírnir* XCIX (1925), 65–106.

man's complaint appeared to have much of hypochondriasis in it[1] –
He had last summer some connection with Jergenson, in the
transactions carried on at Reikiavik, & certain pecuniary disappoint-
ments attending the failure of this scheme, threw him into a
despondent, melancholy state – D[r] K. requested me to prescribe for
him, which I did. –

Sunday – May 13 – The day was so wet and gloomy that we were
unable to remove to any distance from the house. We should have
gone to the church, had service been performed there, but M[r]
Severtsen went to preach this day at a chapel in the island of Viidoe.
We were honoured this morning by a visit from the present Governor
of Iceland – a son of our lately acquired friend M[r] Steffensen.[2] He was
formerly governor of the Southern district of the Island[3] – but since
the events of the last summer, his office has been extended to the
government of the whole island.[4] He resides[5] about 20 miles from
Reikiavik on the opposite side of the Bay. He was now coming to the
town to give sentence in some legal cases & we received a message
from Viidoe on Saturday, mentioning his intention of calling upon us.
He accordingly came about 12 o'clock, accompanied by his brother[6]
(the governor of Westerland)[7] & three young men, one of them his
own son[8] – the other two, his brother's children.[9] The elders of this
party very much resembled in manners, appearance & dress the better
class of English farmers – The Governor, or *Etatsraad*, a Danish title
equivalent to Counsellor of State, speaks English with tolerable
fluency. He was taken prisoner two years ago by an English vessel of
war, when going to Copenhagen, & carried into Leith – but was

[1] Holland, 1811, p. 24 accounts for the prevalence of the affliction in Iceland in terms
of 'the condition of life', diet, winter 'incarceration' and the natural melancholic
temperament of the Icelanders.

[2] Magnús Ólafsson Stephensen (1762–1833). See Halldór Hermannsson, *The periodical
literature of Iceland down to the year 1874*, Islandica XI (1918), 16–34; also Þorkell
Jóhannesson, 1933, pp. 166–93.

[3] Holland mistaken. Magnús Stephensen never occupied this position.

[4] After several years legal and administrative experience in Denmark and Iceland, he
was appointed Chief Justice in July 1800, and an acting Governor after Jörgen
Jörgensen's overthrow. See introduction, p. 31, note 3; p. 144; and p. 274, note 1.

[5] At Innrihólmur.

[6] Stefán Ólafsson Stephensen (1767–1820).

[7] He held office from 6 June 1806 until his death.

[8] Perhaps Ólafur Magnússon Stephensen (1791–1872).

[9] Mackenzie (1812), p. 90 claims that it was Magnús Stephensen's two brothers
(Stefán and Björn) who accompanied him. Holland's belief that it was Magnús's two
nephews is more plausible; both Stefán and Björn had sons of the appropriate age.

liberated again in the course of a few days. In his manners he is exceedingly obliging & civil – & he expressed his intention of doing us all the service in his power during our stay in Iceland – One of his nephews, who came with him, has acquired some knowledge of English. He was greatly delighted with a present we made him of a copy of Thomson's Seasons.[1]

We dined this day with Mr Petraus,[2] an agent of Messrs Phelps & Co at Reikiavik. A large and miscellaneous assemblage was present – the *Atastrood* & his son, the *Landfoged* Frydensberg, Mr Simonson, Mr Knutson,[3] with several other Icelanders & Danes – After the healths of their Majesties of England & Denmark had been drank, several appropriate toasts were given to the party – *prosperity to the trade of Iceland; thanks to the British Government for their generosity to the Icelanders* &c The latter of these toasts was suggested by the proclamation relative to Iceland, contained in the London Gazette of March 1810,[4] licensing a trade to the island under certain conditions. This Gazette we brought with us. It was received with infinite satisfaction & delight at Reikiavik & translated into both the Danish & Icelandic languages – Count Trampe's health was likewise given as a toast. There appeared some reluctance on behalf of the *Atastrood* to accept this, & we afterwards heard that no cordiality existed between them – After taking coffee the Governor came with us to our own residence, and looked over the instruments we brought to Iceland – the theodelite, sextant, barometers &c – He appeared pleased with the examination.

Monday May 14th This morning we had an engagement to breakfast with Mr Frydensberg. It was termed *breakfast* but we did not sit down to the table till past 11, & the meal much more resembled a dinner – The party consisted of the Governor, the Bishop, Mr Simonson, M^r

[1] James Thomson, *The Seasons* (1730), a philosophical-pastoral poem which enjoyed widespread popularity in eighteenth-century Europe, not least in Scandinavia. See W. G. Johnson, *James Thomson's influence in Swedish literature in the eighteenth-century* (Urbana, 1936). Mackenzie, 1811, p. 77 quotes from 'Winter', ll.904–9 to describe his first impressions of Iceland. The text presented to Magnús Stephensen may well have been the 1803 edition, containing a lengthy critical essay by Holland's friend John Aikin.

[2] Westy Petræus (b. 1767), a prominent, but less than universally popular Danish merchant in Reykjavík, with other business interests in Hafnarfjörður and Vestmannaeyjar.

[3] There were two Knudsen brothers: Lars Michael (1769–1828), who also married a sister (Margrét) of Stefán Ólafsson Stephensen's wife Marta María, and purchased Westy Petræus's business in 1814; and Adzer Christian (b. 1766), the more commercially powerful of the two and probably the one referred to here.

[4] Hooker, 1813, II, 59–63, and Phelps, 1817, pp. 70–2 print and discuss the proclamation.

Magnuson, one or two other Icelanders, & our own party from the Government House. The first dish set upon the table was Mutton Curry, very well dressed, & accompanied by potatoes & bread, both of them articles of great scarcity in Iceland – A shoulder of mutton baked, was the next dish – This was succeeded by a course of Iceland cheese & butter with American biscuits;[1] & the repast was concluded by coffee. Port, Claret & Vidonia[2] were all set upon the table, & liberally partaken of. The conversation was carried on with difficulty, the Governor and Loptson being the only persons present, who spoke in common the Icelandic & English languages. The Bishop appeared greatly to enjoy the excellence of the breakfast. His corpulence is of the most extraordinary kind; and it is attended by an infinite good humour & pleasantry of character. Mr Fell mentioned to him that some *church wafers* had been brought over in the Elbe for religious services in Iceland – He replied through the medium of an interpreter, '*Tell the gentlemen that the Icelandic church could have relished some wine too;*' and followed the speech by a vociferous burst of laughter.

The management of the meals in an Icelandic family affords more novelty than any other circumstance connected with their domestic habits. Any other bread than that of rye is exceedingly scarce and the common garden vegetables are almost altogether wanting – Fish is the staple article of food, and of this an immense profusion exists within their easy reach – Other circumstances relative to this part of their domestic economy, will afterwards be noticed.

The time of breakfasting led us to delay dinner till a late hour; & in the mean time we took a second walk to the hot springs following the coast to the mouth of the stream and tracing it upwards to the spring. Along the coast we observed the appearances of the lava very similar to those on the other side of the town – Arrived at the hot springs, we collected there a number of specimens, illustrative particularly of the crusts which are formed around the mouth of the spring, & of the substances through which the water passes in rising to the surface. We were struck by observing a strong gush of hot water at the point A in the sketch[3] – a situation in which nothing of the kind appeared when we last visited the spot. In each of the springs, the water gushes

[1] Perhaps deriving from the American trading vessel which reached Reykjavík in 1809, through the full extent of its trading activities is not clear. See above, note 4, p. 95.

[2] A dry white Canary wine.

[3] Refers to lost sketchbook.

out at intervals, & with different force at different times – At the point B in the sketch we noticed a circular swelling or elevation of the ground, with a circular depression at the summit – the outer circumference about 65 yards – the circumference of the depression 16 or 18 – the elevation probably about 15 feet above the level of the stream – The lower and exterior part of this eminence, next to the stream (which alone we had the means of examining) is composed of the same material, as that which encrusts & surrounds the hot springs in the vicinity. These circumstances inclined us to believe that a fountain of boiling water, resembling the Geyser,[1] had, at some former period, existed in this spot – Whether there be any record which favours this supposition, we have not learnt – The inhabitants of Reikiavik are in the habit of washing their cloathes at these warm springs – a convenience highly to be estimated, where there is so great a scarcity of fuel as in Iceland.

In the course of this w[alk][2] we saw a large seal, close to the rocks upon the shore, & prodigious numbers of water fowl – the Divers, Eider Ducks &c.

On our return towards Reikiavik, we heard the report of a cannon fired from the Elbe – Re-entering the town, we found the utmost confusion there – the warehouses of Mess[rs] Phelps & Co guarded by sea men from the ship, armed with musquets & blunderbusses – assemblages of people in different parts of the town – the *Atastrood*, M[r] Frydensberg, M[r] Fell, Savignac & Petraus shut up together in consultation – The cause of this disturbance we speedily ascertained: a storm had burst which for some past time had been brewing – Mess[rs] Savignac and Petraus were left last summer in Reikiavik as the agents of M[r] Phelps. It would appear that these gentlemen had availed themselves of the remoteness of their situation to forward their own interests at the expence of their employers. They of course viewed the arrival of Mr Fell, as a superior agent, with no small concern; and his activity in looking into all the details of their transactions, increased their hostility towards him. This feeling was pretty well smothered for some time; venting itself only in some

---

[1] Geysir in Haukadalur (Árnessýsla), the famed hot-spring which, as much as any other topographical feature, had drawn eighteenth-century travellers to Iceland. Even Stanley, a frustratingly reluctant publisher of material from his 1879 expedition, was prevailed upon to discuss his own visit to the springs. See *Transactions of the Royal Society of Edinburgh*, III (1794), 138–53.

[2] MS reads 'wish'.

little asperities of language – but certain occurrences to day at once threw off the veil. – Savignac & Petraus, after throwing out threats, some of them of a serious nature, seized by force, during Mr Fell's momentary absence, the keys of the warehouses. Immediately a signal was hoisted to the ship – 12 or 15 armed men were sent on shore, – the warehouses were broken open, Mr Fell's locks placed upon the doors – and a strong guard paraded in the vicinity during the night. The meeting with the *Atastrood* & *Landfoged* took place for the purpose of attempting some accommodation – Nothing, however, could be done. The *Atastrood* is a cautious, timid man – a relation moreover to Mr Petraus –[1] and he could not be brought to consent to any of the vigorous measures which justice required – He was extremely averse to the continuance of the armed men in the town, but Mr Fell and Capt Liston would not concede this point – Matters therefore continued in the same state till the morning. We slept with loaded pistols in the house, – a measure dictated by some expressions which Mr Savignac had employed.

Tuesday. May 15 Much of this day was spent in consultations, protests & correspondence respecting the transactions of yesterday. Some letters passed between the Governor and Sir G. Mackenzie on the subject; and both he and Mr Frydensberg were with us several times in the course of the day. Savignac and Petraus persevered in the same measures – refused to acknowledge Mr Fell as a superior agent – or to shew any of their accounts. The guard was still continued over the warehouses – The Governor objected much to this, & in the afternoon sent a protest against the proceeding. To this Mr Fell answered at some length – representing the necessity he was under, as a protector of Mr Phelps's property, of resorting to this measure. It was consented, however, that only two or three men should be on guard this evening, & that their arms should be concealed – The whole of the transactions displayed in a striking light the feebleness & inefficacy of the government of the island.

The day, however, was not wholly occupied by these unpleasant circumstances. We called upon the Bishop in the morning, & sat more than an hour with him, carrying on the conversation chiefly in Latin, which he speaks with much fluency – He gave us a good deal of information respecting the former & present state of the religious polity of Iceland. He is the first bishop of the whole island – the

[1] Katrín, wife of Westy Petræus, was the sister-in-law of Stefán Ólafur Stephensen.

Icelandic church formerly comprehending two bishopricks – those of
Skalholt & Hoolum.[1] He shewed us likewise some valuable
documents respecting the population of Iceland, – of which we were
promised copies – In the course of this visit we were introduced to the
lady[2] of the Bishop, or *Fru*, as she is termed – a title which attaches by
way of distinction to females of superior rank – Some characteristic of
this kind was certainly desirable for the lady in question – as nothing
about her person or manner indicated her elevation in society – She
was, however, in a high degree good humoured & civil – prepared
chocolate for us, & while we were drinking it, shewed us the various
costumes of dress among the Icelandic females of different ages and
situations of life – dressing herself in them for the purpose of better
exhibition.

We obtained at noon to day some good observations of the sun, &
ascertained the latitude of Reikiavik with much exactness, making it
64° 8′ 46″ – This result almost precisely agrees with that laid down in
the best maps & charts.

The evening was wholly given to gaiety – We had determined
some days before to give a ball to the good people of Reikiavik, by
way of conciliating their affections, & observing their fashionable
customs. This was the day fixed upon, & the *annoncement* was made
accordingly – special invitations were issued to our own friends, & a
more general license given to all the inhabitants of the town. We
learnt from Loptson, our informant as to all the news of the place,
that much expectation was excited, & many preparations making for
the evening by all the beaux & belles of Reikiavik. The ball was
given in the club-room[3] – an apartment neither spacious nor
splendid, but nevertheless the best which the place affords – The
party began to assemble between 8 & 9, & at 10 o'clock there were
60 or 70 people in the room; the greater number inhabitants of
Reikiavik – some, however, from Hafnafiord & other places in the
neighbourhood. We were honoured by the presence of the
Governor, the Bishop & his lady, M[r] & Mrs Frydensberg, & all the
other *fashionables* of the place. One of the principal belles was a Miss

[1] Skálholt and Hólar.
[2] Sigríður Halldórsdóttir (1768–1846).
[3] *Klúbburinn* (The Club), also known as Scheelshús, after its owner, the merchant
Henrik Scheel (b. 1750).

Jonsen,[1] the destined bride of Jergenson, had he retained his dignities as Governor of Iceland. The dancing began soon after 9, to the music of one fiddle, the *Government drum*, & a pair of triangles. Each gentleman took out his partner strictly according to the English fashion – and all the arrangements for the country dances were made in the same way. The figures also of the dances much resembled those common in England, but they were accompanied by tunes of a miserable description, & miserably played. We had hoped to see at this ball some peculiar fashions of Icelandic dress; but in this we were considerably disappointed. With the exception of three elderly matrons, (one of them the Bishop's Lady,) who were dressed in the Icelandic costume of peaked caps, long waists, ornamented lacing &c, all the females in the room were habited in dresses precisely similar to those of the English – in the middle classes of life – The whole scene much resembled a country ball-room in England – At 12 o'clock, as many of the party as were able to procure seats, adjourned to the supper room – where a collation was set out, as splendid as circumstances & the country would admit of – cold mutton, beef, & hams, cheese, butter, biscuits and wines – After supper, some of the ladies, Mesdames Frydensberg, Klog, & Simensen gave us several Danish songs, in which they were joined by the Governor & others of the gentlemen present. In return we made up a sort of clumsy chorus of *God save the king*, with which all the party seemed much pleased – Just before we rose from the table to make room for a second party, the glasses were filled with wine, & the ladies commenced in unison a lively little air, in which the health of Sir G. Mackenzie was given, with an acclamation corresponding to the English *huzza*. This done, each one rose, touched their glasses with Sir G.M.'s, & drank off the wine. – After supper dancing was resumed, with the introduction of Waltzes among the country dances; and the assembly did not break up till half past four in the morning. We both began and concluded our gaieties by the light of the sun – At 3 o'clock the candles were dismissed, as wholly unnecessary to us – While the dancing went forwards, the elders of the party were smoking & drinking punch in

[1] Guðrún Einarsdóttir Johnsen. A remarkable girl, eventually befriended and then betrayed by John Parke, the British consul in Reykjavík after 1811, who brought her to London and then abandoned her; she received help from Holland, whom she had first met in Iceland, and from the Stanley family of Alderley, for whom she may have worked during 1814, and with whom she subsequently corresponded. See Wawn, 1985.

an adjoining room. Some of them left the house a little less steadily than they entered it – Among others, the *Right Reverend Father, the Bishop of all Iceland* was observed to be somewhat affected by the potations of the evening.

In the course of the Ball, we were exposed to much difficulty from our inability to speak the language of the country. With our partners, both in dancing & at the upper table, we were compelled to converse by signs alone – the awkwardness of which was, on many occasions, very sensibly felt.

Wednesday May 16th This morning afforded a partial termination to the unpleasant circumstances, which had occurred during the preceding days – The Governor called, to request that Sir G. Mackenzie would be present at a conference between the contending parties. This conference lasted for several hours – After considerable difficulty, an adjustment was made, very favourable upon the whole to the interests of Mr Fell, Messrs Savignac and Petraus being convinced that nothing could be effected by violent means. The guard was now taken off the warehouses & tranquillity restored to the town.

By way of practice, we pitched our tent this morning on an open piece of ground at the back of the house –

Thursday May 17 – This day we devoted a second excursion to the island of Viidoe – A strong northerly wind prevented our taking a boat from Reikiavik. We therefore walked along the coast for three or four miles, & crossed over a narrow straight which here separates the island from the Mainland – The old Governor, or *Geheimer atastrood*,[1] received us with the same mixture of hospitality & form, as on our former visit to him. We explained to him that it was our object to examine minutely the mineralogy of his island. Having received his assent, & promised a return to dinner, we set forth with our hammers & bags, & made a circuit of the whole island – with much interest, as regarded the observation of its mineralogical features. (See opposite page).[2] In the course of our walk, we saw

[1] Gehejme-etatsrood. An honorific title granted to the former Governor, and similar in import to the British title of Privy Counsellor.

[2]HH The mineralogy of Viidoe presents some singular appearances. – To the E of the landing place along the shore, is a vein of highly crystallized Greenstone, on each side of which is an Amygdaloidal rock, fragmented so as to give the appearance of a sort of *tuff* –The cavities of this amygdaloid contain zeolite & calc spar. Further on, the amygdaloidal rock is much intermixed, with a substance which may perhaps be

several eagles hovering over our heads. We were again much struck by the prodigious number of Eider ducks frequenting the rocky shores of the island – Returning to the house, we dined with the old man, talked to him about his titles, his family & furniture, and left him, as we had every reason to believe, very well satisfied with his guests – He gave us a long narrative of a daring robbery committed in his house two years ago by some sailors, belonging, as he stated, to an English ship of war, commanded by Cap^{tn} Gilpin – From some circumstances, we were led to believe that the outrage was committed by the crew of the vessel which Baron Hompesch[1] had with him in the North Seas. The master of this vessel was a man of the name of Gilpin; from which the mistake of Mr Steffensen probably originated –[2] Restitution was obtained of a considerable part of the property thus plundered.

---

termed *volcanic tuff*. Of this C1 & C2 & C3 are specimens – C2 shews the junction between the tuff & amygdaloid. The tuff usually appears in veins in the amygdaloid – some times the latter seems to occur in included masses of large side & a rounded form^G – the tuff forming the boundary of the masses of amygdaloid. Above these included masses appear in one place some irregular columns of greenstone. – On the opposite side of the island (which is about ½ a mile across) the appearances are very different – The general character of the rocks along this shore is very similar to those appearing at Reikiaviik – they exhibit all the appearances of having been acted upon by heat under some modification or other. – their position is above that of the amygdaloid, & trap tuff. In several places they are intersected by veins of greenstone, probably the same as those which appear on the opposite side of the island – 12 to 20 yards in thickness – Of this greenstone C5 is a specimen. – The volcanic rock on this shore assumes columnar appearances in several places – C6 from a column of this rock – A compact basalt appears in one place with the greenstone – Further along this shore, on the edge of a narrow isthmus, where the island is nearly divided into two portions, more greenstone occurs in singular concretions of an oval or irregular globular form – Still further, & approaching the S. side of the island, we saw the greenstone arranged in columns, inclined at a considerable angle, & three or four feet in thickness. These columnar concretions are composed entirely of tabular distinct concretions, 3 or 4 inches thick – The whole affords a singular assemblage – C7 is a specimen of this greenstone.

[1] Little is known of the shadowy 'Baron Hompesch'. The name suggests Dutch origin; he may have been the owner of the *Salamine*; he is referred to as 'Generallieutenant Hampesch' by Jörgen Jörgensen in a letter to Ísleifur Einarsson, dated 14 January – see Jón Þorkelsson, 1892, p. 145.

[2] The British privateer *Salamine*, under Captain Thomas Gilpin, was berthed in Hafnarfjörður and then Reykjavík July 23–August 8 1808; various unauthorised acts of plunder (including the attack on Viðey) were performed by Danish and Irish crew members, the spoils from such raids being however returned almost immediately. Gilpin supervised the seizure of some 35,000 rix-dollars belonging, he believed, to the Danish government, but destined for use as poor relief and for schools. This money was eventually returned to Iceland, through the intervention of Bjarni Sívertsen and

The mineralogy of Viðœ presents some singular appearances. — To the E of the Landing place along the shore, is a vein of highly crystallised Greenstone, on each side of which is an amygdaloidal rock, fragmented so as to give the appearance of a sort of tuff. The cavities this amygdaloid contain zeolite & calc spar. Further on, the amygdaloidal rock is much intermixed, with a substance which may perhaps be termed volcanic tuff. Of & C3 is C1 & C2 are specimens — C2 shews the junction between the tuff & amygdaloid. The tuff usually appears in veins in the amygdaloid — Sometimes the latter seems occur in included masses of large side & a rounded form — the tuff forming the boun-

dary of the masses of amygdaloid.
Above these included masses appear
in one place some irregular colum-
of greenstone. —

On the opposite side of the island, which is about ½ a mile across, the appearances very different. The general character of the rocks along this shore is similar to appearing at Reikiavik — they exhibit all the appearances of being acted upon by heat under some modification or other. — their position is above of the amygdaloid, & trap tuff. In several places they are intersected by of greenstone, probably the same as those which appear on the opposite side the island — 12 to 26 yds in thickness — of this greenstone C5 is a specimen. — the anic rock on this shore assumes columnar appearances in several places. C6 a column of this rock — A compact basalt appears in one place with the enstone — Further along this shore, on the edge of a narrow isthmus, where the land is nearly divided into two portions, more greenstone occurs in singular erections of an oval or irregular globular form — Still further, & approaching S side of the island, we saw the greenstone arranged in columns, inclined at considerable angle, & three or four feet in thickness. These columnar concretions composed entirely of tabular distinct concretions, 3 or 4 inches thick — the le affords a singular assemblage — C7 is a specimen of this greenstone.

Columnar & tabular distinct
Concretions — Viðœ.

G. Field sketches at Viðey

Friday May 18 We had an opportunity this morning of witnessing the marriage ceremony of the Icelanders – it was performed in the church or cathedral of Reikiavik – The bride, a young woman dressed in the Icelandic costume, was seated on one side of the church with an elderly woman, probably her mother, by her side. The bridegroom, a fisherman by occupation, was habited in coarse blue cloth, with seal skin shoes, fastened by cross bands of white tape, and his striped garters likewise crossed externally about his legs – He sat on the opposite side of the church attended by several of his friends. The priest, Mr Severtsen, stood at the altar before them – The ceremony was begun by a general chaunting, not exactly of *Orphean mould*. This was followed by a prayer and long exhortation to the bridal couple, who were brought for this purpose to the foot of the altar. – The minister then addressed three questions to each of the parties, beginning with the man – the nature of these questions much resembles those in the English matrimonial service – This done, he laid his hands upon their shoulders, joining their hands, & bestowed a benediction upon them. They were then taken back to their seats – & the service concluded by a repetition of the chaunting. In walking from the church, the bride preceded at some distance the bridegroom, each being attended by their friends of the same sex.

The coldness of the weather & violence of the wind prevented our making any excursion into the country to day – We called upon several of our friends in the town; the Bishop, Mr Frydensberg &c – From the former we received in the evening a very handsome present of a fine sheep, which had been brought for this purpose from some distance in the country. This is only one instance of many similar acts of kindness which we received from our friends in Reikiavik. Almost every day the arrival of some article, valuable in housekeeping, as bread, eggs, milk &c attested their good will towards us. To Madame Frydensberg we were particularly indebted in this way – The great deficiency in our domestic economy was the want, or rather perhaps the improper management of *fuel*. The wetness of the last summer in Iceland has interfered with the

---

(probably) Sir Joseph Banks. See Historical Manuscripts Commission, *Bathurst MSS.* (London, 1923), pp. 72–4, an account of the raids by a Scottish merchant resident in Reykjavík, Andrew Mitchell; also Jón Þorkelsson, 1892, pp. 13–14, 121–2, 145, 149; Hooker, 1813, II, 10.

preparation of the turf, the common fuel of the country, and it was difficult at this time to procure a sufficient quantity of this article for our domestic purposes. – Coals, which we procured from the ship, there was some difficulty in the use of, in the stoves by which our rooms were heated. Owing to these circumstances we suffered a good deal from the cold during the present week. A northerly wind, continuing for several days, brought with it much severity of weather; and for two or three successive mornings we found water, that had been kept in the kitchen all night, covered with ice, ¼ of an inch in thickness. The Thermometer, placed near the window in our sitting room, frequently indicated as low a temperature as 34°.

Saturday May 19. The greater part of this day was occupied in preparations for our first journey from Reikiaviik, the commencement of which we had fixed for Monday –

Sunday 20th. Nothing of moment occurred to day – with the exception of another ball at the Club-House – The Sabbath of Iceland commences at 6 o'clock on Saturday evening, & ceases at 6 on Sunday. After this hour on the latter day every amusement & occupation proceeds as on ordinary days – and the evening of Sunday is that usually selected at Reikiaviik for their balls. These meetings were supported by a small subscription from each member of the Club – an extra sum being paid for tea, coffee, or any refreshments which may be taken. The number of people present at this ball was by no means so large as on Tuesday evening – and there was no supper – but the party did not break up till a late hour in the morning. The music, dresses, & other circumstances about the ball, were much the same as on the preceding evening.

Sir G.M. received this evening a very polite Latin epistle[1] from the

[1]HH Perillustri Nobilissimo viro, Domino G.Mackenzie –

Hic tibi, vir nobilissime, exhibeo exscriptum invitationis publicæ Lectoris nostri ad examen, quod in schola nostra, (quæ nunc unica in Islandia est) sequenti hebdomade habendum est. Si tibi, tuisque, vel unica hora a propriis negotiis vacaverit, summo nobis honori ducemus, si nos Tua et illorum præsentie dignari velis. Tuæ singularis humanitatis observantissimus cultor

20th Maii 1810 –   Geirus Vidalinus

[To the most illustrious and most noble man, Sir G.Mackenzie.

Oh, most noble sir, here is for you a copy of a public invitation to the examination conducted by our Reader which will take place next week in our school, which is now the only one in Iceland. If you and your companions have even a single hour free from your own affairs, then we would consider it a great honour to us, if you should deem us worthy of your and their presence. The most dutiful respecter of your singular humanity

20 May 1810   Geir Vídalín]

Bishop, inviting us to attend certain examinations at the public school at Bessasted, some day in the course of the week. (See opposite page) –[1] Inclosed in the letter he sent a paper, containing the order & arrangement of the examinations for the several days in the week. It was matter of congratulation to us that this invitation coincided so well with the plans for our journey.

Monday May 21. On this day we commenced our excursions into the interior of Iceland. It was the scheme of our first journey to survey the *Guldbringe Syssel*; pursuing first the southern coast of this district, & returning to Reikiaviik by the northern side of the peninsula – In pursuance of this plan, our first stage was to Havne-fiord[2] seven or eight miles from Reikiaviik – The morning was occupied at home in the completion of our preparations for travelling – Our party consisted of five persons – there being with us, besides Loptson, a young man, recommended by the Bishop as an excellent guide & assistant in our journey – His name is Jonson –[3] a native of the eastern coast of Iceland, but educated at Bessested for a minister. He is unacquainted with English – but speaks Latin with facility.

Horses are essential appendages to travelling in Iceland; & the native horses are in every respect admirably adapted by nature & education

---

[1]HH Ad Examen Publicum Alumnorum Scholæ Bessastadensis audiendum die 21, et seq. Maii 1810, ita ordinatum.

Die Lunæ –	hora antemerid.	8–12 – 2 Class. In Auct. Latin Interpret.
	h.pomerid.	2–6 – 2 & 1 Class. In Stylo Latino
Die Martis –	h.antemerid.	8–10 – 2 Class. In Theologicis secundum Niemæierum
		10–12 – 1 Class. In Auct. Latin. interpret.
	h.pomerid	2–4 – 2 & 1 Class. In Lingua Danica
		4–6 – 2 & 1 Class. In Stylo Danica
Die Mercurii	hor.antm.	8–10 – 2 Class. In Auth. Græcis interpret.
		10–12 – 1 Class. In Auth. Græcis interpret.
	h.pomerid.	2–3 – 2 & 1 Class. In Declamatione
		3–6 – 2 & 1 Class. In Stylo Islandico
Die Jovis	h.antm.	8–10 – 2 Class. In Novi Fæd. Exegesi
		10–12 – 2 Cl. In Analysi Hebraica
	h.pomer.	2–4 – 1 Class. In Reliq. dogmatic. juxta Niemæier.
		4–6 – 2 & 1 Cl. In Arithmetica
Die Veneris	h.antemer.	8–12 – 2 & 1 Cl. In Historia & Geographia.

Omnes rei scholasticæ Patronos, Fautores, et Amicos, qua par est observantia, invitamus.

Steingrimus Jonæus
Lector Theologiæ

[2] Hafnarfjörður.

[3] Probably Jón Jónsson Austmann (the Easterner) (1787–1858), graduated from Bessastaðir 1809· consecrated as priest 1812. See Pjetur Guðmundsson (ed.), *Annáll nítjándu aldar*, 3 vols. (Akureyri, 1912–34), I, 124.

to this purpose. We take five of them with us in our journey. A greater number could have been desirable, but the difficulty of procuring them in proper condition at this season of the year is very considerable – & at this particular time was enhanced by the severity of the preceding winter,[1] & by a disease which prevailed among the horses during the winter months. The luggage we take with us on our journey, comprizing tent equipage &c, is sufficient to load all our five horses – and as regards ourselves, we commence our travels in Iceland with the independence & freedom which pedestrians always enjoy.

[1] During the Icelandic winter of 1809–10, the weather was worst in the South. See Jón Espólín, 1821–55, XII (Part 10), 43–4.

JOURNEY TO THE GULDBRINGE SYSSEL[H]

We left Reikiaviik at 1 o'clock – Our road[1] led us for two or three miles over a wild desolate tract of country, covered with fragments of rock – We enjoyed some fine retrospective views of Reikiaviik Bay, of the Faxe Fiord, and of the range of mountains which bound these bays to the north. Reaching the shore 3 miles from Reikiaviik, we coasted along the upper extremity of an inlet which the sea here forms; and again entered upon a tract of country, every where covered with loose rocks & stones – When about a mile from Havnefiord, we were delighted by the first view of genuine Icelandic lava – a vast body of which here makes its appearance, extending from some point within the country (the situation &c, of which we could not then ascertain) to the sea at Havnefiord – To eyes, unused to the sight, nothing can be conceived more singular than the aspect of this bed of lava – A vast & confused mass of rocky matter, having a general elevation of level above the surrounding country, but thrown within itself into every possible variety of strange & abrupt shape, is the general appearance presented to the sight. In following a narrow & rugged path across the Lava,[2] we

[1]HH From Reikiaviik for 2 or 3 miles in a S.E direction, the ground covered with rocks, similar in general character to those on the shores in the vicinity of the town – Arrived at the inlet of the sea, we found there a conglomerate, with a base of clay & including fragments of amygdaloid & basalt; & also of rocks similar to those at Reikiaviik – This conglomerate covered immediately by gravel & the peat of the surface – Below it, a stratum of indurated clay continuing shells & intersected by many fissures – on both sides of which fissures the clay assumed small columnar appearances – a Slaty sandstone appeared under the clay, & below this we found the Reikiaviik rock – Ascending the hill on the other side of the creek, we found upon the surface the rock, which assumes the lowest position at Reikiaviik. Below this, a little further on appeared *basalt*, having an irregular columnar disposition along the shore.

[2]HH The bed of Lava, which meets the sea at Havnefiord, is a branch from the extensive tract of volcanic country, which occupies the greater part of the south-western angle of Iceland. – Its breadth at Havnefiord is somewhat more than a mile – The exposed surface of the bed presents great ruggedness & irregularity – large scorified masses are projected upwards into every variety of form – The fracture of this superficial rock exhibits an extremely vesicular structure – It contains much of the olivine which we had observed in the rock at Reikiaviik, & a good deal of quartz (Specimens from Havnefiord). The part of

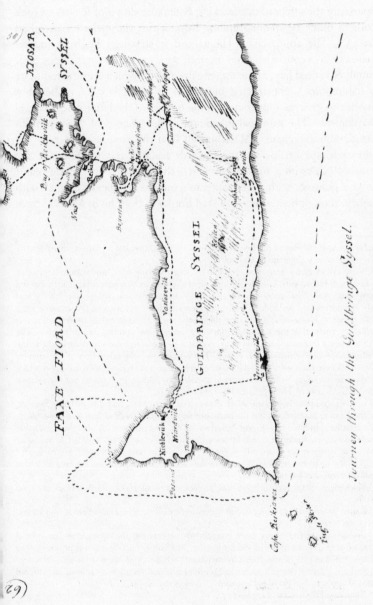

Journey through the Gullbringe Syssel.

H. The route through Gullbringusýsla

113

observed numerous fissures, caverns & hollows – some of them apparently the effect of the cracking & sinking down of masses of rock – others much resembling craters from which the melted matter had flowed – The approach to Havnafiord is striking.[1] High & rugged masses of lava concealed from us, until we were almost at the edge of it, a small & retired bay, at the upper extremity of which are situated 15 or 20 habitations – constructed like those at Reikiaviik, of timber, but superior in general appearance, to the houses of the latter place. This is Havnafiord – The principal inhabitant of the place is M[r] Severtsen,[2] a considerable merchant – M[r] S himself is at this time in England –[3] or rather perhaps on his voyage towards Iceland, but we found at his house M[rs] S,[4] with a son & daughter – the former a fine young man,[5] modest, polite & with a well cultivated mind – He speaks English with fluency, though he has never visited England. Both he & Miss S.[6] have

---

the lava, which appears in the lowest situation, on the shore, has a more compact texture than that above. – (Specimens marked H).

We were informed by Atatsrood Stephensen, when staying with him at Innreholm, that an historical record exists, of the formation of the lava in this particular district having taken place in the year 1000 – a year noted also as being that in which Christianity was first introduced into Iceland. – While the chiefs & principal men of the country were deliberating at Thingvalla, concerning the admission of the new religious system, it was notified to them that the Lava was bursting forth in the country to the south – The Heathen party instantly cited this as an evidence of the indignation of their Gods, at the attempt made to overthrow their power. The advocate for the admission of Christianity claimed 'Where then were your Gods when the place was covered with Lava, on which we are now standing.' – If this historical anecdote be authentic, it points out the relative dates of the Lavas of Thingvalla & Havnefiord.

NB It was subsequently told me by Mr Severtsen of Havnefiord, that this anecdote regards, not the Lava at Havnefiord, but the beds intervening between this place & Kiebleviik.

[Ed. Neither Holland nor Bjarni Sívertsen is in agreement with the then available scholarly record: *Kristni saga*, ed. Hannes Finnsson (Copenhagen, 1773), Ch. 11, p. 91 places the volcanic fire in the Ölfús district, well to the East of Krísuvík. Snorri Goði's retort to the heathens reads – 'What were the Gods angry about when the lava on which we now stand was burning?']

[1] Mackenzie, 1812, facing p. 98 has a colour print of Hafnarfjörður from his own sketch.

[2] Bjarni Sívertsen (1763–1833). See Sigurður Skúlason, *Saga Hafnarfjarðar* (Reykjavík, 1933), pp. 254–74.

[3] Bjarni may already have been engaged in negotiating the restoration (completed 1812) of funds pirated from Iceland during the 1808 Gilpin raid. Bjarni was no stranger to Britain. He was one of the Icelandic merchants whose ships were detained under war regulations at Leith 1807–1809; Sir Joseph Banks helped secure their release and offered financial support. See Halldór Hermannsson, 1928, pp. 41–52.

[4] Rannveig Filipusdóttir (1744–1825).

[5] Sigurður Sívertsen (b. 1787).

[6] Járngerður Júlía Sívertsen (c1788–1824).

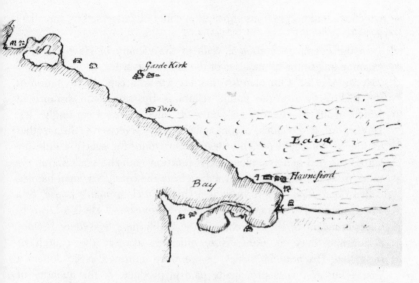

I. Lava fields near Hafnarfjörður

resided at Copenhagen some years.[1] We were introduced to them at the ball at Rekiaviik, & received an invitation to visit the family as we passed through Havnafiord – Availing ourselves of this invitation, we went immediately upon our arrival to M[r] S's house, & were received with a cordial hospitality which was infinitely pleasing. This habitation is by far the most comfortable we have seen in Iceland –[2] possessing not only neatness, but some degree of elegance also in its furniture & internal arrangements. In the sitting room there are three pier glasses –[3] two also in the principal bed room of the house – The dinner, which was served up with the utmost neatness, consisted of a large dish of hashed mutton, accompanied by London porter – and pancakes; the latter manufactured with all due dexterity, and having the very valuable addition of currants to their substance. We slept in beds of Eider down – washed ourselves with Windsor Soap, and in short enjoyed luxuries,

[1] There is no record that Sigurður was ever a student in Copenhagen. See Bjarni Jónsson, *Íslenzkir Hafnarstúdentar* (Akureyri, 1949).
[2] In restored form, the house survives at Vesturgata 8, Hafnarfjörður.
[3] Full-length mirrors.

115

which we had no previous conception could be possessed by travellers in Iceland.

In the evening we took a walk in the vicinity of Havnafiord, to examine one of the boundaries of the bed of Lava.

Tuesday May 22ᵈ Our plan for this day was to accept the invitation of the Bishop to visit the public school at Bessasted, the distance of which from Havnefiord is only 3 miles. We accordingly left Havnefiord at 9 o'clock, accompanied by Mʳ Severtsen – the weather as fine as we could possibly desire. Our route for nearly a mile lay across the bed of Lava, close to its junction with the sea.[I] About 1½ miles from Havnefiord, we turned up from the coast to a small hamlet, called *Garde Kirk*,[1] where there is a church, a clergyman's house, & a few cottages. The clergyman's name is Magnuson –[2] He is a Dean or Superintendant of the churches in the Guldbringe Syssel; & besides performing duty at *Garde Kirk*, officiates also at the church of Bessasted. His nominal salary, as we were informed, is 80 dollars a year – but as this is principally paid in produce, & the quantity of produce given is in proportion to a former lower rate of value, the real amount of the salary is considerably greater. He has besides a large extent of pretty good land annexed to his place as minister.[3]

We called on Mʳ Magnuson, & sat a short time with him. His present habitation cannot boast of great comfort, but he has nearly completed a new one at a short distance, which will have superior advantages. He has a small library of 100 or 150 vols. Among the books we noticed translations of Pope's Works[4] & Young's Night Thoughts into German prose.[5]

From *Garde Kirk* we proceeded to Bessasted,[6] which is situated on the Ness or promontory, stretching from Havnefiord in a N.W. direction into the Faxe Fiord – From the convenience of the situation

---

[1] Garðar.

[2] Markús Magnússon (1748–1825), priest at Garðar 1781–1825, and provost of the region.

[3] Mackenzie, 1812, p. 100 was less impressed with the provost's prosperity: 'we shall spare our readers, that they may not partake the pain inspired by the most squalid indigence in a clerical garb'.

[4] Jón Þorláksson, *Tilraun ad snúa á Islendsku Pópes Tilraun um manninn* (Leirárgarðar, 1798), or the Danish translation upon which Jón's work was based. See Richard Beck, *Jón Þorláksson: Icelandic translator of Pope and Milton*, Studia Islandica, XVI (1957).

[5] *Dr. Eduard Young's Klagen, oder Nachgedanken*, 2 vols. in 4 (Brunswick, 1763–9), a work of ubiquitous European popularity. See L. M. Price, *English literature in Germany*, University of California Publications in Modern Philology, 37 (Berkeley, 1953), pp. 113–21.

[6] Bessastaðir.

for fishing, a number of cottages are scattered about on the peninsula, even to its extremity. The quantity of fish caught in the Bay of Havnefiord, & along the whole of this coast, is prodigiously great. All along the shores, large piles are erected of split cod-fish, covered with boards, & these weighted down with square fragments of Lava.

Bessasted, strictly so called, consists only of a few buildings – a large Church, the School house – the habitation of the head-school-master, & one or two cottages – We called first upon the Rector of the school, whose house is placed at a short distance from the church (see Sketch Book)[1] – His name is Jonson.[2] He is still a young man, apparently not more than five & thirty, pleasing in his countenance & manners, most friendly in his attentions, and speaking Latin with a fluency & elegance of idiom which considerably surprized us. He studied at Copenhagen, & acquired there much credit as a scholar – I examined his Library with some attention, as it is esteemed the best collection of Theological works in the Island. – I found there the works of Michaelis, Mosheim, Heinzius, Reinhard, Brucker, Lowth, Griesbach,[3] with numerous other authors of minor note on ecclesiastical history, polity and doctrine. There are not many English books in the collection. – We were introduced to Mr Jonson's wife – a pleasing good looking woman.[4] Before leaving the house, coffee was handed to us.

Proceeding in company with Mr Jonson, to the church, we were much interested by a minute examination of the interior of this edifice;

[1] This no longer survives.

[2] Steingrímur Jónsson (1769–1845), shortly to transfer to Oddi. Holland's favourable opinion was shared by Mackenzie, 1812, pp. 102, 311–13; by Ebenezer Henderson, *Iceland; or the journal of a residence in that island during the years 1814 and 1815*, 2 vols. in 1, (Edinburgh, 1818), I, 338; Hooker, 1813, I, 351–5, was more struck by the squalor of the school and its scholars, and had sympathised with Jörgensen's proposed reforms.

[3] A collection largely and unsurprisingly Lutheran in spirit, and empiricist rather than dogmatic in approach. Holland would probably have known of Robert Lowth (1710–87) as an influential prescriptive grammarian rather than as a biblical scholar; the works of Johann Jacob Griesbach (1745–1812), a biblical-textual scholar, were known in England, whilst some of those of the philologist and biblical scholar Johann David Michaelis (1717–91) and the ecclesiastical historian Johann Lorenz Mosheim (1694–1755) were already available in English translation before 1810; works by the historian of philosophy Johann Jacob Brucker (1696–1770) were not translated until 1825. Franz Vollmar Reinhard (1753–1812) enjoyed less prominence; 'Heinzius' is difficult to identify – two prominent seventeenth century editors bearing the name are primarily known for editing classical Latin texts rather than for their theological works.

[4] Valgerður Jónsdóttir (1771–1856), widow of Bishop Hannes Finnsson (1739–96), for whom Steingrímur Jónsson had worked as a secretary.

M^r J affording us in Latin all the requisite information. The church was built in at[1] which time the Governor of Iceland had his regular residence at Bessasted, in the building, now the School House.[2] An elevated seat in the Church is appropriated to him. – The construction of the church is much superior to that of Reikiavik; a steeple, however, which was begun, is not yet completed. At the door of the Church, is a stone with the figure of Paulus Stigotus,[3] a former governor of Iceland, who died AD 1566. – The figure is cased in armour – About the Altar of the church, there is a good deal of ornamental work in painting – over the altar an indifferent painting of the Holy Supper – In a vault on the northern side of the Church, we were shewn lying in a wooden coffin the body or rather mummy of a lady, named Anna Wilhelmina Klog,[4] the niece of a former governor of Iceland.[5] She died, according to the date on the Coffin, in 1778. – On each side of the Altar, we observed a voluminous epitaph – one of them an Anagram in Latin verse – Two wooden pillars, painted in a tawdry manner, form the entrance to the body of the Church. They support a cross piece, on each side of which is a large gilded ball – & between them a crown with the cypher of Christian 7th of Denmark.[6] The pulpit is likewise ornamented with much gawdy painting.

Leaving the Church, we proceeded to the School House, which is immediately adjoining. (See Sketch Book) Here we were met by our friend Bishop Vidalin, habited in his episcopal robes; and he with two or three of the schoolmasters, attended us through the building – About the edifice itself, there is nothing striking externally – the interior is ill fitted up, & betokens nothing of convenience or comfort. We first went into the school-room, where we found the scholars, 23 in number, engaged in translation from the Danish into the Icelandic language, this

[1] Awkwardly expressed. Holland means simply 'the church was built at the time when . . .'

[2] The schools at Skálholt and Hólar dated back to the Reformation; the Skálholt school was transferred to Reykjavík in 1785; that at Hólar was abolished in 1801; the Reykjavík school was moved to Bessastaðir in 1805, where it remained for 41 years.

[3] Páll Stígsson, sent out as Governor (1559–66) by King Frederick II to supervise trade: drowned in May 1566. See Finnur Jónsson, 1772–8, III, 6–7; Kristján Eldjarn, 'Legsteinn Páls Stígssonar og steinsmiðurinn Hans Maler', *ÁHÍF* (1978), 83–90 (with picture); also Sveinbjörn Rafnsson, 1983, II, pp. 617–18.

[4] Unidentified. Mackenzie, 1812, pp. 102–3 says there were two coffins, with bodies of a mother and daughter.

[5] Steindór Steindórsson, 1960, p. 75 suggests Lauritz Andreas Thodal, the first resident governor of Iceland (1770–85), whose stepchild bore the family name Klow/Klogh.

[6] Christian VII of Denmark reigned 1766–1808.

forming the subject of their Tuesday's examination. The greater number of them seemed to be from 15 to 20 years of age – stout, well looking youths – After visiting the eating room, kitchen, & dormitories, about which there was nothing remarkable, we were conducted to the library, a small & dirty room on the 2^d story, lighted by a window of six panes. The collection of books here may perhaps amount to 12 or 1400, among which are a few good editions of the classics. The number of manuscripts is very small, & of no value – The number of German books is considerable – there are a few French works, and two or three English – The state in which the whole library is kept clearly evinces the small use at present made of it – A cloud of dust followed the dislodgement of every book from its place of repose. – a circumstance upon which the Bishop commented with his usual vivacity & good humour.

Behind the building which forms the present schoolhouse, a new range of buildings has been begun upon, with a view to an enlargement of the Institution. The war with Denmark, among its other consequent calamaties, has been the means of entirely suspending this scheme – from the want which it creates in Iceland of all the materials for building – (For an account of the History &c of the School, see page 116 – Vol. II).[1]

Having seen every thing about Bessasted, we commenced our return to Havnefiord –[2] In our way thither, we called at the house of a Mr Einerson,[3] a gentleman who for some time officiated as Governor of Iceland,[4] previously to the arrival of Count Trampe in the island. He is

[1] See below pp. 299–301, material incorporated in Mackenzie, 1812, pp. 309–35.

[2] HH

Reikiavik to Havnefiord	7
Excursion to Bessasted	7
Havnefiord to Krisevik	28
Excursions from Krisevik	12
Krisevik to Gründevik	15
Gründevik to Kieblevik	15
Kieblevik to Havnefiord	25
Havnefiord to Reikiavik	7
	116

[3] Ísleifur Einarsson (1765–1836), acted as Governor, whilst Trampe was abroad, from July 1807 until mid-summer 1809, having previously held other legal and administrative posts; opponent of Jörgensen in 1809· appointed one of three acting governors after the insurrection; subsequently Chief Justice until his death; one of the signatories of the letters in note 1, pp. 274–6 below.

[4] Holland no doubt presented to Ísleifur Einarsson the introductory letter provided for him by Rasmus Frydensberg, and included in the MS Journal (I, 48) at this point:

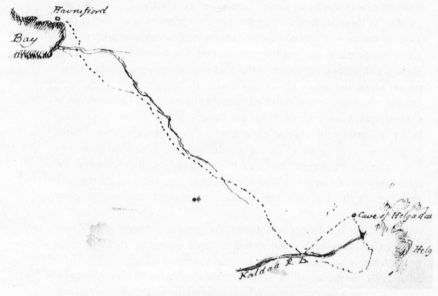

J. The route to Helgafell in Gullbringusýsla

a man of activity & judgement – and has made much improvement on the land in the vicinity of his house by clearing it of stones, enclosing with walls &c. Improvements[1] of this nature might be carried to a much greater extent in Iceland & with the aid of draining, would render beneficial a great deal of land, which is now almost useless.

Translation of the letter of Recommendation written by M[r] Freydensberg, *Sysselman of Guldbringe.*
'Sir G.Mackenzie Bar[t] is come from Scotland to Iceland for the purpose of examining the natural curiosities here – the mountains, lava, hot water springs &c. He & the other gentlemen who are travelling with him, will first make a journey through Guldbringe Syssel: and as they are strangers in the places where they are going, it is my earnest request that all good & respectable people will pay all attention to them; and shew kindness to these strangers, as good & hospitable Icelanders usually do to travellers; doing every thing in their power to help their journey:- for instance, shewing them the road from place to place & providing food for their horses – For this purpose, I give this letter open to the hand of the Baronet to shew to the people'
Reikiaviik. 21st May 1810   Frydensberg

[1] The notion of 'improvement' was fashionable amongst the British gentry at this time; Jane Austen satirises its architectural and landscaping excesses in *Mansfield Park* (1814); Holland's interest was in the sobrieties of agricultural improvement. See Holland, 1808, especially Chapter 12.

K. Lava beds in Gullbringusýsla

We did not get back to Havnefiord until 6 o'clock, being detained some time by the collection of specimens among the Lava. – It is worthy of remark that we were writing at 11 o'clock this night, by the light of the sun.

Wednesday 23^d – Early this morning we recommenced our journey, taking a guide with us. – Our route for 3 or 4 miles lay in a S.E. direction, along the valley of the small stream, which enters the sea at Havnefiord.^J The bottom of this valley is occupied by lava – the breadth of which varies here from a few yards to ¼ of a mile. The rugged peaks of erupted matter are covered with moss, & occasionally afford an appearance not unpicturesque – Four miles from Havnefiord, we came to a surface more completely scorified, & broken into rugged masses of larger size.¹ We have observed appearances in the volcanic rocks, over which we were travelling, which had not before occurred to us – Large rounded elevations of rock forming various spherical segments, shewed themselves on the surface – as if, while the matter composing² these rocks was in a state of viscidity from heat, some force from beneath had operated, & raised here and there the superficial crust into these peculiar forms.^K This idea receives confirmation from an observation we made that all these rounded

¹ᴴᴴ The appearance & structure of the Lava to the head of the valley, about 4 miles from Havnefiord, resemble those of the lava in the immediate vicinity of this place. Here it becomes much more completely scorified on its upper surface, & exhibits evidences of more complete fusion – In a low ridge of rocks which we passed at this place we observed some appearances of stratification – as if the rocks had been acted on from below & their structure changed by the heat, without a disturbance of position – The internal appearance of the rock resembles the more compact specimens of Lava from Havnefiord.

Between the Kaldaá & the Cave, every part of the surface bears marks of great volcanic action – the bare rock every where heaved up into various singular forms – all the intervening hills covered with loose scoriæ and cinders – The cave of Helgadal has evidently been formed by one of these heavings of the surface, when in a state of scoric fusion, & the various configurations which appear on the top & sides of the cave have been formed by the partial flowing of the viscid matter, & its exposure at the same time to the external air. (See Specimens from the Cave)

² Difficult to decipher – it could read 'comprising'.

elevations are mere crusts of rocky matter – having cavities beneath them, frequently of great extent – Entering some of these caves, we found that the lower surface of the superficial crust was covered with small pendulous portions of rocky matter, a circumstance shewing that at the time the cavity was formed, the crust above must have been in a soft or viscid state.

Pursuing our way over this same rugged tract of volcanic country, we came about 12 o'clock to the banks of the Kaldaá;[1] – 6 miles from Havnefiord. It had been recommended to us by Mr Magnuson of *Garde Kirk* to visit a cave at a short distance from this place; & accordingly, taking the luggage off the horses, we turned them out to graze on a small grassy spot by the stream, and ourselves proceeded towards the cave. We found it to be merely a larger cavity of the same description as those we had before seen – formed by the elevation of a superficial rocky crust, so as to leave a hollow beneath. With some difficulty we proceeded to the extremity of the cavern, which we found by admeasurement to be 55 yards in length. The average breadth may be about 5 yards. The height varies from 3 to 6 feet. The bottom of the cave is almost entirely covered with ice. The lava or scoriated rock assumes some singular varieties of form on the sides, bottom & roofing of the cave; occasionally resembling the richly ornamented cornice of a room – It is more than probable, from the appearances we observed on the surface, that there are numerous caves in this district of still greater extent & of similar formation (See Sketch of the Entrance of the Cave).

We returned to our horses & luggage by a circuitous route, & enjoyed by this means some most interesting observation of this very singular district – Every thing around this spot wears the marks of some vast convulsion of nature – which has been able to accomplish the fusion, elevation, or removal of all the rocks formerly situated in this vicinity. Traversing some hills of considerable elevation, covered entirely with scoriæ, we came to an extensive tract of bare rock, as level on its surface as the smoothest bowling green, & composed of large plates or crusts of the same volcanic product, as that which we had before been crossing – On the south-eastern side of this rocky plane, (which is about a mile in length & ½ a mile in breadth,) rises almost perpendicularly from the level, the mountain *Helgafell* –[2] composed, as

---

[1] Kaldá.

[2]HH The mountain of Helgafell rises perpendicularly from a flat plain of bare lava. The conglomerate of which it is composed, has for its basis, a loose friable sandstone – the included masses are chiefly volcanic scoriæ of various sizes – The height of Helgafell from

we found by examination, of a conglomerate rock. Behind this mountain, at the distance of a few miles, lies a long range of mountains,[1] forming a conspicuous object from Reikiaviik, Havnefiord & other parts of the coast. These are at present covered with snow – On our return from Helgafell to the Kaldaá, our route lay over a tract, still more rugged & more completely devastated by fire than any we had yet seen. Several large caverns, open to day, & the superincumbent crust much elevated above the surface, occurred to our notice. The interior of these cavities is lined with matter almost completely vitrified, & disposed in a variety of singular stalactitic forms.

So much time was occupied in this excursion, that we decided upon pitching our tent at the place where we had left our horses, & remaining there all night. There was nothing intermediate between this, & the travelling forwards the same day to Kryseviig,[2] a distance of 14 miles, as neither water nor pasture occur between the two places. We accordingly set up our tent on a small piece of level ground close to the Kaldaá, fixed our bed-steads & made as many comfortable arrangements for the night, as circumstances would admit of. Our guides pitched their Icelandic tent (a humbler covering, though scarcely inferior in comfort) on the other side of the stream. The horses grazed around us, on a small piece of pasture ground by the water's edge.

Thursday 24th Our first night under a tent was rendered exceedingly uncomfortable by the cold, which all our arrangements of cloathing &c could not exclude. The morning presented the additional discomfort of a heavy rain – This did not, however, prevent us from striking our tents, and resuming our journey southwards –[3] It would be difficult for

---

this bed of lava is probably about 800 feet – its elevation above the sea probably 1000. – The mode of formation of this conglomerate, it is difficult to explain. It appears certain, however, that the scoriæ included in its substance must have been the product of some volcanic eruption prior to that which formed the beds of Lava beneath the mountain. – The arrangement of the beds of this conglomerate rock at Helgafell, and in other parts of the same range to the south is extremely varied and irregular.

[1] Apparently the range containing Bláfjöll and Heiðin há.

[2] Krísuvík.

[3]HH Our route between the Kaldaá & Kriseviig presented much the same appearance as we had observed the day before. It conducted us for the first 10 or 12 miles over the same great tract of lava – some times spread out into wide plains, in other places contracted considerably by high ground, composed of the same conglomerate rock, as that of Helgafell. A range of hills composed of this conglomerate, (which might perhaps be called *Volcanic tuff*) extends from Helgafell towards the S.W. Three or four miles from the southern coast of the Guldbringe, it assumes a westerly direction, & extends along the peninsula nearly as far as Grundeviik.

the imagination to picture to itself a more dreary, desolate tract of country, than that over which our route of this day conducted us – Every step of the way was made over land desolated by the agency of fire – Sometimes we traversed eminences, composed entirely of small scoriæ or cinders – sometimes passed over large & level tracts of the bare volcanic rock – sometimes crept along the edge of the same rock, jutting out into a thousand singular and abrupt forms – Not a single habitation occurs in the way – not one indeed in the whole distance between Havnefiord & Kryseviig – No stream, or source of water appeared until we came within 2 miles of Kryseviig; and we eagerly availed ourselves of some unmelted snow, which here and there remained in the clefts of the rocks, to satisfy the thirst, which exercise & the sultriness of the day had created. The non-appearance of streams in this district, is doubtless owing to the numerous clefts & cavities which occur among the volcanic rocks, which prevent the water from collecting into any one channel. The Kaldaá, though a considerable stream, where we passed the night, is nevertheless completely lost among the rocks about ¼ of a mile below –

We were more fortunate in the weather this day than the morning had led us to expect. As a specimen of an *Icelandic road*, the whole route between Havnefiord and Kryseviik[1] is strikingly characteristic – though perhaps somewhat an exaggerated representation of their average quality – These *roads*, as they are termed in Iceland, are merely narrow tracks, along which one horse can pass abreast, & which are generally filled either with water or fragments of stone – Sometimes, in tracts of bog, or bare rock, even these disappear; and the only direction to the traveller is the situation of some mountain or the opening of some valley – About half way[2] between the Kaldaá & Kryseviik, we found at

---

The Lava south of the Kaldaá is exceedingly abrupt & rugged – shewing numerous cavities & hollows, much resembling ancient craters – Ascending about 5 miles from Kriseviik, the conglomerate hills, which in the previous part of the way, we had kept on the left hand, we found in one of the hollows near their summit, a vast collection of fragments of lava, (many of them of large size,) much more compact than any we had before seen. From their locality these fragments must have been derived from some eruption of lava over the surface of the conglomerate – the exact spot where this eruption occurred we were not able to ascertain. – A small fresh water lake appears near this spot – in a very elevated situation among the conglomerate hills. It is not unlikely that this may be the site of some ancient crater.

[1] The description fits the most used nineteenth-century route between Hafnarfjörður and Krísuvík, the Undirhlíðarvegur. See Ólafur Þorvaldsson, 'Fornar slóðir milli Krísuvíkur og Hafnarfjarðar', *ÁHÍF* (1943–8), especially 84–7.

[2] 'About half way … in full bloom': written by Holland on the facing page (MS I, 54) and marked for inclusion in the main text at this point.

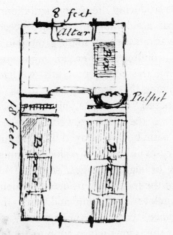

L. The church at Krísuvík

a short distance from the track, a collection of bones, evidently belonging to the human skeleton, with some fragments of clothes, apparently the dress of a female – One guide informed us that a woman travelling this way about 18 months before had been lost – it was supposed among the snow – These were doubtless the remains of the poor sufferer.

About 6 miles from Kryseviig, we observed on the rocks to the left, some beautiful plants of the Gentian,[1] in full bloom. For the first 8 or 10 miles from the Kaldaá our route lay principally along the bottom of valleys, covered with the matter of volcanic eruptions – having a long range of conglomerate hills on our left hand. At this spot, by an alarmingly precipitous path, we ascended these hills; and traversing a rugged mountain district,[2] covered with fragments of lava & conglomerate, came in view of a great plain, which intervenes between this high land & the sea. Previously to descending upon this plain, we turned off from the path to see a boiling spring at a short distance – The appearances on this spot were most singular – A circular bason 9 or 10 feet in diameter, is filled almost to its rim, with a thick turbid fluid, of a blueish colour, through which a quantity of steam rushes upwards with

[1] *Gentiana* (Linn.); Mod.Ice. *Maríuvöndur.*
[2] Along the western side of Sveifluháls.

prodigious force, producing the utmost agitation and disturbance. This vapour, which has a sulphureous smell, proceeds not only from the bason, but from various crevices in the ground in the vicinity. The fluid, filling the bason, is doubtless water, holding in suspension a quantity of blue clay – whence this colour proceeds, we had not at the time, the means of determining. No water appears to rise out of the bason, nor any stream to proceed from the neighbouring rocks –

Our descent into the plain shewed us several other sulphureous springs near our path, but we delayed their examination for the present – We reached Kryseviik' about 5 o'clock – a miserable looking place, consisting of six or eight cottages, scattered irregularly over some rugged ground, at the foot of an insulated eminence, which rises out of the plain. – A church forms the only addition to the size & splendour of the place – an edifice,[L] constructed of timber – 18 feet in length – 8 in breadth, & under the beams which support the roof, 5 feet 8 inches in height – It was our first scheme to make this building our place of residence, while we remained at Kryseviik, & the keys were for this purpose put into our hands, but a survey of the interior soon decided us against this plan. – A number of the most serious disqualifications were here combined – dirt, darkness, the odour of fish in different stages of the drying process &c &c. The floor too of the church was so uneven, that we were unable to fix our bed-steads upon it – and as another hindrance, the contained space, small as it was, was completely crowded with old boxes, wood & various articles of furniture – The pulpit in this singular edifice, is placed on one side, but looking towards the door of the church:- from its relative situation to the roof, the minister must either sit down, kneel, or stoop while performing religious services.

After taking a dinner of fish upon the altar of the church, we proceeded to pitch our tent on a flat piece of ground below the village. The principal farmer in the place, M[r] Gudmundson,[2] engaged to supply us with milk & some other articles of food, during our stay at Kryseviik. This is a tall, athletic, good looking man, who has received an education at Reikiaviik, & is now about, as we understood, to enter into the church, – leaving his farm for this purpose in the course of a short time. His habitation is a good specimen of the Icelandic farm

' Coloured engraving from Sir George Mackenzie's sketch in Mackenzie, 1812, facing p. 113.

[2] Guðni Guðmundsson (1777–1843); at school in Reykjavík 1795–1801; consecrated as priest 1812.

house. Externally, at a short distance, it looks as if a number of grassy eminences had been irregularly heaped up, a door placed in one – a window in another – an unclosed opening in a third. Entering the habitation by a long, & dark passage, the walls of which are covered with dried fish, many apartments present themselves – not to the eye indeed, for nothing is to be seen – but to the hand of the stranger, feeling his way along the walls. These rooms are disposed without any regularity, & correspond in number to the eminences which appear in the external view. – The whole has much resemblance to a rabbit warren on a large scale.

Friday 25th Our breakfast this morning, which was furnished us from the farm house, consisted of milk, rye bread, butter, and cheese – After this meal, we issued forth with hammers, bags, & a horse for the carriage of specimens to the Sulphur Springs – the most interesting natural object which has yet engaged our attention in Iceland. These springs, & the beds of Sulphur connected with them, are situated on the ascent of a ridge of hills, 2 miles to the NE of Kryseviig – The tinge of yellow, which they communicate to the surface & the clouds of steam and vapour which rise from the spot, may very distinctly be seen at the distance of many miles – We noticed them when coasting along the Guldbringe in our voyage to Reikiaviik – At Kryseviig, the noise attending the boiling of the springs may distictly be heard. –

Proceeding to the foot of the range of hills, & ascending a short way, we passed over several small beds of sulphur, mixed with much clay – Out of these beds which were so soft, as scarcely to bear the pressure of the foot, vapour ascended in numerous places. A very delicate thermometer, placed at the mouth of the apertures emitting these vapours, rose to 212° – Proceeding somewhat higher, we came to the first great spring, or that most to the west – Of this spring we took sketches at different distances (See Sketch book.13.14.15).[1] In general appearance, it resembles, on a larger scale, the spring we had seen the preceding evening – a vast cauldron, full of a thick turbid fluid, which is thrown into violent agitation & occasionally forced to a considerable height, by the rapid rising of a dense column of steam from beneath – By the continuance of this action, a wall, 2 or 3 feet in height, & composed of the same kind of clay, which is held in suspension in the water, has been formed around the bason. Owing to

[1] Coloured engraving from Sir George Mackenzie's sketch in Mackenzie, 1812, facing p. 116.

this circumstance, & to the nature of the surrounding surface, which is composed of the same clay & sulphur, & is so soft as not to bear the pressure of the foot, we were unable to approach nearer to the bason than within 3 or 4 yards. As accurately as we could judge at this distance, it is about 15 feet in diameter. – no water appears to issue from it, the wall or rim being perfect all round – The smell of the vapour issuing through the fluid is strongly sulphureous – its quantity & force of emission are not constant, but vary considerably – not, however, at any regular intervals of time – Another circumstance preventing our close approach to the bason, & rendering it difficult to walk even at some distance, was the heat of the surface, & the quantity of sulphureous vapour issuing forth from numerous crevices in the beds of sulphur & clay. This emission of vapour we observed to take place almost at the summit of the hills, on the ascent of which the springs are situated.

In the immediate vicinity of the bason, just described, which is the largest of the kind at Kryseviig, are several others – exhibiting the same phenomena, but in a less remarkable degree – The hollow or cleft in the mountain, in which the whole are situated, present a *tout-ensemble* of the most singular kind – If a foresight of the infernal regions of mythological story were desired, this would be the spot where the wish might best be gratified.

Ascending further up the mountain, in the course of the same hollow, we came to a very extensive bed of sulphur – much purer than any we had before seen – almost entirely free indeed from the admixture of clay – From the appearance of the mineral in this repository, it seems certain that it has been formed by sublimation. The greater part of it is deposited in loose feathery flocculi–[1] with here & there an appearance of crystallization, where an enclosure between two layers of semi-indurated[2] clay has formed a basis for crystals. Much heated sulphureous vapour issues from the whole of the bed – The superficial crust is very warm; & this removed, the heat becomes so great, that the hand can scarcely be retained for a moment in contact with the sulphur – From this spot, we obtained some fine specimens of Sulphur, which were not, however, procured without difficulty & much hazard. The bed of the mineral is so soft, as to require the utmost caution in treading over its surface: – Occasionally, in spite of all caution, the foot sunk a few inches

[1] Flakes.
[2] Hardened.

into the bed – an accident attended not only with inconvenience, but also with much pain, from the degree of heat present at this depth.

This sulphur bed is situated in the highest part of the cleft or valley which here traverses the mountain – Below it, on one side are the springs or basons we first visited – on the opposite descent, another assemblage of springs of the same description. The bed itself has in all likelihood been formed by the penetration upwards of vapour, highly heated, & holding in this state a quantity of sulphur in solution, which is deposited upon coming into contact with the colder air, in the form it here assumes –

Crossing carefully this bed of Sulphur, & traversing obliquely the declivity of the mountain towards the east, over beds of soft clay impregnated with sulphur, we arrived at the most striking of the Kriseviig springs, that called   [1] (See Sketch Book.16). The bason here, out of which the steam rises, is by no means so large as the one we first saw; but the quantity & force of the vapour is infinitely greater. It issues from the ground at the lower part of a deep cleft in the mountain, with a degree of impetuous violence, which is sufficient to throw a column of water several feet into the air – & attended with a noise, which may be heard at the distance of two or three miles. The column of steam[2] may frequently be seen rising perpendicularly to the height of at least a hundred feet, before it is dispersed into the air. This force, however, is subject to much variation – sometimes the vapour recedes to a certain extent for a few minutes – then breaks out again with renewed force & impetuosity. The difficulty of approach to this spring is as great, as to the others, & from the same causes – We obtained however a bottle full of the water, which proceeds in a small stream from the spring: its external characters present nothing remarkable. – In the vicinity of this spring, we observed, (what does not occur elsewhere in this district so remarkably) large incrustations of a mineral, appearing to be *Selenite*, on various parts of the surface – variously tinged, according to the proportion of iron which it contains – Of this we collected some very fine specimens.

Several other sulphureous springs, of the same general character, but less remarkable, occur in a valley still further to the east. Here also beds of Sulphur appear, mixed with clay in various proportions. In the same

[1] Name omitted in MS.
[2] Coloured engraving from Sir George Mackenzie's sketch in Mackenzie, 1812, facing p. 117.

vicinity, we found on the surface, small incrustations of a saline substance, which appeared from its sensible properties, to be the *Sulphate of Alumine* – The formation of this mineral, in a situation of this kind, may readily be explained.[1]

In the plain below the hills on which the springs are situated, are two small lakes, one of which is called the *Groyna Vatn*,[2] or *Green Lake*, from the peculiar colour of its water – Another lake of considerable size, called the *Kleifar Vatn*,[3] appears 2 or 3 miles to the east.

Earthquakes are frequent in this district – very inconsiderable, however, in extent. They usually follow the long continuance of rainy weather.

We returned to our tent about 5 o'clock, after a very interesting walk. We here found a dinner provided for us by the people of the farm house – a large vessel of rice milk – some slices of Mutton ham, & rye bread.

Saturday 26th Having examined the Sulphur district, we devoted this day to an excursion along the coast. Kriseviig is 2 miles from the sea – The level plain which intervenes (varied only by two or three

---

[1]HH The theory of these *sulphureous springs* (if *springs* they may be termed) at Kriseviig, is an interesting object of enquiry – They are situated in a country decidedly of volcanic origin – The high ground on which they appear, is composed principally of the *conglomerate* or *volcanic tuff*, which has before been noticed – The source of the heat, which can generate, *permanently*, so enormous a quantity of steam, must doubtless reside below this rock – Whether it be the same which produced the volcanic phenomena may be doubted – at least, if the Wernerian theory of volcanoes be admitted – It certainly seems most probable that the appearances depend upon the action of water on vast beds of pyrites – The heat produced by this action is sufficient to raise an additional quantity of water in the form of steam, which makes its way to the surface, & is there emitted through the different clefts in the rocks – The Sulphates of Lime & Alumine, appearing upon the surface, are doubtless produced, in process of time, by these operations – In corroboration of this view it may be observed, that the quantity of steam issuing from the springs at Kriseviik, is always greater, after a long continuance of wet weather; and that whenever earthquakes occur on this spot, it is during the prevalence of weather of this kind.

Some years ago, the Sulphur beds at Kriseviig were made an article of commercial importance and a refinery established on the spot – a detailed account of this, & of other circumstances connected with the Mineralogy of this district, is given in a work published in Copenhagen in 1780, in 2 quarto vols., entitled 'Travels (*Oeconomisk*) in the North-western, Northern & North-eastern parts of Iceland, by Olaus Olavius–' [Ed. *Oeconomisk reise igiennem* (Copenhagen, 1780)] At the close of the 2d vol. of this work, the Sulphur Mines are described in a paper of some length by Ole Henschel [Ed. pp. 667–734]. The same work contains a description of the *Surturbrand District* in Iceland by Christian Zieners [Ed. pp. 737–56].

[2] Grænavatn.
[3] Kleifarvatn.

M. Field sketch near Krísuvík

insulated hills) is covered almost entirely with fragments of the
conglomerate rock, & of lava, – with here & there the occurrence of a
tract strewed over with scoriæ & cinders – The rocks along the coast
are bold & abrupt; presenting to the sea a perpendicular face, in some
places not less than 200 feet in height. These rocks are the resort of
innumerable sea-fowl – particularly of the *Fulmar* – the clefts and
ledges of the rock were completely whitened by their numbers. This is
the time of the year when they lay their eggs; and to procure these,
the inhabitants of the coast employ the means usual in such situations
– being let down the rocks by a rope, suspended over a wooden
pulley at the summit.[1]

[1]HH This coast is interesting in a mineralogical view. – In one large & precipitous
promontory, 2 or 3 miles from Kriseviig, we observed beds of the compact lava,
occurring in the conglomerate rock – Half a mile further to the west, in a small bay, we
found the appearances which are sketched in page 62.M Eight distinct beds of lava, BB,
having a regular horizontal arrangement, & being nearly of the same thickness,
occurred over the black conglomerate, A in the position there marked. The average
thickness of the beds might possibly be 6 or 7 feet – The upper surface of each was
scorified, affording evidence of a separate exposure to the air, while in a heated state –
Appearances, similar upon the whole, though with a more confused intermixture of the
conglomerate & lava occurred further along the coast sometimes one appearing above,
sometimes the other – The conglomerate here shewed more decided marks of its
connection with the volcanic phenomena, than we had before observed. All the
fragments contained in it were scoriæ – the sandstone forming the basis very loosely
compacted – occasionally appearing to be disposed in layers, as if originally deposited
by the sea, & raised to its present situation by some force from beneath – The
conglomerate shews different shades of black, red & grey – in one situation the red rock
lies immediately above that of a black colour.
Four miles from Kriseviig, we came to a vast bed of loose rugged scoriæ, coming
down towards the sea in a direction nearly N & S, & about a mile in width. Below
these scoriæ, we observed in two or three places near the sea, the compact lava making
its appearance. Two [sic] specimens (KS1, 2 & 3) this compact lava. 1 (KS 4) the
conglomerate from the shore.

In the course of our walk, which extended 3 or 4 miles along the coast, towards the west, we observed some collections of driftwood, which had been gathered along the shore, & carefully raised to the top of the rock. The wood was fir or pine.

While sitting at dinner in our tent to day, a woman from one of the adjoining cottages came in, holding a wooden bowl, full of milk, in one hand – a snuff hornn in the other – wwhich she alternately held towards us – Our interpreter,, Loptson, being absent, we did not apprehend her meaning in these gestures. We afterwards found that it was an offer to barter her milk for a replenishment of her snuff-box. Before leaving Kriseviig we gave her some tobacco, with which she was highly delighted – In making her thanks, she shook each of us by the hand – the custom in Iceland on all such occasions.

Sunday. 27th Striking our tent at an early hour, we set off this morning for Grundeviig.[1] This place is situated upon the coast, to the west of Kriseviig, & is probably about 15 miles distant.

Distances, however, are known with very little certainty in Iceland. The usual mode of reckoning, (& in such a country, undoubtedly the most useful method) is by the number of hours occupied in a journey – Where the distances are better known, they are estimated by the Danish mile, equal to 4 English. – The road from Kryseviig to Grundeviik passes through a country singularly barren, wild & desolate. Sometimes we traversed vast beds of rugged Lava; sometimes crossed extensive tracts of ground covered with cinders – in other parts of our way, passed along the edge of mountainous declivities, covered with gravel or larger fragments of rock – Excepting the moss, which here & there shewed[2] itself upon the Lava, or in small patches upon the lower part of the mountains, not the slightest appearance of verdure presented itself to the eye: – we did not meet with a stream of water in the whole distance – the valleys were all covered with sand, or with scoriæ & volcanic fragments. – In the course of our walk, we overtook a *Handel*, or merchant, travelling towards Grundeviik, with a cavalcade of 4 or 5 horses – his wife seated upon one of them – Two miles from Grundeviik, descending towards the shore, we passed a small hamlet, called *Hueren*.[3] All the inhabitants crowded together to look at us in passing. From this place to Grundeviik, the coast is covered with

[1] Grindavík.
[2] MS originally read 'appeared'; corrected reading indistinct – probably 'shewed' but possibly 'strewed'.
[3] Hraun.

numerous small cottages, inhabited by fishermen – to whose industry & success the many heaps of fish lying along the shore for the purpose of drying bore an ample testimony – The cod & the hallibut are the fish principally caught here – Mistaking one of these small assemblages of habitations for Grundeviik, we entered a house, – in which we found a venerable old man,[1] apparently 80 or 90 years of age, his beard flowing to a great length. This was the only instance we had seen in Iceland of the beard being worn – We received here some milk, & many external marks of civility & kindness.[2]

Arrived at Grundeviik, we gave our letter of recommendation[3] from Mr Frydensberg, to Mr Jonson,[4] the principal inhabitant of the place, & a man of considerable property, which he has acquired by his farm & by fishing – His house is a long, irregular range of building, adapted not only to his own use, but also to the accommodation of a number of the people who come down from the interior every spring for the purpose of fishing (See Sketch Book.19). Besides this range of building, there are many other habitations, both in Grundeviig, & along the coast, appropriated to this purpose – among others, one very large building, called the *Bud*,[5] fitted to contain a great number of people (See article Fishing)[6] – Mr Jonson is an old, & respectable man – As the principal farmer in the place, he is called the *Bondi* – The part of his house, inhabited by himself, resembles the common stile of farm-houses in Iceland, with some little superiority, however, of accommodation. Like the others, there is scarcely sufficient light in the interior to enable one, who is a stranger in the place, to find his way from one room to another.

---

[1] Mackenzie, 1812, p. 120 identifies this old man as bearing the same name ('Jon Jonson') as their intended host. *MÍ 1801:Suð.*, 1978, p. 322, cites two men bearing this name at Járngerðastaðir (Grindavík): one aged 55, the other 71. By 1810 the latter may well have been Holland's 'venerable old man', whilst the other may have been the man for whom the party had a letter of introduction. The *MÍ* entry indicates that the two men lived in close proximity; Holland's journal indicates a separation of some two miles. See Mackenzie, 1812, p. 118.

[2] HH 2 or 3 miles from Grundeviik, upon the shore, we found numerous fragments of pumice stone, most of them rounded. Likewise rounded fragments of black scoriæ, so completely vesicular as to float upon the water – the country between Kryseviig & Grundeviig presented no novelty in its mineralogical characters – A ridge of mountains, composed of conglomerate, stretches along the peninsula – connected with the range between Helgafell & Kriseviik – These mountains are intersected by tracts of lava & scoriæ. (Specimens of Pumice, from the plain E of Grundeviik – Also with vesicular fragments of lava filled with crystals).

[3] See above, note 4, pp. 119–20.   [4] See above, note 1, p. 133.

[5] Mod.Ice. *búð*, 'booth'.

[6] No such article extant; no equivalent section in Mackenzie, 1812.

This being the period when a number of people are down upon the coast for the purpose of fishing, and moreover the day being Sunday, a large assemblage crowded around us while we were pitching our tent; curiously examining every part of the process; & observing also with much minuteness our dress & different movements. At one time there were more than 30 people present, men, women & children; and many of them continued about the tent till a late hour. We found upon enquiry that we were the only Englishmen, who had visited Grundeviik, during the long period to which Mr Jonson's memory carried him back – He recollected to have once seen a Frenchman there, who made his escape from an English vessel in one of the Icelandic harbours. – It was an additional circumstance of surprize here, as well as in every other place we visited in this journey, that we should be travelling on foot – To this mode of passing through the country, even the lower classes in Iceland are wholly unaccustomed; & Loptson interpreted to us various expressions of astonishment, which our plans excited.

Our tent was pitched this evening behind Mr Jonson's house, which was of infinite service to us as a protection from the easterly wind.

Monday 28th This morning we struck our tent under the discomfort of a heavy rain accompanied by a high wind – The original plan of our journey included Cape Reikianes as one of the objects to be visited – principally on account of certain varieties of *Bole* which are found here – there are also two or three sulphureous springs on this promentory, resembling those at Kriseviig – In consequence of the state of the weather, and the difficulty of procuring pasture for the horses in the vicinity of the Cape, we were induced to resign this part of our scheme, & to direct our course immediately to *Kieblevüik*, on the northern side of the peninsula of Guldbringe – The distance between Grundeviig & Kiebleviig is probably 15 or 16 miles – the intervening country dismal & desolate in the highest degree, though different from that we had before traversed. The mountainous part of the Guldbringe ceases at this point of the peninsula, and a tract of flat land stretches to the west, occupying the whole space between the Skagen[1] and Cape Reikianes. No part of this district is probably more than 150 or 200 feet above the level of the sea. It appears to be entirely of volcanic formation, resembling greatly in appearance, the country near the Kaldaá; the ground every where covered with fragments of lava, & large beds of

[1] Garðsskagi.

this substance occasionally appearing upon the surface, with elevations & cavities beneath, such as were formerly described.[1]

We reached the northern coast of the Guldbringe peninsula at Niardviik,[2] a considerable fishing village, (See Sketch Book 22) situated on the western side of a small bay – Kiebleviig is about a mile still further to the west – a place, which on our first arrival in Iceland, we should have deemed miserable in a high degree, but which now, after some acquired knowledge of the villages or small towns in the island, & more especially, after traversing so many miles of country totally destitute of habitations, we regarded with a sort of admiration & pleasure. A wooden house at present appeared a most desirable place of residence – Of 15 or 20 habitations thus constructed, & a few cottages built up with turf, the town of Kiebleviig consists. It is situated at the upper part of a small bay – having in the background the same tract of barren, desolate country, which here stretches across the peninsula.

Arrived at Kiebleviig, we went to the house of M^r. Jacobæus,[3] a Dane, and the principal inhabitant of the place. We found that he expected our arrival, having heard of us from Kriseviig – We were received with the utmost hospitality, and assured that our letter of recommendation from Mr Frydensberg was wholly unnecessary. Mr Jacobæus is one of the most considerable merchants in Iceland; and had much commercial connection with Denmark; though this trade has of course suffered greatly from the war between England and Denmark. During Jergenson's temporary government of Iceland, he exacted 8000 dollars from Mr J., which have not yet been repaid to him. – Mr Jacobæus saw Sir J. Stanley several times during his visit to Iceland –[4] Madame J.[5] is also a native of Denmark – a pleasing, good humoured woman – civil & hospitable in a high degree – & moreover an *excellent cook* – The house is one of the best we have seen in Iceland – As is the case in most of the Icelandic houses, the best sitting room & the best bed room are one and the same – The luxury of Eider-down, as a stuffing for the mattrass of the bed, we found here, as well as in the houses at Reikiaviik & Havnefiord – Upon our arrival, we received, as is the custom in the Danish families in Iceland, some coffee, of excellent

[1] The fragments of Lava, 2 or 3 miles from Grundeviik presented a variety in appearance which we had not before exactly met with. (A specimen from this place).
[2] Njarðvík.
[3] Christian Adolph Jacobæus (b. 1768). A prominent merchant with important trading interests in both Hafnarfjörður and Reykjavík as well as Keflavík.
[4] There is no mention of this in any of the Stanley expedition journals.
[5] Regine Magdalena Jacobæus (b. 1780).

manufacture, with rye-bread & fresh butter – Our tent-bed-steads were erected for the night in a large room, which forms part of an adjoining building.

Tuesday 29ᵗʰ We passed this day at Kiebleviig. The country in the vicinity furnished nothing whatever worthy of observation – Both in external appearance, & in actual mineralogical character, it much resembles the neighbourhood of Reikiaviik –[1] Our host, Mʳ Jacobæus, we found to be a man of sense and information – and we derived from him many valuable facts respecting the statistics and commerce of Iceland. He was in the island during the great volcanic eruption in 1783, & was himself a witness of some of the extraordinary phenomena which preceded & attended this event – the appearances near Cape Reikianes – the earthquakes &c. (See page 8)[2] – Neither Mʳ nor Madame J. speak English – so that all conversation was of necessity carried on through Loptson. He had some previous acquaintance with the family; having formerly, when with Dʳ Klog, come over from Reikiaviik to inoculate their children with the Cow pock. We learnt from Madame J. a singular fact, that during 16 years of residence in Iceland, she has not once left Kiebleviik – not even to visit the metropolis of the island.

Kiebleviig is noted as one of the best fishing places in Iceland – especially for the cod, which during the early months of the year, March, April, & May, is caught here in prodigious abundance, & of very large size – The fishing banks lie at a very short distance from the mouth of the Bay. All the largest fish are caught with the net. During the interval from the middle of March to the end of April, the use of the hook & line is prohibited, from a fear of alarming the fish, & driving them from the banks. The number of fishing boats belonging to Kiebleviig, is 16 or 17 – of a size sufficient to carry 7 men each. The usual product of the season's fishing, is estimated at 5 or 600 fish for each man. The fish, upon being caught, are split, & collected in heaps for drying – each heap being covered with deal[3] boards, & these weighted down by large stones. The present fishing season & that of last year have been more than usually productive.

We dined to day upon Sago Soup, (a dish very common in the better

---

[1] ᴴᴴ The rocks along the shore & behind the town, exhibit the same general appearances & have evidently undergone changes the same as those which have occurred at Reikiaviik – (2 specimens from the promontory on the eastern side of Kiebleviig Bay (D 1 & 2).

[2] See above, note 4, p. 82.   [3] Redwood.

houses in Iceland) & mutton. Potatoes were likewise brought to the table as a great luxury – We soon discovered that they came from England by the same conveyance as ourselves. The wine, drank at Mr Jacobæus's table, is the same as that we had seen at Viidoe – a sort of thin claret. As another luxury, London bottled porter was also produced, procured from England during the last year.

Wednesday May 30th We had intended to prosecute our journey this morning; but in consequence of Sir G.Mackenzie feeling himself unwell, we were necessarily detained at Kiebleviik a day longer. – I walked this morning along the edge of the shore to Niardviik. While taking a sketch of the place, three or four of the inhabitants came up, accosted me, & remained some time, looking at my procedure. A little boy who came with them, was sent off to one of the houses – & returned with a large bowl of milk, which was presented to me – the boy having previously motioned the drinking of my health, & taken a little of it himself – This is a frequent custom in Iceland. There was something pleasant & interesting in the manner of these people – much curiosity & observation, without impertinence or awkward intrusion. The men, like the Icelanders in general, were tall & well made, their hair light coloured and very long – with ruddy complexions –

Niardviik is very considerable as a fishing place, and is much resorted to during the fishing season by people from the interior of the country.

A dish was this day introduced upon Mr Jacobæus's table, which we had not before seen, but which is common in Denmark, called .' It consists of a sort of gravy soup, having rice in it, & containing besides, a number of small cakes, composed of flour, milk & eggs –

Thursday. May 31st In consequence of a tremendous storm of wind & rain, we were not only prevented from leaving Kiebleviik, but necessarily detained in the house during the whole of this day. We esteemed ourselves fortunate in having the shelter of so hospitable a roof.

Friday June 1st This morning, though the wind still continued high, with frequent showers of rain, we set off on foot for Havnefiord, which is distant from Kiebleviig about four & twenty miles.² – This day's travel

' Name omitted in MS.
²|||| The country between Kiebleviik & Havnefiord much resembles in mineralogical character that between Grundeviik & Kiebleviik – with the intervention, however, of two more considerable beds of Lava, than any which occur in the latter distance. In the bed of lava nearest to Havnefiord on this side, an appearance occurs, which though we had often

was in every respect by far the most difficult we had yet encountered – When a mile from Kiebleviig, in consequence of some mistake about the luggage, I waited ½ an hour for the horses, which were behind us – expecting speedily to rejoin my companions, who proceeded on their way. In this expectation I was disappointed. Before I had walked far alone, I found that all traces of the path were utterly lost – & that I must depend entirely upon my general knowledge of the bearings of the country, for a secure progress in my way. For five hours I proceeded tolerably well, though in a very zig-zag direction, & over a country desolate & barren in the extreme, & so completely covered with fragments of lava, as to render walking very difficult. At this part of my way, I came to a bed of lava, about a mile across, & much more rugged & abrupt than any that had before occurred in our journey. Unable still to find any track, I crossed the lava in the shortest direction that I could take, a task of such extreme difficulty & even danger, as to create a feeling of the most lively pleasure, when the obstacle was surmounted – The deep chasms & rents which occurred on every side, in some places open – in others deceiving the eye by a slight covering of moss – were the most alarming circumstances in the route – To the difficulties arising from the ruggedness of the rocky matter – the loose scoriæ &c, our previous journey had fully inured me – I was happy in making my way to a small cottage about a mile beyond the lava, where I procured some milk, & a direction into the road. I reached Havnefiord at 9 o'clock in the evening – & was infinitely surprized to find Sir G.M., & M^r. B. not yet arrived there. – They made their appearance ½ an hour afterwards; and gave a narrative of difficulties & hazards fully equal to those which I had experienced –[1] Loptson & Jonson did not arrive with the horses until midnight. It was with the utmost difficulty that the poor animals had got through their day's journey.

Saturday June 2^d We spent the morning of this day at Havnefiord – engaged in taking sketches of the place & its vicinity – After dinner, we

---

before observed it, is here particularly striking – the occurrence of small undulations or wavings on the surface of the rounded elevations which present themselves in the Lava – These undulations assume much variety of form, & clearly evince the viscidity of the substance at the time the appearances were produced.[N] Near the bay of Havnefiord, upon the shore, some striking columnar appearances occur in this bed of lava – Over the columns, the surface of the rock is completely scorified. (Specimens from this place – E1 from some depth below the surface of the column – E2 – the scorified surface).

[1] Mackenzie, 1812, pp. 123–4.

terminated our journey by walking from Havnefiord to Reikiaviik. The impression with which we now entered the latter place was widely different from that which attended our first arrival there. Then every thing appeared mean, miserable & desolate – At the present moment, the contrast with what we had lately seen in the interior of the country was sufficient to give to the place a certain semblance of magnificence – something of life, population & activity to which our eyes for the last fortnight had been little accustomed.

N. Field sketch at Hafnarfjörður

We found the Elbe still lying in Reikiaviik Bay – Some further difficulties had occurred during our absence in the loading of the vessel, from the continued interference of the Atastrood – but these were not of much moment, & speedily surmounted. – We again took up our residence in Count Trampe's house, with some slight changes in our domestic economy – Another housekeeper was procured from Havnefiord – our former assistant in this way, having entered into the matrimonial state; & being gone, in consequence of this, to reside at Kiebleviik.

***

Sunday June 3ᵈ Nothing of moment occurred to day – We made our calls in Reikiaviik & were welcomed back by our friends there with much cordiality.

Monday June 4 This day a salute was fired from the Elbe, and a dinner given on board the ship – Mʳ Frydensberg was invited, but from prudential motives declined the visit.

Tuesday 5ᵗʰ We dined to day with Mʳ Frydensberg, meeting there Dʳ Klog, & two or three other inhabitants of Reikiaviik – The dinner, according to a practice common in Iceland, was served upon the table by Madame F. herself – The first dishes appearing were two tureens – one of gravy soup – the other composed of the Iceland Lichen boiled in milk –[1] To this dish sugar is taken, according to the taste of each individual – A plover pie succeeded – This was followed by baked mutton and potatoes, & the dinner concluded by some dishes of pastry, & English cheese –

Wednesday 6th At 10 o'clock this morning we were summoned to the beach by the intelligence that a vessel was seen entering the Bay – We found it to be a Danish galliot called the *Bildal*,[2] direct from Liverpool, which place she left on the 10th of May. She had been kept more than a fortnight on the coast of Iceland by opposite winds – & had even been as far to the north as the *Breyde Fiordur* during this period of delay. M[r] Severtsen[3] of Havnefiord came as a passenger in this vessel – a young man too of the name of Flood,[4] a Dane, who was formerly a sort of Secretary to Count Trampe in Iceland, & went with him to England last Autumn – He brought us a packet of letters from Count Trampe – one addressed specially to Sir G.M. – friendly & polite in the highest degree – the others being letters of introduction, which he had promised us previously to our leaving England – One of these letters was addressed generally to all those of office, authority, or property in the island (See opposite page):[5] – the remainder, individually, to Mr Frydensberg, M[r]

[1] *Cetraria Islandica* (Linn.); Mod.Ice. *Fjallagrös*. Boiled with milk and sugar, or taken as tea, the grass was believed to have beneficial medicinal properties, a claim viewed sceptically by Holland in Mackenzie, 1812, p. 403.

[2] MS superscript erasure *Bildudald*. The vessel was owned by Ólafur Þorðarson Thorlacius of Bildudalur. See below, note 1, p. 203.

[3] Bjarni Sívertsen. See above, notes 2–3, p. 114.

[4] Jörgen P. Flood [n.d.]. Traded in Reykjavík, 1803–14; received citizenship 1811.

[5] HH *Copy of a Letter from Count Trampe to Sir George Mackenzie*

London – April 20th 1810

Sir,

Agreeable to my given promise, I have the honour hereby to forward to you.

1st – A general order to all official men, as well clerical, as others of the civil power & whomsoever else it may concern in Iceland, to give you every assistance in your intended scientific tour through the island.

2[d] – A letter of introduction to the Bishop of the country, whom also I have requested to guide you as to the determination of your travelling route, and to acquaint you with such men of the Clergy, as are able to afford you any literary information.

3[d] – A letter of introduction to the Assessor Einersen, who is one of the Deputy-Governors in my absence.

4th – An introductory letter to the Land-Foged Frydensberg – He is by me directed not to permit your being in any pecuniary want – Therefore in case you should be placed in any such, then be friendly pleased to address yourself to this gentleman, who for my account will let you have what money you want, taking for the amount your bills of 3 months date, payable to Mess[rs] Corbet, Borthwick & C[o] in Leith.

Simonson, the Bishop, Mr Einerson, Mr Thoransen,^{1} & the Hamptman^2 Steffensen, brother of the *Atastrood*.

The arrival of the *Bildudald* effected a sort of revolution in the Government of Iceland – important in name; but puny in all its appearances & events – The *Atastrood*, (whose conduct was more than dubious during the occurrences of the last summer, and whose official situation appears to have been solely derived from the appointment of Captn Jones of the Talbot)^3 experienced at this time the precariousness of all human grandeur – Official letters arrived from Count Trampe, deposing him from his situation, & appointing in his stead three deputy governors of the Island – the Assessor Einerson, (whom we had visited at Bessasted) – the Land-Foged Frydensberg, & Mr Thoransen, – sub-governor of the northern & eastern districts – This change in state affairs appeared to diffuse considerable satisfaction through the metropolis of Iceland. The *Atastrood* is little liked or respected – especially by the Danish inhabitants of the place – to whom his conduct last year gave much umbrage.

Our own situation, if at all affected by this change of Governors, is favourably affected rather than otherwise – With Mr Frydensberg we continue on the best terms, & receive from him the utmost civility & assistance to our plans. Mr Einerson appears similarly disposed. He

---

5th – An introductory letter to my private agent Reikiaviik, Mr Simonson, Merchant, who will make preparations for your accommodation in my house in Reikiaviik during your stay there: & will also, with your permission, take upon him the ordering of your travelling equipage, procuring of horses &c &c. And I should wish that you in matters of this nature would make use of him. He is a very fair man, & agrees with me that principle, which is not the general one, that strangers ought not to pay more than our own people.

6th – An introductory letter to the Sub-Governor for the Northern & Eastern district, Mr Thoransen in case of your coming within the same, which you most likely will do.

7th – An introductory letter to the Sub-Governor for the Western district, Mr Stephensen, in case of your coming within the same, which I suppose you will.

I hope these letters will prove useful to you & present my best wishes that the tour may afford you & your companions entertainment & satisfaction. I shall conclude this letter by reminding you of your good promise of communicating to me, when the tour is finished your observations & remarks.

Sir, your very humble Servant

Fred^c Trampe

^{1} Stefán Þórarinsson (1754–1823). Regional governor in the South and West from 1804; one of the joint acting governors after Jörgensen's overthrow in 1810.

^{2} *amtmaður*, a regional governor. In this case Stefán Ólafsson Stephensen.

^{3} On this and other aspects of the 1809 insurrection, see introduction, pp. 24–7.

came over to Reikiaviik this morning and was initiated into his new dignities.

Thursday 7ᵗʰ Mʳ Einerson called upon us this morning – attended by Mʳ Gudmundsson of Garde Kirk, arrayed in a wig of vast dimensions, and a cock & pinched hat – Mʳ E. gave us much information relatively to a journey, which we at this time have in contemplation to Eya Fiord¹ – in the north-eastern part of Iceland. With this district he is well acquainted, & he assures us of the practicability of the journey thither – In relation to the same object, we went this morning to the Bishop's, to meet Mr Polassen² – an inhabitant of the vicinity of Katlegaia-Jokull,³ and a sort of medical practitioner in this part of the country. He is a man of considerable general information, & intimately acquainted with the Geography & Natural History of Iceland. His manners are simple & pleasant – he speaks Latin with facility. We obtained from Him the promise of a detailed direction for our route – first on an excursion into the Borgar Fiord – afterwards for the longer journey to the northern parts of the island.

Friday 8ᵗʰ We devoted this day to the acceptance of an invitation from the old Governor Steffensen to visit him at Viidoe. Since our return to Reikiaviik we have received from him many testimonials of kindness. Immediately after our arrival, he sent us the present of a fine sheep, with 200 Eider Duck eggs – The same number of eggs was sent on Thursday evening, & two of the Eider-fowl for the purpose of stuffing.

We went to Viidoe this morning by water – in a boat of Icelandic construction, & by no means pleasant or secure as a mode of conveyance – Arrived at Viidoe, we were surprized & pleased by the sight which met our eyes on landing – On every part of the shore, & on the green plot of ground which surrounds the Governor's house, a prodigious number of Eider-Ducks were sitting on their nests – so completely deprived of their usual habits of wildness & shyness, as to allow themselves to be stroked & even lifted from the nests without apprehension or resentment – The number of these nests within 200

¹ Eyjafjörður.
² Sveinn Pálsson (1762–1840). Lived at Vík í Mýrdal from 1809 until his death; physician, naturalist, traveller and scholar. See Þorkell Jóhannesson (ed.) *Merkir Íslendingar*, 6 vols. (Reykjavík, 1947–57), III, 113–59. Holland sent Sveinn a copy of his *De morbis Islandiæ* and received in return a glowing letter of appreciation – MS Þjóðskjalasafn, Varia VI, dated 12 September 1812.
³ Kötlugjá.

yards of the house, was probably not less that 12 or 1500 – Some of them were placed immediately under the window of the habitation, one or two within the church near the house – the greater number on the small eminences between the house & the shore. In one place, on the side of a small bank, a number of holes had been prepared for the reception of the nests – arranged in tiers one above another – In each of these a nest had been constructed, carefully lined, as is the habit with these birds, with the down plucked from their bodies. Where' the duck leaves her nest for a short time in going out for food, she completely conceals her eggs under a covering of the down. At many of the nests, the drake was standing by the side of the duck – much more shy, however; & refusing to let anyone touch him – but keeping in the vicinity of the nest till the intruder departs.

The old Governor was much pleased with the notice we took of his Eider-Ducks. They are a source both of satisfaction & profit to him – About 3000 Eggs are taken every year from the nests on the island, & 70 lbs of Eider Down. The Down is usually taken from the nests three times in the course of the season. – the Duck plucking herself twice to supply its covering – the Drake afterwards performing the same part. Six or seven eggs are generally laid in one nest – The number of Eider-Ducks in the island of Viidoe, is upon the whole increasing, though not rapidly. The Eagle is their great enemy at this season of incubation, & a considerable number had already been thus destroyed in the present year – In our last visit to Viidoe, we had seen two eagles hovering over the rocks along the shore. These Sir G.M. saw again to day & fired at one of them, but without success.

At dinner every thing proceeded much in the same way, as we had seen it when formerly at Viidoe – The old man appeared in his court dress, & shewed as much fondness for the soothings of flattery as ever – After dinner, he introduced to our notice (somewhat mal-apropos) a small volume, containing a Memoir of his late wife – with some poems composed to her Memory.² This was presented to Sir G.M.

On our return to Reikiaviik, going near the shore to pick up some birds which had been shot, the boat was overset by the awkwardness of the boatmen, & we were plunged into the water. The accident was

---

' Steindór Steindórsson, 1960, p. 107 apparently reads 'when' (Mod.Ice. *þegar*); but MS, though indistinct, appears to read 'where'.

² Magnús Ólafsson Stephensen, *Minning frúr stiptamtmannsinnu Sigríðar Magnúsdóttir Stephensen* (Leirárgarðar, 1810).

productive of no more serious inconvenience than the wetting of our cloathes.

We found at Reikiaviik a letter from the Atastrood to Sir G. Mackenzie, in reply to one which had been sent over to Innerholme[1] in the morning, to know if it would be convenient to him to receive us at his house in a day or two from this time (see opposite page).[2] The character of the Atastrood is well seen in his epistle – a large portion of vanity, with a good deal of weakness of mind; and moreover much disappointment (badly garnished over) at the change in the Government which the arrival of the Bilderdald had produced.

Mr Polassen sent us to day a scheme of the route which he proposed

---

[1] Innrihólmur.

[2]HH *Copy of a Letter from Atastrood Steffensen to Sir G. Mackenzie.*

Innerholm. 8th June 1810

Dear Sir,

With the greatest pleasure I'll always wish for the honor to see you, dear Sir, & your respected companions here in my house, whenever you please, as I cannot but approve your resolution soon to travel through Borgar-Fiord, where I hope you'll find more things worth seeing.

But I hope too that you, Dear Sir, will permit me frankly to confess, that only the next week till the 17th this month is as well to me, as to your journey through this part of our Island, less convenient than any other time in the summer; because I'll be myself employed with business whole this week, through delivering all papers appertaining to the Government in a due manner & form, and accomplishing some public accounts – Besides you'll find all horses before said day still very meagre, and I consequently first at that time be able to furnish you with some useful horses, the number of which according to your necessity & wish, I do desire a friendly notice of before. But if it may be convenient to you, dear Sir, to put off your journey to said day the 17th instant, or in the mean time to see what remarkable things Kialdarnes, or Kios, & especially the mount Esien could shew, where some minerals of various species are to be found, I'll afterwards be able to conduct & wait upon you through whole the Borgarfiord from the 17th to the 30th – after which same time my office as Lord Chief Justice of Iceland claims my presence at Reikiaviik in the Higher Court General for 3 days – But from the 17th to the 30th June, you'll easily be able to see every thing remarquable in Borgarfiord, & see too perhaps the finest part of whole the country, & even worthiest seeing, because of the natural history.

You are in the right, Dear Sir, that I am very glad and happy being relieved of the troublesome Government & of all risk. When Count Trampe last year was confined, & usurpers did assume the Government by committing much violence, here I sole did not hesitate to risk every thing, even my own liberty & life, for the release of my country, calling to its aid the generous British Captain Alexander Jones, who by the agreement of 22[d] August, charged me with the Government, as the first remaining officer in this island, & as no other at that dangerous time had any prerogative nor courage to administer such an office.* I wrote immediately a humble letter to my King, containing the story of events by us, & my declaration that I only for the release of my country did thus expose me to all danger & risk, being ready to administer justice, until the confined to our adoption through Borgar-fiord,[1] & afterwards to Eyafiord, Myvatn &c.[2] It was given much in detail, & written in Latin of considerable elegance.

Saturday 9th Nothing of moment occurred to day. We were occupied in writing letters for the conveyance of the Elbe to England.

Tuesday 10th We had proposed going to the church to day, but the indisposition of Mr Severtsen, the minister, prevented the performance of service. In this respect there appears little observation of form or regularity of proceeding at Reikiaviik. The service begins at an uncertain time, and a Sabbath frequently passes away without any attendance whatever at the church.

Monday 11th – This day (Whit Monday) is a holiday in Reikiaviik. We had an opportunity in the morning of seeing the ceremony of confirmation gone through at the church. The ordinary service of the day was first performed – begun by prayers, singing & lessons from the Bible, & concluded by a sermon, somewhat more than ½ an hour in length – all the service in the Icelandic language. The first part was performed by the minister, Mr Severtsen, standing before the altar – habited in a white gown, and this covered with a sort of *toga*, or short

---

Governor Trampe might return, or order any thing about it, or his Majesty's own order should be got. 'Tis only for a short time that Count T for particular reasons has made over the administration on his behalf meanwhile to a commission of three persons during his absence, of which Mr Frydensberg, as an inferior judge, is the last; until the King's order can be got, probably at the arrival of a new Governor from Denmark, who soon can be expected, but Count Trampe hither never more. I did even thereby declare to my King himself, that not a single pence of salary, would be desired of, or received by me for the administration, as I never wished for this office afterwards, knowing my own to be the next; but much more quiet & without risk – more fit to a scientifical man, & my rank too, as his Majesty's Counsellor of State & Lord Chief Justice – even higher than that of a constituted commissioner of the Government for the mean-while, which here exists none – and I do heartily rejoice that neither fear for risk & loss, nor duty in my present office obliges me to further claims & controversies concerning the indemnification for what here happened last year. The business & pleasure of which, & the risk quite to neglect it, I do willingly concede to my relievers.

Every thing which I may be able to afford to your service, Dear Sir, if you'll only please to honour me with your order about what you want or desire, shall with the most ready duty & pleasure be procured & executed. –

I have the honour with utmost respect to be, dear Sir, your faithful most obedient *Stephensen*

*N.B. *This dangerous & eventful period* was brought about by the arrival of a London Soap Boiler at Reikiaviik – in a vessel with letters of marque!

[1] Borgarfjörður.

[2] Mývatn.

cloak hanging over the shoulders, & ornamented with broad bands of blue-stuff with gold lacing. The singing or chaunting was performed by ten or twelve men, placed round the included space before the altar, & might boast much more of noise than harmony of sound – The sermon was delivered from the pulpit – the minister habited in a black gown – The whole of it was previously written, but read with much emphasis & some oratorical display: of the matter we were in no degree qualified to judge – Bishop Vidalin made his appearance in church just before the sermon – walked along the middle aisle and seated himself within a small railing in the space before the altar. He was dressed in his episcopal robes – After the sermon, Mr Severtsen resumed his station at the altar in his first dress, & the children to be confirmed were ranged in a semi-circle about him – the boys & girls separately – 12 of the former, 11 of the latter – dressed in all the splendour of attire which circumstances afforded to them. An exhortation, equal in length to the sermon, was first read by the minister. He afterwards proceeded to catechise the children individually at considerable length – the questions, as they were translated to us, much resembling those common in the English catechisms. After the questions had been proposed, & answered by each child, the confirmation was given by the minister laying his hand upon the child's head – The service closed by another exhortation, & a prayer – the minister kneeling in the midst of the children – The Bishop was a spectator during the whole of the service – He had, however, his own separate occupations in taking snuff, chewing tobacco, & spitting[1] – We were interested by the sight which the body of the Church afforded – It was completely crowded with people, as well from the town, as from the neighbouring country – all in their very best suits – The females sat on the left hand side of the church – almost every one of them dressed in the proper Icelandic costume – the men on the opposite side – We did not observe any of the Danish inhabitants of Reikiaviik to be present in the church.

There was a ball this evening in the town, at which we presented ourselves. It was well attended, but no thing of novelty occurred to our notice in the appearance & customs of the meeting. The dancing, music, drinking & smoking were carried on much in the same way as

---

[1] Mackenzie, 1812, p. 93 took disapproving note that 'the unrestrained evacuation of saliva seems to be a fashion all over Iceland'.

on the two former occasions when we visited the place – The only addition to the proceedings was a song composed by Mr Magnuson,[1] (clerk to Mr Frydensberg) in celebration of the praises of Count Trampe. This was sung in chorus by all the people, both male & female, in the rome [sic] & the health of Count T. afterwards drunk with repeated huzzas.

Tuesday–Wednesday–Thursday – *12th–13th–14th* – In the course of these days nothing particular occurred – A material alteration, however, was made in our plans for future travelling through Iceland. This change took place from a conviction which conversation with our friends in the town, (Mr Frydensberg particularly) produced, that it would be impossible to execute in one summer all the plans we had laid out for ourselves – We were induced therefore to think of resigning the most remote & difficult of our proposed journeys – that to Eya fiord – & of taking up in its stead an extension of our journey into the Borgar fiord – proceeding by land to Snæfield's Jokull,[2] – Stappen's Hafn[3] &c To the adoption of this plan we were still further led by meeting with a Mr Clausen,[4] a merchant of *Olafshavn*,[5] in the vicinity of Snæfield's Jokull, who strongly recommended this route to us, & offered us his assistance, as far as possible, in carrying our projects into execution. Mr Clausen is a Dane – an active, pleasant man, & better informed on scientific subjects than any one we have yet seen in Iceland – He came to Reikiaviik to adjust some commercial transactions with Mr Fell, as the agent of Phelps & Co., an adjustment into which many subjects of dispute unfortunately intruded themselves.

On Wednesday morning I received a note from Mr Polassen,[6] begging my attendance on a daughter of Mr Severtsen the minister of Reikiaviik. I walked thither in the course of the day – & afterwards proceeded to the Ness, to speak with Dr Klog, who was in previous attendance, on the subject. The child I found to be very seriously ill,

[1] Finnur Magnússon. See above, note 1, p. 95.
[2] Snæfellsjökull.
[3] Arnarstapi.
[4] Holger P. Clausen (1780–1826).
[5] Ólafsvík.
[6HH] Dr.H.Holland, ut filiolam pastoris Templi Reykiavicini domini Severtsen ægrotantem, data occasione, concomitante interprete, visitare velit, humillime rogatur –
a Paulsonio
[Dr.Henry Holland is most humbly asked by Sveinn Pálsson that at a suitable opportunity, accompanied by an interpreter, he should visit the little daughter of the pastor of the church at Reykjavík, Brynjólfur Sívertsen, who is ill.]

& another daughter also much indisposed. I was much pleased with the manners & good sense of Madame Severtsen,[1] as I observed them in this visit to her family.

Mr. Jacobæus of Kiebleviik dined with us on Wednesday.

---

[1] Steinunn Helgadóttir (1770–1857).

SECOND JOURNEY

Friday 15th We commenced this morning our second journey into the interior of Iceland – the general scheme of which was to pursue a route through the southern parts of Borgar-Fiord Syssel to Snæfield's Jokull, & to return by the northern part of Borgarfiord, & by Thingvalla–Vatn[1] to Reikiaviik – For the execution of this journey riding horses are indispensably necessary, & we accordingly provided ourselves, by the assistance of our friend Mr Simonson, with three of these – adding two also to the number of our luggage horses. The whole of our travelling establishment now comprized 10 horses. Loptson & two guides[2] attended us.

After bidding farewell to our friends in Reikiaviik, we crossed the Bay in the boat belonging to the galliot Bildudald, Capt Kielson[3] accompanying us. We were cheered from the Elbe, as we passed under her stern. When about half over the Bay, which is here 7 miles across, a violent storm of wind & rain came on. The surf of the sea was thrown so much into the boat, that we were almost completely wetted through, before we reached the opposite shore[4] – The horses had set out a couple of hours before us – the route by land passing round the head of the Bay – a circuit of 15 or 16 miles to the place where we landed.

On leaving the boat, we continued our course along the shore

[1] Þingvallavatn.
[2] Mackenzie, 1812, p. 131, 'Gwylfr and Gudmundr by name'.
[3] Unidentified.
[4] HH The rocks on this side of the Bay of Reikiaviik exhibit a character widely different from those we have before seen in Iceland. Here the evidences of volcanic formation almost if not entirely disappear, & every thing appears to belong to the Flœtz Trap Formation of the German school.
Near the place of our landing, we found near the shore an open face of rock, 8 or 10 feet in height, exhibiting a singular assemblage of distinct concretions, filled with crystals of zeolite &c. (F1). These occur in the rock F2. F3 lies over them, exhibiting a slaty structure – Mount Esian appears to be composed of greenstone & basalt, containing veins of jasper, calc spar &c – The substance, of which F4 is a specimen taken from a fragment in the plain below, appears about half way up the ascent of the mountain. Numerous fragments of this, of jasper, chalcedony, agate, zeolite, calc-spar &c, are scattered over the plain down to the shore.

towards the west, a good deal inconvenienced by the heaviness of the rain, but contriving nevertheless to procure some good specimens from the neighbouring rocks. A plain gradually ascending from the sea for about a mile, conducts to the base of a lofty mountain called *Esian*,[1] which rises with a steep & in some places almost perpendicular ascent to the height probably of 1800 or 2000 feet. This mountain forms a striking object from Reikiaviik – we had seen it even when coasting along the southern shore of the Guldbringe Syssel – Approaching the mouth of the *Hval Fiord*,[2] an inlet of the sea which runs deeply into the country in a NE direction, we waited two hours for our horses, sheltering ourselves, as far as it was possible, under a small ridge of rocks, which here rises out of the plain – Wearied at length of our situation, we directed our course towards *Brautar-holt*, a small village (if a single farm house & church can be so termed) situated on the point called *Kialiarnes*,[3] which forms the eastern boundary to the entrance of the *Hval Fiord* – Here we arrived at 10 o'clock, every thing about us wet & uncomfortable, as well from the rain, as from the morasses which we crossed in the course of our walk – We were glad to find the church a tolerably comfortable one – constructed precisely on the same plan as that at Kriseviik, & not very greatly superior in size – but neater & more respectable in its internal appearance – The farm-house[O] is of the common Icelandic construction, most resembling externally a groupe of mole-hills of large size – The dirt & smell within were so intolerable, that we gladly availed ourselves of the church as our place of habitation for the night, & here upon the arrival of the horses about 11 o'clock, we erected our bedsteads. The people of the house brought us a large dish full of Eider duck eggs for our evening's repast.[4]

Saturday 16ᵗʰ – We breakfasted this morning on boiled fish & rice milk, furnished from the farm house & eaten on the altar – The wetness of the morning, & various interruptions in loading the horses delayed the commencement of our day's travel until 2 o'clock. We then set forth, following a track at the foot of the hills, which bound the Hval Fiord on

---

[1] Esjá. [2] Hvalfjörður.
[3] Kjalarnes. Holland's facing page (MS I, 80) note reads: 'This name is derived from the Icelandic word *kialur* – a sharp point or ridge keel'.
[4][HH] The farm at Brautar-holt keeps 9 Cows & about 100 Sheep – A small island is included in the farm, whence about 30 lbs. of Eider down are annually procured, as well as the Eider duck eggs. The rent of the farm is 10 rix-dollars. The owner of the farm, however, is allowed to keep a certain number of cattle upon the tenant's land during a part of the year.

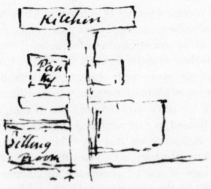

O. A farmhouse at Brautarholt in Kjósarsýsla

the eastern side[1] – and ascending occasionally to some height for the collection of specimens &c. The Hval Fiord in its general appearance greatly resembles some of the Lochs, or arms of the sea in Scotland – It stretches about 20 miles into the country, and has an average breadth of 3 or 4 miles. The mountains which bound it on each side are lofty, & for the most part rise steeply from the water's edge, affording considerable variety & magnificence of scenery – When about 6 miles on our road, we left the banks of the Fiord, & mounting our horses pursued a path to the right, among the mountains – The country here afforded some singular features. The valley along which we passed was about a mile in width,

[1]HH The mountains on the eastern, or rather southern side of Hval Fiord, have the same general mineralogical character as Esian, being in fact continuous with it – They exhibit however more of the peculiar structure of the trap formation, & well illustrate the derivation of the term – shewing a series of steps or stairs, in some places very perfect, from the bottom to the top of the mountain – Many jaspers, chalcedonies, zeolites &c occur also in this part of the hill. (F 6)

A singular vein, composed of a rock, of which F7 is a specimen (somewhat too vesicular), traverses this range of hills on the S.Side of Hval Fiord for some miles – appearing here & there, where its side is disclosed, like a perpendicular wall. About 5 miles from Brautar-holt this vein may be examined to advantage by ascending the course of a stream, which runs through a deep cleft in the rocks. Here the vein is cut transversely & each of the surfaces is exposed to view. Numerous veins of Jasper appear in the vicinity of this great vein, of which F8 are specimens. – There are other veins also composed of a sort of trap, the sides of which exhibit appearances similar to specimens C1,2,&3 from Viidoe. A specimen from this vein I gave to Sir G.Mackenzie.

In the hill behind Houls we found numerous fragments of pitchstone (F9) – which appeared to come from a bed of this mineral, traversing the hill horizontally above 100 feet from its summit. – The lower part of this hill is likewise covered with fragments, of which F10 are specimens – Between Houls & Hvamr, a good deal of rock occurs, exhibiting a sort of transition from greenstone to pitchstone (F11) – also some columnar greenstone near the shore –

tolerably fertile though swampy & containing many habitations. The mountains on each side rose abruptly to a great height, & many of them, even at this time of the year exposed a surface covered entirely with snow. The evening was clouded and gloomy, & we suffered considerably from cold, while in this part of our road. – Leaving the defile in the mountains, we came upon an open plain, so completely swampy that it was with the utmost difficulty we could proceed upon our horses, adroit as these animals are in Iceland in overcoming difficulties of this nature. Our luggage horses & guides we had left behind – but we fortunately encountered a peasant on horseback, who officiated as our guide, though without any means of mutual intercourse or communication – Our projected quarters for the night were at Houls[1] – a farmer's house on a small creek which runs southwards from the Hval Fiord – At the upper extremity of this creek, a river[2] rapidly pours down its waters, which were at this time so much swelled by the rains, that we found it necessary to cross the creek, where about 1/4 of a mile in width. The tide being low, we accomplished this without any great inconvenience – passing near to, but without disturbing it, a large eagle – sitting on a rock about half way across the water – The luggage horses did not arrive till 11 o'clock – much fatigued by the badness of the road.

The farm house & its inhabitants at Houls we found to be in every respect more comfortable than we had before seen them in Iceland – The farmer, M[r] Gudmunson,[3] has indeed an office which raises him somewhat above the common class – He is the *Hreppstiore*,[4] or police officer of the parish – his duties in this situation being the preservation of order & decent conduct among the inhabitants – attention to the state of the poor &c. – He has a pretty good farm;[5] a neat good looking woman for his wife,[6] and as

[1] Neðri-Háls í Kjós. One of a cluster of four similarly named farms at the foot of western Reynivallaháls.   [2] Laxá í Kjós.   [3] Loptur Guðmundsson (1776–1858).

[4] Hreppstjóri. Holland in Mackenzie, 1812, p. 290 writes of 'the Hreppstiorà, whose jurisdiction is a parochial one, and whose duty is particularly to attend to the condition and maintenance of the poor, and to assist the proceedings of the Sysselman in all that relates to the preservation of public order'.

[5] His farm keeps 9 or 10 cows, two or three horses, & more than 100 sheep – The rent 27 rix dollars a year – Under this, however, is included a share in the profits of the adjoining river, which is noted for its salmon – a *Lax river*, as it is termed in Iceland. Each farmer, whose lands come down to the river, is allowed by his terms with the landlord to fish for salmon in the part of the stream opposite to him – The fish are caught by making dams at the side of the stream below the falls – The number caught suffices for little more than their own use. – The garden connected with Mr Gudmundson's farm at Houls is the neatest we have seen in Iceland. When we were at Houls, they were employed in planting out cabbages, which is done here when the plants are very young.

[6] Carítas Oddsdóttir (b. 1777).

comfortable a house as the mode of construction will well admit of. Accommodation for the night was furnished us in one of the rooms, where there was just sufficient space for our reception.

Sunday 17th Salmon & boiled milk were provided for our breakfast this morning by the good people of the house. We presented Mrs Gudmundson with a small packet containing thread, needles, scissors &c; these highly gratified & pleased her – Recommencing our journey, under the escort of Mr G., we regained the shores of Hval Fiord, & proceeded along the foot of the mountains to a place called *Hvamr*,[1] three miles from Houls. The upper reach of the Hval Fiord, varied by several islands & promontories, presents a landscape, which if a little softened by the addition of more verdure on the banks, & the foliage of a few trees, would really have much claim to the epithet of beautiful.[2] At Hvamr we decided upon crossing to Saurbar,[3] on the opposite side of the Fiord, leaving our horses to perform their journey round its upper extremity – We passed over in a boat, rowed by two Icelanders – not without some little risk from the smallness of the vehicle, & the swell upon the water – which is here about 3 miles across – At Saurbar which is situated on a gently rising ground on the northern side of the Fiord, we found a very neat church, with a comfortable house adjoining it – belonging to the minister Mr Hialtalin[4] – By this good man we were received with infinite kindness & hospitality – He is a man apparently about 60, with a pleasing countenance, good manners, & much general information – He has been the minister at Saurbar for 24 years,[5] – with 30 dollars per ann., his house free of rent, & as much land as suffices to keep a pretty good stock of cattle & sheep – The interior of his habitation is tolerably comfortable, though by no means equal in convenience or cleanliness to the lowest class of English farm houses – The sitting room contains a stove, (an article of furniture not common in the country habitations in Iceland) and is furnished with a small library, containing probably about 100 books.[6]

[1] Hvammur.

[2] The word is not used idly by Holland. Its meaning embraces qualities of variety, charm, repose, softness and proportion. The idea of 'the beautiful' was much analysed in the eighteenth-century, most influentially by Edmund Burke, *A philosophical enquiry into the origin of our ideas of the sublime and the beautiful* (1757).   [3] Saurbær.

[4] Jón Oddsson Hjaltalín (1749–1835). Priest at Saurbær 1786–1811.

[5] From May 1786.

[6] Jón Hjaltalín had a long established reputation as a prolific composer and collector of ballads, short verses, hymns and prayers, many of which were anthologised. Extant autograph manuscripts of Jón's reveal a taste for European literature in translation, as well as for native saga and verse. See Lbs MSS 848 4to, 984 4to, 1754 8vo. Such interests were doubtless fully reflected in the '100 books'.

The minister's wife[1] appears to be an active managing woman – It is his second matrimonial engagement. He has had 23 children, of whom 13 are now alive – One of his daughters[2] has married the Amptman Stephensen – another of them is wife to M[r] Gudmundson, our host of the preceding night.

The church at Saurbar[3] is superior in convenience, & neatness to most of the country churches in Iceland – It is calculated to hold about a hundred people. Having, with the permission of M[r] Hialtalin made our arrangements for passing the night *before the altar*, where there was ample room for fixing up our beds, we returned into his house to supper, & had some pleasant conversation with him relatively to the books in his library – the concerns & management of his parish &c. – In relation to the latter subject, he allowed me to take a copy of a couple of pages from his Parish Register – a very interesting book, in which he has made an annual & most minute record of every circumstance relating to every individual in his parish. (See opposite page)[4] This Register has been regularly continued since he entered upon his present situation. The translation which I have given was obtained through the medium of M[r] Hialtalin's Latin, & may be considered as correct. He shewed us also some other more general documents respecting the parish of Saurbar, from which it appears that out of a population of varying from 200 to 210, the average annual number of births is 7, of deaths 6 or 7 – of marriages the ratio is below 1. There are 15 married couple in the parish – Two illegitimate children only have been born in it, within the last 24 years. The extent of the parish is 16 English miles in length, by 10 in breadth – M[r] Hialtalin shewed us from his Library some curious manuscript books of Sagas[5] – executed with infinite labour, & neatness – Our supper consisted of a dish of fish, marked up with milk, & butter and of rice milk – both very excellent.

Monday 18th After a comfortable night within the walls of the church, we resumed our journey – taking the road down the western side of the

---

[1] Gróa Oddsdóttir (c1774–1834).

[2] Holland's mistake. The second wife of Stefán Stephensen (1767–1820), after the death of his first wife Marta María in 1805, was Guðrún Oddsdóttir, sister of Jón Hjaltalín's wife.

[3] Bright's sketch is printed in Mackenzie, 1812, p. 139.

[4] See Appendix D.

[5] Perhaps, for instance, *Laxdæla saga* (Lbs MS 979 4to, c1760–70), which has 'I.Hjaltalin' written at the foot of the final page (p. 154); or, if Holland is using 'saga' in a less exclusive sense, Lbs MS 1249 8vo (c1800), a compilation of *rímur*, folktales and Eddic poetry.

Hval Fiord, to Innreholme,[1] the residence of *Atatsrood Steffensen*, whom some time before we had promised to visit. The day's walk, which was one of 10 or 12 miles presented nothing very remarkable – We arrived at Innreholme at 5 o'clock – a large assemblage of buildings, situated near the shore,[2] on a plain interposed between the mountain of Akrafiall[3] and the sea – We were received with considerable form by the Atastrood, & his family – ushered into the best room of the house, – & had coffee, wine, biscuits & English cheese set before us – This was only the prelude to a more sumptuous entertainment – At 8 o'clock, a dinner was brought to the table of salmon, mutton & potatoes, sago jelly & cream, with very good port wine & London porter – While giving our appetites to all these good things, we were surprized by hearing musical sounds, of no mean excellence, coming from an apartment above – the first of such sounds, we had heard in Iceland, save & except only the miserable scraping of fiddles in the Reikiaviik ball-room. – Upon enquiry we found that the performers were the Atastrood's eldest son & daughter – the instrument was one entirely new to us. – It is called in Iceland *Lang-Spil*[P] – 4 Chords[4] strung upon a long wooden box, & played by an instrument resembling a fiddle-stick – The effect of the music is sufficiently pleasant, when heard from a distance; – the tunes played were principally Danish & Norwegian, with a few native Icelandic airs. This is not the only music in the family – The Atastrood himself performs on an organ which he brought with him from Copenhagen a few years ago – not indeed with much skill or taste, but still sufficiently well to furnish a little amusement to those around him.

The family at Innreholme consisted, as we found it on our arrival

---

[1] See Edward Dayes' picture in Steindór Steindórsson, *Íslandsleiðangur Stanleys 1789* (Reykjavík, 1979), plate 9, facing p. 32.

[2][fH] On the shore near Saurbær the rock of which F12 is a specimen, is met with, occurring apparently as a vein – About a mile further on, an amygdaloid rock appears, running into the sea – containing much rock crystal & calcareous spar. Near Indreholm, the mountains again assume the remarkable appearance, which we had observed on the opposite side of the Hval Fiord, exhibiting in a still more remarkable degree the appearance of steps or stairs, rising with a precipitous ascent to the height probably of 14 or 1500 feet –

On the shore west of Indreholm, a tuff appears, covered by an amygdaloid rock, from which are taken the specimens marked F13, containing cubic zeolite &c.

[3] Akrafjall.

[4] Mackenzie, 1812, p. 145 notes that there are three strings, as in the accompanying line drawing; also found with one or two strings. Unlike the *fiðla* ('fiddle') they have a finger board for altering the notes.

P. A *langspil*

there, of the Atastrood – his Lady or the Fru Stephensen; [1] two sons, one about 20, [2] the other 16 or 17 – a daughter, [3] whose title is *Frukin*, a degree higher than that of *Jung Frau*, a young lady of property, left under the cure of the Atastrood, *Jungfrau Gudrin* by name [4] – a little boy, [5] son of the Amtmand Steffensen & nephew of the Atastrood – and another youth about the same age, – a son [6] of the Amtmand Thoransen of the northern district – The head of this family, the Atastrood, *Counsellor of State in Denmark, & Chief Justice in Iceland* is a tall, tolerably good-looking man, not very brilliant in his understanding or acquirements, but nevertheless having a very exalted opinion of his own merits. His titles, his literary works, his house & his lands furnish an abundant theme of conversation to him, and are introduced on every convenient occasion. The books of different descriptions which he has written & published are not fewer than 20 in number. – moral, political, historical &c &c [7] – Nor is the *cacoethes scribendi* [8] yet in its wane – a work is at this time in the press on the *Polity of Iceland,* [9] which the Atastrood often alluded to with paternal fondness – Of his house & grounds he has certainly some reason by comparison to feel proud. The situation is peculiarly fine, under the brow of the precipitous mountain of Akrafiall & commanding in front a view of the entrance of the Hval Fiord, the Bay of Reikiaviik, & the distant mountains of the Guldbringe Syssel – The house is a building of considerable extent, & as elegant as Icelandic houses usually are. Two small gardens are connected with it, in which an

[1] Guðrún Vigfúsdóttir Scheving (1762–1832).

[2] There seems only to have been one son, Ólafur Magnússon (1791–1872).

[3] Þórunn Magnúsdóttir (1793–1876).

[4] Guðrún Egilsdóttir (1784–1863).   [5] Unidentified.

[6] It is not possible to identify which of Stefán's several sons Holland is alluding to.

[7] Listed by Holland in Mackenzie, 1812, pp. 325–6. See Halldór Hermannsson (1918), pp. 16–32.

[8] The passion (or itch) for writing. The phrase is from Juvenal, *Saturæ*, ed. C. H. Pearson and H. A. Strong (Oxford, 1892), p. 74, VII, l.52.

[9] Probably *Instrúx fyrir hreppstjórnar-menn á Íslandi* (Leirárgarðar, 1810). Prepared coincidentally in the wake of the Jörgensen insurrection in 1809, the work urges clarification and restructuring of administration in the countryside, drawing the attention of local law officers to changes in current statutory law. Material from this volume was incorporated in the more substantial *Hentúg handbók fyrir hvörn mann* (Leirárgarðar, 1812). See Gísli Ágúst Gunnlaugsson, *Fátækramál Reykjavíkur 1786–1907* (Reykjavík, 1982), pp. 19–20.

attempt is made to raise cabbages and potatoes; – with what degree of success the autumn will shew – The pasture around the house is very fine, but speedily degenerates into swamp on every side except towards the sea. The farm which the Atastrood holds in his own hands will keep about 25 cows, and 300 sheep – His property in the neighbourhood & in other parts of the island is very considerable.

The *Fru Steffensen* is a lady somewhat *en bon point*, with an amazingly ruddy complexion – As we had no means of conversing with her, except through an interpreter, it would be difficult to pronounce upon her character & qualities – The daughter is a tall, romping girl, who greatly entertained herself with the awkwardness of our attempts to speak the Icelandic language. Equally amused in the same way was the *Jungfrau Gudrin*, a lady somewhat inferior in beauty to the *Frukin*, but having the accomplishment of singing in a key, which might match the most shrill of the peacock tribe. The cleanliness of these young ladies cannot, consistently with truth, be praised very highly. The habit of frequent spitting was less disturbing to our sight than a certain complaint upon the hands, for which the aid of sulphur might advantageously be called in. The careless exposure of this, shewed of how little moment it was considered by themselves – In truth they were so well countenanced by those around them, that it was next to impossible any shame or restraint should exist.

The Atastrood has a very good library – We found a number of English books in it – novels, poetry, philosophy & history, with several Collections of detached pieces in poetry & prose. He has also some good classics and a valuable collection of Icelandic works of different dates. In another room above stairs, he shewed a smaller collection of books, belonging to the Icelandic Society,[1] of which he has at present the principal direction.

Tuesday 19th – We spent this day at Innreholme. In the morning, the tide being low, we walked over to a small island near the shore, belonging to the Atatsrood, & completely covered with Eider Ducks. The sight was even more surprizing here than it had been at Viidoe, from the very great number of these birds collected in one little spot. With the loose stones on the island, places had been constructed for the reception of their nests, every one of which was occupied. About 40 lbs of Eider down are annually procured from the island.

After dinner to day, we had the music of the organ, the lang-spil, the flute

[1] Hið íslenzka Landsuppfræðingarfélag (The Icelandic Society for National Enlightenment); later (1798) called *Islands Uppfræðingarstiptan*, and enjoying after 1800 Danish royal favour, with the title *Konungleg*.

& the voice. The Atatsrood appeared greatly satisfied with the applause we gave to his concert, and presented us with the music of several of the airs which had been performed.

Wednesday 20th. This morning we devoted to the ascent of the mountain Akrafiall[1] – an undertaking arduous & difficult both from the height &

[1]HH The mineralogical phenomena presented by the mountain of Akrafiall were equally unexpected and interesting. From the external appearance of the hill we had concluded that it was composed entirely of a series of beds of greenstone or basalt. In this surmise we found upon examination that we had greatly erred.

Ascending the mountain to the height of about 150 feet from its base, we found no exposed surface of rock, but were surprised to meet with numerous fragments or scoriæ, & of a rock much resembling the compact lava we had seen at Kriseviik & in other parts of the Guldbringe syssel. – The first distinct bed we met with was the amygdaloidal rock FA1 – Immediately above this lay a thin layer of FA2 – not more than a foot in thickness – To this succeeded a bed of the amygdaloid rock FA3. – FA4 next occurs – & to this succeed 8 or 10 beds of amygdaloid, with two or three of a rock having more of the character of greenstone, interposed. (FA5,6,& 7).FA7 is a specimen from the 11th bed. – Many of the beds of amygdaloid are much decomposed – Between most of the beds a thin layer appears of a substance, resembling sandstone in appearance – produced perhaps by the decomposition of the amygdaloid at this part – A vein of trap-tuff traverses several of the beds in a direction transverse to their longitudinal extent, the included fragments being principally amygdaloid.

When arrived at the 16th or 17th bed, reckoning from below, the appearances become very different. – The beds, of which FA8 & 9 are specimens occur at this place; & above them a thin bed of FA10, apparently forming a sort of jasper – immediately over which we found a *bed of Lava*, about 20 feet in thickness, the lower surface contiguous to the jasper, much scorified – FA11 are specimens of this surface of the Lava FA12 of the junction between the Jasper & the bed above – FA13 of the Lava about 6 feet above the lower surface of the bed. The structure & internal appearance of the Lava are greatly similar to those of the compact lava, which we found on the shore west of Kriseviik – Above this bed of Lava, a long series of beds of the same substance occur, much resembling it in all their characters – exhibiting the same scorified appearance on their lower surface, & having like it, a structure somewhat schistose or slaty. FA14 is a specimen of the lowest part of the 2^d bed of Lava. FA15 is a specimen from the middle of the 3^d – FA16.17.18.19.20 are specimens taken from different parts of the still higher beds – Having passed in our ascent 4 or 5 beds of Lava, we found an amygdaloidal rock; lying, however, in a situation which rendered it doubtful whether it was actually interposed between beds of the volcanic rock – Just above the amygdaloid, we noticed the very curious fact of a vein of complete clinkstone, of which FA21 is a specimen, intersecting the Lava, the surface of which latter rock was scorified on each side of the vein. F22 is taken from the surface of Lava adjoining the vein above. Sir G.M. has a specimen taken from a fragment, but apparently belonging to the outside of the vein, in which one surface exhibits an appearance resembling specimens C1 2 & 3 from Viidoe.

FA23 occurs in a thin bed or layer, between two beds of lava, near the summit of that part of the rock, where we ascended – Above all the beds of Lava, appearing externally at this place, we found the conglomerate or tuff rock, of which FA 24 are specimens – Arrived at the summit of the rock, by walking ½ a mile to the left of the place of ascent, we obtained a much greater elevation, & found 3 or 4 beds of Lava lying above the Conglomerate Rock – The specimens FA25 are from the highest bed in the Mountain of Akrafiall. The Conglomerate here greatly resembles what we had seen so extensively in the Guldbringe Syssel.

Descending the mountain a mile to the west of the place of ascent, we found all the beds of Lava, affording the same appearances, as have been already described. About ⅔ of the way down the descent of the precipice, the Amygdaloid Rock appears. Below a bed

steepness of the hill; but so very interesting from the mineralogical phenomena it enabled us to observe, as entirely to do away with all sense of danger or fatigue. Our progress to the summit, delayed as it was by the collection of specimens &c, occupied more than four hours. Arrived at the pinnacle of the mountain, and proud of the labours of the day, we erected a pile of stones on the edge of the precipice, in commemoration of our arrival there – a monument of vanity which the next storm would doubtless overwhelm – The descent of the mountain was even more difficult than our progress upwards – Not only the specimen bags, but every pocket being filled with specimens, each step was made with fear & trembling – nor did we any of us escape the trivial misfortunes of bruises, sprains &c. – Arrived again at Innreholme, we greatly surprized the Atastrood by the intelligence that Lava existed so near to the confines of his domain. He had previously been totally ignorant of the fact. – (For the mineralogy of Akrafiall, see page 88 [Ed: note 1HH, page 158]) –

---

of this, from which FA 26 is taken, appears a bed of the Conglomerate or tuff FA 27, containing apparently no fragments or lava or scoriæ like FA 24, but including only fragments of amygdaloid – The bed is about 12 or 15 feet in thickness. Below it the amygdaloid FA 28 occurs, & beneath this again a bed of FA 29, of great thickness, & forming the slope of the lower part of the hill.

Connecting the appearances on the mountain with those previously observed on the shore at Innreholm (see page 87 [Ed: see note 2HH, p. 155]) it may be remarked that the tuff or conglomerate, which there lies below the amygdaloid, is considerably similar to that represented by specimen F27. The amygdaloid itself greatly resembles those occurring in the lower beds on the ascent of the mountain.

The height of Akrafiall above the sea (which approaches within a mile of its base) is probably not less than 2000 feet (2050 is the exact height). The face of the mountain presents at the point of greatest elevation, from 35 to 40 distinct beds, receding progressively backwards from the perpendicular, so as to afford the appearance of a flight of stairs. – Observed from the foot of the mountain, no distinction appears between the beds of lava & those of amygdaloid. – their thickness varies from 15 to about 20 feet. The bed of Conglomerate FA 24 may probably be about 20 feet in thickness. The number of beds of Lava at the highest part of the rock, may be reckoned at from 20 to 25 –

The discovery we made of this singular structure of Akrafiall, led us to the belief that the mountain of Esian, & those on the opposite side of Hval Fiord, similar in general appearance, are to a certain extent similarly composed. This supposition is confered [?] by the circumstance of our having discovered scoriæ on the side of the hills between Brautarholt & Houls. It is possible, had we ascended still higher, that we might have found beds of lava, as on the corresponding opposite mountain of Akrafiall.

As respects theory, the points most important in the structure of Akrafiall appear to be – the occurrence of beds of lava in this lofty & almost insulated situation – the appearance of the conglomerate intervening between beds of Lava – the vein of Clinkstone traversing these beds – & the appearance in two or three places of an amygdaloid rock having Lava both above & below it – if indeed our observations were accurate as to this latter point.

The afternoon of the day was fully occupied in the package of our various specimens. Those already collected on our journey sufficed to fill a large cask, which we committed to the care of the Atastrood to be sent to Reikiaviik – In the evening, by the invitation of the Atastrood, we made a survey of the whole of his habitation; from the display of the wonders of which he appeared to derive very great delight. Its interior very greatly resembles that of a large English farm-house – more barren, however, in articles of furniture, and very deficient in cleanliness & comfort. The kitchen in all Icelandic houses is peculiarly remarkable for its want of cooking & other utensils; and bespeaks no small ingenuity in the cooks of the country, who can manufacture good dinners with instruments so meagre & miserable – In our circuit of the house, we did not omit even the bed rooms of the ladies, by whom we were attended in this part of our progress – A servant maid in England would have cast a contemptuous sneer, upon the apartment, the bed, & bed-apparel of the *Frukin* & *Jungfru Gudrun*, and, in truth, not without some show of reason – While examining this room, the ladies displayed to us some little articles of their own manufacture, purses, bags &c, which we of course were obliged to applaud in very exalted terms.

After our sincerity had been sufficiently taxed by their various exhibitions, we were at length dismissed from the task of praise. Music & supper concluded the evening; – the latter, like all the other meals here, served upon the tables by the ladies of the family; who waited in a sort of anti-room during the meal, looking in occasionally at the door, & amusing themselves with various comments upon us; – so, at least, we judged from external appearances.

Thursday 21st. On the afternoon of this day we recommenced our journey,[Q] attended by the Atastrood, & the son[1] of the Amptman Steffensen. Our first stage was to Leira,[2] about 8 miles from Innreholm – formerly the residence of the Atastrood himself – at present occupied by M[r] Scheving,[3] Sysselman of Borgar-fiord, who married a sister[4] of the Atastrood – Our road for 4 miles led us back upon the same track which we had pursued from Saurbar to Innreholm.[5] Here turning to the left, we crossed a part of a widely extended plain, intervening between

[1] Unidentified.
[2] Leirá stands next to the site of the printing house at Leirárgarðar.
[3] Jónas Vigfússon Scheving (1770–1831), moved to Leirá 1803, and had served as *sýslumaður* since 1802.
[4] Ragnheiður Ólafsdóttir (1774–1826).
[5] Another of Holland's spellings for Innrihólmur.

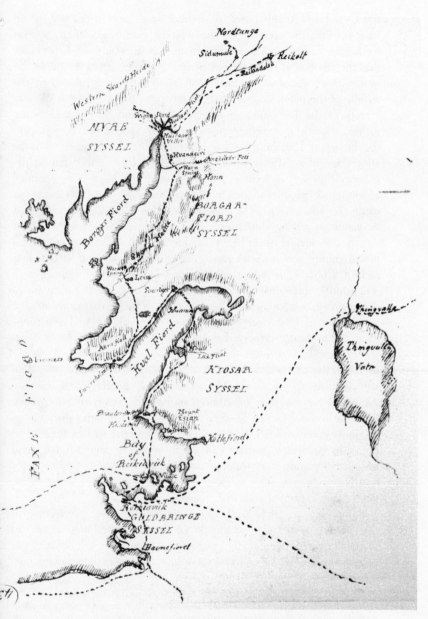

Q. Route from Reykjavík to Hvítárvellir

the Hval Fiord at this point, & another small arm of the sea, which runs up into the country on the western side of Akrafiall. Several fresh water lakes appear on this plain – & it would seem probable that the sea has at some former period extended across it, giving the mountain of Akrafiall an insular situation – Leira is placed in the middle of the plain, on one of the driest parts of its extent. It consists merely of the habitation of the Sysselman, and of a church – the former considerably resembling in general appearance & structure the house at Inderholm – the latter neat & respectable, with the appendage of a gallery, which we had not before seen in any of the country churches in Iceland. The land about the place is in tolerable condition & produces grass of good quality – The farm keeps 20 cattle & 200 sheep. The foxes have this year committed great devastations among the latter – The Sysselman Scheving, who met us on our arrival is a heavy, awkward, red haired man, with a physiognomy which shews just sense enough to prevent the running against a post – his lady a tall & somewhat handsome woman, with much more shrewdness of countenance – dressed in the costume of the country, excepting the *head-piece* for which was substituted a simple cap of blue cloth with a tassel from the top – The sitting-room in the house displayed much more of decoration than is usual in Iceland. The cornices formed of wood coloured red & neatly carved – the chairs covered with a sort of tapestry &c &c – Coffee was handed to us soon after our arrival, & this was speedily succeeded by a supper of salmon, mutton, & a sort of jelly, made from the Iceland Lichen & eaten with cream – The latter dish was of the most excellent kind. It is made by steeping the Lichen for several hours in successive portions of warm water to take off the acrid taste; then cutting it as small as possible, & afterwards boiling it for two hours in milk. This is eaten either warm & cold – when in the latter state, it formed a sort of mucilaginous jelly.

Before supper, Sir G.Mackenzie observed in a causeway leading to the house, a singular fragment of stone, resembling much an incrustation, & containing numerous vegetable impressions & petrefactions – Upon enquiry we found that there is a hot spring[1]

[1]HH We found the temperature of one of the springs to be 134° – the other 138°. The specimens F14 are from the incrustation which is forming on the rock, immediately below the springs. This rock is greenstone, which appears elsewhere above the surface in various parts of the plain – F15 are specimens of the incrustation, taken from the large bed of similar fragments, which lies at a short distance from the springs. This bed of fragments extends over 80 or 100 yards of surface, with a breadth of 15 or 20 yards.

near Leira, in the vicinity of which we were told that a large assemblage of these stones appear – After supper, we set off by the light of an Icelandic midnight, to visit this spring, under the guidance of the Atatsrood – We found it on an open part of the plain about a mile to the NW of Leira. The hot water issues in small quantity from two holes in the rock, & runs down to a stream which flows just below. A considerable cavity in the rock close to one of the springs, through which the hot water runs, has been used as a bath.[1] About a hundred years ago, a magistrate of the district suddenly died,[2] while bathing in this place. We found an incrustation in a state of incipient formation on the rock below the springs – A hundred yards further to the NW, a large bed appeared of fragments exactly resembling that we had found at Leira, evidently the incrustations derived from some spring or springs formerly existing on this spot. No other vestige, however, of such springs is to be seen at the present period – On our way back to Leira, we observed another similar assemblage of fragments, about ½ a mile from the Sysselman's house –

This walk was finished exactly at 12 o'clock at night, on the 21st of June – Though the sky was covered with thick & lowering clouds, the light was sufficient for the perusal of the smallest type without difficulty or inconvenience.

Friday 22[d] We resumed our journey at 12 o'clock this morning, still accompanied by the Atatsrood & his nephew, & with the addition to our party for a few miles of the Sysselman Scheving – Not much splendour was connected with the horse equipage either of the *Lord Chief Justice of Iceland,* or of his brother in law, the Sysselman. Mounted on two sorry poneys – their legs almost coming into contact with the ground – the Sysselman with one stirrup only, & a bridle of the most strange & uncouth manufacture, they afforded figures to which the pencil of Hogarth or Wilkie[3] alone could have done justice. The whole cavalcade, in truth, might well have served for a humorous representation of the modes & accoutrements of Icelandic travelling.

[1] Probably Leirárlaug.
[2] Árni Oddsson, drowned March 1665. See Jón Helgason, *Borgarfjarðarsýsla sunnan Skarðsheiðar. FÍÁ* (1950), pp. 86–7.
[3] William Hogarth (1697–1764); David Wilkie (1785–1841). Wilkie had by 1810 yet to achieve Hogarth's celebrity, but had been elected an Associate of the Royal Academy in 1809 and enjoyed considerable popularity in society circles.

At the distance of a few hundred yards from the Sysselman's House, we stopped some time to examine the interior of the Leira printing office[1] – the only establishment of this nature in the whole island. Formerly there were two – one at Hrappsey – the other at Hoolum[2] – These were given up – and the office at Leira established in the year 1794. The establishment is at present supported by the Icelandic Society (for an account of which see Vol.2[d]).[3] Two men are employed in the office, and have a pretty constant occupation – They have eight founts of types – 6 of the German or Gothic, 2 of the Roman character – Also a few types of the Greek character – The press is constructed much in the usual way – the printer's ink is made on the spot of lamp black, & oil. The building is altogether a miserable one – situated on a piece of swampy ground, & greatly inferior in appearance to an English cottage. It has latterly been much injured by the winter floods, & it is now in projection to construct a new building on the same spot – the execution of which is only delayed from the scarcity of timber in Iceland during the period of war – In one room of the Printing office, are kept some of the books which have been published by the Society – These are sold on the spot by M[r] Schagfiord,[4] the head-printer. We purchased a few of them – among others, as a literary curiosity, a translation of Pope's Essay on Man into Icelandic verse[5] – They are at present engaged here in printing a work of the Atastrood's on the Polity of Iceland.[6]

Arrived at the northern extremity of the great plain on which Leira is situated, we began the ascent of the Skards-Heide[7] – a lofty range of mountains separating this plain from the still more

[1] On printing at Leirárgarðar, see Benedikt Benedikz, *Iceland* (Amsterdam, 1969), in the series, 'The Spread of Printing' (Colin Clair, ed.).

[2] Hólar in Hjaltadalur.

[3] No account in Journal MS. The society is discussed briefly by Holland in Mackenzie, 1812, pp. 325–35.

[4] Guðmundur Jónsson Schagfiord (1758–1844), who worked at Leirárgarðar 1795–1815.

[5] See above, note 4, p. 116.

[6] See above, note 9, p. 156.

[7] Skarðsheiði. HH: The many fragments of scoriæ & of compact lava which we observed in different parts of the Skards-heide clearly prove that beds of lava, similar doubtless to those of Akra-fiall, exist in these mountains. In various places, some of very great elevation, we noticed large collections of white stones, of which F16 and 18 are specimens, scattered over the surface. F18 is from the vicinity of the hot springs, which we visited in our descent on the northern side of the Skards-heide – Much of a

extensive district of flat country along the banks of the Hvitaar Fliot,[1] & the shores of the Borgar Fiord. In its progress across this lofty ridge, the road attains an elevation of probably not less than 1000 feet above the sea. The mountains on each side of the pass rise to a much greater height – some of them were almost entirely covered with snow. In this part of our journey we observed (but were less surprized by it now than we had been a day or two before at Akrafiall) the evidences of volcanic phenomena having occurred among these mountains – Arrived at the highest point which the road attains in crossing the ridge, we enjoyed a singular and widely extended view of the great plain of the Borgar Fiord, the river Hvitaar & several other streams making their way through it in circuitous courses, & entering the arm of the sea, properly called the Borgar Fiord, which extends itself far up into the country – On the right hand, in descending from the mountains, we observed and were interested by a very singular mountain, called *Horn*[2] – of very great height, & possessing a more perfect pyramidal form than could have been conceived to belong to any mass of such vast size, & formed by the operations of nature alone – Its resemblance to an artificial pyramid was rendered still more striking by the perfect & regular structure of the beds composing the mountain; these appear externally, shortening by steps to the summit of the cone. An examination of these upper beds (were it possible,) would probably shew that they, in correspondence with Akrafiall, & other mountains in this district, are of volcanic formation – On the same side of our road, & at the distance of a few miles, we saw the lake of *Skoradals*

---

green-coloured substance also appeared on these mountains – sometimes in small fragments, sometimes in a decomposed state, as clay or earth. It would appear to be the same formation as the specimen F4 from Mount Esian – the base of these mountains belongs to the trap formation, under the varieties of basalt, greenstone, clinkstone & amygdaloid. Some fragments of pitchstone occurred to our notice on the ascent of the hill – While descending on the northern side, we found on an amygdaloid rock, the specimens of chalcedony &c marked F17.

The appearance of the mountain composing the Eastern Skards Heide is peculiarly remarkable for the number and distinctness of the beds presented to the eye, & for the regularity of the *trap* or *stair form* which these beds assume.

[1] Hvítá.

[2] Horn; known as Skessuhorn, apparently after a giantess (*skessa*) who lay in wait to prey on travellers. MS indistinct but may read 'Honn'; Mackenzie, 1812, p. 152 spells it 'Honn', no doubt copying direct from Holland's journal.

Vatn,[1] extending several miles between the mountains to the eastward – When nearly arrived at the level of the plain, we turned a little aside from the road, to see some warm springs, which gush out from several places on the side of the hill – At the one we first saw, the water issues out in a considerable stream – the temperature, as tried just below the place of egress, is 100° of Fah[t] – In another place, where the thermometer was plunged into the cavity whence the water rises, the temperature shewn was 132°. We did not observe any incrustation in the vicinity of these springs – Just below them a considerable river pursues its course through the valley, after having descended from the rocks above by a series of very fine cascades – These falls are called in the Icelandic, *Anakilsdr-Foss*[2] – the latter word signifying a fall of water in this language. While crossing this river, which was rendered somewhat difficult by its depth & rapidity of current, we observed some wild ducks, of a species we had not before seen – They are called in Iceland *Straumönd*[3] – a very handsome bird, seen on many of the streams, particularly those which are most rapid, during the summer, but going out to sea in the winter season.

The termination of this days journey[4] was at *Hvanneiri,*[5] the residence of the Amtmand Stephensen, brother of the Atastrood, & governor of the Vesterland, or Western district.[6] The latter part of the way was rendered extremely difficult, by the depth of the bogs we traversed, & the number of small streams it was necessary to cross – In some places the horses sunk so deep into the swamp, that it was with much labour they extricated themselves – in other places it was absolutely necessary to dismount before we could proceed forwards – The house at Hvanneiri & the church there, resemble in all respects the common description of such buildings in Iceland. The *Amtmand* himself we did not find at home, being with his eldest son on a journey into Snæfields Syssel. His

[1] Skorradalsvatn.

[2] Andakílsárfossar.

[3] Harlequin Duck, *Cosmonetta histrionica* (Linn.)

[4][HH] In our way from Leira to Hvanneiri we overtook several cavalcades of horses & men, returning from the coast into the interior of the country, loaded with fish – their stock for the winters consumption – In some of these parties there were as many as 10 or 12 horses, each with his respective burthen.

[5] Hvanneyri.

[6] Stefán Ólafsson Stephensen's term of office extended from 1806 until his death in 1820.

wife,[1] however, & eldest daughter[2] were at Hvanneiri, & received us very hospitably. The former (a second marriage) is the daughter of a country priest.[3] The evening being very wet, we remained within doors, amusing ourselves with some English books which we found in the Amtmand's library – A supper of salmon & veal was served up to us in the accustomed Icelandic manner – the females of the family, (as is always the case when strangers are present & any degree of form is thought necessary) not appearing at the table – Borgar Fiord is particularly noted for its salmon – the rivers which run through the district being admirably well adapted to this fish – This, however, is not the only circumstance from which it derives celebrity. The Atastrood, whose mouth was ever open in its praises, (& in the praise of Inderholm beyond all other places in this favoured land) gave us a long catalogue of perfections. The *pastures of Borgar-fiord* are the best in Iceland – the *cattle & sheep* are of the finest kind – the *salmon* are pre-eminent – the *fishing off the coast* is very good – & finally there is a great abundance of Eider Ducks & *Seals*. To these remarkable qualities we added from our own observation, that of containing a prodigious number of *wild swans*[4] – Standing at the door of Amtmand Stephensen's house we counted on the marshy plain reaching down to the shore, not fewer than 40 of these birds – & flocks still larger are very frequently seen in this place.

Saturday 23ᵈ. – A travelling breakfast in Iceland is almost a dinner in quantity & quality of food – A dish of salmon was first brought to the table, accompanied by *wild sorrell*,[5] dressed much in the same way as *Spinach* – To this succeeded a plate covered with small cakes, made of flour, butter, eggs & sugar; & coffee more excellent than any we had before seen in Iceland. – The breakfast was finished by Sago Jelly, and a large tureen of the richest cream – Rye-bread & American biscuits were produced as appendages to the meal – There was especial reason to expect excellence of cookery in this house, – as the former wife of the Amtmand was the author of a Cookery-book in the Icelandic language[6]

---

[1] Guðrún Oddsdóttir (1780–1838).

[2] Sigríður Stefánsdóttir (1792–1827), married Ólafur, only son of Magnús Stephensen.

[3] Oddur Þorvarðsson (1744–11804); priest at Reynivellir from 1779. MS erasure reads 'Mʳ Hialtalin of Saurbar'.

[4] Whooper swan, *Cygnus musicus* (Beckst.); Mod.Ice. *Álft*.

[5] Perhaps Mod.Ice. *Túnsura*, or *Heimula*; *Rumex acetosa*, or *Rumex domesticus* (Linn.).

[6] See above, note 4, p. 91.

– This valuable production we each purchased a copy of at the Leira printing office.

Taking leave of our kind entertainers with the accustomed form of salutation, we proceeded across a dismal tract of swampy ground to *Hvitaar-Vellir*,[1][R] where there is a ferry over the river Hvitaar[2] – The only mode of getting the horses across this stream which is broad, deep, & rapid, is by swimming them after the boat – While this process was going on, we went to the house of a Clergyman,[3] who lives near the Ferry – the *Provost*, as he is termed, or Superintendant of the churches in the Borgar-fiord Syssel – Here coffee was handed to us – Previously to crossing the river we made our adieus to the *Atastrood*, whose guidance of our travels here ceased – We certainly were indebted to him for an abundance of attention, civility & kindness – and by his foibles we were very little disturbed. – After having passed the Hvitaar, we proceeded on foot for about a mile to another branch of the river, which it was necessary to cross – the ferry boat being rowed up the stream to meet us here. The guides & horses with considerable difficulty forded the river a short distance below – where its breadth was about 150 yards – The remainder of our day's journey, though short, was rendered tedious & uncomfortable by the occurrence of a heavy rain, & by the nature of the country over which we passed – The whole of the extensive flat or valley of the Borgar-fiord, celebrated as one of the finest pasture districts in Iceland, may not improperly, from our own experience of it, be termed a vast morass – such a tract as in England it would be deemed prudent to make a circuit of 40 miles for the sole purpose of avoiding. Across these bogs a track of path is rarely to be seen – Every thing is left to the discretion of the guide, who selects the route which seems to him the most secure – The horses likewise are admirably well instructed in the art of crossing a tract of country of this kind – They manage their feet with the utmost adroitness, placing them wherever it is possible, upon the little spots of elevated ground, which afford the firmest footing; and recovering themselves speedily, when sinking down to any considerable depth. The termination of our days journey was at *Svigna Skard*,[4] where we took up our abode in the house

---

[1] Hvítárvellir.

[2][HH] From an amygdaloid rock on the western bank of the river at *Hvitaar Vellir*, were taken the specimens F19.

[3] Mackenzie, 1812, p. 155 identifies 'Arnar Jonson'. Arnór Jónsson (1772–1853) was provost in Borgarfjarðarsýsla 1807–11.

[4] Svignaskarð.

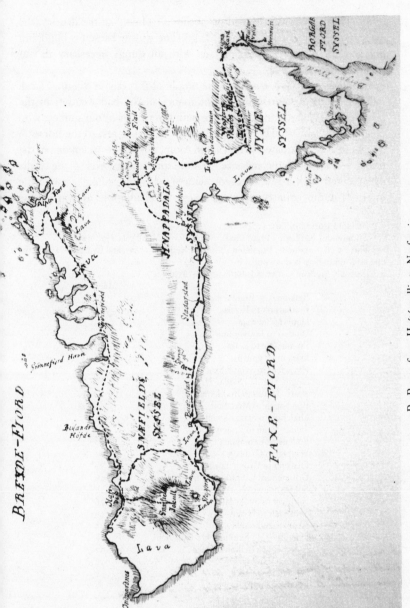

R. Route from Hvítárvellir to Narfeyri

of an elderly woman,[1] the widow of the Sysselman[2] of the district (the *Myre Syssel*) who died about a year ago. The widow herself is blind, but her son[3] & daughter[4] provided us with all things necessary to our accommodation.

Sunday.June 24th.[5] We remained the whole of this day at Svigna-Skard, induced so to do, partly by a continuance of the bad weather of the preceding day, partly in compliance with the wishes of our guides; who pleaded the Sabbath day, & the necessity of giving rest to the horses – We were accommodated with a small room, the only wooden one in the house – just of sufficient size to hold our three beds – the walls ornamented with a few tattered pictures – In proceeding towards the interior of the country more neatness & cleanliness appear in the

[1] Halldóra Þorsteinsdóttir (1748–1821).
[2] Guðmundur Ketilsson (1746–1809), *sýslumaður* in Mýrasýsla 1778–1806.
[3] There were three sons: Þorsteinn (b. 1783), Ketill (b. 1787), and Eggert (b. 1791): the one referred to here is unidentifiable.
[4] Probably Guðrún Guðmundsdóttir (1782–1850).
[5] HH

	Miles
Reikiaviik to Brautar-holt	10
Brautarholt to Houls	12
Houls to Saurbar	6
Saurbar to Innreholme	10
Innreholme to Leira	7
Leira to Hvanneiri	16
Hvanneiri to Svigna Skard	8
Svigna Skard to Stadar-Hraun	18
Stadar-Hraun to Roudemelr	10
Roudemelr to Miklaholt	8
Miklaholt to Stadar-sweit	13
Stadar-Sweit to Boden-stad	12
Bodenstad to Stappen	8
Stappen to Olafsvig	14
Olafsvig to Grönnefiord	16
Grönnefiord to Stikkesholm	26
Stikkesholm to Narfeyre	16
Narfeyre to Snoksdalr	26
Snoksdalr to Hvam	20
Hvam to Sidumula	8
Sidumule [MS Sidulume] to Hvanneiri	18
Hvanneiri to Reikolt & back	32
Hvanneiri to Leira	16
Leira to Innreholm	7
Innreholm to Reikiaviik by water	12
	349
Excursion to Snæfield's Jokull	16
Total	365

domestic habits of the people. Fish is here an article of greater scarcity, & the offences to the sight & smell which are always found in habitations where this is the principal food, decrease with its decreasing quantity. A dish was brought to us for dinner to day, which we had not before seen in Iceland, – made from cream curdled by sour whey, & the curds mashed up with fresh milk.[1]

Monday–June 25th – We rose this morning at 2 o'clock, & began our days travel at four, under the guidance of a peasant of the country, in addition to the two men who were with us. Our route lay over the *Western Skard's Heide*,[2] an elevated chain of hills, forming the western boundary of the great valley of the Hvitaá – Had it not been that the morning was gloomy & a thick sleet falling upon us, we might have derived considerable pleasure from the objects which presented themselves in our ascent towards the mountains. For three or four miles we skirted along the banks of a river, the Glufurá,[3] which pursued a precipitous course between high rocky cliffs, fringed with birch-wood. By this term, *trees* are not [to] be understood – these being wholly unknown in Iceland[4] – but a small stunted shrub, which rarely rises more than 3 or 4 feet from the ground, spreading itself, however, to a considerable extent along the surface. Even these petty attempts at forest scenery are very rare – The wood, (if such it may be called) which we now traversed, is said to be one of the most extensive in the island. A portion of it is alloted to each farmer & inhabitant of the vicinity, whence they procure charcoal for their domestic consumption.

The route across the mountains was varied & interesting, though the characteristic features of the scenery were extreme desolation & solitariness – Several small lakes appeared in the hollows between the hills, – from which there issued large & rapid streams, forming numerous cataracts in their passage downwards towards the plain. In crossing these rivers we frequently encountered much difficulty from the strength of the current, which the horses were almost unable to

---

[1] *Skyr*, a thick-set yoghurt.
[2] Skarðsheiði vestri.   [3] Gljúfurá.
[4] Holland invariably draws attention to such trees as are to be found in Iceland. His sympathies are clearly with Dr. Johnson who noted that whilst 'plantation is the least expensive of all methods of improvement' (p. 7), those living in areas (such as Scotland or Iceland) governed by an 'unsettled state of life and the instability of property' (p. 7) might be forgiven for observing the long delay between seed and timber and for concluding that 'plantation is naturally the employment of a mind unburdened with care and vacant to futurity' (p. 116): Samuel Johnson, *A journey to the Western Islands of Scotland (1775)*, ed. J. D. Fleeman (Oxford, 1985).

stem. Six or seven miles from *Svigna-Skard*, when nearly at the summit of our ascent, we came somewhat unexpectedly to a tract of lava, occupying a hollow between the higher mountains, & stretching in a westerly direction towards the plain on the eastern side. This lava[1] presented all the singular characters of that we had seen at Havnefiord, & in other parts of the Guldbringe Syssel – a rude, irregular assemblage of rocky masses, broken into every possible variety of form – in some places giving an accurate resemblance of groupes of houses, fortifications, &c. – The external crust was every where completely scoriated, & occasionally disposed in a variety of singular contorted forms. We had no opportunity of ascertaining whence this lava is derived – whether it has been erupted from some single crater, or thrown up from various places in the surface which it now covers – Keeping our course along its edge for a few miles, with a gradual descent, we came to a small grassy plain, situated at the foot of the mountains. Here we remained an hour or two for the purpose of giving rest to the horses, occupying ourselves meanwhile in gathering specimens from the adjoining rocks – Resuming our journey, we entered upon an extreme district of flat country, intervening between the mountains and the sea, occupied partly by lava – in other places being merely a morass. The track led us under the mountains, by a small hamlet called Hraundalur,[2] to another wide valley[3] opening out from the north, likewise occupied by a bed of Lava, resembling that of

[1]HH The first part of the ascent of the Skards-Heide presented rocks of amygdaloid & greenstone, principally the former, which continued till we reached the Lava. At the commencement of the Lava, the amygdaloid borders upon it for some way. Half a mile further, a conglomerate rock appears, forming considerable heights above the road – resembling a good deal the conglomerate of Guldbringe Syssel, but containing, as far as we observed, no included scoriæ. The Lava itself is similar in all respects to that at Havnefiord. F20 is a specimen of it. The length of the bed, in the direction in which we pursued it, is probably 5 or 6 miles – its average breadth nor more than ¼ or half a mile – but there are other collateral beds connected with it, the extent & direction of which we had not the means of ascertaining. – At *Hraundalur*, where the lava passes down upon the flat plain which intervenes between the mountains & the sea, the road is carried below an amygdaloidal rock, which forms a precipice on the right hand two or three hundred feet in height – This amygdaloid is disposed in beds and contains much Zeolite. F21 is an average specimen of the rock. A mile beyond *Hraundalur*, a bed of *amygdaloidal porphyry* occurs near the summit of the rock. F22 are specimens from massive fragments of this porphyry, fallen into the plain below.

The bed of Lava at Stadar-Hraun resembles that in the Skards-heide. No continued extent of Compact Lava appears in either place.

2 miles from Stadar Hraun, there is a mineral spring, from which we procured two bottles of water.

[2] Syðri-Hraundalur. [3] Hítardalur.

Skards-heide. In the midst of this lava, we found our destined place of abode for the night, the minister's house & church of *Stadir-Hraun*,[1] situated in a small grassy spot, entirely environed by rugged volcanic rocks. The minister, Mr Olav,[2] we found getting upon his horse to accompany a short way the Sysselman of the Myre Syssel,[3] who had been with him at his house. He is a tall, awkward man dressed in a very uncouth way, & having little that belongs to the clerical manner or habit – He gave us, however, a cordial welcome, willingly allowed us to make the church our sleeping place, & with the assistance of his wife[4] furnished an excellent supper of boiled milk, upon the altar.

The evening was remarkably cold, the wind blowing over the mountains from the north – From the door of the church we had a fine view of Snæfield's Jokull, the size of the mountain now greatly enlarged from our nearer approach to it.

Tuesday June 26th. We passed a cold & uncomfortable night in the church at *Stadir-Hraun* – At 7 in the morning we resumed our journey, attended by the minister as a guide – Crossing by a rugged & circuitous track the bed of Lava[5] & fording a deep & rapid stream[6] which forms its westerly boundary, we came to the foot of a lofty range of hills, which limits the valley on this side – From [the] base of these hills, & on the side of Stadar-Hraun, there rises a very singular insulated hill,[7] evidently of volcanic formation. It is apparently about 300 feet in height, conical in its form, & the summit formed by a rugged, seemingly scorified, mass of rock, projected perpendicularly from the general mass of the hill – The sides are covered with small scoriæ or cinders – This hill is celebrated as having been in days of yore, the

---

[1] Staðarhraun.

[2] Holland's mistake. The priest at Staðarhraun 1797–1817 was Daníel Jónsson (1769–1842).

[3] Pétur Ottesen (1778–1866); *sýslumaður* in Mýrasýsla 1807–28.

[4] Vigdís Sigurðardóttir (1771–1830).

[5]HH Upon some parts of *Stadar-Hraun Lava*, the birch shrub, mentioned in p.101 [Ed: p. 171] grows with considerable luxuriance – affording an appearance in this situation not wholly unpicturesque.

[6] Hítará.

[7] Grettisbæli, west of Fagraskógarfjall. HH: At the foot of the conical hill described in the opposite page [MS I, 103], we [Ed: MS he] found several fragments of the volcanic rock, of which F23 is a specimen – Also a good deal of the conglomerate rock, which he had seen in the Guldbringe. – The range of mountains extending from this place to *Kolbenstadr-Fiall*, appear to be composed of amygdaloid, greenstone & basalt, arranged in a very extensive series of beds – From the hill which lies directly south of *Kolbenstadr Fiall*, we procured some fine specimens of zeolite. Several veins of greenstone intersect the beds of amygdaloid in this hill – *Kolbenstadr Fiall* is similarly composed.

retreat of an Icelandic warrior,[1] known in the songs of the country; who took refuge here from his enemies; & assisted by one friend[2] in the valley below, contrived to maintain himself in this situation for 2½ years. Thus the story goes – *Valeat quantum valere possit.*[3]

Skirting along the foot of the range of mountains, with a wide extent of flat country, a great part of it covered with Lava, stretching down towards the sea on the left hand, we came to the opening of another wide valley from the north.[4] – this, like all the others, we had lately seen, being completely occupied by Lava or swamp. At the place where the valley opens out to the plain, near the middle of it, there appears a small insulated eminence, so shaped as greatly to resemble a crater – surrounded on every side by Lava. Several other appearances of the same kind occur in different parts of the valley – the sides of these eminences being covered with red scoriæ – rendering it probable either that lava has actually flowed from these places, or that they must have been open to the emission of smoke, vapour & flame from the great heated mass below – This valley is bounded on the eastern side by a magnificent range of mountains – the highest of which, called *Kolbenstadr Fiall*,[5] probably about 2000 feet in height, presents a very extensive series of beds; many of them, particularly those near the summit, affording very perfect columnar appearances –

At 1 o'clock we stopped for a short time at *Kolbenstadr*,[6] a small hamlet, situated in the middle of the valley – Here, after partaking with us in a dinner of cold lamb & milk in the church, our good minister left us, & we proceeded under the guidance of a farmer,[7] who lives at *Kolbenstadr* – The remainder of our day's journey, which was about 4 miles lay principally across the Lava, which presented a surface even more rugged than any we had before seen. In some places it appears to have a level of 50 or 60 feet above the plain – Its termination, or rather origin up the country, we had not the means of observing. It occupied the lower part of the valley upwards, as far as the sight could reach – *Roudemelr*,[8] the place where we stopped for the night, is singularly

[1] Grettir Ásmundarson. See Guðni Jónsson (ed.) *Grettis saga Ásmundarsonar*, *Íslenzk fornrit*, VII (Reykjavík, 1936), pp. 186–98.

[2] Björn Hítdælakappi Arngeirsson.

[3] H. P. Jones (ed.) *Dictionary of foreign phrases and classical quotations* (Edinburgh, 1910), p. 121, cites, without attribution, *valeat quantum valere potest*, 'let it pass for what it is worth'.

[4] Hnappadalur.   [5] Kolbeinsstaðafjall.

[6] Kolbeinsstaðir.   [7] Perhaps Jón Jónsson (b. 1777).

[8] Rauðamelur. One of several place names in the area derived from the red (Mod.Ice. *rauður*) scoriæ noted by Holland.

situated below a large, and rugged mass of lava. It consists of a farm house, a few scattered cottages, and a church – the latter an edifice lately erected – of the same construction as all the country churches in Iceland; about 25 feet in length, 12 or 14 in width; a timber front, & the remainder of the building composed of stones & turf – In the space before the altar, at the upper end of the church, we as usual fixed our beds; converting the altar itself to the various purposes of a table. Over the altar[1] in all the Icelandic churches is placed a painting of the *last supper*. In some of the country churches we observed this to be used as a sort of drawing board, on which are inscribed with chalk the Psalms to be used on different days.

In the evening, we took a walk under the guidance of the farmer[2] at Roudemelr[3] to see a spring, which has acquired considerable celebrity in this part of Iceland; being called in the language of the country *Öl Kielda*,[4] or the *Ale Spring*. It is situated about 2 miles to the north of *Roudemelr*. We found two very small basons of water, through which a large quantity of air rushed upwards with considerable force. This air was evidently *carbonic acid gas*. With this gas the water of the wells is very strongly impregnated, giving a most agreeable sharpness & pungency to the taste; resembling soda water, after it has been exposed for a minute or two – Whether the water contains any other saline ingredients we were not at this time able to ascertain – we filled, however, a bottle with the water. – The temperature of the spring was 45°, precisely the same as that in an adjoining stream. – No water appeared to flow from it – or if at all, the quantity is very minute. No other remarkable appearance occurred in the vicinity of the spring –

On our return from the spring, we found in the church at *Roudemelr*, our destined place of abode for the night, a dirty squalid being, in the form of a man[5] who from his countenance, figure & habit, might well have passed in England for the meanest description of beggar – This, to our astonishment, we found to be an Icelandic divine upon his journey.

[1] 'Over the . . . different days' is written by Holland on the MS facing page [I, 104] and marked for inclusion in the main text at this point.

[2] Magnús Þorleifsson (1751–1818).

[3]HH The Lava immediately above *Roudemelr*, presented some little variety in its appearance, containing a greater abundance of the crystals which we had observed in the Lava at Havenefiord – F24 are specimens of this Lava. F25 is a specimen from a bed which occurs a few hundred yards from *Roudemelr*, terminating abruptly in a face or front, which presents the appearance of extremely regular columns, pentagonal in form. The diameter of the columns is about 3 feet. The longest are from 15 to 20 feet in height. The extent of this face of rock may be about ½ a mile.

[4] Ölkelda.   [5] Unidentified.

It was our immediate wish, though perhaps an uncharitable one, to remove him from the church, every bench of which he was bedewing with tobacco & spittle. This after some little time we effected. Still, however, he kept about the door, putting his face in occasionally, & observing very attentively all that we were doing. At length, to our great relief, the night removed him to his tent, which was pitched at a short distance from the church.

Wednesday 27th. This morning we breakfasted on a large dish of warm curds & whey brought us from the farm house.[1] – A young man,[2] a friend & former school fellow of Loptson made his appearance at Roudemelr. He had heard of Loptson's being in this part of the country, & came a distance of 15 miles to see him. We purchased three horses this morning – 2 at 8 dollars each – the third for seven dollars – One of them was procured from the minister who had infested us so much the preceding evening, and another exchanged with the same venerable personage – a balance of *½ a dollar* being made in his favour on the score of a swelling upon the back of our horse! – These important bargains arranged, we began our journey in a fog so thick, as wholly to prevent our seeing any thing of the country through which we passed[3] – Judging, however, from the immediate vicinity of the path, there was little reason to regret this circumstance. During the whole of our journey to Miklaholt, which was our resting place for the night, we were engaged in traversing either lava, plains covered with rude fragments of stone, or deep & almost impassable bogs. – The bogs which occurred during the greater part of the way, presented the most formidable obstacles. The farmer from *Roudemelr* came with us as our guide to Myklaholt; but in the last two miles of the way, was obliged to be himself guided by a young man, procured from a farm house on the road. Even with this double security, we had the utmost difficulty in

[1]HH We examined the interior of the farmer's house at *Roudemelr*, previously to leaving the place. It contains 4 apartments – the kitchen, with turf walls covered with seal skins, sheep skins &c – a long bed-room, containing 7 or 8 beds – one store room, in which are kept milk, Lichen, butter &c – another, occupied by the wool obtained from the sheep on the farm – The winters stock of Lichen for the family was two large hogsheads full – Since the war began, the practice has been introduced of grinding the Lichen by a hand mill, instead of cutting it. Treated in this way, it is said it does not require steeping previously to being used.

[2] Unidentified.

[3]HH The state of the weather prevented us from observing minutely the mineralogy of the country through which we passed to day – It appears to consist principally of amygdaloid & basalt. We crossed one bed of Lava, not far from Roudemelr, about ¼ of a mile in breadth, terminating somewhat abruptly near the place where the path crosses it.

surmounting the impediments before us. The horses frequently plunged so deeply into the swamp, as to render their situation one of considerable hazard; and every step before us was made with fear and trembling. No better idea can be given of the general difficulty of the road, than by stating that five hours were occupied in travelling 8 miles, the whole distance between Roudemelr & Myklaholt.

In the course of our ride, we passed three or four Icelandic tents, pitched in situations which afforded a little pasture for the horses – these were feeding around the tents. Some of these parties were going down to the coast for fish – others returning loaded with this article, so valuable in the domestic economy of the Icelander. Their stoppage was occasioned by the state of the weather; of this the Icelanders appear to be much more apprehensive, than might have been expected from their other habits of life.

At Myklaholt[1] we found a church of good size, well suited to our night's abode – also a minister's house where we received upon our arrival some pretty good coffee, and very great civility from the minister, Mr Bakman,[2] & his wife. The former is a tall, stout, well looking man, seemingly of great simplicity & goodness of heart. He has a small collection of books – His house contains one tolerably good room, with little more furniture, however, than a bed, two tables, a bench, & a few boxes. His fondness for snuff enabled us to gratify him much by the present of a small canister of this article. Equally pleased was his wife with a packet we gave her, containing scissors, needles, thread &c. They had never before seen Englishmen, & minutely enquired from Loptson respecting our manners & habits of life.

Thursday 28th. This morning we commenced our preparations for departure at an early hour – all the people of the place assembling as usual around us, and attending very closely to our several proceedings. Mr Bakman, the minister, prepared himself to attend us as a guide – his dress for this purpose greatly resembling that of an English sailor; with

[1]HH The parish of Myklaholt extends along the coast for nearly 20 miles, with an average breadth of 3 or 4 miles – The population is about 300, out of whom there are 40 married couple. There are two churches in the parish – one at Myklaholt, the other at Roudemelr – The salary is 48 dollars per annum, with a house & small extent of land, sufficient for the keep of 4 cows and about 80 sheep. From peculiar circumstances this salary is at present divided among three ministers. Mr Bakman, who does all the duty of the parish, has only 16 dollars a year with the house & land. He officiates every third sunday at Roudemelr.

[2] Jón Hallgrímsson Bachmann (1775–1845). Assistant priest to Magnús Sigurðsson (1769–1812); the third recipient of a priestly stipend was Magnús's father Sigurður Magnússon (1733–1816), 'pastor emeritus'. See *MÍ 1801: Vest.* (1979), p. 57.

a larger proportion of rags, however, than usually appertain to it – Our day's journey was to Stadar-sweit,[1] 12 miles from Myklaholt – The route presented nothing that was new or interesting. The first half hour was occupied in crossing the bog, by which Myklaholt is on every side surrounded. In doing this, we had the advantage for some part of the way, of what is called in Iceland *a bridge* – a number of loose fragments of stone thrown upon the bog in the line of direction required, where by continual passing they had been sunk deeply down, the hollow bbeing completely filled with water. – Having passed the bog, we pursued the course of a small river for some way, crossing & recrossing it many times – On this stream we saw a number of water-fowl – two of which Loptson shot – apparently the *teal*[2] & the *widgeon*.[3] Tracing the river to its mouth, & passing it there by a deep ford, we pursued the remainder of our way along the shore, crossing some sands of considerable extent – About 6 miles from Myklaholt, we left *Hnappadals Syssel*,[4] in which we had been travelling for the last three days, & entered *Snæfields Syssel*,[5] which forms the peninsula, terminating towards the west in the great mountain of *Snæfield's Jokull* – The lofty range of hills which run along the peninsula towards the Jokull, are distant between Myklaholt & Stadar-sweit about 3 miles from the southern shore. The intervening space is a flat plain, appearing to have been at some former period, the sands of the sea; now forming an excellent pasture, on which a great number of cattle & sheep are kept – *Stadar-sweit*[6] is situated on a small elevation in the middle of this plain; a small assemblage of buildings, comprizing the church, the minister's house, & one or two small cottages – the whole in a much more respectable stile than the villages to which we had lately been accustomed. The minister, Mr Jonsson,[7] is a

[1] Staðastaður.

[2] *Querquedula crecca* (Linn.); Mod.Ice. *Urtönd.*

[3] *Mareca penelope* (Linn.); Mod.Ice. *Rauðhöfðaönd.*

[4].Hnappadalssýsla.   [5] Snæfellsnessýsla.

[6]HH The parish of Stadar-Sveit has about the same extent as that at Myklaholt. It contains nearly 500 people, divided into 80 families. There are two churches in the parish – at Stadar-Sveit & at Buderstad. Service is performed at the latter only every fourth Sunday. The nominal salary of the minister, Mr Jonsson, is 100 rix-dollars per annum – Besides this he has his house free of rent, and a farm which keeps 12 cows & a considerable number of sheep.

[7] Guðmundur Jónsson (1763–1836), priest at Staðastaður 1797–1836.

HH (MS I, p. 110): When at Innreholm a packet arrived from Reikiaviik, containing a letter from Bishop Vidalin to Sir G.M, & inclosing two letters of introduction from the Bishop – one of them to Mr Jonsson of Stadar-sveit – The Bishop's letter to Sir G.M. ran thus.

'Dominum perillustrem nobilissimum Mackenzie saluere jubet Geirus Vidalinus –'

man of 50 or 60, a respectable looking person, clad in a gown of coarse blue cloth, with a cap of the same material. He is *provost* of the Snæfield's Syssel[1] – has a good salary, a good farm, & a good house. His wife[2] was formerly a servant of the old Governor at Viidoe – Our arrangements for sleeping were made as usual in the church – a pretty large building, constructed entirely of timber, & having, moreover, a gallery, which is not common in the Icelandic churches – Attached to the church floor, we found a massive *copper* ring, of curious manufacture, & having some characters inscribed upon it. We learnt upon enquiry that this had been obtained from a tumulus at Kirkiaholt,[3] on the road between Stadar-sweit & Budenstad.[4] The period of opening the tumulus we could not ascertain; but as the story stands, it was discovered that there was a large chest under it, in attempting to obtain which, the ring broke off – A superstitious alarm being connected with this accident, no further attempt was made to procure the chest – the ring was fixed on the church door at Stadar-Sweit. Sir G.Mackenzie purchased it from Mr Jonsson for three dollars.[5]

– 'Exigua hæc epistolia, ut data occasione, Præpositis Toparchiæ Borgarfiordensis et Snæfellsnæssensis tradantur enixè rogo, certe persuasus ut, me vel non rogante quidquid in eorum potestate situm est, lubentissimè serviant, ad iter tuum facilitandum. Arnorus Jonae tibi quæ in Borgarfiordo visu digna sunt indicabit Gudmundus verò Jonæ facilem tibi præbebit antiquum montis hujus incolam Dominum Bardum Snæfellsas, cuius sine auspiciis mons Snæfells Jokul vix ne vix quidem superari potest.'

To Right Honourable
Sir George Mackenzie *Bart*

[Geir Vídalín greets the most illustrious and noble Sir George Mackenzie. I strenuously ask that these letters should be given, when you get the chance, to the *sýslumenn* of Borgarfjörður and Snæfellsnes. I am certain that even without my asking, they will do whatever is in their power to facilitate your journey. Arnór Jónsson will show you the things which are worth seeing in Borgarfjörður, and Guðmundur Jónsson will give you a good introduction to the ancient inhabitant of this mountain – the deity of Snæfellsnes – without whose favour the mountain of Snæfellsjökull can scarcely – not even scarcely – be conquered].

[1] Holland apparently mistaken. Guðmundur Jónsson had been provost in Árnessýsla 1792–7; he did not become provost of Snæfellsnessýsla until 1816. See Sveinn Níelsson, *Prestatal og prófasta á Íslandi* (Second edition, Reykjavík, 1949–51), p. 157.

[2] Margrét Pálsdóttir (c1780–1821).

[3] Kirkjuhóll.   [4] Búðir.

[5] Einar Haukur Kristjánsson (ed.), *Lýsing Snæfellsnes frá löngufjörum að Ólafsvíkurenni*, *FÍÁ* (1982), p. 37 for a fuller account: two men sought to raise the chest; one jumped into the tumulus to lift it; his companions on the surface said that the chest would emerge 'if God allowed'; the man in the tumulus retorted that the chest would emerge 'whether or not God allowed it', whereupon the ring broke and the chest fell on the impious wretch and killed him. HH: We learnt afterwards from M[r] Jonson himself, that he did not attach much credit to the anecdote respecting the ring.

In the evening, Sir G.M. & Loptson shot two large birds, a species of red-throated *Diver*[1] on a marshy pool below the church. This was done with considerable difficulty – from the skill of the birds in diving. A prodigious number of *terns*[2] frequent this pool, from which their eggs are procured in great number.

A fine evening afforded us some magnificent views of Snæfield's Jokull, & the range of mountains occupying the middle of the peninsula. The hills immediately behind Stadar-Sweit, which are probably not less than 2000 feet in height, are peculiarly striking & picturesque in their forms, & the shades of the evening gave additional effect to the scene. The summits of these mountains are still almost entirely covered with snow – Snæfield's Jokull is thus cloathed for nearly ⅔ of its height.

Friday 29th – This morning was brought to us a breakfast of salmon trout, the eggs of the *tern*, and milk – a repast of much excellence – Previously to setting out, we were occupied for some time in arranging with the Provost for the purchase of certain books &c – He would willingly have made most of these things presents to us, had we allowed of it. After these matters were concluded, he disappeared for a time, & met us again so much altered in his dress as scarcely to allow the recognition of his person. He was now habited very much in the stile of an old English farmer of the better class, and his whole appearance had very much the same character – He had thus prepared himself to accompany us to *Buderstad*, our next stage; a road with which his offices as a minister have made him well acquainted. In the course of our day's journey, I had much conversation with him in Latin, & found him to be a man of good common sense, and very extensive information connected with the natural history, agriculture & statistics of his native island. He was formerly [3] a secretary to Bishop Finnæus[4] at Skalholt & well recollects to have seen Sir John Stanley[5] there, when on his journey to Hecla. He likewise retains some remembrance of Sir Joseph Banks, & the companions of his voyage to Iceland.

The road from Stadar-sweit to Buder-stad is upon the whole the best

[1] *Colymbus septentrionalis* (Linn.); Mod.Ice. *Lómur.* MS has 'red throated' written above 'species of Diver'.

[2] *Sterna macrura* (Naum.); Mod.Ice. *Kría* or *Perna.*

[3] Prior to his consecration as priest in June 1790.

[4] Hannes Finnsson (1739–96). Bishop of Skálholt from 1785. See Jón Helgason, *Hannes Finnsson* (Reykjavík, 1936).

[5] Stanley continued to correspond with Bishop Hannes after his return to England. See Lbs MS 30 fol.

we have seen in Iceland. It passes along the shore the greater part of the way, commanding in front a fine view of Snæfield's Jokull, & the hills about Stappen – The vast mass of the former mountain was seen to the greatest advantage from this low level, and gave additional incitement to the scheme we had previously formed of attempting its ascent – Half way between Stadar Sweit & Buderstad, we turned aside from the road, to examine a warm spring at Lysiehols,[1] under the mountains. The spring itself is called *Lysieholslaug*, or the *bath* of Lysiehols. – It considerably resembles that we had before seen at Leira; presenting a similar incrustation with many vegetable impressions in its substance – A fragment of this incrustation[2] was found at Stadar-sweit, which led to our enquiries respecting the spring. The temperature of the water is inferior to that at Leira – being only 96° – Around the spring, in a circular space, about 50 yards in diameter, a complete coating of the incrustation has been formed – A still larger space, covered with fragments of the incrustation, occurs at a short distance; – but no present appearance of a spring on this spot.

About ½ a mile beyond Lysiehols, a considerable bed of Lava[3] descends from the mountains & diffuses itself over the plain below. This was the first instance we had seen of a stream of Lava actually descending from the hills – In appearance the Lava in no respect differed from those we had before seen.

At a short distance from Buderstad we turned aside from the road, to see another mineral spring – of the common temperature – but having a taste considerably saline – We procured 2 bottles of water from this spring – two also from the spring at Lysiehols –

In approaching Buderstad, it was necessary to cross, by deep fords, several creeks, which run up from the sea at this place. Buderstad itself is situated on a small inlet of the sea, immediately under a bed of lava – a situation which would have surprized us more, had we not previously visited Havnefiord – the site of which is in many respects considerably similar. – We found the place to consist of one *brick-house* (the second edifice of this kind we have seen in Iceland)[4] a timber house, or rather

---

[1] Lýsuhóll.
[2]HH The specimens of the incrustation at Lysieholslaug are marked F26. – The temperature of the spring is 96° – Under the mountains in the vicinity of the spring, we found numerous fragments of a highly crystallized greenstone, of which F27 is a specimen – Of this, it would appear that the mountains are composed – The bed of Lava near the spring resembles entirely those we had before seen – The Lava which occurs at Buderstad contains much of what we suppose to be Augite – Of this F28 are specimens.
[3] Bláfeldarhraun.   [4] The other was on Viðey.

warehouse, a church, and several turf cottages. – The inhabitant of the brick-house is a Mr Gudmundson,[1] a merchant, who has commercial connections at Copenhagen, at Reikiaviik & at Havnefiord – He had been prepared to receive us by Mr Clausen, who having reached Olafsvig by sea some time before, was good enough to send over a message to Buderstad, to notify our probable arrival there. Mr Gudmundson is an Icelander – a friendly, hospitable man, shewing us every possible attention & civility – We found from conversation with him that the war between England & Denmark had been greatly injurious to his trade – Three years have now elapsed since any vessel has come from Copenhagen to Buderstad; though previously to this time, it was usual for one or two vessels to enter the port annually[2] – This privation of the accustomed intercourse is severely felt by the inhabitants of the interior, who are greatly in want of corn, timber, iron &c. The warehouses at Buderstad, and other ports in this part of Iceland, are filled with the commodities of the country – fish, oil, fox-skins &c, which it is impossible at the present time profitably to dispose of.

In various places, both in our first, and in the present journey, our persons & pursuits had been curiously & minutely examined by the Icelanders – In no place, however, did we observe this curiosity more strongly manifested than at Buderstad. A short excursion which we made this evening into the Lava, with our hammers & specimen bags, was attended by a numerous groupe of women and children, who followed all our steps, & allowed not a single movement to escape observation – It was a matter of much surprize to them that we should be collecting fragments of what they deem so little valuable. This astonishment was further increased, as was evident on their countenances, when following our steps into the house, they saw us wrapping up the specimens of Lava in paper – Whether they considered us *very wise* or *very foolish* we had no means of determining. – While the females & children of the neighbouring cottages were thus occupied, Loptson had collected round him a group of men, to whom he was narrating all the wonders of Scotland – a theme with him perfectly inexhaustible.

Our adieus with the old Provost, Mr Jonsson, were very kind – He expressed an earnest wish to hear from some of us, when returned to

[1] Guðmundur Guðmundsson (1772–1837).

[2] Búðir was at this time the major trading port for Southern Snæfellsnessýsla and Mýrasýsla.

England – a request which it was impossible to put a negative upon, after the great & various kindness we had received from the good man. *Saturday–June 30ᵗʰ* – After a night, disturbed only by the crowing of a cock, who slept in the same apartment with us; and after a breakfast of coffee, mutton, cheese & rye bread, we resumed our journey. – attended, as a guide, by the son of the man,[1] who accompanied Sir John Stanley in his ascent up Snæfields's Jokull. – Our day's journey was to Stappen,[2] a distance of only 8 or 9 miles. The road is altogether strange & singular. For the first three miles it passes over the bed of lava,[3] under which Buderstad is situated. This lava presents a more broken, abrupt, & irregular surface than any we have before crossed. The track we pursued over it, is one of danger as well as of difficulty – rugged in the extreme, & in many places so steep as to render it extremely hazardous for the passage of horses. Numerous clefts & cavities of great depth present themselves on every side – Many caves are found under the surface of the Lava, similar in appearance & mode of formation to that of Helgadal[4] – We penetrated to the extremity of one of these, which is probably 30 or 40 yards in length.

Having, after much time & labour, reached the other side of the Lava, we came to the shore of the Bay[5] of Stappen – Here the appearance of a long extent of sandy beach, induced us to halt for some time, for the purpose of measuring a base, with which by the aid of the sextant, to ascertain the height of Snæfield's Jokull. This was the more desirable; as in the early part of the journey, one of our barometers had been broken – which rendered the accurate barometrical measurement impracticable, even admitting the success of our attempt to attain the summit of the mountain – A base of 400 yards was measured on the sand, & the angles taken by the Sextant with all due regard to accuracy of proceeding[S] – The day was peculiarly favourable for this purpose – fine, clear & calm – *Snæfields Jokull*, the precipitous cliffs of Stappen, & the range of mountains to the east of the Jokull,[6] were seen in their

---

[1] Unidentified. On Stanley's 1789 ascent, see West, 1970–6, I, 78–84.
[2] Arnarstapi. [3] Búðahraun.
[4] See above p. 122. [5] Breiðavík.
[6]ᴴᴴ The range of mountains extending eastward towards the Jokull, continued between Buderstad & Stappen, to present much the same character as before. They are probably composed entirely of beds of amygdaloid, greenstone &c. In some places lava appears on the summit of the mountains. On the shore, on the eastern side of the Bay of Stappen we found numerous rounded fragments of pumice & volcanic scoriæ, doubtless brought there by the sea – F29 are specimens of these – Between the two beds of lava near Stappen, a conglomerate rock appears, similar to that universal in the Guldbringe Syssel –

utmost grandeur. The whole scene was one of Alpine character &
magnificence.

We were somewhat surprized to find the mountain of *Snæfields Jokull*
actually forming a part of the volcanic district – On the western side of

S. Sextant readings at Snæfellsjökull

the Bay of Stappen, a large bed of Lava[1] descends from a mountain
which forms a part of the Jokull; and still further to the west another
stream of Lava[2] comes down upon the plain through the hollow which
intervenes between the Jokull & the hill of Stappen – About half way
up the mountain, we remarked[3] amid the snow what appeared as a
crater, or a bursting of the surface. This we noted as a spot to be
examined, if the ascent of the mountain so far were found to be
practicable.

The latter part of our road was highly interesting – Besides the views
we enjoyed of the mountains on the right hand, the path conducted us
on the edge of the precipitous cliffs,[4] which terminate the beds of lava
on the side of the sea. Numerous streams, coming down from the
hills, are projected over these cliffs, forming cascades of considerable

---

the included fragments principally scoriæ. It forms the sides of a deep cleft or valley,
between the Lavas; indicating strongly from its general structure, that it has originally
been formed in the sea. The sandstone, which is the basis, is extremely loose & friable.[T]
The cliffs along the shore on the eastern side of Stappen are formed of the compact lava
which here, as in so many other places lies beneath the rough, scoriated covering of the
bed.

[1] Hnausahraun.

[2] Probably Klifhraun. The principal lava flows further to the west are, in succession,
Háahraun, Drangahraun, Beruvíkurhraun, and Neshraun.

[3] MS appears to read 'remalked'.

[4] Sölvahamar.

T. Field sketch near Arnarstapi

grandeur. Some of those streams we crossed only three or four yards above the place of their fall.[1]

The situation of Stappen, where we arrived at 6 o'clock, is singularly striking. It is placed on the edge of the cliffs, which continue forwards along the shore, and which here form by their curvature, a beautiful little bay or haven, with depth of water for vessels of any size. These cliffs are probably about 100 feet in height, and present very striking columnar appearances – Their effect is greatly added to by the presence of several lofty masses of insulated rock, at various distances from the shore; which insulated rocks are entirely formed by assemblages of columns, arranged in every possible direction; & with the utmost variety of size & form. – To the north, at the distance of about a mile, rises the steep & rugged mountain of Stappen-fiall,[2] terminating upwards in a high conical peak. Behind this appear the summit & eastern side of Snæfields Jokull, covered with eternal snows.

At Stappen, as at many other places on our journey, we found our arrival expected & doors open to receive us – The Handel or Merchant of the place, Mr Hialtalin,[3] is brother to our former worthy host at Saurbar – Him, however, we did not see – At the commencement of the war, he was taken prisoner, & carried into

[1] MS has an asterisk, but no facing-page material to which it could specifically refer.
[2] Stapafell.
[3] Hans Hjaltalín. Mackenzie, 1812, p. 171 notes that Hans returned to Arnarstapi in 1811, and was there to greet Henderson in 1814. See Henderson, 1818, II, pp. 35–6.

England – Thence he contrived to get into Norway, where he was about 1½ years ago. Since that time no intelligence what ever of him has reached Iceland. His wife, Madame Hialtalin,[1] with a family of six children, continues to reside at Stappen, where she carries on the business as well as lies in her power. She is a native of Denmark; a woman of good & somewhat genteel manners – and apparently an excellent manager in her domestic concerns – Her house is, upon the whole, the best we have yet seen in Iceland, – The Government House in Reikiaviik not excepted – The rooms are large, convenient, & well furnished. In the larger sitting room there are two pier glasses – The best bed room has a range of windows, extending its whole length – a bed of considerable elegance & much comfort, and a handsome glass chandalier hanging from the cieling – Soon after our arrival, coffee was handed to us, & at 9 o'clock we sat down to a dinner of fish & the curds of milk. – M^d Hialtalin informed us that she lived at Stappen, at the time Sir John Stanley[2] visited this place. She well recollects him, & described minutely to us the various circumstances which occurred during his stay here.

Sunday July 1st Had the morning been favourable, it was our intention to have occupied this day in the ascent of Snæfield's Jokull. In this scheme we were disappointed by the state of the weather. The morning threatened rain, – and the mountain was completely enveloped in clouds. – Although failing in this plan, we spent a most interesting day in surveying the very singular features of the shore in the vicinity of Stappen[3] – in collecting

---

[1] Sophía Katrín Hjaltalín. See Helgi P. Briem, *Sjálfstæði Íslands 1809* (Reykjavík, 1936) p. 275.

[2] West, 1970–6, I, 78, and note 139. Hans Hjaltalín was then 'the principal man in the place'.

[3]HH The occurrence of such columnar concretions, as those of Stappen, in a rock which has been thus affected by heat, is a fact singular & interesting. – That it has been acted upon in this way no doubt can exist. F30 are specimens taken from two different columns at the distance of a few feet from their base. – F31 are specimens taken from the scoriated termination of two different columns. – No direct proof, however, appears that the matter composing these columns has ever been in such a state of liquidity as actually to have flowed & concreted from this state. It is perhaps possible that its present state may have been produced by the vicinity of beds of real lava, or by streams of this substance which have flowed in amongst it – It is an argument against this supposition that there appears at the place, whence the specimens were taken, the Conglomerate sandstone rock, containing included scoriæ, & lying under the rock which presents the columnar appearances. Of this Conglomerate F32 is a specimen. The mountain of Stappen Fiall is likewise composed of Conglomerate with the same sandstone basis.

The bed of Lava which occurs ½ a mile to the west of Stappen, is considerably different in its structure from any we have yet seen. The Lava contains very few crystals, has a darker colour, & the vesicles occuring in its substance are differently arranged. – F33 are

specimens – taking sketches &c. The views which Mr Baynes[1] took on this spot when with Sir J.Stanley at Stappen, we had seen in Edinburgh – Upon the whole we found reason to think them very accurate, though conveying the impression of scenery on a larger scale than the reality displays – The columns, though in general extremely regular & perfect, are not, however, of any very great size – & the grandeur of their effect is wholly lost, when seen from any considerable distance – The most striking points of view occur on the shore about ¼ of a mile to the W, or rather to the S of Stappen – Here the columns are of greatest size, & most perfect in form – Their height from the water's edge may be estimated at 40 feet – their direction is in some places perpendicular – in others much inclined. This variety of position occurs most strikingly in the small detached islands along the coast. Some of these islands are wholly composed of columns horizontally arranged – others present an arrangement which the language of German mineralogists would call *diverging radiated*[2] – others display a more confused & irregular structure, the columns being arranged in fasciculi in every possible position & with great variety of size. – A short way south of Stappen, the sea has worn two vast caverns in the rock,[3] where the columns, perpendicularly placed, & having a height

---

specimens from the external scoriæ of this lava. F34 is a specimen from a rock, of which there is a considerable abundance in that part of the lava, nearest the sea – perhaps also in other parts of the bed. The surface of this rock is covered with scoriæ, like the common lava. – F35 has the same general situation, & is likewise covered with scoriæ. Where these rocks are in contact with the scoriæ, their internal structure presents a splintery or slaty appearance – Following downwards the steep descent of the lava towards the sea at this place, the rocks appeared on the face of the precipice, of which F36, 37, 38 are specimens. Still further down occurs in considerable quantity, the slaty rock, of which F39 is a specimen. It would seem as if there were a gradual transition in structure from F34, through F36, 37 and 38 to this slaty rock. How this has been effected, it may be difficult to conceive. Some of the varieties of the rock in this particular place, greatly resemble the specimens F10 from the mountain behind Houls on the Hval Fiord.

It may be worthy of remark that the columnar appearances at Stappen occur only in the rock on the shore, intervening between the two beds of Lava–

[1] John Baine. His account of his 1789 journey with Stanley survives in two manuscripts (Lbs MS 3887 4to – copy made by Stanley himself; another copy is privately owned by Mrs. Marianne Vestdal of Reykjavík). Many of Baine's drawings from the expedition are reproduced in Steindór Steindórsson, 1979. Little is known of Baine's life. He was a mathematician, astronomer and draughtsman who taught in Edinburgh for much of his life.

[2] A divergent or radiated mineral has long, narrow, flattish plates or scales diverging regularly from a centre. See Robert Townson, *The philosophy of mineralogy* (London, 1798), p. 147.

[3] Stapagjár. The two main ones are Eystrigjá and Miðgjá.

of about 30 feet, are seen to the utmost advantage – The singularity & grandeur of the effect are aided by the circumstance of the superincumbent rock having fallen in at each of these caverns; thus affording to the spectator above the appearance of a great & deep bason formed with an almost artificial regularity of structure. The best point of view, however, of these caverns, is from the surface of the sea beneath; where the eye, looking upwards through these vast natural arches, catches the summits of the mountains beyond – A still more singular & interesting specimen of this scenery occurs further along the coast. A prodigious mass of rock,[1] almost insulated in its position, stretches out at a right angle with the line of the coast. Through this rock, the sides of which are perfectly perpendicular, has been worn a great arch,[2] probably not less than 25 or 30 feet in height, & having an horizontal diameter considerably greater. The landscape seen through this arch is in a high degree picturesque & pleasing. In the fore-ground there appear, rising out of the sea, numerous columnar masses, with the utmost variety of form. In the distance is seen a part of the lofty range of mountains, which occupy the whole length of the peninsula between the two great Fiords. The columnar structure is less striking at this spot than in other places along the shore; but is still sufficient to add much to the singularity of the scene.

One of the most wonderful circumstances, however, about the shores of *Stappen-hafn*,[3] is the *nature* of the rock in which the columnar appearances are found. We had previously expected to meet with basalt or green stone; but in lieu of these, we found a rock, greatly resembling in appearance & structure some of the compact lavas we had before seen, & moreover exhibiting in numerous places completely formed scoriæ – not only at the base of the columns, but also in their interior structure – We had before seen at Reikiaviik, Viidoe, & in other places, columnar appearances in rocks which have been subjected to the action of heat. Nothing, however, which might be compared with the singular phenomena of this kind exhibited by the vicinity of Stappen.

Our morning's walk led us to another great bed of Lava, which descends from the Jokull upon the plain, & makes its way to the sea;

---

[1] Perhaps either Kríuklettur or Gatklettur.

[2] Sketched by Mackenzie, 1812, facing p. 172, along with Richard Bright's sketch of a cave (p. 173).

[3]HH On the shore at Stappen, we saw several large sharks, which had been caught by the fishing boats, & dragged on shore. One of these measured 14 feet in length –

affording another proof of the former volcanic character of this mountain. The termination of the peninsula on the western side of the Jokull, is likewise covered with many beds of lava – In setting out on our journey, we had little expectation of meeting with so vast a tract of volcanic country in this part of Iceland – We have not yet travelled 20 miles together in the island, without meeting some appearance, which decidedly indicated the action of fire.

In the afternoon, we took a boat, & examined from the sea the columnar rocks along the shore – The evening was extremely fine, & we enjoyed a magnificent view of the whole range of mountains extending from the Jokull to the point of Akranes.

The attention of our worthy hostess & her family continued unintermittingly. They could scarcely conceal their astonishment, however, that we should think it worth while to take so many fragments from their rocks, and to pack them up carefully in paper. They minutely enquired from Loptson what use we should make of them in England, and could scarcely credit the fact that they were merely intended to satisfy the curiosity of ourselves & others.

Monday–July 2ᵈ – Another cloudy morning again disappointed our scheme for the ascent of the Jokull. Delaying therefore the execution of this project for the present, we this morning set out for Olafsvik,[1] on the northern shore of the peninsula; with the intention of paying the visit to Mʳ Clausen,[2] which we had promised when we saw him in Reikiaviik. On leaving Stappen, Madame Hialtalin paid us the compliment of putting up the Danish flag on her warehouses – There are three roads from Stappen to Olafsvik – the longest taking the western side of the Jokull – another passing along the eastern side,[3] close to the foot of the mountain – the third likewise on the eastern side, but at a greater distance from it – we decided upon taking the last, which conducted us over a part of the range of mountains to which the name of *Kam-skard*[4] is given – The ascent to the summit was a laborious one, but we found ourselves recompensed for it, by a noble view which we obtained from this elevated spot, of the whole of the great bay called the *Breyde Fiord*[5] or *Breyde Buglen* – bounded to the north by the mountains of Dale[6] & Bardæstrand Syssels[7] – The descent on the northern side of the mountains was made by a path still more

---

[1] Ólafsvík.
[3] Jökulháls.
[5] Breiðafjörður.
[7] Barðastrandarsýsla.

[2] See note 4, p. 147.
[4] Kambsskarð.
[6] Dalasýsla.

rugged than that which carried us to the summit – When nearly at their foot, we were struck by a very fine range of basaltic columns, forming a precipitous barrier to the channel of a mountain stream; which just above this spot falls from the summit of a rock in a fine cascade. These columns are remarkably perfect – a part of the range probably 50 or 60 feet in height. – Reaching the shores of the Breyde-Fiord, we proceeded westwards for about 2 miles – Olafsvik[1] is situated on this part of the coast, at the bottom of a small bay;[2] a high mountain rising almost perpendicularly in the back ground. It consists of six or seven wooden buildings, and 14 or 15 small cottages, inhabited by fishermen. – Of the wooden buildings only two are houses – one inhabited by M[r] Clausen – the other by a factor in his employ – The remainder are warehouses, or *pack-houses* as they are called in Iceland, all belonging to M[r] Clausen.

We were received by this gentleman with the utmost cordiality & kindness, & introduced to Madame Clausen;[3] a lady who has more gentility of person & manner than any other female we have seen in

[1]HH Our route from Stappen to Olafsvig presented few mineralogical novelties. F40 is a specimen from the bed of Lava to the east of Stappen, which shews its entire similarity to the bed westward from this place. They both descend from Snæfield's Jokull, on the southern side of the mountain, & probably, if traced upwards, might be referred to the same source. – F41 is from an exposed face of rock about half-way up the mountains – The rock contains much Augite – A large extent of surface on this part of the mountain is covered with fragments, of a white slaty stone, greatly resembling F10 from Houls, & F16 & 18 from the Eastern Skards-heide. Also many fragments of a friable green-coloured stone, similar to F4 from Mount Esian – F42 is a friable green-coloured stone, similar to F4 from Mount Esian – F42 is a specimen of the white stone. – Near the summit of the ascent, basaltic rock occurred, intersected by veins of jasper – On our descent from the mountain about half way down, we found many fragments of a volcanic rock, differing from any we had before seen – of which F43 is a specimen. The source of these we had not the means of ascertaining – Several mountains, however, apparently of volcanic character appeared at some distance from the road – one especially in the right hand, which had much of the semblance of an ancient crater.

Near the foot of the Kam-skard, a singular face of rock presented itself. It may be divided into three different parts – F44 is a specimen of the lowest part of the rock, which lay just above the level of a stream – apparently true basalt – Over this is placed a confused conglomerate mass, containing fragments of basalt, or scoriæ &c, & above this occurs the rock F45 – the lower surface of which exhibits a scoriated appearance as in the specimen F46. – In this upper bed of rock, which likewise appears to be basaltic, the range of columns occurs, which is noticed in the Journal. (Attention must be paid to these specimens, as there is some error in the numbers upon them.)

[2]HH The hills on the coast near Olafsvig are almost entirely composed of the Sandstone Conglomerate containing scoriæ – In some places, the ascent immediately above the shore displays a singular assemblage of rolled masses, heaped together to a considerable height, with scarcely any other basis than a little loose sand interposed.

[3] Valgerður Pétursdóttir (?b. 1776).

Iceland – His family consists besides only of one little boy,[1] – Mr Clausen is esteemed a man of large fortune & may probably be considered as the principal merchant in the island. He is a native of Denmark, & was brought up at Copenhagen in the continental trade. Obtaining, however, by his first marriage,[2] a commercial property at Olafsvig, he came over to Iceland, & has since divided his residence between Olafsvig & Copenhagen. – He has passed three winters at the former place – Besides the large warehouses which he possesses here, he has different establishments on other parts of this coast, where factors reside in his employ. The nature of his trade is the same as that of other Icelandic merchants. He collects for exportation, fish, oil, tallow, fox-skins, & the various woollen manufactures of the island – & sells to the inhabitants, both in a retail & wholesale way, different articles of foreign produce or manufacture, procured from the continent of Europe. The war between England & Denmark has been greatly detrimental to this trade. Besides the intercourse with Denmark much profit was formerly derived from the exportation of fish to France, Spain & the ports of the Mediterranean Sea; a branch of commerce which is now entirely suspended. The intercourse with England has not yet acquired a sufficiently settled footing to relieve these evils – M[r] Clausen's warehouses are crowded with goods for which a market is wanting – He reckons that he has lying by him, (either under cover, or collected into large heaps upon the shore) many hundred thousand fish, salted or dried – Of the woollen goods, manufactured in Iceland, his stock is proportionally large. He has about 50,000 pair of mittens, or woollen gloves; and almost an equal quantity of stockings of different qualities of fineness. – It is M[r] Clausen's intention to go to England in the Autumn, and either to spend the winter there, or to proceed to Copenhagen – He has never yet visited Britain, and is desirous to see something of the country.

Tuesday July 3[d]. The morning of this day giving a fair promise of clear, settled weather, it was determined to signalize it by the ascent of Snæfield's Jokull[3] – or at least by the attempt to attain this object – success being declared quite impossible by all who heard of the project – Sir G.Mackenzie declined making one in the expedition – The party consisted of Bright & myself – attended by Loptson, one of the guides

---

[1] Hans Arrebo Clausen (1806–91).

[2] Apparently Holland's mistake. Holger Clausen was married only once.

[3] Mackenzie, 1812, pp. 175–80, offers an extended account of the ascent attributed to Richard Bright.

who came with us from Reikiaviik, & a man from Olafsvig' – The latter was called a *guide*, but in fact could only officiate as such to the foot of the mountain, his spirit of adventure never having carried him beyond this point. He set out with us, however, under a promise on his part, that he would continue with us, as long as we ourselves chose to proceed in the undertaking.

Furnished with provisions, brandy, specimen bags, a large hammer, & walking staffs spiked with iron, we set forth on foot at 11 o'clock – The distance to the foot of the mountain, as it is called, or to the place where the snow begins, is about 6 miles, a steep ascent all the way, & the country wild, desolate & rugged in the extreme. By dint of hard walking, we accomplished this distance in two hours, and at 1 o'clock found ourselves on the verge of the snow, which occupies probably about two thirds of the height of the mountain – above the level of the sea. This covering of snow is not one which the winter creates, & the summer destroys – It remains from year to year – from century to century – scarcely affected by the vicissitudes of weather or of the seasons. – Standing at the foot of this vast & singular ascent, there was something in the prospect before us, which might have created alarm & despondency, had we been less determined to perseverance in our object – Allowing ourselves, however, only a short interval of rest & preparation, we recommenced our labours, & entered upon the dreary waste before us, without any track or previous knowledge to guide our footsteps – assuming the summit of the mountain as the object to be attained, & pursuing a direction towards this, as straight as it was possible to take. For the first part of the way, we found the surface of the snow tolerably hard & firm, & had little conception of the distance which intervened between our feet & the solid rock beneath. Having proceeded, however, about ½ a mile, we discovered that we were treading on a surface less secure than we had supposed. A cleft presented itself in the snow, 3 or 4 feet in width, & at least 30 in depth. The formation of this chasm would seem to have taken place from a shifting in the mass of snow on the lower side, probably arising from some alteration in the surface of the rock beneath. Many such occurred in the remainder of our ascent – some of them so narrow as to allow our passing over them with the assistance of our poles – others considerably wider, & rendering it necessary to make a circuit to avoid the danger of passing directly across –

' Unidentified.

In the progress of our ascent, we stopped occasionally for a few minutes, as well to obtain a little rest, as to examine the widely extended view which opened out on every side of us–. The state of the day, however, was not at this time particularly favourable for distant prospect – A belt of clouds gathered round the lower part of the mountain, & admitted only partial views of the more remote horizon. These clouds, however, formed in themselves a striking & magnificent object – rolling their broken masses beneath us, and disclosing at intervals portions of the great landscape beneath. The views towards the north were the most distinct, comprizing the whole of the Breyde Fiord, covered in its upper part with a multitude of islands – & bounded on its northern side by ranges of mountains, which the eye might pursue almost to the point where they lie beneath the Polar Circle –

After a constant & laborious ascent of 2 hours, we found ourselves at no great distance from the summit of the mountain – Three peaks or summits presented themselves before us – two of them about the same height, & very abrupt, – the third about 100 feet lower, & with a less steep ascent – Convinced of the impracticability of ascending either of the first summits, from the deep chasms & rents which appeared round their base, we decided upon attempting the last, an undertaking, however, of no small difficulty & hazard, – At the spot, where the steep ascent of the peak commenced, a vast chasm in the snow presented itself – apparently 50 or 60 feet in depth, & 10 or 12 feet in width, stretching on each side as far as we were able to see. To pass over by a leap was impossible, as the bank of snow rose almost perpendicularly on the other side. After walking some way along the edge of the chasm, we discovered the means of crossing it by the snow – a mass of which had fallen over the chasm, forming a sort of bridge, 3 or 4 feet in width. With some difficulty we effected a passage across – & exerting all our strength for the remaining part of the ascent, which was infinitely steep & laborious, we at length attained the summit of this peak of the mountain – exactly 2 hours and 17 min' after our entrance upon the snow.

Though the belt of clouds round the middle of the mountain, now becoming every moment more dense, prevented the enjoyment of distant views from this elevated point, yet was the scene singular and interesting in a high degree – There was, however, before us an object still unattained; & we experienced a feeling of mortification, in looking

' Difficult to decipher, but apparently 'min'.

to the peak which lay beyond us, rising to a somewhat greater height than the one on which we now stood. The attainment of this object, however, we were convinced, was wholly impossible, at least from the part of the mountains which we had ascended – A precipitous slope in the snow conducted the eye to a vast chasm intervening between the two summits; of the impracticability of crossing which we were at once aware. We convinced ourselves, however, by a minute and *impartial* inspection that the additional height of this summit can not be more than 100 feet. An additional inducement to have attained this 2^d peak, had the thing been possible, was the appearance of the bare rock in two or three different points of its surface. In one place, the rock presented a perpendicular face of considerable height rising abruptly from the mass of snow beneath. The examination of these rocks would have been highly interesting to us, in relation to the mineralogical character of the mountain.

Eghert Olafsen, in his travels through Iceland, gives the narrative[1] of his own ascent of Snæfield's Jokull, of which he says he attained the summit.[2] He remarks that at this point, the compass was very greatly affected – its indications being extremely irregular & wholly erroneous. – If this be an accurate statement, Olafsen must doubtless have ascended to the higher summit of the mountain, as on the place to which we attained, I observed the needle to be perfectly uniform & accurate in its movements – We were surprized by the height at which the thermometer stood,[3] even at the summit of the mountain. The

---

[1] Eggert Ólafsson and Bjarni Pálsson, *Reise igiennem Island*, 2 vols (Soroe, 1772), I, 283. An English translation of a truncated French version (1802) of the work appeared in 1805, but there is clear evidence (see, for example, note 2, p. 265 below) that Holland had access to the original.

[2][IIII] At the time of ascending the Jokull, we were led to believe from various sources of information that its height above the sea was between 6 & 7000 feet. This however would appear to be an exaggerated statement, though supported by the Trigonometrical calculation, which *Eggert Olafsen* made on the spot. The later & doubtless more accurate observations of the Danish lieutenants |Ed. See note 6, p. 77|, now engaged in the survey of Iceland, make the height to be not more than 4554 – or according to an observation from another base, 4584 feet – If this mensuration be accurate, *Snæfield's Jokull* is by no means the highest mountain in Iceland.

[3][IIII] Thermometrical Observations in the ascent of Snæfield's Jokull.

At 11 o'clock	at Olafsvig	58°
12	halfway to the snow	56°
1	entrance upon the snow	43°
2	— — — — —	42°
3	— — — — —	39°
3.17m	on the summit	33½°

lowest point, at which I observed it, when not in contact with the snow, was 33½ of Fah[r].

It is said, that from some points of the channel, which lies between Iceland & Greenland, – the mountain of Snæfields Jokull may be seen on one side, and a high mountain in Greenland on the other. – It is difficult to ascertain how far this is an accurate statement. The distance between the two lands at this point cannot be less than 80 leagues.

We were prevented from remaining more than 10 or 12 minutes at the summit of the Jokull, by observing a thick fog coming rapidly upon us. We descended as speedily as possible to the chasm which we had before crossed. The danger we had experienced here on our ascent, was wholly insignificant, compared with that to which we now were exposed. Speaking individually for myself, I may say that at no former moment had I ever been placed in a situation equally hazardous. The bridge of snow which had before just borne our passage over it, was now by the pressure & sinking of the feet, become so weak, as not to allow the weight of the body to be continued upon it. Without the assistance of the poles we brought with us, our safe return would have been almost impossible – As matters stood, we at length succeeded in placing ourselves securely on the other side – not, however, without much fear & trembling while thus hazardously engaged – Scarcely had we passed this chasm, when we became enveloped in the fog, which was so dense, as not to allow us to see more than the immediate track we were pursuing. In the whole descent, we followed accurately the trace of our ascending footsteps – excepting in one instance, when we went off a few hundred yards to the left, to examine an assemblage of loose stones, which formed a bank, elevated a few feet above the level of the snow. We were surprized to find the greater number of these fragments either scoriæ or pumice[1] – with minute fragments of what appear to be pitchstone – The interesting nature of this fact, in relation as well to the nature of the stones themselves, as also to the

No barometrical observations were made: One barometer had been broken in the first day's journey from Reikiaviik, & so much risk attended the carriage of our other, from the mode of travelling in Iceland, that we deemed it prudent to send it back from Innerholme.

[1][HH] When approaching Stappen from Buderstad, we had noticed in the eastern side of *Snæfield's Jokull*, at about ⅔ the height of the mountain, the appearance of a burst or crater of great extent – In ascending the mountain from Olafsvig, we passed within half a mile of this spot, but were unable to reach it, from the numerous fissures in the snow which occur in this part of the mountain.

mineralogical character of the mountain, will readily be perceived. (See page 126)[1] The situation of this assemblage of fragments is at about ⅓ of the height of the mountain from the line where the snow begins – or probably about 3000 feet above the level of the sea.

The remainder of our descent was made without delay & with much rapidity. We reached Olafsvig soon after 6 o'clock – after an absence of only 7½ hours in the whole excursion.

[1]HH The specimens of Pumice from this spot are marked F47 – F48 are found in small fragments on the same place – F39 & 40 are brown & yellow scoriæ, which form the greater part of the collection. F51 is a specimen of a white stone found together with the others – F52 is a singularly shaped stone which occurred on this spot – F53 is from an assemblage of loose stones of this kind a short distance only above the line where the snow begins.

F54 are specimens from the Conglomerate Sandstone Rock which occurs between Olafsvig & the foot of the Jokull – Two of these specimens are intended particularly to illustrate the probable sub-marine formation of this rock.

(There is an error in marking these specimens – the numbers are given upwards from 37, instead of 47).

VOL. II[1]

Wednesday – July 4th – This day we passed at Olafsvig, recruiting our strength after the labours of the proceding day. We found from Loptson that the story of our ascent to the summit of Snæfield's Jokull, received very little credit from the people of Olafsvig, and that no assertions of our guide could convince his neighbours of the fact. The poor fellow himself, a talkative good-humoured man, was infinitely proud of the exploit, and doubtless added some embellishments to his tale of wonders. Ἡδυ τοι σωϑεντα μεμνησϑαι τυονων [?][2]

In the course of the morning, Mr Clausen brought to me several patients for medical advice – The nearest practitioner is at Stikkesholm,[3] about 40 miles distant from Olafsvig – Of course, the difficulty of procuring medical assistance in this situation is very great.

The weather was so warm as to induce Sir G.Mackenzie & Bright to bathe this morning in the sea.

Thursday July 5th – It had been our original plan to leave Olafsvig this morning but the solicitation of Mr Clausen persuaded us to remain with him a day longer. Our stay in his house was productive of more gratification to us than any other visit we had made in Iceland. The utmost license was afforded to us in the choice of our occupations, and we were in no degree disturbed by the intrusive curiosity, which in several other places had greatly interfered with our comfort. – Mr Clausen speaks English with considerable fluency, though instructed solely by himself, & never having visited England – The greater

---

[1] Volume 2 of the Journal MS has, on its initial facing page, a complete itinerary of all three journeys undertaken within Iceland. It incorporates the material from note 2, p. 119; note 5, p. 170 above, and from note 1, p. 228 below, though adding one 6 mile excursion to the third journey. It notes the total internal mileage travelled as 776.

[2] 'But it is pleasant after rescue to remember travails'. Holland's incomplete, uncertain and, at times, illegible transcription derives from a line in Euripides' lost play *Andromeda*. See A. Nauck, *Tragicorum Græcorum Fragmenta* (London, 1856; second edition, Leipzig, 1889), p. 399 – the line in its complete and correct form reads ἀλλ᾽ ἡδύ τοι σωϑέντα μεμνῆσϑαι πόνων.

[3] Stykkishólmur.

number of his English books are at present at Copenhagen – the only books he has now by him, are a collection of voyages, and a volume of Roderick Random.[1]

In the evening we walked along the shore west of Olafsvig, with the view of killing, if practicable, some of the seals, which are very numerous upon this coast – We saw a considerable number of them near the shore, but though many shots were fired, they were wholly without avail. The usual time of killing the seals is when they are sitting upon the rocks at low-water. – There are two species upon the coast – one of them much large than the other, called the Greenland-Seal[2] – The evening was so perfectly clear & fine, that I was induced to sit up during a part of the night, with the view of seeing the rising of the sun, & ascertaining with exactness the length of time it remained under the horizon – The situation of Olafsvig is more favourable for this purpose than any other place we have yet visited in Iceland. That part of the Bardæstrand Syssel,[3] which lies immediately opposite, on the northern side of the Breyde Fiord, has not great elevation above the horizon, & does not interfere much with the exactness of the observation. – The sun remained under the horizon exactly 2 hours & 35 minutes, giving as the time of its rising 17½ minutes after one. – During the whole of the time it was below the horizon, its rays were distinctly visible, and the light, even within doors, sufficient for any occupation whatsoever. The sun rose with much splendor, about 20 degrees east from the true north, richly gilding with its beams the waves of the intervening sea. The whole scene was striking and magnificent. (See Register for this day).[4]

July 6th This morning we left our hospitable entertainers at Olafsvig & resumed our journey[5] The scheme of the route before us was to pursue

[1] Tobias Smollett, *Roderick Random* (1748), itself a comic fiction 'collection of voyages'.
[2] *Phoca groenlandica* (Linn.); Mod.Ice. *Vöðuselur*.
[3] Vestur-Barðastrandarsýsla is immediately north from Ólafsvík across Breiðafjörður.
[4] See Appendix A.
[5]HH The ride from Olafsvig to Gronnefiord was extremely interesting in a mineralogical point of view. The columns upon the coast about 3 miles from the former place, are composed of a rock, which must certainly be regarded as belonging to the trap family, as will be seen in the specimens F 55 – An amygdaloid rock containing Zeolite, calc-spar &c, forms the basis of the columns – Of this F 56 is a specimen. The columns not only present the appearance of scoriæ at their lower extremity, but actually contain scoriæ in the heart of the rock – a fact highly interesting in relation to our ideas of their mode of formation – I have no good specimen to shew the internal scoriated structure – F 57 are specimens of the scoriæ from the lower part of the columns. F 58 is a specimen of the appearance which most of the columns assume in coming into contact with the amygdaloid beneath. Sir G.M. has a good specimen of the scoriæ from the heart of a column.

the southern side of the Breyde Fiord as far as Snoksdalr[1] – then to proceed to Kalmanstunga by the way of Reykolt,[2] and to return to Reikiaviik by the lake of Thingvalla.[3] In pursuance of this plan, our first day's journey was to Grönnefiord,[4] a distance from Olafsvig of 16 miles – The northern shore of the peninsula is in every respect much more Singular & interesting, than that adjoining the Faxe-Fiord, – which we before had traversed. – Three miles from Olafsvig we were gratified by the view of some very splendid columnar appearances upon the coast; very greatly superior to the scenery of the same kind which occurs in the vicinity of Stappen – The columns are longer, more perfectly formed, & assume in many places still more singular varieties of position and curvature – They are seen to the greatest advantage in some small bays or inlets occurring on this part of the coast – Here they present in many places a perpendicular elevation of 50 or 60 feet, forming a magnificent barrier to the waves of the sea, which break at their foot upon a columnar pavement of regular and curious structure: The singularity of the scene is added to, (though perhaps not the harmony of effect) by a prodigious assemblage of sea fowl; whose nests are constructed upon the ledges & broken parts of the columns. The whole rock is absolutely whitened by their numbers. They are of the species of Gull commonly called the *Kitti-wake*,[5] a bird of considerable elegance of form & colour. While admiring their numbers, and the economy of their rocky habitations, two large eagles appeared, hovering over the spot – All was immediately commotion and disturbance – Vast flocks of the gulls rose from their nest, & the ear was almost stunned by their screaming.

From the amygdaloid below the columns we procured some good specimens of zeolite – F 59 are specimens, shewing a singular variety of calc-spar which recurs in this rock. F 60 are specimens of the zeolite.

Further along the coast in the same direction, the mountains approaching close to the sea, & having an almost perpendicular face of 8 or 900 feet, display a singular alternation of beds, apparently consisting of columnar amydaloid & the conglomerate rock, of which so much appears in this part of Iceland. The lower bed of Conglomerate contains scoriæ in great abundance – The lower part of the columns exhibits a structure apparently much scoriated – but from the steepness of ascent it was not possible to procure any specimens from this spot. – Beyond the pass of *Buland's Höfde*, the beds of amygdaloid above the road contain much zeolite. – The remainder of our way exhibited mountains, composed of beds of amygdaloid, greenstone, & having their summits for the most part formed of the sandstone conglomerate. The beds were for the most part horizontally arranged. – the conglomerate rock much worn & presenting numerous peaks & rugged edges.

[1] Snóksdalur.
[2] Reykholt.
[3] Þingvallavatn.
[4] Grundarfjörður.
[5] *Rissa tridactyla* (Linn.); Mod.Ice. *Rita*.

These columns present also mineralogical phenomena of the most singular kind, & we spent two or three hours in their careful examination.

Continuing our route along the coast, we came to *Buland's Höfde*,[1] the name given to a place where the road is carried for ½ a mile along the side of a mountain, falling precipitously towards the sea. A more difficult and dangerous track can not well be conceived. The face of the mountain is not less than 1000 feet in height; an elevation almost perpendicular – having just inclination enough from it to retain a covering of gravel & fragments of rock – The path,[2] about 2 feet in width, & without the least security on the side of the precipice, is carried round the mountain, at a height of 3 or 400 feet above the sea, the waves of which wash the loose rocks that have fallen from the precipice above. Several lives have been lost in this place – We were told that in winter the road is absolutely impassable – an assertion which may easily be credited. Beyond this spot, we left the shores of the Breyde Fiord, & pursued a path among the mountains to the right hand, passing the head of an arm of the sea, which runs deeply into the country from the Fiord – The mountain scenery in this part of our road was exceedingly fine – much superior to that on the opposite coast of the peninsula. The mountains are very lofty, & the conglomerate rock of which many of them are composed, is broken into clefts & caverns, so as to give the finest effect of light & shade. One very singular insulated mountain[3] was in the vicinity of Grönnefiord – completely *table-formed*, as viewed either from the east or west – a sharp cone or pyramid, as we saw it in passing along its northern side.

Grönnefiord is situated upon the upper part of the arm of the sea from which it derives its name; surrounded on every other side by mountains of great height, – and having much of the picturesque in their forms. Intervening between the shore & the foot of the mountains is a large tract of fine pasture land, through which a stream makes its way, after having been precipitated from the heights above by a series of falls – The Handel's House is situated on the beach, is built of timber, & though not equal to some of those we had lately seen,

[1] Búlandshöfði.

[2] Þrælaskriða. HH: The pass of *Buland's Höfde* resembles much that of *Penmaenmawr* in N.Wales. It is, however, from the nature of the road, infinitely more difficult & dangerous.

[3] Kirkjufell. Mackenzie, 1812, p. 183: 'called Sukker-Toppen (Sugar loaf) in the charts'. See, for example, Hans Erik Minor's 1788 map of the Snæfellsnes peninsula: Haraldur Sigurðsson, 1971–8, II, p. 208.

afforded us nevertheless very good accommodation for the night. We found the Handel, Mr Müller,[1] on the point of relinquishing his situation at Grönnefiord – A' sloop belonging to Mr Sivertsen of Havnefiord was at this time in the Haven, in which M^r M, his wife, & their goods and chattels, were about to be transferred to Reikiaviik – here he is going to establish himself as a merchant. We took the opportunity of this conveyance to disburthen ourselves of the mineralogical specimens, collected between Olafsvig & Grönnefiord, which were by no means few in number.

Saturday July 7th. After a series of salutations, *among both males & females* of the family, we recommenced our journey this morning – The plan of our day's route was to proceed if possible to *Stikkes-holm*, a distance of about 25 miles – This to travellers in Iceland, impeded, as we were, by a long cavalcade of baggage horses, is a serious undertaking, & ought not to be attempted unless with some necessity or peculiar convenience attached to the plan. The road fortunately was good, & free from the impediment of bogs – otherwise the accomplishment of the journey in one day would have been wholly impossible.

From Grönnefiord, the route conducted us through the mountains for the purpose of avoiding the many deep arms of the sea which run up from this coast[2] – A few miles from Grönnefiord, we left the road to view a fall of water[3] from the mountains on the right hand – a singularly striking spot, as well from the height of the waterfall, as from the magnificence of the surrounding scenery – One part of the deep and

[1] Ole Peter Christian Möller. See Klemens Jónsson, *Saga Reykjavíkur* (Reykjavík, 1929), p. 167.

[2]HH On the shore near Grönnefiord, we observed a vein of basaltic rock, the sides of which shewed the same appearance as specimens C 1,2 3 from Viidoe – (A specimen from this place, not numbered). The cleft in the mountains at the waterfall presented some singular mineralogical appearances. The basis of the rock appears to be a sort of trap-tuff, which is intersected in every possible direction by veins of basalt, & other varieties of whin-stone, containing much calc spar, & so numerous, as to give a singular striped appearance to the whole surface of rock. Besides these veins, a good deal of the white stone occurred (apparently in thin beds) of which we had seen so much at Houls & in other parts of our journey – Is this a decomposed greenstone? – The rock in some of these veins shewed a distinct tendency to columnar concretion.

F 61 is a specimen from the Lava which we crossed between Grönnefiord & Stikkes-holm. The character of the country about this place much resembles that of the vicinity of Roudemelr, which indeed is not distant more than 10 or 12 miles. The appearance & structure of the mountains are very similar to those appearing in Kolben-stadr Fiall; as in that mountain, columnar appearances occur in many of the beds, especially near the summit. The volcanic tract immediately below, has likewise very much the same character as in the great valley at Roudemelr.

[3] Perhaps Grundarfoss in the Grundará, or, further on, a fall in Kolgrafafjörður.

wide cleft which is here formed in the hills, is filled with snow – This has been hardened into one vast, compact mass, beneath which, as under an arch, the waters of the stream, after being precipitated from a height of 150 feet, rush downwards with a rapid and imperious course –

A short way beyond this waterfall, we crossed the neck of a steep & lofty mountain,[1] intervening between two arms of the sea – Our descent on the eastern side, brought us to a large tract of Lava,[2] evidently proceeding from the mountains in the middle of the peninsula, & stopping at this place, where it meets the inlet of the sea. This bed of Lava presented exactly the same characters as the many we had before traversed – Having crossed it by a better path than usually occurs in these situations, we ascended an eminence, entirely covered with red scoriæ & cinders; having to the right hand a conical hill, evidently of volcanic origin, & covered in the same way – Many similar hills meet the eye in this tract of country – rising from amidst the rugged lava beneath. – The deep hollows which appear on some of them render it more than probable that the scoriæ with which they are thickly covered have been erupted from the very place where they now appear – The whole scene presented on this spot is singularly wild, rugged and desolate.

Previously to passing another bed of Lava, which probably has the same origin as the former, we stopped on a grassy bank to give some refreshment to ourselves and our horses. – We procured milk from an adjoining cottage, and made our rustic meal on the turf, our horses grazing around us. Including the singular natural scenery, which environed us, the groupe would have made no bad subject for the pencil.

The remainder of our way to Stikkes-holm presented nothing particularly interesting, excepting some fine views of the Breyde Fiord, which is here much contracted in width, & covered with numerous small islands. The number of these islands is reckoned to be about 150, nor does this appear to be an exaggeration. From many points of view, the Bay has much the appearance of a lake – not wholly unlike the lower part of Loch Lomond, though with much more desolation & barrenness of the surrounding objects. We did not reach Stikkes-holm until after 11 o'clock – our baggage horses not till one. It is situated at the extremity of an isthmus running far into the sea, and the road to it is

[1] Probably Gjafi, with the 'two arms of the sea' being Kolgrafafjörður to the West and Hraunsfjörður to the East. The familiar route past Gjafi was via Tröllaháls.

[2] Berserkjahraun, beyond Hraunsfjörður.

rendered tediously circuitous by numerous creeks, which it is necessary to wind round in approaching the place. The immediate vicinity is striking & picturesque. The shore is steep, rocky & abrupt, several small islands appear at a short distance, some of them presenting columnar appearance of considerable regularity. The place consists of four or five large wooden buildings, & a few adjoining cottages, the whole belonging to M[r] Thorlacius[1] of Bildudald – The principal inhabitants are two merchants, & a surgeon; the latter[2] a son of M[r] Hialtalin of Saurbar – He studied at Copenhagen, – and was about to settle in some town in Jutland; when, according to his own account, he was ordered by Count Trampe to take his present situation in Iceland, at that time vacant. He has at present the charge of a very extensive district here, for which he receives only £12 per annum. His professional profits during the full year of his residence here, which is just expired, amount scarcely to £6, and for this sum he has had to go through much labour & fatigue – I had much conversation with him in Latin, which he speaks with facility. His medical information is good, & he has communicated some valuable facts respecting the diseases prevalent in Iceland – His wife, Madame Hialtalin,[3] is a Danish lady – They lodge at present in the house of M[r] Benedicsen,[4] one of the merchants[5] at Stikkesholm, but are building a house for themselves at Helgafell,[6] a few miles distant –

We were received at Stikkes-holm, as at Stappen & Olafsvig, with the compliment of the Danish flag. We took up our abode in the house of Mr Benedicsen, a man of mild & pleasing manners, & disposed to show every kind of hospitality. He is a native of Iceland & has never been out of his native country.

Sunday.July 8[th.] This day we remained at Stikkes-holm, occupied in

[1] Ólafur Þórðarson Thorlacius (1762–1815), a prosperous merchant with operations in Ísafjörður, Bildudalur in the North-West, as well as in Stykkishólmur.
[2] Oddur Hjaltalín (1782–1840), son of Jón Hjaltalín (see above, note 4, p. 153); studied in Copenhagen 1803–7; physician in Stykkishólmur 1807–39; published books on agricultural, medical and botanical subjects.
[3] Dorothea Georgina Bornemann (1771–1831).
[4] Bogi Benediktsson (1771–1849), commercial manager for Ólafur Þórðarson Thorlacius in Stykkishólmur 1807–26; author of the exhaustive *Sýslumannaæfir* (Reykjavík, 1881–1932).
[5] The other was Jón Kolbeinsson (1765–1836).
[6] A celebrated hill a mile to the west of Stykkishólmur. HH: The rocks on the shore about Stikkesholm appear to be principally basalt or greenstone, containing veins of greenstone, & of calc spar. – F 62 is a specimen from a vein, taken to shew the appearance of its sides. F 63 is a specimen from another vein in the vicinity –

walking, writing & taking sketches of the place. The difference between
Sunday and another day is not very conspicuous in Iceland – and less so
in the mercantile places than in any other – No business was done in the
early part of the day; but the only occupation of the people seemed to
be loitering about the houses & on the shore. In the evening, one of the
pack-houses was open, & several men at work in it – Previously to the
war, Stikkes-holm was a place of considerable trade, three or four
vessels from Norway or Denmark generally coming to the port every
year. The only vessel which arrived last year was one from Norway, &
none has yet appeared here in the present summer. The fishing at
Stikkes-holm is a very considerable one, beginning somewhat before
that in the Faxe-Fiord, and continuing for two or three months –

Though treated with much civility by M[r] & Madame Hialtalin, we
had nevertheless reason to believe that their dispositions towards the
English nation at large were not very favourable. M[r] H. had been
present at the late unfortunate attack upon Copenhagen – his house &
much of his property had been destroyed in the bombardment of the
place. He shewed us an umbrella, broken by a shot whilst he was
sleeping under it,[1] in a tent – Some anecdotes too were given us of ill
treatment which was received from the captains of two English vessels
of war, on their passage from Denmark to Iceland – It was an
unpleasant office to listen to these narratives, without the means of
vindication for our countrymen; & melancholy to see a man, whose
acquirements might have enabled him to rise in the world, unwillingly
forced into this remote situation, where his best exertions are scarcely
competent to the livelihood of himself & his family – Both M[r] Hialtalin
& M[r] Benedicsen spoke much of the distress produced in Iceland by the
war between England & Denmark; & seemed to consider the English
Order in Council[2] as likely to afford only a very partial relief. They
made many enquiries respecting the present state of affairs on the
Continent, of which they had been during the last year, in almost entire
ignorance – The intelligence of the marriage of Napoleon with the
princess of Austria,[3] appeared to astonish them much.

Our dinner to day consisted of boiled rice, & a dish of *tern's eggs*. The

---

[1] Jón Espólín, 1821–55, XII (Part 10), 12 notes that whilst 1600 Danes were killed or
injured during the 1807 British attack, only one Icelander in Copenhagen was hurt.
Holland here reveals that a second Icelander was very lucky.

[2] See above, note 4, p. 99.

[3] Marie-Louise, daughter of Francis II of Austria. The wedding took place by proxy on
11 March 1810, with the civil ceremony following on April 1. See J. H. Thompson,
Napoleon Bonaparte: his rise and fall (Oxford, 1952), pp. 303–6.

females of the family did not sit down to it. – At 9 o'clock a supper was set out of smoked mutton, rye bread, and butter.

Monday 9ᵗʰ. – This morning we left Stikkes-holm, accompanied by Mʳ Hialtalin who offered to officiate as our guide to Drapühlid Fiall,[1] a mountain about 6 miles distant from Stikkes-holm, in a direction nearly south.[2] This mountain we had originally been recommended to visit by Count Trampe, and his recommendation was seconded by that of our friend, Mʳ Clausen – The hill is minutely described by Olafsen in his travels through Iceland[3] – who mentions having found there some curious petrefactions as well as the Surtur brand, & the Iceland Agate, or Obsidian – We spent some hours upon this mountain, & collected thence a number of specimens. No petrefactions occurred to our notice, though there were appearances in some of the stones, which might possibly have been mistaken for these – The Surturbrand we found in considerable abundance, but no decided specimens of Obsidian. (See opposite page).[4] Mʳ Hialtalin remained at the foot of the mountain

---

[1] Drápuhlíðarfjall.

[2]HH On our way from Stikkesholm to Drapühlid Fiall, we observed a good deal of the *Betula Nana*, growing to the height of about a foot from the ground.

[3] Eggert Ólafsson and Bjarni Pálsson, 1772, I, 288–92: none of this material appears in the truncated English translation *Travels in Iceland* (London, 1805).

[4]HH The mountain of *Drapühlid Fiall* presents some singular mineralogical phenomena – Seen from some distance, its surface appears of a white or reddish-white colour. This appearance is owing to its being entirely covered with fragments of a white stone resembling those, of which we had seen a large assemblage at Houls & in other places on our route. These fragments present considerable variety of colour & appearance, some of them spotted like those at Houls – others perfectly white – others again presenting various shades of yellow & red. It is probable that all these varieties are merely different degrees of decomposition of the original rock – In ascending the mountain, which we did on the northern side, we found several species of Fossil Wood of which F 64 are specimens. These were lying among the fragments of decomposed rock. Endeavouring to ascertain the true situation of the [Ed. 'Surturbrand' erased – left blank] we ascended nearly to the summit of this face of the mountain. Here we found a bed of pearlstone, probably about 20 inches, or 2 feet in thickness – F 65 are specimens from the upper part of this bed. Below it passes by a gradual transition into F 66. Beneath this again appears a singular sort of tuff, containing fragments of pearlstone & *surturbrand*, & also exhibiting some appearance of scoriæ. From this situation it is probable that the pieces of Surturbrand found below, were derived – We traced the bed of pitchstone, (if such it might be termed) very distinctly for 20 or 30 yards its position being nearly a horizontal one. Beyond this on each side it was less distinctly marked, – though observed to extend itself considerably further – Immediately over the pitchstone, & passing gradually out of it, is the substance, of which F 67 is a specimen – This again passes into the rock of which F 68 are specimens – From this part of the rock are doubtless derived most of the loose stones which cover the surface of the mountain below. – The height of the place on the mountain where the pitchstone appears is probably about 800 feet – The hill rises to a considerably greater height behind, but this part of it we had not leisure to examine. On

Beds of greenstone

Drápühlid Fiall from the East.

U. Drápuhlíðarfjall

during our ascent. Upon our return, we found a man with him, whom we learnt was the Sysselman of the Snæfield's Syssel,[1] a rough looking mortal, with accoutrements altogether much below those of an English farmer. He lives under a promontory[2] near the sea, a few miles west of Stikkes-holm. He came to the foot of Drapühlid-fiall, for the express purpose of meeting with us, to deliver the compliments of the *Amtmand Stephensen*, with a message from him, to request that we would, if possible, take his house, at Hvanneiri, in our way back to Reikiaviik. The Amtmand has just been travelling through this district, & had left directions with the different Sysselmen, to shew us all the attention in their power, wherever we might come. His information of our being in this part of the country had been procured from the Atastrood, who intrusted me, when at Hvitar-Vellir with a packet to convey to him in the Snæfield's Syssel. This packet, (which contained also printed copies of the English Gazette, with the Order in Council relative to Iceland), I left to the care of the minister at Myklaholt,[3] to be conveyed to the *Amtmand.*

At the foot of Drapühlid Fiall, we arranged our specimens, & enjoyed a draught of excellent milk, brought to us in a wooden pail from an adjoining cottage – The whole groupe upon the grass,

---

the eastern side, as seen from *Narfeyre*, there appear, (especially in the lower part of the mountain,) a distinct series of beds probably of greenstone –

In the valley on each side of *Drapühlid Fiall*, a bed of rugged lava descends from some part of the mountains behind – These beds of lava terminate before reaching the sea –

The shores of the Alpta Fiord presented mountains of considerable elevation, belonging to the trap-formation – composed of a series of beds, & these intersected by numerous veins, apparently of the same rock.[U]

[1] Sigurður Guðlaugsson (1764–1840); *sýslumaður* in Snæfellsnes 1806–17.

[2] Hallbjarnareyri.

[3] See above, note 2, p. 177.

including the Sysselman, & the Surgeon, would have made a good subject for a picture – These good people left us here, and we pursued our journey to Narfeyre,[1] situated on the eastern shore, & near the mouth of an arm of the sea, called the Alpta Fiord,[2] which runs deeply into the country at this place – The necessity for passing round this Fiord rendered our route a very circuitous one; and it would have been still longer, had not the ebbing tide allowed us to cross the lands near the head of the Fiord. We arrived at Narfeyre at 6 o'clock, and found there a farm house & a church; in the latter of which we immediately decided upon taking up our abode for the night; greatly preferring this to the trouble & inconvenience of pitching our tent. This was the 7th time of sleeping beneath the roof of a church since the commencement of our journey – The edifice, exteriorly, & interiorly, precisely resembled those we had before inhabited – In the loft or gallery, Loptson pointed out to us a substance lying upon an old painted chest, the description of which a little surprised us. It was a mass of fat taken from the human body, & destined to medical purposes:- if Loptson's information may be credited, to the cure of asthma, & other pulmonary complaints – This is not an uncommon practice in Iceland – When a grave is opened, & any of this substance found in it (probably produced by the conversion of muscular substance, into a sort of spermasiti) it is eagerly seized upon, & laid up for future use. – Was not this a practice among the vulgar in England formerly?

Tuesday 10th. This morning we set out at an early hour. Previously, however, to mounting our horses, we went into the farm-house to examine the process of weaving, as conducted in Iceland, – the sister of the farmer's wife exhibiting to us her performance at the machine.[3] The whole procedure is rude & laborious. The general arrangement of the threads (which are *coarsely spun woollen*) is much the same as in the common loom, except that the weft is placed in a position nearly perpendicular. No shuttle is employed, but in lieu of it, the thread intended to be placed on the weft, is passed by the hands between the double row of threads – It is then stretched & brought to its proper position by a small stick scraped over the threads externally – and is afterwards still further tightened by a piece of *whale's rib*, broad and flattened at one extremity, which is passed between the rows of threads in different places, and struck upwards against the weft with

---

[1] Narfeyri.   [2] Álftafjörður.
[3] See illustrations of eighteenth-century Icelandic looms in Elsa E. Guðjónsson, 'Fjórar myndir af íslenska vefstaðnum', *ÁHÍF* (1977), 125–34.

considerable force. This is the whole process which is repeated regularly in the same way – The piece upon which the woman was at this time employed, was a sort of rug or bed covering, three yards in length, composed of red & yellow threads – The completion of this piece, if steadily worked upon, occupies 3 days; or about a yard each day – These manufactured articles are exchanged by the country people for fish &c. One rug of this kind may be exchanged at a rate somewhat below 2 dollars – the people manufacturing them providing all the raw materials – This weaving machine was placed in the bed chamber of the house, to which we ascended for the purpose of examining it. This apartment, as is usual in the Icelandic farm houses, is a very long one, and contains 5 or 6 beds – all the family sleeping together in this place.

Our day's journey[1] was to Snoksdalr,[2] a distance of about 25 miles, as nearly as we could surmise. It is [a] matter of extreme difficulty in Iceland to procure accurate information with respect to distance, as we frequently found to our great inconvenience. The best method of enquiry is that respecting the time which will be occupied in riding between two places; & this, as might be expected, is very uncertain, depending upon the time which the person questioned, may himself take to accomplish this – Our progress on the road was rendered exceedingly slow, by the necessity of having the baggage horses always within a short distance of us, so that a distance which we were assured might be travelled in 5 or 6 hours, frequently occupied us 10 or 12 – This day our journey was continued, with the interval of only an hour's rest, from 8 in the morning till the same hour at night – With the exception of some fine views of the Breyde Fiord, nothing that could be deemed interesting was offered to us during the whole day. The road[3] conducted us through a country barren, wild & desolate in the highest

[1] HH From Narfeyre, there is a singular view of the great cluster of islands in this part of the Breyde Fiord. By the eye alone it is scarcely possible to estimate their number. These islands are the resort of innumerable Eider-Ducks – large flocks of which are seen in different places along the shore.

[2] Snóksdalur.

[3] HH The country between Narfeyre & Snoksdalr is wholly uninteresting in a mineralogical point of view. It belongs entirely to the Flœtz trap formation, exhibiting beds of green stone & basalt – we did not observe any amygdaloid – Judging from the distant observation we had of the mountains on the opposite side of the Breyde Fiord, it is probable they belong to the same formation as well as the whole tract of country intervening between Snoksdalr & the North Sea – No lava is met with in the district forming the northern part of the Vesterland – comprehending the Syssels of Bardæstrand, Isafiord, Strande & Dale – It may therefore be presumed that the whole of this country is composed of greenstone, basalt, and other rocks of the trap-formation.

degree – not a single object occurred to diversify or enliven the scene, – except indeed an *Iceland wood*, through which we passed a few miles from Narfeyre; – an assemblage of birch shrubs trailing along the ground to the height only of a couple of feet – Passing a small hamlet with a church, called *Breida bolstadr*,[1] we came upon the shore of the Fiord,[2] which to the east of the islands, expands greatly on the northern side, having much of the appearance of a vast lake. – Pursuing our course along the southern shore for 10 or 12 miles, we came at length to the eastern extremity of the bay, and ascending a hill from this point, arrived at Snoksdalr, distant about 2 miles from the coast. During the latter part of our ride we suffered exceedingly from cold. – A high wind blew from the north east almost directly in our faces, coming over a tract of country of no great height, which here intevenes between the Breyde Fiord & the North Sea. – The direct distance between Snoksdalr & the nearest inlet[3] of the great ocean, which bounds Iceland to the north, is not more than 30 or 40 miles, and owing to this circumstance, the situation of the place is much exposed to cold & tempestuous winds. The latitude of Snoksdalr we had not the means of ascertaining on the spot, nor is it marked with accuracy in the maps. In the map attached to Magnusens travels in Iceland,[4] it is placed in 65°15′ – In that, which was copied from the German collection of maps,[5] the latitude is set down at   [6] – By a connection with Minor's Chart,[7] which may undoubtedly be considered the most accurate, but which does not extend further along the Breyde Fiord than Stikkesholm, it would appear that the real latitude is about 65°12′[8] –

At Snoksdalr we found a tolerably good farm house[9] & a church – In

---

[1] Breiðabólsstaður.   [2] Hvammsfjörður.   [3] Hrútafjörður.

[4] Both the book and the map remain unidentified and may be the products of Holland's confusion. It is not clear, however, which books and maps he may have been confusing. Ólafur Olavius, *Oeconomisk reise igiennem de nordvestlige, nordlige og nordostlige kanter af Island,* 2 vols. (Copenhagen, 1780) has no maps; Eggert Ólafsson and Bjarni Pálsson, 1772, have no relevant maps; on the maps in von Troil, 1777, 1780 and Niels Horrebow, 1752, 1758, Snóksdalur is not marked, and had it been marked, it is clear that it would not have been at 65° 15′. Árni Magnússon and Páll Vídalín compiled detailed notes on the geography and economy of all regions of Iceland, but no particular map is associated with their work, which, in any case, was not published until 1913–43.

[5] Probably the maps of Johann C. M. Reinecke (1768–1818). See Haraldur Sigurðsson, 1971–8, II, 197–9.

[6] Omitted in manuscript.

[7] Haraldur Sigurðsson, 1971–8, II, map facing p. 208.

[8] Mackenzie, 1812, p. 190 notes that the latitude of Snóksdalur is 'about' 65° 5′. Its latitude is in fact about 65° 1′.

[9]HH In the farm-house at Snoksdalr, we found a table, made from a single piece of Surturbrand, which was procured in the Bardæstrand Syssel – This table Sir G. Mackenzie purchased at the price of eight rix-dollars.

the latter we fixed our quarters for the night, no difference appearing in the edifice from the many we had before inhabited, except the substitution of the *Slaying of Stephen* for *the Last Supper*, as a picture for the Altar piece. We were supplied from the farm house with much excellent milk, & a large dish of curds & whey; made by curdling the milk while warm, & continuing the boiling for some time afterwards.

Wednesday 11th. We remained this day at Snoksdalr; not induced to do so by any peculiar beauty or comfortableness of the place – but merely that we might recruit ourselves & our horses for the next day's journey, which we expected to be one of much length. The vicinity of Snoksdalr presents nothing that is interesting either to the mineralogist, or to the lover of picturesque beauty. In the morning I took alone a long walk northwards from the place, with the view of ascertaining as far as possible the general character of the country in this direction. From an eminence which I ascended with this view, nothing was seen towards the north but long ranges of hills, stretching into the distance – having nothing of the picturesque in their forms, & exhibiting the utmost desolation & barrenness of surface – A country more dreary & repulsive can scarcely be imagined.

Our abode in the church during the day was by no means comfortable. A continuation of the wind from the North East rendered the weather exceedingly *cold*; & we suffered much from this cause, in a building, ill sheltered against the inclemencies of weather, without any fire, & with a flooring so damp & rotten as scarcely to bear the weight of our bed-steads. The thermometer, even under the roof, at no time in the day, shewed a temperature of more than 45° – Nor were we much prepossessed in favour of our neighbours at the farm-house – They supplied us indeed with an abundance of milk, but some discoveries we made as to their cleanliness of domestic economy, greatly diminished the satisfaction we might otherwise have had in this beverage – We were induced to betake ourselves to the utensils in our own kitchen, upon ascertaining that the spoons belonging to the house were cleaned by the simple process of passing them through the mouth, & afterwards wiping them upon a dirty wadmal' gown – Other anecdotes of the same kind might be given to illustrate the habits of the family; and we soon discovered that it was wise to keep out of the way of discoveries of this nature – We were informed that

---

' Mod.Ice. *vaðmál*, a rough, home-spun cloth.

Count Trampe formerly slept in this church on his way to Stikkes-holm – what his accommodations in it were, we had not the means of learning.

Tuesday 12th. This morning we rose at 2 o'clock and resumed our journey before 5 – three hours being always necessary by the tardiness of our guides for the completion of our preparations for travelling – Our route conducting us over a rugged hill to the north of Snoksdalr, brought us into a long & wide valley, called *Middalur*,[1] which is entirely used as meadow land. It is divided into no fewer than 30 portions, connected with different cottages; – the property in the land being divided to the same extent. Many of these wide valleys occur in the Dale Syssel[2] – from which circumstance the district derives its name –

Entering another valley, which meets Middalur from the south, & pursuing its course for 2 or 3 miles, we began the ascent of the *Brautar Brekkar*,[3] a high mountain ridge which separates this valley from another. – The ascent, from its length and steepness, was one of considerable labour – the descent, which is still more steep & abrupt, was accomplished with more ease, but not without some degree of hazard, both to ourselves & to the horses. Having reached the level of the valley beneath, we eat our breakfast on the turf by the side of the stream; and afterwards, aided by the shelter of the mountain behind, & the warmth of an unclouded sun, made ample amends for the deficiency of our night's rest, by an hour's very comfortable repose upon the grass. Previously to leaving England, scarcely could we have conceived it possible that we should sleep on the ground among the mountains of Iceland, with snow not more than a hundred feet above us.

Following the course of the valley for a few miles, we stopped at the foot of a very lofty insulated mountain, on the left hand of the road, greatly resembling in appearance the mountain of Drapühlid, which we before had visited – It is nearly conical in form, & covered to its summit with the fragments of white stone, which render the appearance of the former mountain so remarkable. No hill of the same character occurs in the neighbourhood, nor any which possesses the same elevation & form – In the valley at its foot, we collected

[1] Miðdalur.
[2] Mod.Ice. *dalur*, 'valley'.
[3] Brattabrekka.

specimens, which shewed its similarity in other respects to the Drapühlid Fiall – The name of the mountain is *Beule*.[1]

We took up our quarters for the night at Hvam;[2] a church & farm house situated on the side of a valley, which affords fine pasture & some tolerably good meadow land. A considerable river called Norder-o[3] runs through it, which we forded many times on our road. At Hvam we fixed our quarters in the church, procuring as usual much excellent milk from the farm-house. In this church there was no altar piece; but in lieu of it, a singular marble[4] carving, representing the Deity in a human shape, folding his hands over a figure of Christ suspended from the cross – with the people of the house, though apparently in meaner circumstances, we were better satisfied than we had been with those at Snoksdalr.

Friday 13th – It was the plan of this day's journey to proceed to Reikolt, to examine the very singular hot-springs for which this place is celebrated. We set out from Hvam at 6 in the morning, attended by the farmer[5] as our guide – an oddly formed, but merry & active little man, who by dint of constant knocking of his knees against the sides of his horse, made a miserable & awkward animal proceed with a degree of speed, which it required some exertion on our part to equal. A fall from the horse, with a long roll upon the ground, little discomposed him. He got up again, & proceeded with as much agility as ever. – We acquired from him, though with considerable difficulty, some information respecting the district inn which he resides. The valley of the Norder-o, in which Hvam is situated, is divided into many small portions of land,

---

[1] Baula. HH: In the valley at the foot of Beule, we observed numerous veins of pitchstone, irregularly traversing a rock of trap-tuff, which likewise contains many veins of calc-spar. Of this pitchstone F 69 are specimens. Some of the veins have a thickness of several feet. The appearance of this pitchstone in this mountain, together with the occurrence of the decomposed white stone on its surface, shew its similarity of general character to the Drapühlid Fiall – A still further circumstance of coincidence is the occurrence in this mountain of a substance resembling the Surturbrand – This we did not find *in situ*; but were shewn a few small specimens of it at Hvanneiri by the Amtmand Stephansen. E 70 is a small fragment of this.

About 2 miles from Hvam in a south westerly direction, We observed two beds of rough lava, coming down from the mountains. The mountains in this part of the country display very strikingly the *trap-formation*; exhibiting in many places a long series of stairs. – each step presenting in part a bare face of rock, the lower ones covered above with a fine verdure. The effect of this contrast is here & there very singular.

[2] Hvammur.   [3] Norðurá.

[4] MS has 'marble' written above 'wooden' apparently as a correction, though 'wooden' is not crossed out.

[5] Steindór Steindórsson, 1960, p. 186 identifies Jósep Þorsteinsson (1776–1860).

connected with different farm-houses & cottages. Much of it belongs to the church at Hvam – the rents paid partly in produce, proportioned to the number of cattle kept – partly in money – a fixed sum in a ratio to the quantity &c of the land. Our guide had been in his farm only one year.[1] As the land was in bad condition when he came to it – (or rather the buildings, for in Iceland the improvement of land is scarcely ever thought of) no rent whatever was paid to the church this year – the general practice in Iceland under similar circumstances.

Crossing a rugged, but not lofty chain of hills,[2] which forms the southern barrier of the valley of the Norder-ò, we came to an *Iceland wood*[3] of considerable extent, & considerably more respectable in appearance than any we had before seen – The birch shrubs (*Betula alba*) of which it is composed, attain here & there a height of nine or ten feet – This, however, is rare – the average height is not more than 3 or 4 feet. – Beyond this wood we passed by a hamlet, called *Nord-tunga*,[4] where there is a small church, the duties of which, as it is in the same parish, are done by the minister of Hvam. – The ascent of another low range of hills, brought us in view of the great valley of the Hvitaar – the river flowing in a circuitous course through it, & dividing the Myre Syssel from that of Borgar Fiord. The lower part of this valley, near the mouth of the Hvitaar, we had before traversed. It was now our plan to cross the river by a ford at *Sidumule*,[5] & to proceed thence to Reikolt. This plan, however, underwent a material alteration, in consequence of a visit we paid at *Sidumule*, to a gentleman of the name of Ottesen,[6] Sysselman of the Myre & Hnappadals Syssels,[7] who resides at this place. This personage we had before seen for a few minutes at *Stadir-Hraun*; & had received from him an invitation to his house, should it fall within our route. He presented to us an appearance & manner greatly superior to those of any of his brother Sysselmen, we had yet seen; and we found him to possess besides much sagacity & intelligence of mind. He is a young man, & has only lately been inducted into his office; to the duties of which, however, if we might judge from his conversation, he seemed in every way fully competent. We obtained from him a good

[1] Previous occupant was Einar Þórðarson (b. 1721). See *MÍ 1801: Vest.*, 1979, p. 163.

[2] Grjótháls. HH: The low ranges of hills beteen *Hvam* & the valley of the *Hvita-ar*, belong to the trap formation. Some fragments presented themselves, having an apparently scoriated structure. We did not observe, however, any actual appearances of Lava.

[3] See above note 4, p. 171.   [4] Norðtunga.

[5] Síðumúli.   [6] See above, note 3, p. 173.

[7] Mýrasýsla and Hnappadalssýsla.

213

deal of information,[1] as well as respecting the particular district over which he presides, as also regarding the general offices & conditions of the Sysselmen in Iceland. All his statements were made with a degree of plainness, simplicity, & precision which at once gave them a title to our full credit – His house is a tolerably good one – & the appearance of his dairy, which displayed 24 wooden vessels, filled with milk & cream, bore testimony to the excellence of his farm. He has a small library consisting of 90 or 100 vols – We found in it several translations from English works – among others, a translation of Sir Charles Grandison[2] into Danish – a translation of Addison's Cato[3] into the same language, &c.

While at Sidumule, the consideration of several circumstances, particularly the difficulty of crossing the river Hvitaar at this place, induced us to make a change in our plans. – and to determine upon going down the valley to Hvanneiri[4] with the view of proceeding thence to visit the hot-springs at Reikolt. It happened fortunately, that the Sysselman, at the time of our arrival at Sidumule, was likewise setting out for Hvanneiri – the services of a guide were therefore unnecessary to us. –

The whole of our route to Hvanneiri lay along the valley of the Hvitaar, the course of which river we pursued for 14 or 16 miles – crossing it about 8 miles from Sidumule by a ford,[5] which was rendered

---

[1] HH Mr. Ottesen shewed us the register book which he keeps as Sysselman of the Myra & Hnappadals Syssels, & allowed the full examination of its contents. From this book we found that there are in the two syssels, taken conjointly, 259 farm-houses or cottages & 303 farmers – it happening in many cases that more than one farmer resides under the same roof. – The revenue derived to the Government from the 2 Syssels did not amount last year to more than 252 rix-dollars. – this being the common average for the district. The Sysselman collects this money from the farmers in a ratio determined by the number of cattle which each farm keeps – or rather indeed collects a given value of produce, which he himself is obliged to dispose of to the merchants, & to convert into money for the uses of the Government. He retains, as his own share the 3ᵈ part of the sum collected – from this however, it is necessary for him to pay the various expences attending the collection & disposal of the produce obtained from the farmers – Last year, owing to the peculiar circumstances of the Icelandic trade, he lost some money in the disposal of the goods which were collected for the revenue.

The land in the Myre & Hnappadals Syssels is better adapted to Sheep than to cattle. – On the two largest farms in the Myre Syssel, those of Sidumula & Svigna Skard, about 18 cows are kept – On one farm within the district, there are about 500 sheep – In the *Myre Syssel* there are 7 parishes – in *Hnappadals Syssel* only three.

[2] Samuel Richardson, *Sir Charles Grandison* (1754).

[3] Joseph Addison, *Cato* (1713).

[4] Hvanneyri.

[5] Steindór Steindórsson (1960), p. 193, suggests Langholtsvaði.

not a little difficult by the width of the stream & the depth & rapidity of the current. In the course of our ride, it was necessary to cross a great extent of boggy land, some parts of which were both difficult and hazardous – It was impossible, however, to be under better guidance than that of Sysselman Ottesen. – *Myre Syssel* derives its name from the bogs it contains – & it was a natural supposition that the prefect of this district should be intimately acquainted with the best means of traversing these in safety. – Some miles from Sidumule, we examined a hot spring on the western bank of the river – the heat of the water about 165° – Passing by *Hvitaar Vellir*, where we had formerly crossed the river[1] with our horses, we arrived at Hvanneiri in the evening – At *Hvitaar-Vellir*[2] we were informed that the Amtmand Stephenson had gone to Reikiaviik a few days before, & was not yet returned – a piece of intelligence which mortified & disappointed us; as it seemed to render likely a failure of our scheme for visiting Reikolt on the following day. – Proceeding with this impression, it was a matter of great satisfaction to us, in arriving at Hvanneiri, to find the Amtmand standing at his door to receive us – & a still greater & more unexpected pleasure to see with him, our good friend M[r] Fell – The coincidence in this case was a remarkable one. The *Amtmand* & Mr Fell arrived at Hvanneiri from Reikiaviik about 5 minutes before we reached it from the opposite quarter, each party little looking for the other at this time, and in this place. – M[r] Fell's object in coming over the *Borgar Fiord* was to examine the salmon fishery in this district – to ascertain its general productiveness – and to make, if desirable, some agreement for the produce of this year – Another addition to the party at Hvanneiri was made by the Sysselman of the Dale Syssel, M[r] Ottesen,[3] brother to Mr Ottesen of Sidumule – a man of singular uncouthness of physiognomy, but possessing much good-

---

[1]HH The river *Hvitaar* derives its name from the colour of the water, which is a sort of milky-white. This colour continues both during the summer & winter. It is the common opinion in Iceland that it appears only in those rivers, which arise from the Jokulls – or the mountains which are covered with snow during the whole year – The colour in question is doubtless derived from a portion of white clay, held in suspension in the waters of the stream. – The waters of the river Hvitaar are in great part derived from the neighbourhood of the mountain, called *Eirek's Jokull* –

[2]HH At *Hvitaar-Vellir* we saw for the first time this summer, *the mowing of grass*. This however was only in the immediate vicinity of the Provost Jonsson's house – the grass on the common meadow land being by no means ready at this time of the year.

[3] Holland's mistake. Skúli Magnússon (1768–1837) was *sýslumaður* in Dalasýsla from 1804–37. Pétur Ottesen's one brother, Lárus, was a merchant in Reykjavík.

natured shrewdness & humour. – He came from Reikiaviik with the Amtmand.[1]

All this numerous assemblage brought together into one small house, and added to a family consisting in itself of nearly 20 people, it was a matter of immediate consultation how we should all be disposed of for the night. Though not expecting the luggage horses till a very late hour in the night, it was our own wish to have waited their arrival, that we might erect our own beds in the house. The assiduous attention of the good people of the family prevented us in this intention. Mattrasses, filled with Eider-down, were disposed upon chairs in the sitting room, & in an adjoining apartment – and upon these we passed the night – How matters were arranged in other parts of the house, we had not the means of knowing – but judging from the quantum of noise in the room over our heads, a large and singular assemblage must have passed the night in this place. Those refinements in social life, which with us prescribe a separation of the different members of a family during their hours of rest, are considered of very little importance in Iceland. During our former visit at Hvanneiri, we had made a similar observation of this kind. The young *Frukin Stephansen*, eldest daughter of the Amtmand – the Atastrood – and our associate Loptson were all lodged together in the same room. At the present time, it is probable from their greater number, that there was a still more promiscuous grouping of the inhabitants of the house.

We were glad to have the opportunity of knowing something more of the *Amtmand Stephansen*, whom we had before seen only for a few minutes at Reikiaviik – Of all Icelanders whom we have yet met with, he most resembles an Englishman in his countenance, dress, & manners; – it might perhaps be nearest the truth to compare him with one of the highest class of farmers[2] in England. He is a man greatly superior in every respect to his brother the Atastrood; though not equally vain, or equally anxious to display his various qualifications – His manners are simple, pleasant, & unassuming – He possesses excellent common sense, and as much literary information, as is sufficient to render his conversation agreeable. – His inability to speak

[1] Stefán Ólafsson Stephensen. Skúli Magnússon's close association with the Stephensen family helped to restore his position after the collapse of Jörgensen's 1809 administration, which he supported. See Benedikt Benedikz, 'Grímur Thorkelín, the University of St. Andrews, and Codex Scardensis', *Scandinavian Studies*, 42 (1970), 385–93.

[2] Holland attributes 'intelligence and respectability of character ... judicious and rational spirit of improvement' to the great farmers of England and compares this favourably with the heedless conservatism of the small farmers: see Holland, 1808, p. 100.

English was in some measure compensated to us by his knowledge of the French, which he speaks tolerably well[1] – In his library, there are a few French books, but none of much value – The *Amtmand* is one of the greatest farmers in the island. He has 50 cows, 40 horses & 2 or 300 sheep. An appendage exists to his house, which is not known elsewhere in Iceland. This is a small windmill,[2] for the purpose of grinding corn – rude indeed in construction, but amply sufficient for the services of its present situation – The Amtmand's family is a large, & still increasing one – His present wife was formerly, as we understood, a servant in the house. Her manners & appearance are not particularly good; but she appears an active manager in domestic concerns.

Saturday 14th – This day Sir G.Mackenzie & I executed our intention of visiting the hot springs of Reikolt – Bright was detained at Hvanneiri by the occurrence of a slight indisposition. The direct distance of Reikolt from Hvanneiri is probably not more than 12 miles; but the circuitous nature of the route lengthens this to at least 16 – For the first few miles we were accompanied by the Amtmand, Sysselman Ottesen, & Mr Fell. The latter left us at Hvitaar Vellir, for the purpose of examining the salmon fishing on the river – the Amtmand & Sysselman accompanied us as far as the ford over the Hvitaar, which they crossed here on their way to a place called *Hvitaar*[3] in the Myre Syssel; where a judicial court was held on this day. The eldest son[4] of the Amtmand remained with us as our guide to Reikolt – a youth of about 16 years of age – and possessed of abilities of no common sort. The facility and elegance with which he speaks Latin, & the great progress which (with the assistance of his uncle, the Atastrood) he has made in the English language were less surprizing to us than the extreme shrewdness & accuracy of his remarks on all subjects which occurred in conversation. It is the intention of the *Amtmand* to send this young man by the first secure opportunity to Copenhagen – to prosecute his studies at the University there.[5] There is every probability that at some future period, his native

[1] Mackenzie, 1812, p. 200 notes Stefán Stephensen's fluency in French; only Steingrímur Jónsson at Bessastaðir displayed comparable command of the language.

[2] Mills were introduced to Iceland at the end of the eighteenth century. Wind mills were much rarer than those driven by water. See Þór Magnússon, 'Skýrsla um þjóðminjarsafn Íslands 1976', *ÁHÍF* (1977), 162–3.

[3] Unidentified as a specific place as opposed to the name of the river. Just possibly a reference to Hvítsstaðir in the Álftaneshreppur of Mýrasýsla.

[4] Ólafur Stefánsson Stephensen (1791–1854).

[5] Ólafur studied in Copenhagen 1814–17.

country will derive credit from his talents,[1] & advantage from his public service.

The excursion of the day was, upon the whole, productive of more gratification to us, than any other part of our journey. The weather was remarkably fine & the objects offered to our observation more than usually singular and interesting. Our road to Reikolt lay principally along the valley of the Hvitaar, upon the eastern side of the river – About 10 miles from Hvanneiri, we left this valley, & entered that of the *Rekiadals à*,[2] a considerable stream, which joins the Hvitaar from the east. – In the course of our ride the mountains to the north of this district formed magnificent objects in the distant view. The mountain, called *Eirik's Jokull*,[3] appeared pre-eminent over the rest;– covered with snow for more than half its height – On entering the valley of the *Reykiadals à*, the vicinity of the hot-springs was announced to us by the rising of columns of vapour in various parts of the valley. The first springs at which we arrived, were those of   ,[4] on the left[5] bank of the river – They are situated on a sort of platform, or elevated surface, formed by the bare rock – & probably about 20 yards in length by 10 or 12 in breadth. From apertures in this surface there rush out in numerous places streams of hot water, with much violence of ebullition, & the issue of a vast quantity of steam – Five of these springs[6] are of more considerable size than the others, & throw jets of boiling water to the height of two or three feet into the air – Where access could be obtained to any of the little basons from which the water issued, the thermometer indicated the boiling temperature. A considerable quantity of incrustation appeared about the springs, from which we obtained a few specimens.

Proceeding up the valley about a mile further, a still more interesting form of the same natural phenomenon was offered to our notice. In the middle of the channel of the river *Reikiadals-à*, an insulated rock appears, 8 or 10 feet in height, about 12 yards in length, & 5 or 6 in width – On this rock there are three boiling springs, one of which threws up a jet of water with so much violence, as to render it

[1] He became a judge and administrator in Denmark, and never seems to have returned to Iceland.
[2] Reykjadalsá. HH: This name is derived from the Icelandic words *Reikur*, Smoke – *Dale*, valley – & *à*, a river – It signifies therefore *the river of the smoking valley*.
[3] Eiríksjökull.
[4] Name omitted in MS.
[5] Original MS reading 'right' corrected subsequently by Holland.
[6]HH F 71 are specimens of the incrustation which appears about these springs.

hazardous to approach within a few feet of the aperture – Another of these springs rises from a bason, 2 or 3 feet in diameter, & 9 feet in depth, the water of which is in a state of evident & continued ebullition – It is a singular circumstance that the edge of this bason is not distant more than a couple of feet, from the perpendicular side of the rock, out of which the springs arise – Out of a small bank of gravel, continuous with the rock in the channel of the river, hot water bursts forth in several places, and another spring appears on the southern bank of the river, at a short distance from the spot. This singular assemblage of springs bears the name of *Vellines-hver*.[1]

The church & minister's house of Reikolt[2] are situated about 2 miles further up the valley – We proceeded to this place for the purpose of examining an ancient bath,[3] which has been constructed here for the reception of the hot water from an adjoining spring. The bath is of very simply construction – a circular bason, 12 or 14 feet in diameter, & 3 or 4 in depth – with one channel for the admission of the hot water from the spring – another for its exit – The temperature of the water, entering into the bath, we found to be 112° – The average temperature of the bath, probably about 100° – The hot-spring is 100 yards distant. It affords a considerable stream of water, the level for carrying which to the bath is not ill-constructed. – This bath of Reykolt was constructed by the celebrated *Snorro Sturleson*,[4] nearly 600 years ago. – At the present time it appears to be little used.

The minister of Reykolt[5] was not at home, but we saw his wife,[6]

[1] Vellinesshver. Sketched by Mackenzie, 1812, p. 195.

[2]HH At Reikholt, we were shewn a small fragment of porphyry, with green felspar – resembling the *verd-antiqua*. We were informed that it was found in the mountains to the north of Reikholt – a circumstance which produced some regret that our present plans did not admit of visiting this district of country. It was our original scheme to have proceeded northwards from Reikholt to Kalmanstunga, & thence to Surtshellir; with the view of examining a cave in the latter place, – which has acquired some celebrity from the report of Eghert Olafssen, in his travels – Finding reason, however, to believe that it was nothing more than an extensive cavern in the Lava, of which we had already seen several examples, we were led to resign this place, – as occupying more time than we could well bestow upon it. In *Husafell*, a mountain a few miles north of Reikholt, it is said that pitchstone is found in considerable quantity.

[3] Snorralaug.

[4] Snorri Sturluson (1178–1241), Iceland's most famous medieval man of letters and politician who lived and was murdered at Reykholt. The bath, and its linking passageway into the main buildings, are now restored. See Þorkell Grímsson, 'Gert við Snorralaug', *ÁHÍF* (1960), 19–45.

[5] Eggert Guðmundsson (1769–1832). After working for Magnús Stephensen at Leirá, he was consecrated priest in 1792 and served at Reykholt 1807–26.

[6] Guðrún Bogadóttir (1770–1850).

who brought us in the way of repast, two large basons filled with cream – an excellent specimen of the goodness of the pasture in the valley of the Reikiadals-à –

We commenced our return towards Hvanneiri on the northern, or rather western side of the river. Proceeding a mile or two, we came to a small hamlet, called *Storruleikia*,[1] where several hot springs issue from the ground. One of these in particular affords phenomena highly singular & interesting. The hot water bursts out, not in a direction perpendicular to the surface, as is the case in most of the other springs, but from the lower part of a small eminence, through an horizontal channel – A few feet above this aperture, another appears, from which no water issues but a large quantity of steam, rushing out with much impetuosity, and a noise resembling that from the open valve of a steam engine. The singular circumstance about this spring is its intermittence at intervals – Observing it for a short time, we were surprized to see the exit both of the water & steam suddenly cease, & remain suspended for one or two minutes. After this interval, a rushing noise was heard, the water began to flow again, & nearly at the same time, the steam to issue from the aperture above. The repetition of this process we witnessed several times. – The theory of the phenomenon would seem to be the following. A large reservoir below is connected by a narrow pipe with the external aperture – The water in this reservoir brought into ebullition by the ingress of steam, a portion of it is probably thrown into the pipe, where it is supported for some time by the steam below – During this interval, neither the water nor the steam appear from the external apertures. The steam, however, constantly increasing in quantity, soon acquires sufficient power to force the water along the pipe – and at the same time that the water begins to flow from the aperture, the steam also makes its appearance. The circumstance of the water & steam having different apertures is probably merely accidental, from the particular situation of the place.

This spring is made of some avail to economical purposes – In a small bason, just below the spot where the hot water issues from the ground, we observed two large pans, one containing milk, the other filled with curds: these belonged to the cottages above – Use is made of the heat which is communicated through the ground from the water & steam passing beneath. A small building has been erected a few yards above the spring, where clothes &c are dried, without any expence

---

[1] A mistaken form of Sturlureykir.

from fuel – The temperature of the room, at the time we were in it, was 73° – that of the air out of doors, 45°.

The most singular assemblage of hot springs, however, in the valley of the *Reikiadals à*, are those of *Tunga-hver*,[1] about a mile below *Storruleikia*. When distant two or three hundred yards from them, we were struck by the appearance, amid the mass of vapour, of a fine jet of water, apparently 12 or 14 feet in height. – While looking attentively upon the spot, & speculating upon the height of the column, we were amazed by its sudden disappearance, while another column of water, of less height but greater density, rose in its stead at a short distance. – Scarcely had we arrived at the place, & dismounted from our horses, when the phenomena were again reversed – the shorter column disappeared, & the one, first seen, again rose to its former height. By remaining on the spot about ½ an hour, we witnessed eight or ten of these remarkable alternations, which were repeated with the utmost regularity, & apparently at equal intervals of time – An examination of the spot, in which the phenomenon occurred, shewed two distinct apertures distant about a yard from each other, – or rather indeed two basons from which the water rose – One of these basons is considerably larger than the other, but is divided apparently into two parts by a ridge of rock which crosses it in the form of a bridge, not preventing, however, the free communication of the crater below. – Out of the smaller division of this bason the higher column of water is thrown; greater height probably depending upon the particular position of the arch which passes across the bason – In the larger division, the water rises only two or three feet – in the other, occasionally to the height of 13 or 14. – the rising in each division precisely at the same time – The jet of water from this bason continued 4 or 5 minutes; then gradually sinks down, & nothing but a slight ebullition appears in the water thus brought down to its natural level – When beginning to subside, the opposite process goes on in the bason or aperture near it – The ebullition becomes more violent, the water rises gradually to the edge of the bason, & soon is thrown up into the air in a column probably 5 or 6 feet in height. This column presents a more considerable body of water than the higher spout – but its periods of elevation are not continued for so long a time.

The theory of this singular phenomenon it is difficult to give – It is clear that the two springs must have the same common origin below –

---

[1] Deildartunguhver. See Mackenzie's sketch in Mackenzie, 1812, p. 199.

but the circumstance determining the exit of the steam first by one pipe, then by another, & this at regular intervals, it is not easy to define – This[1] alternation of the two springs is a permanent appearance – nor does it seem to be affected by the changes of the seasons.

The springs of *Tunga-hver*, are *not* remarkable only for the phenomenon just described. They are still further singular from their number, & from the peculiar situation in which most of them are placed – Arranged in a row at the foot of a perpendicular face of rock, they might be taken at some distance for an assemblage of vast caldrons, artificially thus placed – Looking from the overhanging edge of the rock above, the effect is singular in the extreme. The whole number of hot springs on this spot is 16 – the greater part of which throw columns of different heights into the air.

The minute observation of all these various natural wonders, detained us so long, that we did not reach *Hvanneiri* until a late hour in the evening. The day had been fine, & in every respect favourable to the excursion – from which we derived more than ordinary satisfaction & pleasure.

Sunday 15th. The plan which we laid out for this day, was to proceed, in company with Mr Fell to Innerholme, and thence to procure if possible, a boat for Reikiaviik the same evening – This being a road we had before travelled, nothing new was offered to our observation in the course of the journey – The *Amtmand* accompanied us a few miles, on a horse, which is considered to be one of the best in Iceland, as regards strength & speed. Sir G.Mackenzie mounted him for a short time, to try his paces – On dismounting & expressing his approbation of the animal, the *Amtmand* in a stile of no common politeness, requested that Sir George would accept him as a present; & in despite of all remonstrances, pressed the matter so much, as to render it necessary to comply – The *Amtmand* is celebrated in Iceland for his rapidly travelling – Though a very heavy man, & riding upon roads, of the badness of which it is scarcely possible for any one, not seeing them, to form an adequate conception, he nevertheless with a change of two or three horses contrives to get over a hundred English miles in the course of 24 hours – and has even in some instances accomplished a still greater distance in this time. The peculiar method of trotting of the Iceland horses was seen to the best advantage under his management –

---

[1] 'This alternation . . . seasons': marked for inclusion in the text at this point; written on facing page. See Journal MS, II, 30.

He contrived to make his horse proceed at the rate of at least 14 miles an hour in this pace.

The day was remarkably fine, and we enjoyed some splendid views of the mountain scenery of the Skard's Heide, which we crossed in proceeding to Leira – as well as an extended retrospective view of the great valley of the Borgar Fiord – At Leira we stopped a short time in the house of Sysselman Schaving, & took coffee with him. Independently of our own desire to proceed, we were unable to remain here long, in the fear of disturbing the preparations for a wedding, & wedding dinner, which were to take place this day in the Sysselman's house. Even before our departure the priest & some of the guests had arrived, all arrayed in their holyday suits – and each saluting each, as they respectively came in. It would have given us some satisfaction to have remained as witnesses of the marriage feast; but neither would our time admit of it, nor is it likely that we should have been regarded as welcome guests by the party assembled.

Between Leira & Innerholm we obtained some very striking views of the Hval Fiord, which we had never before seen to so much advantage. Nothing but foliage is wanting, to make the landscape perfect.

Arrived at Innerholm, we found the *Atastrood* & his family just as we had left them a month before – the former as ridiculously vain & insignificantly great as ever – We remained with them only a few hours, during which time, a supper, the organ & the Lang-spiel were provided for our entertainment. At 10 o'clock we went down to the shore to embark in a boat for Reikiaviik, the direct distance of which, across the Hval Fiord, & the Bay, is little more than 12 miles. The boat provided for us in the first instance was so leaky, as to render it impossible to put to sea in her – Another was accordingly launched, & the first one dragged on shore – The latter operation afforded us considerable entertainment. It was performed by a strange miscellaneous groupe of people – including besides our own party a number of persons from the house who were summoned by the Atastrood to assist in the labour, & who being raised from their beds for this purpose, came down to the shore in attire not a little singular & uncouth. Seven women were among the number – at the head of them, *Jungfru Gudrun*, who laboured at the task of hauling the boat, with infinite labour & perseverance. At this moment even the *Lord Chief Justice of all Iceland* forgot his dignities & greatness, & gave all his strength to the humble toil before him.

Our midnight sail of four hours was by no means disagreeable, though we met with some heavy seas in crossing the mouth of the Hval

Fiord – We set foot on the beach at Reikiaviik, at 2 in the morning, after an absence from the metropolis of Iceland of one month & two days – in the course of which time we had traversed altogether a distance of about 335 miles.

We remained at Reikiaviik until the 24th of the month – Nothing of moment occurred during this interval. Little variety occurs either in the occupations or amusements of this place, & the only novelty now offered to our notice was the *Handel*,[1] or Fair of Reikiaviik, which happens only once in the year, & continues from the 25th of June to the middle or later end of July. During this period great numbers of people assemble here from all points of the island, to dispose of their produce, & to purchase from the merchants the various articles necessary for their own use. – A good Handel will frequently bring to Reikiaviik some thousand horses – either wholly or partly laden with goods, – fish, oil, tallow, wool, butter, fox-skins &c – Most of the transactions between the country people & the merchants are conducted in the way of barter. A man brings his fish & wool to the merchant – it is weighed & its value ascertained – and the seller of these goods is entitled to call for articles of an equivalent value from the merchant's shop. Any surplus on either side is paid in rix dollars &c. The goods taken by the country people in exchange, are principally tobacco, spirits, meal, cotton goods, linen, thread, steel &c &c[2] –

Considering the number of people who come from the interior to the Handel at Reikiaviik, very little bustle or disturbance appear in the town at this time. Except in the shops of the merchants, nothing is seen to indicate the busy character of the time. Two or three Iceland tents indeed are sometimes pitched in the vacant ground before the church, but the greater number are always to be found at some distance from the town, pitched in those situations where pasture may most conveniently be obtained for the horses. The men themselves come into the town every day, with a certain number of their horses, to make their exchanges, purchases &c at the shops.

The Handel of this year, though better than that of the last summer,

---

[1] Danish word for 'market'.
[2]HH Some of the country people purchase at the Handel a small quantity of coal, intended for the fuel, wherewith to manufacture their knives &c. They may occasionally be seen tying up this in an old pair of fishing-breeches for carriage into the country.

is, however, by no means equal to those of former years. This may be attributed principally to the present unfortunate war – the evil effects of which are felt in Iceland, as in almost every other part of the habitable world¹ – Very little tallow has been brought from the country to Reikiaviik this year; owing to a deficiency in the produce of butter the preceding summer, which led to the consumption of the tallow in its stead. Some of the country people from the fishing district even purchased this article at the Handel for their domestic use. In the street of Reikiaviik, we saw some little children eating tallow eagerly, without any addition to the nauseous morsel. In general when used, it is eaten with the stock fish in lieu of butter.

A good deal of drunkenness may be seen in Reikiaviik during the period of the Handel – and this habit is too much encouraged by the merchants as an assistance to the disposal of their goods – Among other individuals of the motley tribe who appeared at the Handel with their horses & goods, we observed an old acquaintance in the person of the dirty priest,² whom we contrived to eject from the church at Roudemelr. We saw him once or twice during his stay at Reikiaviik, in a situation little befitting his clerical office. –

Another event during our present stay at Reikiaviik was the fishing of salmon in the *Lax River*,³ four miles to the east of the town – This salmon fishery is the only one in Iceland belonging to the King of Denmark. It is rented by Mr *Scheel*,⁴ the master of the Club-House at Reikiaviik, at the rate of 60 dollars per annum – In the present year he has made a contract with Mr Fell to give him all the salmon caught in the river at 1^d per lb. – The day of fishing the salmon is one of considerable importance at Reikiaviik – Not only those immediately concerned in the business are present – but likewise all the rank, fashion and beauty of the place. – At an early hour in the morning great numbers of people set out from the town for the river – the ladies mounted upon their horses, in a seat resembling a comfortable arm-chair, and galloping along with a degree of courage & hardihood not a little surprizing. The fishery this year was more unproductive, than it has ever before been recollected. At some former periods, not fewer than 5 or 6000 salmon have been taken from this river in a single day – This year only from 900 to 1000 fish were taken from one branch of the

¹ MS reads 'word'. ² See above, pp. 175–6.
³ Elliðaár.
⁴ See below, note 3, p. 103. The practice of renting out salmon fishing rights in the river had begun in 1757.

stream – and a day or two afterwards, 140 from another part of the river. No fewer than 60 or 70 men were employed in the fishing, which was performed by a net dragged up the stream. It is the practice to pay these men by a third portion of the fish caught – which they employ for baits in the sea fishery in the spring.

A disgraceful, but ridiculous *fracas* occurred while the fishing was going on. Mr Savignac, who was one of the party at the river, struck a fisherman for having, as he alledged, purposely thrown a salmon into his face. A verbal dispute of much violence ensued, which drew all the other fishermen from their occupation in the river. Mr Savignac striking the man a second time, was immediately assailed by several of the fishermen, who contrived to throw him upon the ground; & would doubtless, by pressing upon him, have committed some serious injury, had we not interfered[1] to prevent any further proceeding. The business was afterwards brought before the Sysselman[2] of the district, & before the Landfogd Frydensberg, – the fisherman demanding the penalty of 9 dollars which is imposed by the law upon any man striking another. No adjustment, however, was made. – Mr Savignac is dreaded, as well as disliked in Reikiaviik;[3] & not even the *governors of the land* are willing to subject themselves to his resentment. The notice which he sometime ago received to quit his present habitation, he has refused to comply with – and here it appears the matter will rest. The government has neither power nor courage to enforce its legal proceedings.

During our present stay at Reikiaviik, I passed a good deal of time with the Bishop, from whom I derived much valuable information respecting the present state of literature in Iceland, the character & habits of the people &c &c. Our conversations were carried on solely in Latin, & frequently continued for three or four successive hours. The frequent necessity there has been for speaking this language in Iceland, has given me much additional facility in its use, and enabled me to surmount the difficulties which I at first experienced from the extreme dissimilarity of the English and Icelandic pronunciation of the language. – Another most valuable informant, whom I had the good fortune to meet, and with whom I spent much time, was the *Amtmand Thoransen*[4] –

[1] MS indistinct: perhaps 'interfeared'.

[2] Hans Wolner Koefoed (1779–1849); *sýslumaður* in Kjósarsýsla from 1806–12; continued to exercise authority there by proxy until 1814.

[3] See Jón Espólín, 1821–55, XII (Part 10), 46, 56–7, for other instances of Savignac's volatile yet cowardly nature in his dealings with citizens of Reykjavík.

[4] Stefán Þórarinsson; see above, note 1, p. 141.

a man of plain & simple manners, but possessing excellent good sense, & most accurate & extensive information in all matters relating to the statistics & political economy of Iceland – He lives at Eyjafiord, but came over to Reikiaviik at this time, in consequence of his appointment to be one of the three *pro tempore* governors of the island. I obtained from him much interesting information respecting the northern part of the island – from the communication of which he himself appeared to derive no small satisfaction & pleasure.

A good deal of medical business occurred to me, during this short residence at Reikiaviik, increased by the absence of Dr Klog, who had gone over to the Westmann Islands some time before for the purpose of investigating a singular disease,[1] which appears in this place. One of my principal patients was the assessor Gröndal[2] – a man who had obtained celebrity as the first Icelandic poet of the present day.

The plan for our next journey into the interior of Iceland included *Thingvalla*,[3] *the Geyser, Hecla*, and, if it were found possible, the volcanic district about *Kattlegaia Jokull*[4] – Mr Fell associated himself as a partner in our projected expedition, as far as the Geyser; and we received a further addition to the party in Mr Flood, a young man who came over from England in the galliot Bilderdald. He is a native of Norway, & came to Iceland last year, as a sort of secretary to Count Trampe. When the Count was taken prisoner, Flood solicited permission to remain with him on board the *Margaret & Anne*, which was allowed him. He afterwards accompanied the Count to England, attended him in his travels through various parts of the kingdom, & spent the last winter in London. His object in returning to Iceland this year appears to have been, to collect & dispose of Count Trampe's property in the island. It is now well ascertained, & generally known that the Count will not return to the Government of Iceland; and another Governor is expected to arrive either in the autumn of this year, or early in the ensuing spring – Mr Flood will leave Iceland again in the course of a few weeks, – and wishes before his departure to see all that may be possible in this part of the island.

[1] Identified by Holland in Mackenzie, 1812, pp. 405–6 as Tetanus (Mod.Ice. *Ginklofi*); discussed by Holland, 1811, p. 25; the disease was particularly virulent amongst children. Klog's visit to Vestmannaeyjar was noted by Holland: see Mackenzie, 1812, p. 405.

[2] See above, note 3, p. 97.

[3] Þingvellir.   [4] Kötlugjá.

THIRD JOURNEY[1][V]

Tuesday 24th July – Our luggage horses & guides left Reikiaviik on Monday morning; it being our plan to meet them at *Thingvalla* on the evening of this day. – The morning augured ill for the comfort of our journey – The barometer had been gradually falling for several days, and the change of the wind to the easterly quarter the preceding evening brought with it clouds & heavy rain. – During the preceding five weeks we had enjoyed an almost uninterrupted succession of fine, clear weather – A similar instance scarcely occurred to the recollection of the oldest inhabitant of Reikiaviik –

In despite of all ominous appearances, we availed ourselves of an interval of fair weather this morning, to commence our journey. Scarcely, however, had we proceeded ½ a mile, before the rain again came on more heavily than ever. We pursued the road, however, for two or three miles without wavering in our plans. At length, finding the rain become every instant more violent, & seeing a dismal prospect of dense, black clouds before us, we decided upon returning

[1]HH *Eastern Journey*

	Miles
Reikiaviik to Thingvalla	26
Thingvalla to Skalholt	25
Skalholt to the Geyser	16
Geyser to Skalholt	16
Skalholt to Kalfholt	20
Kalfholt to Storu-vellir	12
Storu-vellir to Niifürholt	9
Excursion to Reikiadalr, about	55
Excursion to the summit of Hecla	14
Niifürholt to Hlidarende	25
Hlidarende to Odde	16
Odde to Eyarback	25
Eyarback to Reikiaviik	30
Miles	289

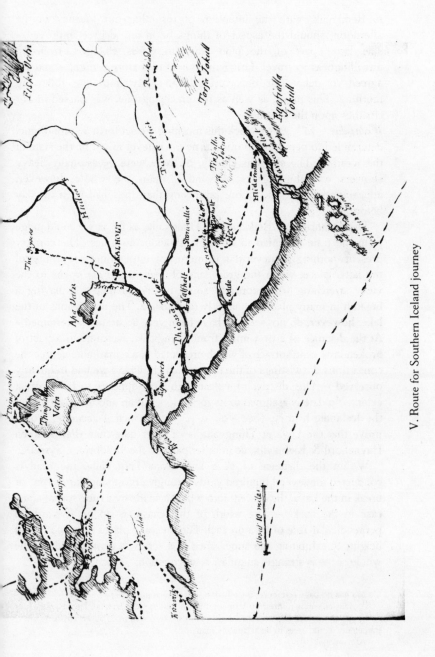

V. Route for Southern Iceland journey

to Reikiaviik, with the intention of resuming our journey in the afternoon, should the aspect of things be in any degree improved – The latter part of the plan was afterwards changed, from an unwillingness to travel during the whole of a stormy night – and we agreed to delay our departure till an early hour the following morning. This night, as well as the preceding one, was passed in our cloathes upon the ground.

Wednesday – 25th. At 5 o'clock this morning we set forth a second time, determined to persevere in our journey, whatever might be the state of the weather. The sky was cloudy, & there were occasionally heavy showers with high gusts of wind – upon the whole, however, appearances were much more promising than they had been the day before –

The distance from Reikiaviik to Thingvalla, as far as we could judge from the time occupied in riding it, is about 26 miles. The country presents nothing whatever that is interesting until within a few miles of the latter place, when the great lake of *Thingvalla-Vatn* opens to the view; stretching from north to south nearly 20 miles, & having a breadth in many places apparently of 10 or 12. The dimensions of the lake, however, do not seem to have been very accurately ascertained – At the distance of 2 or 3 miles from Thingvalla, we came to a tract of broken lava – the surface of which presented in a remarkable degree the contortions & twistings of the rock which elsewhere we had frequently observed – This district of volcanic country appears to be of great extent. No date is assigned to its formation, but an anecdote is given in the Icelandic history, (See Vol. 1, p.   )[1] which if accurate, would prove that the Lava at Thingvalla is of older date than that between Havnefiord & Kiebleviik, & in other parts of the Guldbringe Syssel.

Within the distance of ½ a mile from Thingvalla, the road is conducted for several hundred yards through a most singular chasm[2] or break in the Lava, the descent into which is made by a rude sort of stair-case in the rock[3] – The width of this chasm is 20 or 30 yards, a perpendicular face of lava on each side, in some places 80 or 90 feet in height, & exhibiting the appearance of a series of distinct beds – The whole scene is strange, singular, & uncommon.

---

[1] MS has no page reference: the allusion is to note 2, pp. 112–14.

[2]HH This chasm is noticed by Van Troil in his Letters from Iceland. He describes it as being 105 feet broad, & states the height of the western wall to be about 107 feet. These statements would seem to be accurately made.

[3] Almannagjá.

The church of Thingvalla, connected according to common
Icelandic custom, with the minister's house,[1] is situated on the eastern
bank of a small river,[2] which enters the lake at its northern extremity –
On the opposite side of the stream, & fronting the door of the church,
a complete wall of lava presents itself to the eye, stretching more than
a mile from N to S. – This forms one side of the chasm before
mentioned – The church is situated at a short distance from the Lake,
the views of which, from this side are particularly fine – The depth of
Thingvalla Vatn is very great – in some places a line of 100 fathoms
has been sunk without finding the bottom – It abounds in trout &
char[3] of excellent quality; which are, however, caught only for the
immediate use of the cottages & farm-houses in the vicinity of the
lake.

The church at Thingvellir we found to be more miserable than any
we had before seen in Iceland; that of Kriseviik alone excepted. It is
very small, very dirty, & badly paved with rough fragments of lava.
With some difficulty we contrived to make our arrangements for the
night, by the aid of chests, stones &c. Three of the party were settled
in the space before the altar – The other two near the church door –
We were provided from the minister's house with a good supper of
fried trout & char, with sour curds & cream.

Thursday 26th. Thingvalla has attained celebrity as being the spot
where the judicial assemblies, & other national meetings of Iceland
were formerly held.[4] Few vestiges, however, now remain to mark a
spot so important in the history of Iceland, though not more than 10
years have elapsed since the transference of the judicial courts from
this place to Reikiaviik.[5] A few square fragments of lava, appearing in
small heaps on the western side of the river, opposite to the church,
are the remains[6] of walls, upon which were stretched the tents of the
different magistrates & officers of state, who attended these public
meetings – The only building on the spot was a small wooden house,
in which the consultations of the judicial magistrates were held, and

---

[1] Minister was Páll Þorláksson (1748–1821); served at Þingvellir 1780–1818.

[2] Öxará.

[3] *Salmo alpinus* (Linn); Mod.Ice. *Fjallbleikja*.

[4] MS erasure reads: 'scarcely a single vestige, however, of these ancient glories is
now to be seen – some fragments of lava only excepted, which appear on the western
side of the river, and which are said to be the ruins of buildings, formerly existing in
these places'.

[5] Transfer took place in 1798.

[6] See *FÍÁ* (1930), pp. 33–4.

from which the sentences were announced. – by the *Stifftamtmand* or Governor of the Island – The place where some of these sentences were put into execution, was likewise shewn to us at Thingvalla – On a small island[1] in the river, the male culprits who had received sentence of death, were beheaded with the axe – The females condemned to die, were drowned in a deep pool[2] which appears below the Lava, some way further up the river – The presence of the *Stifftamtmand*, of the *Amtmand*, of the two *Laugmen*,[3] & of all the *Sysselmen* of the island, was required at the general meeting of Thingvalla, – which was held once a year, about the middle of July.[4] At the time of the transference of the court to Reikiaviik, the office of *Laugman* was abolished; and in lieu of it were appointed a *Justitiatius of the island* (the office filled by the Atastrood) & two *Assessors* or *assistant judges*.

An ecclesiastical court also was formerly held annually at Thingvalla at which were present the Bishop of Skalholt – the Provosts from the Syssels of Borgar-Fiord – Guldbringe – Aarnes, & Rangaavalle[5] & two ministers attending the Provost from each Syssel – Their meetings were held in the church of Thingvalla.

We recommenced our journey at 6 o'clock – it being the plan of the day, to proceed to Skalholt,[6] on our way to the Geyser Springs. This route is a circuitous one; but we were induced to adopt it, from the greater convenience of passing the night within the walls of a church – For the first few miles from Thingvalla the road lies along the banks of the lake – entirely over Lava – The views we obtained from the lake, & the mountains which environ it were exceedingly fine – It is probable, however, that the extent of this piece of water is considerably over-rated in the maps of Iceland – Judging from appearances alone, I should conceive that it might be 12 or 14 miles in length, by 6 or 8 in breadth. The district of Lava at Thingvalla is of great extent, probably not less than 7 or 8 miles in width. It does not present the same ruggedness of surface, as many other beds of Lava in

[1] Þorleifshólmi; also called Höggstokkseyri.
[2] Drekkingarhylur.
[3] Mod.Ice. *lögmaður*, 'lawyer'. HH: I have since learnt that the office of *Laugman* was continued for some time after the removal of the Courts to Reikiaviik.
[4] The general assembly (*alþingi*) was originally held for two weeks, beginning on the Friday of the tenth (later the eleventh) week of summer.
[5] Árnessýsla and Rangárvallasýsla.
[6] Skálholt.

the Guld-bringe & in Vesterland, – but is thrown up into rounded elevations of various size, below which hollows & caverns in many places occur. Numerous fissures appear in the rock – some of them of great depth, & having streams of water, flowing at the bottom. The *contortions* & *undulations* of the exposed surface of the rock, appear in a remarkable degree upon this bed of lava.

To the north of the extensive plain, which is here formed by the Lava, lie several ranges of mountains,[1] having a great elevation, & exhibiting much variety of form – One of these mountains, called *Skial-breid*[2] 12 or 14 miles NE of Thingvalla, is said to have a distinctly-formed crater on its summit. The general form of the hill is that of a very flat cone – the upper part covered with snow. – Beyond this mountain, is seen a wide extent of mountain land[3] cloathed with perpetual snows; – this district, according to the accustomed use of the term in Iceland, is called a *Jokull*[4] –

Leaving the track of Lava, 6 or 8 miles from Thingvalla, and ascending gradually to the summit of a low range of hills, a view opened out towards the west, at once extensive & magnificent – Immediately before us lay a valley of great width, & considerable fertility – through which two large rivers pursue their course – uniting their streams below – In the middle of the valley are spread out the waters of the lake, called *Apa-Vatn*.[5] Its western boundary is formed by several ridges, rising gradually over each other – passing beyond which, the eye takes in the celebrated mountain of Hecla – and further to the south, the less celebrated, but much higher mountain of *Eyafialla Jokull*,[6] which we before had seen, when first approaching Iceland from the sea. –

Skalholt is situated in the middle of the valley, in the angle formed by the confluence of the two rivers *Brúar-á*[7] and *Hvitaar*[8] – One of these

[1]HH From their general appearance, it is probable that many of these mountains belong to the *Conglomerate* or *Volcanic-tuff* formation, which prevails so abundantly in the Volcanic districts of Iceland. – The lower part of one of the ridges, which we passed on our road, we distinctly observed to be composed of this Rock.

[2] Skjaldbreiður, 'broad shield'; a 'lava shield' volcano is a flat and regular cone of ropy-lava, which has erupted only once.

[3]HH From the map it would appear that this high mountain range must be that called *Tungur-Fiall Jokull*. |Ed: MS erasure 'Blafelds Jokull'|.

[4] Mod.Ice. *jökull*, 'glacier'.

[5] Apavatn.

[6] Eyjafjallajökull.

[7] Brúará.

[8] Hvítá. To be distinguished from the river of the same name in Borgarfjörður.

rivers, the *Brúar-á*, it was necessary to cross before reaching the place. The stream is of considerable breadth – deep & rapid – We crossed over in a boat, – the horses swimming across – Skalholt is somewhat more than a mile beyond the ferry, having a situation which possesses more picturesque beauty than any other we have seen in Iceland. – Somewhat elevated above the level of the valley, it commands a striking view of the confluence of the two rivers, and towards the west, of Hecla, Eya-fialla Jokull, & other lofty mountains in their vicinity – The place, though usually considered as the capital of Iceland, consists only of a church & farm house. – The church[1] is constructed entirely of wood, & is one of the largest we have yet seen in the island. It is of very recent date; the old cathedral, on the site of which it stands, having been taken down only 6 years ago. – During many centuries, Skalholt was the seat of one of the Icelandic Bishops[2] – an equality of rank existing between the Bishop of this place, & that of Hoolum,[3] in the north of the island. The learned Johannes Finnæus,[4] son to Finnur Jonsson,[5] the author of the Ecclesiastical History of Iceland,[6] was the last Bishop of Skalholt – he died in 1796, & the Bishop of Hoolum[7] dying soon afterwards, application was made to the court of Denmark, to allow a union of the office & revenue of the two sees. This was granted, & the title of Bishop of Iceland given to Geir Vidalin, the present possessor of this dignity – The cathedral of Skalholt has been twice destroyed by fire.[8] The vestiges of the last edifice are still remaining, so far as to allow its extent to be seen, which was considerably greater than that of the present church –

We were much gratified by meeting at Skalholt the *Lector* of the school at Bessasted – *Steingrim Jonsson* – in whose favour we had been greatly prepossessed, when he saw him at his own house in our

[1]HH At the present time, service is performed in this church only every third Sabbath day – in the winter, only one Sunday in four.

[2] From 1056–1796.

[3] Hólar in Hjaltadalur.

[4] Hannes Finnsson. See Kristján Eldjárn, 'Myndir af Skálholtsbiskupum', *ÁHÍF* (1968), 100–4; also note 4, p. 180 above.

[5] Finnur Jónsson (1704–1789). See *ÁHÍF* (1968), pp. 90–100. MS has 'son to Finnur Jonsson, the' added above the line, clearly as an authorial correction.

[6] *Historia ecclesiastica Islandiæ*, 4 vols. (1772–8); a work frequently cited by Holland in his 'Preliminary Dissertation'. Finnur was a prolific author of historical, theological, biographical and geographical works, many of which remain unpublished.

[7] Sigurður Stefánsson (1744–1798), bishop of Hólar from May 1789.

[8] Most recently as far as Holland was concerned, in the devastating volcanic eruptions of 1783.

excursion to Bessasted – He was formerly a secretary to Bishop Finnæus, and on the decease of the latter, married his widow[1] – the second wife of the Bishop – a marriage by which his prospects in life were very greatly improved[2] – I obtained from himself the information that at the time of his becoming a *demissus* from the school, he had not a single dollar in his pocket. By his marriage he became possessor of half the farm at Skalholt[3] – The other part belongs to the sister of his wife, an unmarried women,[4] who lives at the farm-house at the present time.

We fixed ourselves for the night in the church, which was large enough to admit conveniently all our party – It contains several relics of the old cathedral;[5] none of them, however, of much value – A portrait of

[1] Valgerður Jónsdóttir (1771–1856).

[2] HH NB *Skalholt Church.* 29th July. An Icelander is at this moment looking over me, with his head so close to mine, as to keep me in continual dread of the contact – He is commenting upon my writing at as much length & with as great loquacity, as if he were assured that I understood every word of his discourse.

[3] Steingrímur Jónsson was consecrated as priest at Oddi in Rangárvallasýsla in 1811.

[4] Valgerður's one sister, unmarried at this time, was Margrét Jónsdóttir (1776–1857); she suffered a nervous breakdown after the breaking off of her engagement to Jónas Scheving (See above, note 3, p. 160).

[5] HH At the door of the church at Skalholt are some old grave stones, with inscriptions on them –

> Sepulchrum vir pietate, genere, ac doctrina clarissimi,
> Gislavi Magni f. Nomarchiæ Rangarvallensis Præfecti
> Regii, qui placide in Christo obdormivit Schalholti,
> Die 4 Junii Anno MDCXCVI Ætatis LXXVI – Præmissa ad
> Cælites uxore nobilissima
> Ðruda Thorlevi filia.

[The tomb of a man most renowned for piety, family, and learning, Gísli Magnússon, Royal Prefect of Rangárvallasýsla, who died peacefully in Christ at Skálholt June 1696, at the age of 66. His most noble wife Þrúður, the daughter of Þorleifur, went to heaven before him.]

In the space before the altar are suspended two tablets with the following inscriptions –

> ΙΧΟΥΣ
> Priscis nobilibus creatus olim
> Virtutis q. patrum beatus hæ res
> Dilecti genitoris ipsa imago,
> et desiderium piæ parentis,
> Communis q: amor omnium bonorum
> Quos secum sociavit alma fides,
> Et candor sibi nescius fraudis
> Eheu precipiti nimis ruina
> Mortis vulnifico peremtus æstro (?)
> Post vitæ decies duos Decembre
> Mæstæ Thorstenides domus levamen
> Eggertus jacet hac sepultus in urna
> amoris ergo fecit Joh. Widalin

[Born of noble forebears once, and the blessed heir of the virtue of his ancestors, the very image of his beloved father, the longing of his pious mother, and the

Bishop Finnæus, tolerably well executed, hangs on one of the walls. The Bishop is buried immediately under the space before the altar – A trap-door raised disclosed to us his tomb-stone, the epitaph on which, in the Icelandic language, was composed by *Atastrood Stephansen*. – A considerable part of the evening I passed in conversation with the *Lector*, from whom I obtained much information regarding the literature of Iceland, conveyed in a manner, simple, pleasing, & unaffected. – In going to bed this evening we experienced much inconvenience from a source not new to us – A number of people both male & female, stood at the church door & within the church, watching us with the most minute attention – None of the hints we gave them, that their departure would be acceptable, were understood; & at length it was necessary to tell them our wishes directly through the medium of Loptson. – Even then it was difficult to move them from the place, and from the occupation on which they were so intently engaged.

Friday 27th – Our journey to day was to carry us to a spot, long celebrated as one of the greatest natural wonders, not merely in this island, but even in the extent of the known world. – To visit the *Geyser Springs* had been with every one of the party the subject of long &

---

common love of all good men whom dear faith associated with him, and candour ignorant of deceit. Alas, with ruin too headlong he has been taken away by the wounding tempest of death, after twenty winters of life. Eggert, son of Þorsteinn, comfort of a sad house, lies buried in this urn. Jón Vídalín wrote this out of love.|

Hic ego sponsa Dei, felix agnis ministra
Mortua post vitæ munera parva tego(?)
Nomen in orbe mihi nulli Deus arbiter orbis,
Scripsit in auspicuo nomen in orbe meum
Extremis tetigi labris, diræ ascula mortis.
Ne saltem prisca lege, soluta forem
Quandoquidem vixi, lethi mihi prosunt inde,
Inveni nunquam denique posse mori.
Lux igitur formosa vale, lux filia lucis
Qua nunc in cælo candidione fruor.

|Here I, the bride of God, am covered dead after the small gifts of life, I the happy ministress to the lambs. God, the arbiter of the world, wrote me no name in the world, wrote my name in *his* auspices. I have touched with the tips of my lips the kisses of dreadful death, so that I would not be exempt from ancient law, since I have lived; my letters are of advantage to me, and I have found because of them that I can never die. Farewell beautiful light – light, daughter of that light, which now in heaven I enjoy more dazzlingly|.

|ED. (i) Gísli Magnússon (1621–96), a widely travelled author, scholar and *sýslumaður*. His wife was Þrúður Þorleifsdóttir. The family had one tragic connection with Britain – their son Þorleifur died in Oxford in 1679, aged 19. (ii) Jón Vídalín (1666–1720) was priest (1693) and then bishop (1698–1720) at Skálholt. The deceased and his father are unidentified|.

earnest desire – and these wishes were now about to be gratified. – A heavy rain which occurred in the morning delayed our setting out until 1 o'clock – We were accompanied, as a guide, by a son of the late Bishop Finnæus – a fine young man,[1] who has studied the English language assiduously; & speaks it with some degree of facility. – The distance of the Geyser from Skalholt is about 16 miles – the direction of the springs being nearly north of the latter place. The road which, in Iceland, may be esteemed a very good one, conducted us up the valley of a river,[2] which falls into the Hvitaar, a short distance above Skalholt. In our way, we observed several hot springs; some of them near Skalholt – one very considerable spring about a mile from the shore of the *Apa Vatn*.

At 4 o'clock we arrived at the great assemblage of springs, which are named the *Geysers*.[3] Some time before, we had been made aware of our

[1] Either Jón or Ólafur, the two sons of Hannes Finnsson.

[2] Tunguﬂjót.

[3]HH *Situation &c of the Geyser Springs*
The Geyser Springs are placed at the foot & upon the eastern ascent of a steep but not lofty ridge of hill, which has an insular situation in a valley, about 16 miles north of Skalholt. The valley itself is several miles in width, & consists of tolerably good pasture land – About a mile north of the springs is a small hamlet, called *Haukadalr*, with a church. At the distance of not more than 200 yards to the south of the springs, there is a farm house & several others appear in different parts of the valley –
The surface from which the springs arise, at the foot & on the ascent of the insulated ridge, is completely denuded of all verdure, & covered with fragments of incrustation from the springs. Its form is very irregular, & it is difficult therefore to assign its extent in different directions. The longest line which can be traced upon it is one nearly in a direction from N to S – which is probably little less than 350 yards in length. A stream runs at a short distance on its eastern side, which receives some smaller streams from the springs themselves. – (See Sketch p. 58)[W] [Ed. sketchbook missing.]
The *Great or Old Geyser* is situated nearly at the northern extremity of the tract from which the springs arise; the high conical mound of incrustation which has been formed around it, rendering it conspicuous among the rest. The circumference of this mound at its base is not less than 300 yards. The great bason at its summit has a figure approaching to the circular – its greatest diameter 56 feet.– the smallest diameter 46 feet.[X] The pipe, which is not, however, placed in the centre of the bason, has a diameter at its aperture of 16 feet – the diameter within is about ten – The mound of incrustation terminates more abruptly on the eastern side than on any other – and at a shorter distance from the bason – having a perpendicular fall on this side of several feet – Below this runs a small stream, originating in the water from several different springs on the opposite ascent. – Tracing the stream downwards under the edge of the incrustation, several small springs appear on each side, all in a state of ebullition, the water of some of them deriving a white colour from a bole or clay which it holds suspended. The bank on which these springs appear, under the mound of the Great Geyser, is composed in a great measure of *bole* of different colours, with a small quantity of *Alum*, & some traces of *sulphur*.
At the distance of about 130 yards in a direction nearly south from the Old Geyser, is situated the New Geyser, presenting externally only a small & imperfectly formed mound of incrustation – and a pipe nearly circular, about 9 feet in diameter – The incrustation

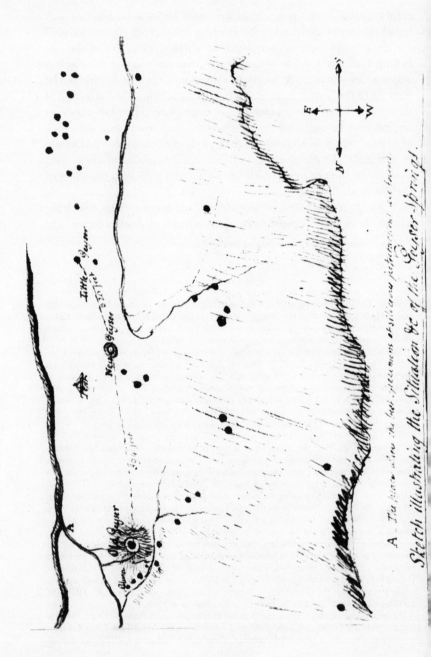

A – The place where the best specimens of siliceous petrifactions are found ◯

Sketch illustrating the Situation &c. of the Geiser-Springs.

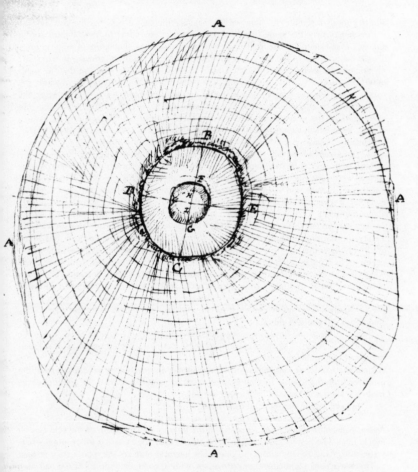

The Old Geyser Spring

AA &c --- About 300 yds --- the circumference of the great Cone.
BC. --- 56 feet --- --- the greatest diameter of the Basın.
DE --- 46 feet --- --- the smallest diameter of the Basın.
EG --- 16 feet --- --- Diameter of the pipe, at its aperture.
IL --- 10 feet --- --- Diameter of the pipe within.

X. Geysir

239

approach, by seeing numerous columns of vapour rising from the ground, the surface surrounding them bare of grass, & every where covered with fragments of a red-incrustation.' Reaching the spot,² we

---

almost entirely resembles in character &c, that surrounding the bason of the Old Geyser.

Pursuing nearly the same line of direction about 100 yards further, a third spring appears, of considerable size, & likewise surrounded by a small quantity of incrustation – This is the principal of the Little Geyser springs as they have been termed – in which the phenomena are precisely of the same kind as in the Great Geyser – except that the water only boils violently without spouting, when the pipe is full. Still further towards the south, numerous hot springs occur, some of them exhibiting in a slight degree the phenomenon of alternate rising & falling – others in a state of constant ebullition – In every part of the encrusted surface among these springs, small apertures or fissures appear, from which vapour issues, having a slightly sulphureous odour. In many places, the rushing of water & of steam below the ground is distinctly heard.

On the ascent of the hill, likewise, to the west of the great Geysers, numerous hot springs, of greater & less size, appear. It is probable that at a former period some of these springs were very much more considerable than at present. This may be inferred from the quantity of incrustation every where covering the surface, & from the great depth & diameter of several of the apertures – One of them in particular, situated on a level greatly above that of the Old & New Geysers, is singularly curious and remarkable – A bason, not less than 20 feet in length, & 8 or 10 in width, is filled almost to its brim with water, in a state approaching to ebullition. The appearances presented in the inside of this bason are highly beautiful. – The water is extremely clear & transparent, & allows the eye to penetrate to a great depth along the perpendicularly descending sides, which are every where lined with an incrustation, projecting outwards into a variety of forms. The bason is traversed about its middle by a narrow arch, appearing to be composed entirely of incrustation, but so slight as to render it dangerous, if not impossible, to cross it in this way – Neither description nor drawing are capable of giving a sufficient idea of the singularity & beauty of this spot.

Two or three of the hot springs are placed very nearly at the summit of the hill to the west of the Geysers. The most elevated of these exhibits some appearances of sulphur, though in very small quantity.

Near the hamlet of Haukadalr, other hot springs appear. There we did not visit, but procured from them some specimens of incrustation; which shew that the qualities of the water are similar to those of the Geyser springs.

' Produced by the clay mineral iron oxide.

²HH *Occurrences at the Geyser Springs during 44 Hours.*

Friday. Arrived at the Springs ¼ past 3 in the afternoon. The bason of the Old Geyser nearly full – The first spouting began ¼ past 5 – ceased at 5.21 – 18 distinct spouts – The water sunk about 10 feet within the pipe – The height of some of the spouts 50 or 60 feet.

The water began immediately to rise again, with frequent ebullitions. At 6 it had risen into the funnel – at 6½ the funnel was full – At 7.40 a second spouting occurred, the bason being then about half full – Few spouts & inconsiderable in height. The water sunk very little after the action had ceased.

At 8.45 the Geyser again rose – continued to spout for 3 minutes – Only two considerable spouts. The water did not sink within the pipe.

At 6 this evening, one of the springs to the south of the Great Geysers continued for some minutes to throw up water to the height of 10 or 12 feet.

At 11.48 several reports were heard from the Old Geyser, & the water ran over the bason, but there was no spouting.

immediately directed our steps to a great circular bason, elevated considerably above the ground in its vicinity, & surrounded by an incrustation of great thickness. This is the bason of the Great Geyser spring – At the time we approached it, it was completely full of water, nearly in a state of ebullition, – the water in several places running over the edge of the bason, & flowing down the side of the flattened cone, on the summit of which the bason is placed – In the middle of the bason, a pipe appeared, having the form of a funnel, or inverted cone, & as we afterwards found, about 16 feet in diameter at the base of the cone – The depth of the water in the bason, taking it in the middle over the aperture of the pipe, is about 3 feet – Having contemplated for some time the general appearances of the spot, and observing no material change to take place, except a very gradual rise in the level of the water, we left the spring & occupied ourselves in observing others in its immediate vicinity. Scarcely had we been absent, however, a quarter of an hour, when several successive reports were heard, proceeding from underneath the ground, & much resembling the noise of distant cannon

---

Saturday
    At 2.30 PM – The same phenomena were repeated in the Old Geyser.
    At 4.5 PM – The New Geyser began to spout – Continued till 7 –
    (During the remainder of this morning the appearances of the Old Geyser were (not particularly attended to, as we were occupied in the tent. There was no (spouting, however, from the spring–
At 1.57 PM the Old Geyser boiled over, with several reports, but without spouting.
At 5.25 – the same phenomenon repeated
At 6.55   –––D°–––––
At 8.35   –––D°–––––
NB. In no instance, where there was merely a boiling over from the bason, did the water sink within the pipe.
At 8.38 immediately after the boiling over of the Old Geyser, the New Geyser began to spout.
At 9.17 it had nearly ceased, the spray just rising above the bason.
At 11.30 many loud reports were heard from the Old Geyser, and immediately afterwards it began to spout to a great height. Nine distinct columns were thrown into the air. The 7th which was the highest appeared to be about 90 feet in height. The water sunk to some depth within the pipe.
Sunday.
At 6.43 AM. The water boiled over from the bason of the Old Geyser, with several reports.
At 9.21. The same phenomenon repeated
At 9.32. The New Geyser began to spout – to a greater height than either of the preceding times – probably not less than 90 feet.
At 10.30 – The spouting of the New Geyser had almost entirely ceased.
    During the whole of this period that one of the Little Geysers, nearest to the New Geyser, continued to display the phenomenon of alternate rising & sinking in its pipe – the water when at the greatest height, boiling with much violence.

– Sir G. Mackenzie, who was employed at the time in collecting some specimens of the incrustation surrounding the bason, very distinctly felt the ground to shake under him – These subterranean noises continued for some minutes – the successive sounds varying in force & in frequency of occurrence. We all immediately hastened to the spot & placed ourselves as near to the bason, as our present ignorance of the phenomena rendered prudent – At this time the water in the bason was in a state of violent & incessant agitation – particularly in the centre over the aperture of the pipe. Almost immediately afterwards the spouting commenced – the water was thrown up in great masses into the air – each successive time with more violence, & to a greater height – immense volumes of steam bursting out at the same time from the bason & from every part of the column – In the course of about 4 minutes the phenomenon was repeated eighteen times, the height of the spouts varying considerably during this interval. Forming a general judgement from a comparison of our several observations, it is probable that the highest column of water thrown into the air at this time, had an elevation of 60 or 70 feet – Immediately after the spouting had ceased, the water, which before had filled the great bason, ran backwards with much rapidity, and in little more than a minute had sunk to the depth of 8 or 10 feet within the central pipe – every appearance of ebullition having now ceased – For more than an hour we remained on the spot, watching the phenomena which successively occurred – After continuing stationary for a short time at its lowest point, the water began very gradually to rise in the pipe – this rising being attended with frequent violent ebullitions, & the discharge of large quantities of steam. In 40 minutes the water had risen into the funnel of the pipe. In $1^h 10^m$ it had filled the funnel, & began to rise in the great bason of the spring.

In the course of the evening, we twice witnessed the repetition of these phenomena, though in a much less considerable degree than at the first time of observation – The second spouting took place at $7^h.40^m$ – two hours & twenty minutes after the first – At this time the bason was only half-full – the spouts were few in number & did not attain any great height – After the action had ceased, the water sunk very little in the bason – At 8.45 the occurrence of subterranean noises announced a third rising of the spring – The phenomena at this time were very similar to those last observed – only two considerable spouts, & the water not sinking within the pipe at the close of the action. –

Our luggage horses did not arrive until a late hour in the evening – We were occupied meanwhile in surveying the various phenomena just described – in examining the other springs in the vicinity, & in collecting specimens of the incrustation surrounding the great Geyser, – specimens also of petrefactions, produced by the flowing of the water from the springs over moss, grass, & other vegetable substances – These petrefactions are found most abundantly, & of the finest kind, on the sides of a small valley, through which the water from the great Geyser makes its way to a stream below – In this situation, they are so numerous, that the greatest difficulty occurring to us was that of selection – The singular quality possessed by the waters of the Geyser, of producing these siliceous petrefactions, has long been known & celebrated – The accurate analysis of Bergman[1] & other chemists,[2] has ascertained, that the water contains a small quantity of silex (about [3] per cent) retained in solution by a certain proportion of potash which is likewise dissolved in the water – This character has been supposed to be peculiar to the waters of the Geyser springs – The observations, however, we have made in Iceland, prove that it belongs to many other springs in this island – and we have in our possession numerous specimens demonstrative of the fact – The hot springs of Leira, Reikolt, Lysiehouls &c, may be mentioned as instances. It is probable that the great spring of *Uxa-hver*,[4] in the northern part of the island exhibits the same quality of its waters. – No where, however, have we seen specimens of vegetable petrefaction, so singularly beautiful, as those met with in the vicinity of the Geysers.

The baggage horses having arrived, we selected a situation for our tent, as favourable as possible for the observation of the phenomena of the springs, as they might successively occur. We were distant from the bason of the Great Geyser little more than a hundred yards. It was arranged that we should keep watch by turns during the night, that nothing might escape our notice during this interval. – For the same reason, we did not undress but slept upon our rugs spread over the floor of the tent – A little before 12 o'clock we were summoned forth, by the occurrence of several loud reports from the Great Geyser. No spouting,

[1] Torbern Bergman, Swedish scholar and explorer; his analysis of Geysir samples from the 1772 Banks expedition to Iceland is in von Troil, 1780, pp. 342–53.

[2] Holland was certainly familiar with the analysis of Geysir samples by Stanley's companion Joseph Black, Professor of Chemistry and Medicine at Edinburgh University. See *TRSE* III (1974), 95–126.

[3] Blank in MS.

[4] Uxahver. Regional earthquakes reduced Uxahver from the most to the least powerful of the group of three hot springs (the others being Baðstofuhver and Syðstihver) in South Þingeyjarsýsla.

however, occurred at this time, but the bason was practically emptied by the waters flowing over its edges. At 2½ the same phenomenon was repeated – At 4 in the morning our attention was altogether arrested by a new & unexpected appearance – Our survey of the vicinity of the Great Geyser the preceding evening had not been very minute, & we had inadvertently pitched our tent at a distance of not more than 30 yards[1] from thhe pipe of the New Geyser,[2] which being surrounded only by a small narrow mound of incrustation, had escaped our observation. At 4 AM, M[r] Bright who was watching in his turn at the door of the tent, saw a column of water thrown up suddenly at this short distance from him. He instantly awakened us, & we all hastened out to contemplate this new phenomenon – The scene was a wonderful one. We saw before us a solid, massive column of water & steam rising from the ground with immense impetuosity, violence & noise to a height of not less than 70 or 80 feet – Nor was this a momentary appearance. The water indeed, which at first formed a large part of the column, gradually lessened in quantity, & in a few minutes almost wholly disappeared. But the impetuous rushing forth of the steam was increased by the removal of the superincumbent pressure, & it burst out with a violence which seemed to tear up the very earth through which it passed.[3]

Our route to Skalholt being the same we had before traversed, presented nothing that could interest or detain us. We had some apprehension that the circumstance of its being Sunday, might prevent our immediate occupation of the church – This, however, was not the case; & the only vestige we observed on the Sabbath at this place, were the priest[4] preparing to set out homewards, & the people loitering about the church, without any other employment than that of observing our motions – The priest, before mounting his horse, came in the church to take some coffee. He is a rough, dirty-looking man, resembling much in appearance & dress a common porter on the quays

---

[1] MS superscript '57 paces'.   [2] Strokkur.
[3] The entry for Sunday July 29 begins at this point. Fell and Flood returned to Reykjavík: Mackenzie, 1812, p. 221. The entry for Saturday July 28 consists of an undated section 'Occurrences at the Geyser Springs'; see above, note 2, p. 240. HH: GS 1 are specimens of different varieties of the incrustation found about the Geysir Springs. GS 2 are taken from the interior of the bason of the Old Geyser just above the pipe – GS 3 are specimens of vegetable substances petrefied by the water from the Old Geyser. GS 4 were taken from the incrustation surrounding the pipe of the New Geyser.
[4] Halldór Þórðarson (1751–1831), a student at Skálholt; consecrated as priest 1781; served at Torfastaður as curate (until 1800) and as priest until 1824.

of an English commercial town. – We were occupied during the greater part of this evening in preparing to forward to Reikiaviik the specimens we had collected at the Geyser Springs; having engaged, to convey them thither, the man who had ferried us over the river Brùar-à – Four horses were found necessary to carry the product of our labours – We were grieved to find on examination, that very many specimens had been greatly injured in their short journey between the Geyser & Skalholt – some of them entirely destroyed – a loss which we had now no means of retrieving.

Monday – July 30ᵗʰ – Two days journey still remained for us to Mount Hecla. Our journey this day was to *Kalfholt,*[1] situated about 2 miles from the eastern bank of the river *Thiors*[2] – This is a very circuitous route from Skalholt to Hecla; but it is rendered necessary from there[3] being no ferry over the Thoirs-á in the direct way. Having crossed over a dangerous & unpleasant bog, we came about 2 miles from Skalholt to the Hvitaar – here a very fine river, as large as the Thames above Westminster Bridge, & carrying down a large body of water to the sea – It derives its name, as well as the Hvitaar in Borgar-fiord Syssel, from the whiteness of the water –, produced by a quantity of white clay which it holds suspended. The horses had much difficulty in swimming this river, from the great rapidity of the current – At a hamlet called *Reikum,*[4] we procured a guide to the ferry over the river Thiors[5] – Formerly there was a ferry over the river near Reikum –, which afforded a much more direct road to Hecla – At present it is necessary to proceed 10 miles further down the river, before it can be crossed – We procured a man[6] as a guide, who lived at Reikum between 50 & 60 years, & who recollected to have seen both Sir J. Banks & Sir J. Stanley. His memory carried him back to the last eruption of Hecla in 1766;[7] concerning which he gave us some information. According to his account, a hot spring,

[1] Kálfholt.
[2] Þjórsá.
[3] MS 'their'.
[4] Reykir: HH: The name of *Reikum*, which is given to many places in this part of Iceland, is derived from the Icelandic noun *Reikur, a Smoke* – At all places so called there are hot springs – *Reikholt* is derived from the same source – Probably Reikiaviik also –
[5] HH The river Thiors exhibits the same whiteness of its waters as the Hvitaar.
[6] Eiríkur Vigfússon (1758–1859).
[7] The most prolonged eruption of Hekla, from April 1766 to May 1768, with one period of intermission.

which there is at Reikum burst out during the time of the eruption.

Our route to the Ferry led us over a wide extent of Lava;[6] not exposing a rough surface like that of Havnefiord; but covered with verdure, except in a few places, where there appeared great bursts & clefts, displaying the character of the rock. We crossed the river Thiors with less difficulty than we had calculated upon from the magnitude of the stream, which is still larger than that of the Hvitaar near Skalholt. At the place of the ferry, it cannot be less than ¼ of a mile in width – probably even more. The stream is rapid, & apparently very deep – From motives of curiosity we took the dimensions of the boat in which we passed over – It was *10½* feet in length, *4* in width at the broadest part, & *13* inches in depth. Two of us only could pass over at once & two horses also at the same time, tied together & following the boat – The ferryman however, was an active, careful, man, & brought us all over in perfect safety. He informed us that in the course of 7 years only one horse had been lost at this ferry; though at some periods of the year – the fishing season, the Handel at Reikiaviik &c, more than a hundred have passed over in the same day.

We arrived at *Kalfholt* at a late hour in the evening, & found there a church & minister's house. In the latter habitation, reside an old priest[2] & his son;[3] the former an old man with a long white beard, and having something venerable in his countenance & manner – At the time of our arrival, he was working in the occupation of a black-

---

[1HH] The Lava between Reikum & the ferry over the Thiors-a presents no variety of character from these we have before seen. – We observed in several places, the Sandstone Conglomerate, which so generally accompanies the Lavas of Iceland, appearing upon the surface – containing fragments of scoriæ.

On the western bank of the river Thiors-á, we observed a bed of what appeared to be well-marked greenstone, scoriated on its lower surface. N 1 is a specimen taken from the bottom of the bed. N 2 is from a bed of sandstone lying immediately below. On the eastern side of the river, there appears a bed of rock, having a perpendicular face exposed, 15 or 20 feet in height. Of this rock N 3 is a specimen, containing amygdaloidal cavities, the crystals in which present a singular glazing of the surface. The lower surface of the bed, like that on the opposite side of the river, is in many places, very much scoriated – as is seen in N 4, where the amygdaloidal cavities, however, still appear. – N 3 is from a part of the bed 4 or 5 feet above N 4 – N 5 are specimens from the same bed, containing small portions of *Steatite*. – Immediately below this rock, there appears a bed of *Sandstone Conglomerate*, containing numerous fragments of scoriæ; the surfaces of many of them completely glazed.

[2] Guðmundur Bergsson (1733–1817), consecrated 1759; priest at Kálfholt 1772–97.

[3] Brynjólfur Guðmundsson (1765–1851), studied at Skálholt and Reykjavík; consecrated curate to his father 1795; priest at Kálfholt 1797–1848.

smith in an adjoining hovel. – His son, who now does duty as the minister of Kalfholt, is an awkward, ungainly mortal, with an expression of extreme stupidity in his features. We found him dressed

Y. Figures at Stóruvellir

in a strange way – his upper garment & breeches of white woollen stuff – black stockings gartered over the breeches – and a white woollen cap rising in a stiff conical form, almost two feet above the head – The salary connected with the church at Kalfholt is only 32 dollars per annum. The farm, however, attached to the living, will keep 6 cows, & a considerable number of sheep. The church is a very poor one, & afforded us but indifferent accommodation for the night. Still, however, we considered it preferable to the tent; the pitching of which always occasioned us much detention & labour. The luggage horses did not arrive until 11 o'clock at night.

Thursday – July 31ˢᵗ. We proceeded to day to *Storu-vellir*,[1] ᵞ a place about 12 miles from *Kalfholt* – The road presented nothing particularly interesting, with the exception of some fine views of the amphitheatre

[1] Stóruvellir.

of mountains, which surrounds the district of flat country forming the valleys of the Bruará, Hvitaar, & Thiors rivers. A few miles from *Kalfholt*, we obtained a distant view of the Westmann Islands – The farms in this tract of country appear to be better than any we have seen elsewhere in Iceland – some parts of Borgar Fiord alone excepted – About most of the farm houses, the people were employed in the hay – in some places they were making it on the tops of the farm houses, where the best part of the crop is generally to be found – The variable weather, & frequent showers which have occurred of late, have done a good deal of injury to the hay lying upon the ground – Much of it has become yellow & rotten – Six or seven miles from *Kalfholt*, having ascended a small eminence, we came in view of a vast extent of flat country, intervening between us & Mount Hecla – the greater part of its surface covered with Lava.[1] *Storu-vellir* is situated in the middle of this valley – on a verdant spot of land which occurs among the Lava – We found here a church of tolerably good dimensions, but very dirty, & crowded with a compound of *villainous smells* – Stock-fish, wool, cloathes & numerous other articles were all brought together here, as a general deposit – The minister, M[r] Steffensen,[2] who lives in a house adjoining the church, is a tall, awkward man, with more lack of information than is common with the priests in Iceland – He made sundry attempts to speak Latin to us; but without much avail, as respected the facility of intercourse. In matters of common life, however, we were informed that he is more at home. He has a good farm, & manages it well – his house, which is a large one, is an excellent characteristic example of the general description of farm houses in Iceland[Z] – Seen externally there appears little more than nine distinct mounds of earth, or hillocks, between which there are several foot paths, & upon which the grass grows with the utmost luxuriance – Examined more minutely, small windows, & circular apertures for the exit of the smoke, appear in various places. Internally the house is a complete cavern – the passages perfectly dark, and the apartments having no more light than is admitted by a single pane of glass – this

[1]HH A considerable part of this tract of Lava is covered with sand, & small fragments of pumice – The minister of Stóru-vellir informed us that formerly none of this Lava was exposed, but that the continued violence of the wind had driven away the sand and disclosed it.

In the course of our progress through the Lava, we observed in many places distinct columnar appearances.

[2] Holland confuses the name. The priest was Stefán Þorsteinsson (1762–1834), first consecrated 1791; priest at Stóruvellir 1794–1811; provost in Rangárþingi from 1807.

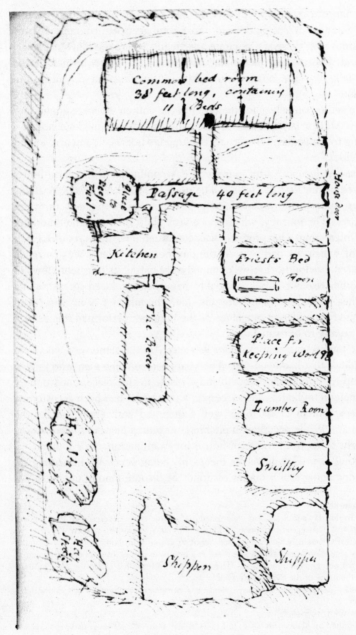

Z. The priest's house at Stóruvellir

Common bed room 38 feet long, containing 11 Beds

Passage 40 feet long

Kitchen

Place to keep Fuel

The Beer

Priests Bed Room

Place for keeping Wool?

Lumber Room

Smithy

Hay Stacks

Hay Stack

Shippen

Shippen

Horse Road

even almost obscured by dust & dirt. The common bed room which is nearly 40 feet in length, divided into 3 compartments, contains 11 beds – Besides this, there is a separate apartment, where the minister sleeps, without flooring or pavement, but having a gutter which opens externally, for the purpose probably of carrying out the dirt from within.

We settled ourselves for the night in the church – being supplied for supper with a large vessel of rice milk from the minister's house – Owing to a mistake in their road, the luggage horses did not arrive until 12 o'clock.

Wednesday.August 1ˢᵗ. Our journey to day conducted us to a farm-house situated at the foot of Hecla – The place is called *Niifurholt*,[1] & is the nearest spot to the mountain where a tent can be pitched, or water procured. The journey, which was a very short one, presented nothing very interesting. Our progress was continued over the tract of Lava, a part of which we had crossed the day before[2] – Hecla was so much obscured by clouds, that we obtained only partial & transient views of it – otherwise we should probably have been induced to take some sketches of the mountain from this side. The minister & his son,[3] who officiated as guides to ourselves & the luggage, performed this service very greatly to our satisfaction.

We pitched our tent at *Niifurholt*, exactly in the same spot where Sir J.Stanley's tent had been placed 20 years before.[4] The man who guided him up the mountain, does not now reside in this place, but we were fortunate in finding, as his successor, a man[5] who had been accustomed to the ascent of Hecla, & is well acquainted with every part of the mountain. While occupied in pitching our tent, a piece of Obsidian was brought to us from the farm-house for examination. This mineral we had long desired to have the means of seeing *in situ*, its mineralogical relations being still a matter of doubt & dispute among geologists of

[1] Næfurholt.

[2]HH In this day's journey also we crossed many large tracts covered with fragments of pumice – We observed too some striking columnar appearances, particularly near the channel of a stream, which we crossed about ½ a mile from Niifúrholt. This columnar form is seen more especially where there is a fissure in a crust of the Lava, exposing to view two perpendicular surfaces. – The river near Niifurholt is called the *Rangaa*, from which the name of the Syssel is derived.

[3] Stefán Stefánsson (1792–1845). Became a priest after studying under Steingrímur Jónsson.

[4] See West, 1970–6, I, 107.

[5] Identified by Mackenzie, 1812, p. 238 as 'Jon Brandtson'; *MI 1801: Suð.*, 1978, p. 159 cites Jón Brandsson as farmer of the neighbouring farm at Háls.

different sects – We made immediate enquiries respecting the place where the specimen in question was found – but were somewhat alarmed by hearing that it was a long day's journey distant from Niifurholt – Still, however, we did not give up the idea of visiting the spot –; to which expedition it was a further inducement that it would afford us the means of seeing something of the vast tract of uninhabited & almost unknown country, which occupies the central part of Iceland, and which has never yet been visited by the foot of the traveller – Upon further enquiry we found that the man at Niifurholt was acquainted with the spot in question, having several times gone this way into the mountains to seek his sheep – Consulting with him on the project, we ascertained the practicability of accomplishing the journey thither & back in 24 hours, each person having two horses with him to forward his progress. This at once decided us. We procured from the guide four horses – three for ourselves, & one for the carriage of specimens &c; & determined upon setting out at an early hour the following morning; provided the weather should not be so fine, as to induce us rather to attempt the ascent of Mount Hecla, & to delay till afterwards the execution of this project. – This point settled we went immediately to bed, that we might be well prepared for the fatigues of the ensuing day.

Thursday August 2ᵈ We arose at 2 o'clock this morning, & finding the morning foggy, with small rain, decided at once upon giving up Hecla for the present, & resorting to the scheme we had formed the evening before. Accordingly at 4 o'clock we were prepared to set forth, in pursuit of *Obsidian*; our party consisting of 4 persons, & 9 horses; each one leading the horse which was to serve him as a relay on the journey. – Loptson was left at Niifurholt in charge of the tent – The journey of this day was altogether greatly more singular & interesting than any other we have made in Iceland – *Reikiadalr*,¹ the spot where the Obsidian is found, is situated among the mountains to the NE of Hecla – at the distance (as we judged from the time & rate of our journey) of 26 or 28 miles from Niifurholt – It may be mentioned as a singular & curious fact that out of this distance not fewer certainly than 25 miles

---

¹ Reykjadalur. HH: It is somewhat doubtful whether this is actually the name of the place in question – *Reikiadals* would imply (according to the analogy of numerous instances in Iceland) *the valley of Smoke*, or of *Hot Springs*. In the valley, at the extremity of which the bed of Obsidian occurs, no hot springs appear. – If, however, this really be the name of the place, it has probably been given from the appearance of a column of vapour, rising from a great waterfall in the Tun-River; which vapour we distinctly observed from the summit of the bed of Obsidian – though then distant from the spot at least 2 or 3 miles.

were travelled over volcanic scoriæ and ashes. – Our route for some way conducted us in a northerly direction along the banks of the river Rangaa. About 2 miles from Niifurholt, we passed a cottage,[1] which is remarkable as being the last vestige of human habitation in this direction towards the interior of Iceland – Beyond this point, all is wild, barren and solitary; a tract unknown even by the natives of the country, except to the short distance to which they occasionally go in search of their sheep. – Continuing our route from the cottage over a surface covered entirely with cinders, we approached a mountain called the *Beur-Fiall*,[2] at the foot of which runs the river Thiors, here pursuing a course nearly from east to west, & carrying down a vast body of water. This part of the river is rendered particularly striking by the occurrence of a long extent of rapids in the stream, terminated by a waterfall[3] of considerable height; – where the water rushes impetuously down the contracted channels which are formed by two vast insular masses of lava rising abruptly from the torrent – Our road became now every moment more wild & singular – The mountains[4] surrounding us, of great elevation & extremely precipitous & abrupt, every where exhibited marks of their having been either affected or actually produced, by volcanic action. On the right hand, a high range

[1] At Merkihvoll.   [2] Búrfell.
[3] Tröllkonuhlaup.

[4][HH] The chain of mountains which is continuous with Hecla on the northern or north-eastern side appears to be composed entirely of the *Sandstone Conglomerate Rock*, containing included scoriæ; & covered in many places with loose scoriæ of a more recent formation. We had not the means of examining the mountain *Beur-fial*, but from appearances, we judged it to be composed of a series of beds, either of greenstone or compact lava, with the conglomerate rock superincumbent & subjacent to them – Most of the other mountains which we passed in our way to Rekiadals would seem to be composed of the same conglomerate – the valleys in the whole of this distance exhibiting a surface covered with scoriæ; & other volcanic products.

The great bed or tract of rocks which it was the object of our journey to visit, is composed solely of Obsidian & Pumice, in various states of connection & affinity with each other, & of certain other varieties of rock, having an intimate relation to these minerals – We were not able, however, to procure from the great mass of rocks, any specimens of the completely black, glassy Obsidian. The greater part of it appears as passing into the state of Pumice – & in various stages of this transition – Many fragments, however, of the perfect Obsidian may be met with, scattered over the valleys in this vicinity.

N 6 are specimens of the Obsidian – N 7 of the Pumice appearing in this spot. N 8 exhibits the transition from Obsidian into Pumice, & other appearances of the connection of these two rocks. N 9 shews an appearance which we observed the Obsidian in several places to assume – greatly resembling a bottle-glass slag – N 10 is taken from the highest point in the great bed of Obsidian & Pumice – We found many scoriæ connected with these minerals *in situ*, as appears in some of the specimens marked N 7.

connected with Mount Hecla to the south, & extending in a direction N. & NE from this mountain, presented a surface entirely covered with volcanic ashes. In one part of this range, a low conical hill[1] appears on the summit of which there is a very distinct crater – the sides of the hill are covered with red scoriæ. The lower ground which we traversed, intervening between the mountains, exhibits a surface entirely composed of cinders, scoriæ, & pumice – varied only by vast rugged masses of Lava, which rise abruptly in various places, & give a singular wildness to the whole character of the scenery – Having reached the northern side of Hecla, the general direction of our course became towards the NE, with a continuance of the same character of country. The morning had now greatly improved, & we enjoyed some striking views of the mountain scenery around us. – Having proceeded about 15 miles, we changed our horses, & moved forwards at the average rate of 3½ miles an hour. – The vast tracts of volcanic ashes which we traversed affording a road more than usually good for Iceland. – Changing our direction somewhat more towards the east, we entered a chain of long, narrow valleys, less barren & desolate than the tract we had before been traversing, but still exhibiting a surface covered here & there with pumice & cinders. For some miles we followed the course of a stream,[2] the waters of which were tinged in a remarkable degree with the white clay, which affects the colour of so many of the Icelandic rivers – At length, at 12 o'clock, when having proceeded, according to the best calculation we could make, about 26 or 28 English miles, we arrived at the spot, which was announced to us by our guide as the termination of our journey. – A valley nearly circular in form, & about a mile in diameter, exhibited at its upper extremity a vast bed,[3] of what appeared at a distance, to be the same rough lava, which had so frequently before occurred to our observation – Approaching the spot, we were surprized & gratified to find that this mass of rock was entirely composed of Obsidian & Pumice; – the former of these minerals giving a brilliant glassy lustre to that face of the bed which is opposed to the valley beneath – The front of the rock on this side has an elevation nearly perpendicular of about 30 feet. Beyond this, however, it rises considerably higher, presenting a surface extremely rugged and abrupt – The extent of the bed is very great, but irregular in its dimensions – in some directions, it extends apparently more than a mile – The

[1] Steindór Steindórsson, 1960, p. 230 tentatively suggests Rauðaskál.
[2] Helliskvísl.
[3] Hrafntinnuhraun. Mod.Ice. *hrafntinna*, 'obsidian'.

appearance & structure of the bed altogether indicate its volcanic formation; & we were enabled to procure some very interesting specimens, illustrative of this fact, as well as of other circumstances connected with the changes & relations of the minerals composing it.

We were occupied more than two hours in the survey of this very singular spot – Ascending to the summit of a peak, which formed the highest part of the bed, we were gratified by the view of a landscape more extraordinary in all its features than any other which had before occurred to our notice in Iceland. The extreme wildness, and desolation of the scenery was its most prominent feature – a desolation derived not only from the absence of every trace of human existence but still more from the many marks of convulsion & disorder in the operations of nature, which present themselves on every side – The whole country around was of volcanic formation – vast rugged rocks, piled up in the most strange & singular forms attested the violence & extent of this action. At the distance of two or three miles, we observed a large crater, apparently more than ½ a mile in diameter – the sides & edges of this vast bason covered with scoriæ of a red colour. – As regarded its extent, the landscape before us was scarcely less remarkable – Looking towards the north, there appears beyond the district of volcanic country, a wide extent of flat, sandy plain, called the *Sprænge Sandur*[1], on the edge of which is the great lake of *Fiske Vatn*,[2] one of the largest in Iceland. This plain is bounded & the view terminated on the northern side by a long mountain range, covered with snow, called the *Hofs* or *Lange Jokull*[3] – This mountain, which has a great elevation is situated very nearly in the centre of the island – somewhat nearer to the northern, than to the southern coast – The road to the Nordland by way of Skalholt passes a little to the west of it – Further to the East, there appears another assemblage of mountains, still more wild & desolate in their character – This is the *Skaptaar-Fiall Jokull*,[4] the tract of country from which proceeded the great volcanic eruption of 1783[5] one of the

[1] Sprengisandur.
[2] Holland's allusion may be to Fiskivötn, now more usually known as Veiðivötn, a cluster of lakes. His map (p. 229) suggests that he has mistakenly named Þórisvatn as 'Fiskivatn'.
[3] These are two separate peaks bearing these names: Hofsjökull and to the west, Langjökull.
[4] Skaftafellsjökull.
[5] Stanley, 1813, p. 95 recalls the eruption and its effects on Europe, claiming that ash had fallen on the Faroes, the Orkneys, Germany, and even severely hampered his own Alpine sightseeing during the summer of 1783. Magnús Stephensen, 1785 was the fullest discussion of this catastrophic eruption available to Holland. Hooker, 1813, II, 125–260 offers a translation of this work, acknowledging Jörgensen's assistance.

most extensive & dreadful of which there has been any record preserved – This vast tract of country, forming the interior of Iceland, & wholly unknown even to the natives themselves, is currently reported to be inhabited by a race of men, differing much from the Icelanders – This story is credited even by some men of accuracy & good-sense, though attended in itself with circumstances of great improbability – The instances adduced of people having occasionally come down from this interior part of the island, to gratify their curiosity & to steal the sheep of those inhabiting the coast, are doubtless wholly undeserving of credit.[1]

After having minutely surveyed all that appeared worthy of notice in the spot which we came to visit, we eat a hasty dinner on a rock of Obsidian, and commenced our return towards Hecla – We did not turn our faces southwards without some degree of regret at the necessity of leaving unexamined the singular tract of country which we had just entered. The difficulties of travelling, however, through this district, would seem to be wholly insuperable. – Not only the want of all tracks or roads, & the occurrence of impassable rivers oppose themselves to such a scheme; but still more the difficulty of obtaining pasture for horses would render it wholly impracticable. Every traveller, however, who visits Hecla should make a point of proceeding forwards to the bed of Obsidian & Pumice at Reikiadalr. We claim to ourselves the credit of being the first to explore & examine this singular spot.

We did not reach Niifurholt again until after 12 at night, – the latter part of our ride being rendered uncomfortable by rain & the darkness of the evening; partly too by the weariness attending a journey of not less than 55 miles –

Friday – August 3^d – We had scarcely expected that the fatigues of the preceding day, would allow us to devote the present morning to the ascent of Mount Hecla – A good night, however, so much recruited our strength, that we could not consent to forego the opportunity which a

---

[1] A reference to *útilegumenn* ('outlying people'), who lived in the wilds of central Iceland including the area of Skaftárjökull. Originally fugitives from justice, (*útlagar*, 'outlaws'), they are later represented as having organised themselves into an alternative society. Magical powers and gigantic stature were frequently attributed to them. Popular superstition was supported by learned testimony. See Jón Árnason, *Íslenzkar þjóðsögur og ævintýri* (2 vols., Leipzig, 1862–4; second edition, 6 vols., Reykjavík, 1954–61), II, 161–293; some of which are translated by G. E. J. Powell and Eiríkur Magnússon, *Icelandic Legends* (London, 1866), pp. 101–231. HH: A man whom we sent up into the *Skapte Fells* to procure some specimens of the Lava, reported in coming down that he had seen one of these men who inhabit the interior of Iceland. His narrative gave him moreover the comfortable appendage of a tent & horses.

more than commonly fine morning afforded us for this purpose – We left Niifurholt between 9 & 10 attended by the same man, who had officiated as our guide the day before; – a clever, active fellow, who may very safely be recommended to any travellers pursuing in future and the same route – Niifurholt is situated at some distance from the immediate base of Mount Hecla, and we were enabled to proceed 4 or 5 miles on horseback; over a tract covered entirely with Lava in crossing which we obtained some fine views of the mountain before us. – The form of Hecla very considerably resembles that of Snæfield's Jokull[1] – the general shape is that of a cone, terminated upwards by three peaks or summits, the middle one considerably higher than either of the others. The height of the mountain is probably about 4000 feet;[2] though I am not sure that any accurate determination has been made of this point – A considerable part of the mountain is covered with snow during the whole year – It has been made a general remark by those who live in its vicinity, that the quantity of snow lying on it this summer is much less than at former periods – a circumstance from which some have ventured to predict the speedy occurrence of some new eruption from the mountain. It is more probable that the thing is accidental in its occurrence – owing possibly to the fineness of the weather during the whole of the summer.

Dismounting from our horses at the foot of this mountain, we commenced the ascent – It was necessary to send the horses back to Niifurholt, as no pasture is to be found near to the mountain. – After ascending a short distance we came to a bed of rough lava, the crossing of which was attended with some difficulty – This lava comes from the southern side of the mountain – when several hollows appear, the form & situation of which clearly indicate their having been craters at some former period – Another stream of lava, connected with this near to its origin, descends from the mountain still further towards the south, & diffuses itself over the plain below. In their general appearance these beds of Lava entirely resemble those in the Guldbringe & Snæfields Syssels – a rude assemblage of rocky masses piled together in every possible variety of form. In the internal characters of the mineral, it

---

[1] Hekla and Snæfellsjökull are both strato-volcanoes, but Hekla is ridge-shaped rather than coned, due to its multiple vents.

[2] 1491m. HH: Van Troil states the height of Mount Hecla, as ascertained by a barometer of Ramsden's, to be 5000 feet – It is probable that this is an exaggerated statement. NB Mr Bayne, who accompanied Sir J. Stanley, ascertained the height of Hecla to be somewhat more than 4300 feet.

differs considerably from most of those we have seen, resembling perfectly, however, the Lava which descends from Snæfields Jokull on each side of Stappen.

Our progress up the mountain[1] was rendered difficult as well by the steepness of the ascent, as by the nature of the surface over which we passed – covered either with cinders & volcanic ashes, or with loose fragments of lava & other erupted stones. – Numerous clefts occurred in our way, many of which it was necessary to cross by the fragments of rock lying over them in different places. The sides of these clefts exhibit masses of scoriæ of various shades of colour – principally reddish brown – Before we had accomplished our ascent to the summit of the southern peak, we found ourselves enveloped in clouds, which at this time began to gather round the upper part of the mountain, allowing only partial & indistinct views of the country beneath – Our progress was greatly retarded by this circumstance, the guide, whom we had with us, having never ascended to the summit, and being almost wholly ignorant of the proper route. At length, after much exertion and fatigue, we attained the southern summit – a narrow ridge of scorified rock, having on each side a precipitous descent of many hundred feet – One of these precipices forms the upper part of the eastern side of the mountain – the other marks one side of a vast bason or hollow, which probably has been the principal crater of the volcano. – The dense masses of cloud by which we were now surrounded, deterred us from attempting immediately the further ascent to the highest peak of the mountain – Fortunately, however, for the success of our undertaking, a

---

[1]HH The circumstance of Mount Hecla being covered with scoriæ, cinders & Lava prevents any accurate investigation of the mineralogical character of the mountain. It is an interesting fact, however, that all the lower eminences which appear at its base, or which indeed may be said to form its base, are composed of the *Sandstone Conglomerate Rock*, containing many included scoriæ. N 11 is a specimen of this conglomerate, taken from the base of the mountain. It appears exposed also in some situations considerably higher up, having the same character & internal structure. It might perhaps be too bold a supposition to state the possibility of the whole mountain being composed of this rock – It is clear, however, that the Scoriæ included in the Conglomerate are of much older formation than the present volcanic rocks which appear upon the surface of the mountain.

The specimens N 12 are from the bed of Lava which we crossed in ascending the mountain from Niifurholt. Its similarity to the Lava of Stappen is very complete – N 13 exhibit another volcanic formation – numerous fragments of which, many of them of great size, are met with in the ascent of the mountain. Some portions of this have a good deal of external resemblance to Obsidian – N 14 are small fragments of primitive rock, found while ascending the mountain, & doubtless ejected in some former eruption. N 15 are specimens of scoriæ &c, of various kinds met with on the mountain. Those marked N 16 are from the summit of Hecla.

short interval of clearer sky occurred – availing ourselves of which, we set forwards towards the completion of our labours. A considerable hollow occurs between the two peaks, the passage over which was rendered difficult, & in some degree dangerous, by the narrowness of the path, along which it was necessary to proceed – a mere ridge of rock, in some places scarcely a couple of feet in width – a precipice on each side of tremendous depth. Another steep ascent succeeded – having accomplished which, we found ourselves on the summit of the mountain – We were singularly favoured at this moment. The clouds by which the peak of Hecla had before been enveloped, were now dispersed, & the vast landscape around us was for some time clearly & distinctly seen – the light clouds which floated below diminishing in no degree the extent or singularity of the view – Towards the north, the landscape comprehended, though at a greater distance, most of the objects which we had seen in the view from Reikiadalr, before described – including, however, in addition, the intervening ranges of mountains, among which, the groupe called *Torfa Jokull*,[1] was particularly conspicuous. – Towards the west, the eye passed over the wide valleys of the Thiossa, the Hvitaar, & the Bruara – the view being terminated on this side by the singularly peaked mountains, which extend from Thingvalla to the neighbourhood of the Geysers. The landscape on the south western & southern side of the mountain comprehended the vast tract of flat country lying along the sea-coast – while that towards the east offered to the eye the great mountain of Eyafialla Jokull, & at a shorter distance the peaked summits of the Tinfialla Jokull[2] – Looking more immediately beneath the pinnacle on which we were placed, the scene was one of singular confusion & irregularity. Every object bore the marks of volcanic action – Numerous eminences appear around the great body of the mountain, all of them covered with scoriæ, and some of them shewing, by their conical shape, & by the hollows on their summits, that they have been formed by eruptions on the very spot. One very remarkable crater[3] of this kind appears on the northern side of the mountain, which we had before observed in our excursion to Reikiadalr. Two or three of smaller size

[1] Torfajökull.
[2] Tindfjallajökull. HH: The situation given to *Tinfialla Jokull* in the map of Iceland is extremely inaccurate. Its real situation is to the South east of Mount Hecla; at the distance probably of 8 or 10 miles from this mountain.
[3] The craters of Hekla are discussed in Guðmundur Kjartansson, *Hekla, FÍÁ* (1945), 114–16.

occur in other situations around & upon the ascent of the mountain – The most elevated, & probably one of the principal craters of Hecla is placed immediately under the higher peak of the mountain, which forms a semi-circular ridge above the hollow – The depth of this crater is not considerable – Estimating from the highest point of the ridge, it probably does not exceed 100 or 120 feet – The crater, along the edge of which we had passed in ascending the mountain is much more considerable in extent & depth – Its figure is irregular, a projection occurring in the middle of one of its sides, which gives the general form of the cavity some resemblance to the shape of a horse-bean. A descent into the crater is rendered almost impossible by the steepness of the sides, and the loose scoriæ and ashes with which they are covered.

While examining the summit of the mountain, I was struck by the appearance of steam, issuing from the ground in two or three places, and on putting my hand to the surface, I found it so much heated, as to render it impossible to continue the contact for any length of time – Reporting this circumstance to my companions, we examined the matter more minutely; and found that a thermometer placed an inch or two below the surface, in the places whence the steam issued, rose to 132, 138, & in one particular spot to 144 degrees[1] – while exposed to the air in the vicinity it did not rise above 39°. This phenomenon was not confined to one particular spot, but occurred in several places around the edge, and upon the descending sides of the summit crater. No distinct fissures appeared, serving as apertures for the exit of the vapour – but in those spots, where it issued in greatest quantity, we observed the fragments of scoriæ to be very loosely put together, so as to afford a ready passage to the ascending steam.

This appearance of smoke & heat on the summit of Hecla was noticed by Sir Jos.Banks & the associates[2] of his voyage to Iceland, in the year   ,[3] when they ascended the mountain[4] – At that time, however, a very short period had elapsed since the eruption from Hecla, which took place in the year 1766. Whether the phenomenon has been noticed since the observation of these gentlemen, I have not been able to learn.

[1]HH Therm. at Niifurholt at 9½ AM – 59°
   At the foot of the Mountain 11.10 – 55°
   At the summit   4.10 PM – 39°
   2 inches below the surface, where the smoke issues – 144°
[2] von Troil, 1780, p. 241.
[3] Blank in MS. It should read '1772'.
[4] Superscript in a different later hand '+ Sir J.T.Stanley'.

The eruption in 1766 was not attended with the emission of any Lava,¹ but solely of smoke, flame, ashes, and volcanic scoriæ. – For some time after the more considerable volcanic appearances had ceased, smoke & flame continued at intervals to be thrown out particularly on the northern side of the mountain – Earthquakes are very frequent in the vicinity of Hecla, though probably not now occurring so often, as in the period more immediately succeeding the eruption, when three or four have been noticed in the same year. More than 18 months have now elapsed since the last observation of this phenomenon.

Previously to commencing our descent from the mountain, we went down into the crater at the summit; an undertaking of no difficulty or hazard. The bottom of this crater is filled with a vast mass of congealed snow – which by the process of melting, gradually proceeding during the summer, has been hollowed beneath in several places, so as to form caverns of some extent. Entering these caverns, we were surprized & gratified by the singular beauty of their appearance – the congealed snow had acquired a bluish transparency of colour, the effect of which in certain points of view, was at once extraordinary and pleasing – The magical palaces of an eastern tale, could not have been better illustrated to the eye. This mass of snow is in some places distant only a few yards from the spots where the steam issues, as before described.

We began our descent² from the mountain at ¼ after 4 in the afternoon. At this time we were again enveloped in clouds & fog; a circumstance which rendered our progress downwards much slower than it might otherwise have been. In any state of the sky, however, it is impossible to descend from Hecla without inconvenience, & some degree of risk; owing to the loose scoriæ & cinders with which its surface is covered, and to the ruggedness of the bed of Lava which it is

¹ Holland mistaken, perhaps following von Troil, 1780, p. 243. See the map of lava emission in *FÍÁ* (1945), attached to an unnumbered page at the end of the volume; more generally Sigurdur Thorarinsson, *Hekla*, (Reykjavík, 1970).

² HH In passing along the SW & Southern side of Hecla, we observed a continuance of the *sandstone conglomerate*, at the basis of the mountain, containing included scoriæ. – Three distinct lava formations seem to be pointed out on this spot – the *first or oldest* that which furnished the scoriæ to the Conglomerate formation – the 2ᵈ, which covers the level at the foot of the mountain – the 3ᵈ, which lies over the Conglomerate, & is evidently of more recent date. – It is possible, however, to reverse in theory the date of the 1ˢᵗ and 2ᵈ formations, here mentioned; or perhaps indeed to reduce the number of formations to *two*; considering the lava which appears upon the level, as having furnished the scoriæ to the Conglomerate.

The Lava upon the level below Hecla, resembles much in structure that of Havnefiord – containing, however, still more of the *white crystal*. The newer Lava, lying over the Conglomerate is very different; resembling greatly that of Stappen.

necessary to cross in the lower part of the mountain – We were further retarded in our descent by a mistake we made in the route; which obliged us to traverse the Lava in a place, where it exposed a surface greatly more rugged and abrupt, than that we had crossed in ascending the mountain – Owing to these, & other delays, we did not reach our tent until a late hour in the evening – The toils we had just undergone, & those of the preceding day, rendered the repose of the night more than usually acceptable.

Saturday. August 4th. It was our plan for the present day to proceed to *Hlidarende*,[1] a place situated in the valley of the *Markar-Fliot*,[2] and distant from Niifurholt somewhat more than 20 miles in a south-easterly direction. At *Hlidarende* lives Mr Thoransen,[3] Sysselman of Rangaavalle, and brother to the Amtmand Thoransen. We had seen him at Reikiaviik, shortly after our arrival from our former journey, and received a pressing invitation to his house, should this fall within the plan of our route – We left Niifurholt at 9 o'clock; and were attended for a few miles by our guide, though his services at this time were wholly unnecessary, Loptson being well acquainted with the road. The poor fellow, however, was so well satisfied with the recompense he had received for his previous services, that he would not be prevented from paying us this compliment. He had just completed too the getting in of his hay – a good crop & in good condition – As there is no vehicle in Iceland for carrying hay from the ground to the place where it is to be stacked, this is done entirely by means of horses – The hay is tied up in bundles of considerable size, & one of these placed on each side of the horses – It is stacked with much care – the stacks being disposed in a space, inclosed round with a high & thick wall, constructed of mud, stones & turf.

Our road to Hlidarende, conducting us by a circuitous route, under the southern side of Hecla, disclosed some new & striking views of the mountain; & enabled us to understand more accurately the direction and extent of the beds of Lava, which make their way downwards on this side. The great tract of flat country which intervenes between Hecla and the sea, aand extends westwards to the estuary of the *Elvas River*,[4] is

---

[1] Hlíðarendi. Mackenzie, 1812, facing p. 254, includes a colour print based on Holland's sketch.

[2] Markarfljót.

[3] Vigfús Þórarinsson (1756–1819). He became *sýslumaður* in Rangárvallasýsla 1789, after earlier service in Kjósarsýsla; continued there until his death. See Jón Skagan, *Saga Hlíðarenda í Fljótshlíð* (Reykjavík, 1973), pp. 132–43.

[4] Ölfúsá.

entirely covered with lava – the rugged surface of which, however, is only exposed in certain places – the greater part of the plain affording pasture land superior to the average quality of what is met with in Iceland. The source of the lava, covering this plain, we were unable very distinctly to ascertain. That a considerable part of it has originated in ancient eruptions from Hecla is more than probable – Some part of it may possibly be derived from *Tinfialla Jokull*, as this group of mountains appears to be connected with the volcanic district – Towards the western extremity of the plain, it may possibly have a connection with the Lava formation of Thingvalla – or with that in the Guldbringe range of mountains, though this is little more than conjectural.

Proceeding in a South easterly direction over this district of flat country, & crossing occasionally tracts of some extent covered with fragments of pumice & other volcanic stone, we came to the *Western Rangáá*,[1] a stream of considerable size – Beyond this river, passing over a high ridge of hill, we came in sight of the valley of the *Markar Fliot*, a wide level, bounded on the eastern side by the magnificent mountain of Eyafialla Jokull, a branch of which mountain also terminates the valley at its northern extremity. The Westmann Islands,[2] at the distance of a few leagues from the place where the Markar Fliot enters the sea, made another striking addition to the very fine view presented to us from our present station above the valley – The *Markar Fliot* itself is a river of large size & of singular character. In the upper part of its course, it descends precipitously from the mountains, – having a remarkable whiteness of its waters from the quantity of clay which it brings down – We learnt too from Sysselman Thoransen that at particular times of year (if I rightly recollect, he particularly specified the Autumn) the water of the river has a strong sulphureous odour – sometimes so powerful, as to be perceptible even from his house, which is at some distance from the stream. Coming upon the flat near the sea, the river diffuses itself into numerous channels – and in different years is subject

[1] Holland mistaken. Of the two branches (Ytri and Eystri) of the Rangá, it must have been the latter (more Easterly) one.

[2]HH The Westmann Islands, as we learnt from Sysselman Thoransen, & afterwards from Dr Klog, belong to the volcanic district – being composed entirely of Lava – Some rough lava appears in the island of Heimaklettur, the largest of the groupe & the only one inhabited. – Dr Klog passed two or three weeks in the islands this summer, for the purpose of investigating the nature & causes of a singular disease, called by the Icelanders *Ginklobe* – a modification of Tetanus which affects infants at a very early age, & invariably proves fatal. This disease is confined to the Westmann Islands (see Dr Klog's paper on the diseases of Iceland).

to great differences of course – sometimes entering the sea under the high range, which extends southwards from the Jokull – at other times forming its estuary 10 or 15 miles further to the west.

Sysselman Thoransen's house, which is situated on the ascent of the hill forming the eastern side of the valley, commands a fine view of the objects just described. We were received by the Sysselman with much hospitality; though with great difficulties of intercourse, as he is wholly ignorant of English, & from want of practice is unable to make his knowledge of Latin subservient to conversation. Our accustomed interpreter, Loptson, was now wanting to us. *Hlidarende*, the place, where we now were, is the place of his nativity & the abode of his parents – His father[1] & mother[2] he had not seen for more than 3 years, during a great part of which time, they had supposed him to be lost by shipwreck. Considering these circumstances, & further that Loptson is an only child,[3] the meeting was as uninteresting, & *unsentimental* as can well be conceived – Neither the *amor patriæ*, nor the στοργη[4] of the Greeks are deeply rooted in Loptson's breast – his native island, since our arrival in it, he has taken every opportunity of reviling – and the indifference shewn about visiting the abode of his parents, has often in a high degree astonished us – There were indeed some reasons of his own for not being particularly anxious on the latter score, which we did not until this time discover – He had practised upon us numerous deceptions with respect both to his father's situation in life, and his own former situation & conduct in Iceland; and doubtless felt some little alarm at the idea of these frauds being discovered – For some time past indeed, we have lost all the confidence in him which we once entertained – & have, moreover, had much reason to be dissatisfied with his conduct as a guide & assistant to us in our travels – His manner & behaviour, now thus placed again among his old friends and associates, were highly ridiculous – though perhaps affording only an exaggerated representation of what is common among other men in similar situations – of what, under certain modifications indeed, may be deemed natural to all. – Dressed out in his gayest suit of *English* clothes, he mustered up ten thousand *petit maitre* airs, the grace, the bow, the shrug, the stride; and displayed a rapid alternation of these accomplishments to the all-wondering eyes of his former companions –

[1] Loftur Ámundason (b. 1758).
[2] Ingibjörg Ólafsdóttir (b. 1746).
[3] Confirmed by *MÍ 1801: Suð.*, 1978, p. 102. Ólafur Loptsson was 27 in 1810.
[4] love.

His father's real situation in life is that of a *workman*,[1] with a small quantity of land attached to his cottage.[2] In real good sense & honesty he seems at least equal to his son, but in *grace*, how far behind!

The Sysselman Thoransen has a large[3] & excellent farm, of which he appears to make the best advantage. – His house entirely resembles those we have before seen, belonging to the same class of Icelanders – In the vicinity of the house, he shewed us a spot of ground of some size, covered with Angelica[4] – a plant which is used as food in many parts of Iceland – A greater vegetable rarity in this country is the *Carroway*,[5] which is only to be found in this particular district. It was introduced here some years ago from Copenhagen by a person who brought a small quantity of the seed over with him. It now grows in great profusion in a part of the meadow land before the Sysselman's house at Hlidarende –

At 10 o'clock in the evening, a supper was brought to us, consisted of baked mutton, without bread or potatoes, and rice milk. We fixed up our bed-steads for the night in the sitting room of the house – a tolerably good apartment, though not so perfectly clean, as might have been desired – Two months travelling in Iceland, however, had greatly inured us to inconveniences of this nature.

Sunday – August 5th Coffee was brought to us this morning, as soon as we rose – and about an hour afterwards, the cloth was laid upon the table for what was termed breakfast – a repetition of the baked mutton, without any other additions than butter, salt, and oil, under the denomination of gravy. – Being desirous of seeing the performance of religious service in the country churches of Iceland, Bright and I went in the course of the morning to a place called *Eyindarmule*,[6] about 3 miles from Hlidarende, up the valley of the Markar Fliot, where there is a small church. We were accompanied thither by Loptson, & by a student, who officiates as a sort of secretary to the Sysselman – a clever, well informed young man. Being furnished with fresh horses by the

---

[1] Holland rather understates Loftur Ámundason's status. *MÍ 1801; Suð.*, 1978 p. 101 identifies him as *reppstÿrer*, (Mod.Ice. *hreppstjóri*), a kind of parish prefect whose responsibilities in this region included overseeing fishing, and commercial dealings.

[2] Nikulásarhús.

[3] There were 27 people attached to the household in 1801.

[4] *Archangelica* (Linn.); Mod.Ice. *Ætihvönn* or *Erkihvönn*. Hooker, 1813, II, 318 notes: 'The Icelanders gather the stems and roots of this plant, which they eat raw, and generally with the addition of fresh butter'.

[5] *Carum* (Linn.); Mod.Ice. *Kúmen*.

[6] Eyvindarmúli.

Sysselman (who is esteemed one of the best riders in Iceland) we occupied no long time in making our way to the church. – According to the accustomed method of Icelandic riding, we proceeded the whole way on full speed – disregarding the various obstacles of bogs, dykes, and streams – Had our time been otherwise than short, we should have preferred a more deliberate progress, as the valley of the Markar Fliot, offers much interesting & picturesque scenery. From the precipitous cliff which forms its western boundary, numerous streams precipitate themselves into the valley – forming cascades of great height & magnificence. One of these waterfalls is very singular in its character. The stream, which is a large one, descending perpendicularly from the summit of the cliff upon a ledge in the rock, about half way down, has in process of time, worn out three or four distinct apertures at different elevations; – through one or more of which all the water is now poured out. In dry seasons, the stream falling down into the hollow or pipe, which has thus been fabricated in the rock, is seen to issue entirely from the lowest aperture. When swelled by rain, it rushes out impetuously at the same time from all the four openings.

Still more striking is the scenery on the eastern side of the Markar-Fliot,[1] where the great mountain of Eyafialla Jokull rises steeply from the very level of the valley; covered with snow for apparently about ⅔ of its height – If the admeasurement of the Danish lieutenants be accurate, this is the loftiest mountain in Iceland, the height of which has hitherto been ascertained. Their estimate (founded upon Trigonometrical observation) gives the mountain an elevation of somewhat more than 5500 feet; – while Snæfield's Jokull, the height of which they likewise ascertained, was found not to exceed 4550 – Judging from appearances alone, I should have said (and my companions made the same observation) that the latter mountain was the higher of the two. It may be noticed that *Eghert Olafsen's* estimate of Snæfield's Jokull (likewise professing to be a Trigonometrical one) makes the height of this mountain very nearly 7000 feet.[2] The difference is an extraordinary one. – Eyafialla Jokull more than any mountain we have seen in Iceland gives the idea of the glaciers of the Swiss Alps. In one or two places upon its western side, vast avalanches have taken place; and the snow congealing in the clefts of the mountain, affords appearances much

[1] Mackenzie, 1812, facing p. 256 has a colour print from Holland's sketch.
[2] More evidence that Holland knew Eggert Ólafsson's work in the original Danish text (I, 288 reads '6862 Fodder dansk Maal') rather than the shorter English version (1805, p. 76 reads '686 Danish feet'). See above, note 1, p. 194 and note 3, p. 205.

resembling the picture which my imagination has drawn of those sublime[1] scenes in Switzerland.

Arrived at *Hyindarmule*,[2] we found ourselves somewhat too early for the service – the interval we occupied in surveying the things & people around us. The situation of the place (which consists only of the church, a large farm house, & one or two cottages) is very fine – beneath the cliff, forming the western side of the valley, and which here presents some striking columnar appearances – The people we found all assembled about the church, waiting the arrival of their pastor – every one dressed in his or her best apparel – the women especially exhibiting dresses in the strict Icelandic costume, & of no small magnificence. The farmers in this district are comparatively opulent among the Icelanders; and the appearance of their wives and children bears testimony to the fact. Through the medium of Loptson & the student, we endeavoured to obtain some articles of dress in the way of purchase. We were unable, however, to effect any thing of this kind – Not that the people were unwilling to sell – but they all pleaded the impossibility, during the present period of war, of replacing any article with which they now parted – The priest at length made his appearance – a tolerably good looking man, from whose countenance we at once premised that he dealt not in religious austerities – and this supposition was speedily confirmed to us. The congregation all assembled in the church (which in every respect was similar to those we had ourselves so often tenanted) the women sitting, as usual on one side, the men on the other – the service began – Psalm-singing, readings from the Bible, and prayers formed the first part of it; during which time, the priest stood before the altar, on which two lighted candles were placed. The part which he took in the service was a very active one – his voice in the Psalms was that of a *Stentor*, and scarcely less stunning in the readings & prayers, which were all given as chaunts. His whole manner in the service had nothing in it that was devotional or serious – though in giving this opinion, some allowance must be made for differences of habit & custom – We entered the church a few minutes after the service had begun, while he was engaged in singing – He beckoned us towards him, & made us take seats on each side of the altar. Shortly afterwards, while still proceeding in the service, he handed to me a snuff box of no small dimensions, inviting me by his gestures to partake in what it was

[1] Awe inspiring and wild. See above note 2, p. 80 and note 2, p. 153.
[2] Holland's eccentric spelling of Eyvindarmúli.

evident he himself considered a very good thing. Snuffing, however, was not his only extra-occupation during the service. A dram bottle, well provided, stood upon the altar; to which while engaged in singing, he had recourse three several times – Just before the sermon, he went out of the church, & motioned us to follow him – Through the Latin interpretation of the student, he then told us, that he should esteem it a great honour to ride to Hlidarende with us, if we could possibly wait till the conclusion of the service – He informed us that he had already shortened the Psalms by 7 or 8 verses, in our behalf, and that he would abridge the sermon, as much as it was possible – We accordingly all went into the Church again – he mounted the pulpit, & with his head almost touching the roof of the building, delivered a discourse of somewhat more than ½ an hour – by the noise of which we were abundantly impressed, though wholly ignorant of the meaning – This was followed by the administration of the sacrament, when he again returned to the altar & with many minutiæ of ceremony, delivered to the people kneeling around, the wafers & wine – being careful himself not to allow any liquor to remain in the cup after the communicants had partaken of it. The whole over, and the people dismissed, he again joined us, mounted his horse, and we set off towards *Hlidarende*, with nearly the same speed as we had used in our progress towards the church – We were not, however, without some interruption arising from our new companion. When advanced scarcely ¼ of a mile from the church, he took a large dram bottle out of his pocket (not the half-emptied one which had before stood on the altar) & after soliciting us to take a part, consoled himself for our refusal by liberally partaking of it himself – This potation was so often repeated, that before we reached Hlidarende, the bottle was nearly exhausted – the priest meanwhile uttering many witticisms on the subject. Urged by the bottle, he even made some attempts to talk to us in Latin – here, however, his conversation soon came to a pause – It must not be understood that this is a general picture of the ministers in the interior of Iceland – Intemperance, though certainly not *unknown*, is not, however, a common vice among them – and the minister in question, *Sæmundar Halfdanarson*[1] by name, is subjected to much reprobation on the score of his defaults in this way.

Returned to Hlidarende, we found Sir G.M. engaged in examining an

[1] Sæmundur Hálfdanarson (1747–1821); consecrated as priest 1774; moved to Fljótshlíð 1780. The church of St. John the Apostle at Eyvindarmúli was one of two to be served in the district. Sæmundur relinquished his post in 1819.

Icelandic female dress – one of those used by women in the higher ranks – This he purchased from the Sysselman[1] at the price of 80 rix-dollars – or 8 guineas, as the rate of exchange now stands in Reikiavik.

In originally planning the present journey, we had indulged ourselves in the hope of penetrating still further towards the east, than the place where we now were – of seeing, if possible, the volcanic districts of Skapte-Fells & Kattlegaia Jokull.[2] Considerations, connected with our return to England, had subsequently induced us to resign this scheme. It now appeared certain that the Elbe, at whatsoever time she arrived in Iceland, would necessarily be detained here until a very late period in the year. Resigning therefore all hopes of this conveyance, we began immediately to consider what other might best be adopted. The chances open to us were so very few, & the evils of spending in Iceland the latter months of the year so very great, that we deemed it proper to neglect no opportunity held out to us – The Brig Flora, (belonging, as well as the Elbe, to Phelps & Company of London) which was lying at Stromness when we were at that place; had been to all ports in the east & north of Iceland – in quest of a cargo – being able to procure a part only of which, she was now coming to Reikiavik, to complete there her loading for England. Just before leaving Reikiavik, we had heard, by an express from the Nordland, that she was to sail from Skage-strand[3] about that time – of course, her arrival at Reikiaviik might be expected in a few days – Having decided upon adopting this conveyance to England, it was now our business to hasten back to Reikiavik as speedily as possible – all the principal objects of our journey being well and fully accomplished – Under these circumstances, we were almost inclined to consider it fortunate that the road by which we were to return, offered nothing interesting enough to

[1] HH We were shown at the Sysselman's the method in which the Icelanders manufacture the figured stuff which they use for saddle cloths, chair cushions &c &c much resembling *tambour-work* when completed – The process, however, is rather that of weaving – different coloured threads being wove in, & the scissors afterwards used to give the figures on the work.

[2] The areas to which Holland refers, short of Skaftárjökull, are probably Lakargígar and Eldgjá (formerly Kötlugjá). HH: Through the medium of Loptson's Father (when we had ourselves given up the plan of visiting Skapte-Fells & Kattlegaia Jokull) we engaged a man to procure us specimens of Lava from these two volcanic districts. – Some were accordingly brought to us when at Hlidarende, but from the ignorance of the man in selection not of the least value. It is more than probable indeed that the fellow, to save himself the labour & fatigues of the journey, had taken the simpler method of procuring some fragments of the lava in the vicinity of his own habitation. This we judged likely from more than one circumstance.

[3] Skagaströnd in Austur-Húnavatnssýsla in the north of Iceland.

detain us – We had now examined every thing in this district which was either new to us, or particularly worthy of notice.

We resumed then our journey after dinner to day; being attended to Odde,[1] the first stage, by the Sysselman & his secretary – The former was good enough to supply us with his horses, that our own might be reserved for the remainder of the journey. The road to Odde, (which is 14 or 15 miles from Hlidarende) led us down the valley of the Markar-Fliot, the hills forming the western boundary of which gradually fall off so as to connect the valley in its lower part with the great tract of flat land lying along the coast. The farms & the pasture in this district are greatly superior to any we have seen elsewhere in Iceland. The farm houses are numerous, & neat in their appearance. A few miles from Hlidarende, we passed the church & hamlet of *Breida-bolstadr*[2] – This is the richest living in the whole island, the nominal salary of the minister being 182 specie-dollars – his real profits from the church much more considerable – *Odde* is situated on the western side of the Eastern Rangaà, at no great distance from the river, & only a few miles from the sea – Arrived here, we found a church of a very superior kind, large, neat, & ornamented with some degree of taste – a very large house too, appropriated to the minister of the parish – At present, this house is occupied by the widow[3] of the late minister,[4] who died a short time ago – his successor, *Steingrim Johnson*, the *Lector Theologiæ* at Bessasted, not yet having taken up his abode here. The living of Odde is among the best in Iceland; and the widow & her family appear to be left in very good circumstances. We were received with much attention & hospitality by her son – a fine young man[5] of good manners & well cultivated mind – Though we did not arrive until late in the evening, it was thought necessary to prepare a meal for us, & a little before 12, a repast of baked mutton, & rice milk was brought upon the table. We were glad to get this over, & to prepare ourselves for the fatigues of the ensuing day, by putting up our beds, & going to rest.

Monday August 6 – At an early hour this morning, we were informed of the arrival of an express from Reikiavik – He brought a letter from M^r

---

[1] Oddi. A colour print from Mackenzie's drawing of Oddi appears in Mackenzie, 1812, facing p. 256.

[2] Breiðabólsstaður.

[3] Jórunn Sigurðardóttir (1751–1834).

[4] Gísli Þórarinsson. (1758–1807); priest at Oddi from 1784 and provost in Rangárþingi from 1792.

[5] Sigurður Gíslason Thorarensen (1789–1865); shortly (September 1812) to be consecrated as priest at Garðar on Álftanes.

Fell, relating chiefly to the arrival & probable time of sailing of the Flora – The intelligence was of such a nature as to induce us to think of using all possible speed in our return to Reikiaviik – We did not leave Odde, however this morning without transacting much business there. – Besides the time occupied in our breakfast, which consisted successively of coffee, mutton, & chocolate, we were employed for more than an hour in making a *handel* or market with our worthy hosts – The old minister had left behind him a number of books, which his family were not only willing, but anxious to dispose of – They were accordingly summoned forth from their dusty respositories for our inspection – & we purchased not a few of them – in despite of the absurdity of buying books even the titles of which we were unable to read – Among other purchases,[1] I made one of the Transactions of the Icelandic Society – in 14 vols[2] –

Our next stage was to Eyarback,[3] distant from Odde about 25 miles. The road which lies over the flat country along the coast, presented nothing that was new or interesting – Crossing the eastern Rangaà by a very steep & difficult ford, & passing over some extensive bogs, we came to the river Thiors, about halfway between Odde & Eyarback – This river is at this place more than a quarter of a mile in width, & very rapid. We crossed it in a ferry boat, the horses swimming after us – This ferry[4] is an extremely inconvenient one, owing to the shallowness of the stream on the western side which renders it necessary to saddle the horses out of the boat, & to ride 150 yards through the water. The bottom of the river is composed of a soft mud, brought there by the waters – This was so deep, as to expose us to some risk & much

[1] Mackenzie, 1812, p. 257 notes Richard Bright's purchase of a 'superb Icelandic Bible'; in fact a composite of two Hólar-printed texts, *Old Testament* (1637) and *New Testament* (1644). The volume, with stamped and gilded leather backs, and wrought metal corners and clasps, is now in the Bodleian library, with a note in Bright's hand describing the circumstances of its purchase.

[2] These publications appeared annually from 1781 under the title *Rit þess íslenzka Lærdómslistafélags*; the contents ranged over a characteristic cross-section of European Enlightenment interests – medicine, agriculture, other practical applications of science, the humanities, and some political and social questions. Holland in Mackenzie 1812, pp. 457–8 lists a representative selection of articles from the series. See also Halldór Hermannsson, 1918, p. 12–16.

[3] Eyrarbakki. HH: When near *Eyarback*, we observed on the right hand at the distance of a few miles, the hot springs of *Reikum*. – We should have visited these had we not seen so many hot springs in our several journeys through Iceland, as to render these natural wonders not only familiar, but even indifferent to us.

[4] Sandhólaferja. A ferry was associated with this spot as early as the settlement period, and a bridge was eventually built in 1895.

difficulty in riding over it – We reached Eyarback at 5 in the afternoon – This place is situated upon the estuary of the *Elves á*,[1] a river formed by the conjunction of the stream coming from the lake of Thingvalla, with the united streams of the Bruarà & Hvitaar from the vicinity of Skalholt. Eyarback is one of the ports of Iceland, included in the Reikiavik commercial district – Previously to the war, three ships usually came there every year from Denmalk [sic] – The harbour, however, is a very dangerous one; insomuch that during the last 20 years, 5 vessels have been wrecked in it – besides others upon the neighbouring coast – In the vicinity of the place, there are a number of fishing cottages, but owing to the nature of the coast & other circumstances, the fishing here is not carried on here to great advantage – The principal exports from the port are wool & tallow, brought from the farms in the interior of the country – Some part of the barter between the merchant here, & the country people, is carried on in an article for which Eyarback is peculiarly noted – This is the sea weed called *Dulce*,[2] of which about *16000 lbs* are procured annually on the shores about this place; & disposed of to the country people, at the common rate of 80 lbs of Dulce for one pound of butter, or 20 lbs of mutton – About 30 barrels of the *Fiüru-grass*[3] are likewise procured annually at Eyarback, and disposed of in the same way. These two plants are used by the country people, as a substitute for bread.

The merchant proprietor at Eyarback is a M[r]. Lambasson[4] – This gentleman being detained in Norway by the war, the business is conducted at present by his wife, & by an agent, M[r] Peterson. We were received by them with great hospitality, & remained at the house a few hours to refresh ourselves, it being our intention to proceed forwards during the night, with the view of reaching Reikiavik the following morning – owing to the state of the tide we were not able to cross the *Elvas á* until midnight – This ferry[5] is rendered formidable by the breadth, depth & rapidity of the river, which is not less than half a mile

[1] Ölfúsá.

[2] Mackenzie, 1812, p. 263 notes that 'Dulse' is a Scottish name for the plant *Fucus palmatus* (Linn); Mod.Ice. *Söl*. Eaten raw or boiled in Scotland, the weed was dried and preserved by the Icelanders and subsequently eaten with fish and butter or boiled with milk into a cream. See also Hooker, 1813, I, 445.

[3] Mod.Ice. *Fjörugrös*.

[4] Níels Lambertsen (b. 1767). Lived at 'Kaufmanshuus' near Stokkseyri with his nineteen year old wife 'Kirstine', a two year old child and his father, and other household members. See *MÍ 1801: Suð.*, 1978, p. 209.

[5] At Óseyrarnes. It served as an important link before the construction of a bridge at Selfoss.

across. The ferrymen, however, are adroit in their business, & our horses swam over without any great difficulty. Every year, as we were informed by these men, several thousand horses cross the river at this place – as many as 900 have been know to pass over in a single day. – The river here is very full of seals, of which we saw many in crossing it. *Thursday. August 7* – Having reached the western bank of the Elvas River we mounted our horses, and resumed our journey towards Reikiavik, which is distant from Eyarback about 30 miles – Proceeding for some miles along the shores of a broad estuary into which the river expands just above the ferry, we began the ascent of the ridge of hills, which extends uninterruptedly from the lake of Thingvalla almost to the extremity of the Guldbringe-peninsula. In making this ascent we enjoyed some very fine retrospective views of the country through which we had lately been travelling – In the distance the range of lofty mountains, beginning to the north of Hecla, & terminated by Eyafialla Jokull towards the south, were clad in the gray shades of morning – Before we lost sight of them by the windings of the road among the hills, they were richly illuminated by the beams of the rising sun – The remainder of our road, a distance of about 25 miles, was entirely over Lava; of which several large beds come down from the higher part of the mountains we were traversing, & diffuse themselves in the intervening valleys, and upon the lower country beneath. The origin of some of these beds we could distinctly perceive in small craters which we passed on our road. – The rugged nature of the surface we were traversing, rendered our progress very slow and tedious; and we did not reach Reikiavik until noon – much fatigued with the labours we had undergone during the preceding 24 hours. Since leaving Odde the morning before, we had travelled little less than 60 miles.

We were now arrived at the termination of our last journey in Iceland. During the whole period of our labours, we had been singularly favoured by the state of the weather. It may be noticed as an extraordinary fact, that in two journeys of a fortnight each, & one of a month's duration, it could scarcely be said that we were detained two days by rain, or prevented by this cause from accomplishing any object which came within our plans. The grand matter of regret was that we had not succeeded in a project, which had engaged our wishes, when first undertaking the voyage to Iceland. This was a journey to the Northern parts of the island, & the examination of a district which has scarcely ever been trodden by the foot of the traveller. The execution of this project, however, we found to be impracticable, without the entire relinquishment of other important objects of the voyage – It is an undertaking, well & thoroughly to execute which, would require to itself the uninterrupted devotion of a whole summer. This therefore must be left to some future traveller in Iceland, & we must retire from our labours in this field, with the satisfaction at least of thinking, that in the district we have traversed, nothing has been omitted, that appeared really worthy of notice, & some facts been ascertained, which may be of importance to the interests & advancement of science. –

Owing to many unforeseen circumstances – delays in loading the vessel – stormy weather &c, our departure on the Flora was delayed much longer than we had expected or wished. Very nearly a fortnight elapsed between our return from the journey to Hecla, & the time of our final departure from Iceland. Few incidents occurred during this interval of impatient expectation. We had entertained hopes that the Elbe, or some other ship from England might arrive previously to this time – the welcome bearer of letters & other intelligence from home. This hope, however, was a fallacious one. The only vessel at Reikiavik, besides the Flora, was a Danish galliot, which arrived in Iceland during our absence in the *Vesterland*, & which was now on the point of returning to Denmark, taking Leith in her way, according to the directions given in the British Orders of Council. This vessel sailed about 10 days after our return – carrying out a number of passengers – among others, our late companion to the Geyser, Mr Flood.

On the Friday evening, succeeding our return from Hecla, a ball was given at the Club house in Reikiaviik – every circumstance about which was precisely similar to those of the Balls we had formerly attended. – On Sunday, we went to a public dinner at the Club-house, given by the merchants & some other inhabitants of the place, as a testimony of their regard & good will to us. – As usual, a number of complimentary toasts went around the table – we thanked them for the honour they did us – & they thanked us for the honour we did them. All went off in a pleasant & friendly manner; *externally* so at least; We had found reason to believe that some of the Danish merchants in Reikiavik were not very favourably disposed either to English men or English interests; and we knew at the time that some of these persons were at the table with us. Nothing, however, occurred, which could draw forth animosity or ill-will on either side – It is neither an exaggeration of fact nor the effect of a partial prejudice, to say, tha the general description of Danish merchants in Iceland is greatly inferior to that of the middle class of shopkeepers in our own country.

During our stay in Reikiavik, we dined once or twice with the Landfoged Frydensberg, who continued unintermitting in his attentions & kindness to us – At his house we always met the Amtmand Thoransen, whom the concerns of the Government still detained at Reikiavik – He is a man of plain & simple manners; well informed on all subjects, & particularly so with respect to the history, topography & economy of his native island.

On Sunday, the 19th of August, we bade a final adieu to Iceland.[1]

[1]HH i). Copy of a Letter from Atatsrood Stephansen to Sir George Mackenzie.

Innraholm 12th August 1810

Dear Sir,

Among several (*instances*) examples of my ill luck, I do certainly mark the last, not to could enjoy the pleasure & honour to find you, my dearest Sir, at Reikiavik, before my return home from that place the 6th of this month – in order to take leave of that noble man, who has honoured our Iceland with a visit for scientifical researches; – my roof with a friendly entry, & confident sleep under it; – myself with his most valuable friendship & even presents – a man whose name & remembrance once perhaps can be even so renowned & beloved in the world, & especially in this island, as that of Sir Joseph Banks, & whose humanity once might prove himself even the same patron of it, under its persevering afflictions. – Even the speedy return of the Danish vessel with Mr Thielsen, & my many letters to Copenhagen, in public & private concerns, besides various other business, do all at present deprive myself of every leisure to think of any thing other – However, I find myself in your debt, dear Sir, not only for your valuable present of the Telescope, but even remembering that I still have not kept my promise concerning some scientifical accounts for your learned work, a list over my own publications & writings, accounts of my society, and of my Spanish sheeps. But I once more do hereby promise you, dear Sir, with the next returning vessel from hence to Leith in this Autumn, or if you rather do order it with Mr Fell, to send you all these accounts. Excuse only at present friendly, that it impossibly before could be done – and accept my cordial thanks for all your humanity & friendship towards us in this season – Permit me, dear Sir, to offer you the small book *De natura et constitutione Islandiæ*, by *Eggert Olafson* [Ed. Eggert Ólafsson, *Narrationes historicæ de Islandiæ formatæ et transformatæ per eruptiones ignis* (Copenhagen, 1749)], of which you did take notice in my house, as curious for your work which I with ardent desire from hence do look out for – But all accounts myself & any other of my countrymen could furnish you with, you'll find all gathered in, or drawn out of my book *Iceland in the Eitheenth Century* – viz. the Danish publication of 1808 [Ed. *Island i det attende aarhundrede* (Copenhagen, 1808)], and in its three annexed tables, which book I have heard that yourself or your companions have already got in Reikiavik – but if not true, I'll take care to procure you one copy, & to send it with my accounts, as myself am no more owner of a single one – You'll certainly find it, dear Sir, worth reading, if you only could understand it – and moreover perhaps worth, that an English translation of the most interesting accounts drawn from it, once might be known even in your happy country.

Your kindness has offered to send me some English books, & desires to know of what sort. Permit me, Sir, afterwards in a letter, by better leisure, to disclose to you my most sincere wish, that only my Society could get any instructive books, even for farmers &

the common people, in concern of that kind of husbandry too, which you know to be applicable to our Island – our cattle, sheeps, economy, & what here may be useful for all my countrymen, in order to improve their means for getting livelihood – and that you, dear Sir, may be pleased to order their payment in any thing from hence which I could afford. Always I'll chiefly esteem it as a singular favour, if my Society, by your friendly recommendation could win the good-will of learned and respected men in Scotland, in order to its some support & scientific honour, & to enable it to forward common instruction and use all over my native soil.

According to your order, I at last have the honour (besides the most kind Compliments from my wife & family) to send my own picture, with the friendly application that you, my dearest Sir, would grant it some place in a corner of your library, in remembrance.

To the R¹ Hble	Dear Sir,
Sir G.Mackenzie	of your most obliged & faithful Servant
Baronet.	Magnus Stephensen

[ii] Letter from the Deputy Governors of Iceland to Sir G. Mackenzie.
Perillustri nobilissimo Domino Georgio Mackenzie salutem plurimam –

Litteras Tuas, vir nobilissime, humanissimas accepimus, et nostri officii erit, incolas regionum, per quas iter fecisti, de singulari tua, et itineris sociorum, humanitate benignitate et grato erga eos animo certiores facere. Te et socios vicissim excusare rogamus, si antiqua illa hospitalitas, quæ incolis huius insulæ a primis usque temporibus propria fuit, vobis alicubi defecerit, et ut hoc verecundiæ, paupertati ac linguæ vestræ, ut & vitæ consuetudinis, imperitiæ, non inhumanitati gentis tribuatur, enixè postulamus –

Accipe denique, Vir Nobilissime! nostras integerrimas grates, pro tua et Sociorum dulci, amica, et urbana conversatione, quam grata diu colemus memoria. Prosperrima Te, Tuosque itineris socios, nostra et insulæ huius incolarum prosequuntur vota.

Reikiavicæ d.13 Augusti 1810
Thoransen – Einarsen – Frydensberg]

[ii] To the most illustrious and most noble Sir George Mackenzie – greetings. Most noble sir, we have received your most civilised letters, and it will be our task to inform the inhabitants of those regions through which you have journeyed of the singular humanity, benignity and gratitude of yourself and your companions towards them. We ask you and your companions in turn to excuse any failings that there may have been of that ancient hospitality which has always been characteristic of the inhabitants of this island from the earliest times. We strenuously request that this should be attributed to modesty, poverty and ignorance both of your language and of your customs of life, and not to the barbarousness of the people. Receive then, most noble sir, our most heartfelt thanks for the sweet, friendly and urbane society of you and your friends, which we shall long cherish with pleasing memory.

The warmest good wishes of one and the inhabitants of this island follow you and the companions of your journey.

Reykjavík 13 August 1810
Bjarni Thorarensen Ísleifur Einarsson Rasmus Frydensberg]

iii) Serenissimæ Majestatis Danicæ et Norvegiæ Regis Præfecturam Islandiæ generalem pro tempore administrantes.

Notum facimus quod perillustris Dominus Georgius Mackenzie Barᵗ de Coul, qui Præfecti huius insulæ et Clavigeri regii, Comitis de Trampe literis salve conductus, cum sociis munitus, huc ineunti hac æstate, vectus est, eo fine, ut res quæ hic sunt naturæ scrutatore dignæ, ipse adspiceret; tam singulari humanitate, benevola liberalitate, morum viro gravi, docto et nobili, digna urbanitate et candore nostratium omnium, quibuscum ei res erat, intimam gratitudinem, favorem, amorem conciliaverit – Ingenuum eius studium nobis etiam in quacunque re auxilio esse, vel ex hoc elucet, quod materiam variolarum

After a detention of two or three days from the unfavourable state of the winds & weather, we were at length summoned on board on the morning of this day – the wind being fair for our departure. – Attended to the shore by a number of our friends in the town, we went off in a boat to the vessel, which was then tacking up & down among the islands in the Bay. Mr Fell accompanied us, and remained with the ship, until the pilot boat put off to the shore.

The minute particulars of the voyage it would be tedious to recount. It was altogether an unfortunate & uncomfortable one. – rendered so by the extreme variableness of the weather & the constant shifting of the wind. Three or four days elapsed before we lost sight of the southern coast of Iceland – during which time, we suffered much from a very heavy swell, consequent upon preceding gales of wind from the W & S.West. The last land we saw in Iceland was the *Vester Horn*,' a headland not far distant from the port of Berufiord^2 – During the seven succeeding days we were out of sight of land, harassed by alternate calms & gales of wind – the latter sometimes very violent, though never of long continuance. In one of these gales the main top gallant mast was carried away, & six of our sails completely destroyed – At

---

vaccinam nescius hanc antea ad insulam nostram allatam fuisse, ipse secum adtulerit, et propria manu aliquot incolarum liberis cum felicissimo successu inoculaverit.

Scripsimus Reikiavicæ die 13 Augusti 1810

Thoransen – Einarsen – Frydensberg

[iii] The current administration of the general prefecture of Iceland in the realms of the serene Majesty of Denmark and Norway.

We note that the very illustrious Sir George Mackenzie of Coul, who was given a safe conduct by the letters of the prefect of this island and royal Governor, Count Trampe, accompanied by his companions, and was borne through these parts this present summer for the purpose of seeing phenomena worthy of investigation – by his singular humanity and benevolent liberality, and by his gravity, learning and nobility, and by his worthy urbanity and candour, he aroused the deepest gratitude and love of all our people with whom he had anything to do. His frank desire to be of help is clear from this fact – namely that he brought cow-pox vaccine, ignorant of the fact that it had already been brought to our island – and with his own hand he innoculated several children of the inhabitants with the greatest success.

Written in Reykjavík   13 August 1810

Bjarni Thorarensen, Ísleifur Einarsson Rasmus Frydensberg]

' Vesturhorn and Austurhorn are both prominent headlands, 25 kilometres apart, with Austurhorn nearer to the eastern fjord Berufjörður. Steindór Steindórsson, 1960, p. 259 links the reference to the more easterly headland; MS clearly reads 'Vester Horn', but Holland had made similar directional mistakes earlier in the Journal, notably note 1, p. 262.

^{2} Berufjörður.

1 o'clock in the morning of the 30th, we just saw land – what we at first supposed to be the small rocky islets, called the *Stack & Skerry*, but which afterwards was found to be the two islands of *Barra & Rona*,[1] situated somewhat more than 50 miles to the west of the Orkney islands – Previously to this time, we had been so much fatigued & harassed by the voyage, that it was our determination to reach the shore by the first practicable means. The destination of the Flora was to London, & thither we had originally designed to proceed with her – as it was necessary, however, for the ship to pass by Stromness, to put out some seamen there, we decided upon landing at this place, & making our way forwards to the Main Land of Scotland as speedily as possible, and by the best method that might be offered to us.

During the whole of the 31st we were steering towards the mouth of *Hoy Sound* & had the wind been otherwise than scanty, might have got into Stromness with the evening's tide. We were not fortunate enough, however, to effect this – and the next morning our hopes were still further sunk by the information that the wind had shifted in the night, & was now blowing very hard from the very quarter in which our course lay. The whole of the 31st was spent in tacking to and fro within sight of the land, with a wind blowing in heavy squalls from the east. At night it blew a complete gale & another of our sails was destroyed. In the morning, the wind, though more moderate, was from the same quarter; but taking advantage of the flood tide, we were enabled to get up Hoy Sound – and cast anchor in Stromness Harbour at 10 o'clock – Four months and a few days had elapsed since we sailed from this place in the Elbe –

We remained two days in the Orkneys, and took this opportunity of riding over to Kirkwall – an excursion which had been unaccountably neglected in our former visit to these islands – On Monday we recommenced our progress southwards – having hired a decked boat to convey us to Inverness or Cromarty – This plan was partially frustrated by the state of the weather. – Apprehending some risk from crossing the Pentland Firth at a late hour in the evening, we did not proceed further on Monday, than the *Long Hope*; a harbour in the island of Hoy – where we passed the night on shore. The following morning we

---

[1]HH These two islands, though often called *Barra* and *Rona*, yet are properly named *Sulisker* and *North Rona* – composed wholly of *Gneiss*. *Rona* the largest about 3 miles round. Its highest point about 500 feet above the sea – Accessible only on one single spot, & that with danger. One solitary family resides here, tenanting the islet from a proprietor in *Lewis*, & under a covenant not easily broken, of remaining 8 years on this wretched spot.

crossed the Firth in safety, with a pretty strong breeze. The wind increased so much, while we were coasting along the shores of *Caithness*, & the sea began to run so high, that we were compelled, very unwillingly, to take refuge in the harbour of *Wick*. – Here, being thoroughly wearied of the uncertainties & discomforts of the sea, we dismissed the boat – & decided upon making our way, as well as might be, over land to Inverness. Partly on foot, partly on horseback – sometimes in chaires – sometimes in boats, we accomplished this journey in somewhat less than six days; – making, however, a circuitous route through Ross-shire; for the purpose of visiting *Geanies*, the seat of Colonel Macleod,[1] & the singularly beautiful place of *Coul*[2], the seat of Sir G.Mackenzie – An excellent coach carried us from Inverness to Edinburgh in two days & a half. No other circumstances than those in which we were placed, could have justified so cursory & transient a view of the romantic country through which we passed. – Every thought & feeling, however, now dwelt upon home, and to attain this object as speedily as possible was at present our sole endeavour & desire.

[1] Donald Macleod, sherrif of Ross-shire. Mackenzie married Macleod's fifth daughter Mary on 8 June 1802.
[2] Between Contin and Strathpeffer in Ross-shire.

APPENDIX A^{HH}

[*Register of Weather*]

1810

May *14th*   At Reikiaviik. Wind from N.E.
Therm. at 10 PM 28°

_____

15th   A clear, cloudless day. Wind N.
Therm. at 8 AM 34°
6 PM 32°
9 PM 28°

_____

16th   A clear, cloudless day. Wind N, &
high
Therm. at 9 PM 30°

_____

17th   Continuance of clear weather.
Wind N. In the evening very high.
Therm. at 8 AM 32°
2 PM 34°
9 PM 29°

_____

18th   The ice this morning ¼ of an inch
thick upon water within doors –
Clear weather continues – Wind
N. and very high –
Therm. at 8 AM 29°
4 PM 34°
10 PM 27°

_____

279

19th Wind from NW. The cold less severe. Between 1 & 2 PM., a fall of snow.
Therm. at 10 AM 38°
10 PM 36°

Full moon today –
High water on the beach at Reikiaviik at ½ past 5. The rising of the water from low water mark 17 or 18 feet
(This by information from Captain Liston)

20th A fine, clear day – Wind W.
Therm. at 9 AM 43°
2 PM 49°
10 PM 36°

21st Travelled from Reikiaviik to Havnefiord
The morning clear – Snow from 3 to 5 PM
Wind S.W.

22^d A clear, calm day – Wind W. Frosty towards evening.

23^d A clear, cloudless day. Wind W. In the evening got towards the N.
From Havnefiord to the stream Kaldaá.
Therm. at 3 PM 50°
9 PM 32°

24th From 6 to 9 A.M., rain with SE wind. In the evening, the weather became clearer, with wind from NNE.
From the Kaldaá to Krisevik.
Therm. at 10 AM 45°

25th   Morning fine & clear with S.
       Wind. In the evᵍ, wind more to
       the E.
       At Kriseviik.
       Therm. at 10 AM 47°
                   8 PM 40°

_____

26th   Morning clear with SE Wind. In
       the afternoon, cloudy.
       At Kriseviig –
       Therm. at 10 AM 50°
                   3 PM 55°

_____

27th   A cloudy day, but without rain.
       Wind SE and fresh.
       From Kriseviig to Grundeviig
       Therm. at 10 AM 46°
                   9 PM 44°

_____

28th   A cloudy day, with frequent
       showers of rain. Wind SE and
       strong –
       From Grundeviig to Kiebleviig
       Therm. at 9 AM 50°

_____

29th   A strong gale of wind from SE,
       attended with rain –
       At Kiebleviig
       Therm. at 9 AM 50°

_____

30th   Wind still from SE, but not so
       strong. Showers of rain. Evening
       tolerably clear. At Kiebleviig.
       Therm. at 10 AM 56°
                   4 PM 53°

_____

31st   A violent gale of wind from S.E.
       with much rain, continuing all the
       day.
       At Kiebleviik

Therm. at 11 AM 50°
4 PM 51°
8 PM 52°

June 1ˢᵗ   The wind from SSW to day. Some
rain in the morning – Cloudy all
day. In the afternoon the wind
dropped.
From Kiebleviik to Havnefiord
Therm. at 9 AM 52°

June 2ᵈ   Wind still SSW & fresher this
morning In the afternoon came to
the S – A fine day.
Returned to Reikiaviik.
Therm. at 10 AM 50°
9 PM 52°

Observations at Reikiaviik
June 3ʳᵈ   The morning cloudy, with frequent showers of rain – A
fresh wind from S – In the evᵍ the wind got more towards
the SW
Therm. at 10 AM 53°
9 PM 47°

June 4ᵗʰ   Wind from SSW – Morning clear. The Afternoon &
Evening Cloudy – Wind fresh in the Evening.
Therm. at 9 AM 58°   Baromʳ at 9 AM 30.311
9 PM 51°

June 5ᵗʰ   Morning rainy – Wind from SW. Very heavy rain in the
afternoon and evening.
Therm. at 9 AM 48°   Barom. at 9 AM 30.01
9 PM 51°

June 6ᵗʰ   A thick, foggy day, with rain. Wind SW.
Therm. at 9 AM 47°   Barom. at 9 AM 29.718
9 PM 50°

June 7th In the morning wind SW, with some rain. At 1 o'clock the wind went round to the NE & in the evening blew fresh with a clear sky.
Therm. at 9 AM 48°   Barom. at 9 AM 29.87
    9½ PM 35°

June 8th A clear, calm day – Wind NW
Therm. at 9 AM 46°   Barom.ʳ at 9 AM 30.14
    9½ PM 48°

June 9th A fine day. Wind SE in the morning NE in the evening.
Therm. at 9 AM 50°   Barom.ʳ at 9 AM 29.815
    9 PM 47°

June 10th The morning fine & clear with NE wind – Some heavy rain from 2 to 5. In the evᵍ wind E
Therm at 9 AM 49°   Barom at 9 AM 29.117
In the sun at 12   72°
In the shade at 12   61°
    at 10 PM   49°

June 11th The weather variable to day. Showers of rain. Wind NE & E.
Therm. at 11 AM 51°   Barom. at 10 AM 29.513

June 12th The weather fine, though somewhat cloudy with occasional showers of rain. Wind NNE
Therm. at 10 AM 55°   Barom. at 10 AM 29.619
    at 9 PM 49°

June 13th Wind to day varying from SE to S. Day fine though somewhat cloudy. A little rain in the evening.
Therm. at 9 AM 46°   Barom. at 9 AM 29.7
    12   52°

June 14ᵗᵍ Much rain in the course of the day – Wind SE & S
Therm at 10 AM 48°   Barom. at 10 AM 29.65

15th From Reikiaviik to Brautar-holt. Morning cloudy. Much rain from 3 PM till night, with wind SE

Therm. at 9 AM 51°   Barom. at 9 AM 29.82

16th The wind very high in the night. The day cloudy with occasional showers. Wind SE & E. from Brautarholt to Houls.

Therm. at 10 AM 53°   Barom. at 9 AM 29.8
   at 10 PM 53°   Therm at 9 AM 54°

NB The Barometrical observations' down to the 13th July, made by Mr Fell at Reikiaviik

---

17th Wind to day between E & NE, still fresh. The day tolerably clear, without rain. From Houls to Saurbar.

Therm. at 10½ AM 56°   Barom. at 9 AM 29.8
   at 10½ PM 51°   Therm. at 9 AM 60°

18th A remarkably fine clear day. Wind SW. From Saurbar to Inderholm.

Therm. at 8 AM 56°   Barom. at 9 AM 29.83
   at 2 PM 65°

At 2 PM in the sun 86° – a slight breeze
   at 10 PM 51°

19th A perectly clear, & calm day. Wind SW. At Indreholm.

Therm. at 9 AM 56°   Barom. at 9 AM 29.83
in the sun at 2 PM 85°   Thermometer 62°
   9 PM 50°

20th A thick misty morning with small rain. The remainder of the day fine, though somewhat cloudy. Wind SW & South. At Innreholm

Therm at 8 AM 49°   Barom. at 9 AM 29.92
Therm at 11 PM 47°   Therm^r 56°

21st The day cloudy but without rain. Wind SW & S. From Innreholme to Leira.

Therm. at 9 AM 49°   Barom. at 9 AM 29.84
   12 PM 50°   Therm^r 54°

' Also the right-hand column thermometer readings.

June 22^d The morning tolerably fine. About noon became more cloudy & rained nearly all the evening. Wind E. from Leira to Hvanneiri

Therm. at 9 AM 53°	Barom. at 9 AM 29.91
at 10 PM 52°	Therm. at 9 AM 56°

23^d Morning cloudy. In the afternoon & evening much heavy rain. Wind SE & E
From Hvanneiri to Svigna-Skard

Therm. at 10 AM 60°	Barom. at 9 AM 29.83
at 9 PM 53°	Therm. at 9 AM 56°

24th A thick, cloudy day, with much rain at intervals. Wind E. At Svigna-Skard.

Therm. at 10 AM 56°	
4 PM 58°	Barom. at 9 AM 29.51
8 PM 55°	Therm^r at 9 AM 54°

25th The day thick & foggy with small rain. Wind E. Weather cleared up about noon, the wind getting round to the North. In the evening, occasional showers, with intervals of clear sky. Wind NNW. A very cold evening. From Svigna-Skard to Stadir Hraun

Therm. at 11 AM 49°	Barom. at 9 AM 30.1
at 6 PM 42°	Therm^r at 9 AM 48
at 7½ PM 39°	

26th The day fine, clear and calm. Wind W & in the evening SSW.
From Stadar Hraun to Roudamelr.

Therm. at 6 AM 43°	Barom at 9 AM 30.325
at 2 PM 55°	Therm. at 9 AM 50°
at 9 PM 44°	

27th A very thick foggy morning, with rain. The fog continued during the whole day. Wind SW
From Roudamelr to Myklaholt

Therm at 10 AM 49°	Barom. at 9 AM 30.33
10 PM 48°	Therm. at 9 AM 54°

28th The morning foggy, but clearing up about 7 o'clock
The remainder of the day very fine. Wind SSW.
From Myklaholt to Stadar sweit.
Therm. at 8 AM 52°
        at 4 PM 61°   Barom. at 9 AM 30.135
        at 11 PM 52°   Therm. at 9 AM 53°

29th At midnight a thick fog came on. The morning foggy but
clearing up about mid-day. The evening cloudy Wind SW.
From Stadar sveit to Buderstad
Therm. at 9 AM 52°   Barom. at 9 AM 30.14
        11 PM 52°   Therm. at 9 AM 60°

June 30th A fine, calm & clear day. Wind in the morning W, in the
afternoon went round to the N.
From Buderstad to Stappen
Therm. at 9 AM 56°   Barom. at 9 AM 30.215
        10 PM 57°   Therm^r. 61°

July 1st A fine day upon the whole, though cloudy and thick in the
morning. Wind Westerly.
At Stappen.
Therm. at 10 AM 57°   Barom. at 9 AM 30.01
        10 PM 56°   Therm^r. 64°

2nd The morning somewhat cloudy. The remainder of the day
clear & fine. Wind NNW.
From Stappen to Olafsvik.
Therm. at 9 AM 54°   Barom. at 9 AM 30.02
At 2 in the sun 80°   Therm – 62°
at 2 in the shade 61°

3rd A warm and upon the whole, a fine day. About noon rather
cloudy. In the evening clear. Wind SW in the morning – in
the ev^g W.
Ascended the Jokull to day   Barom. at 9 AM 29.94
Therm. at 8 AM 56°   Therm^r – 56°
                              The sun set this evening 30°
                              East of North by the Compass.
                              About 4 o'clock by Mr Clausen's
                              calculation.

4th The weather perfectly calm to day, but cloudy, with small rain at intervals. Wind NW.
At Olafsvig.

| Therm. at 10 AM 55° | Barom. at 9 AM 29.74 |
| at 10 PM 49° | Therm. – 58° |

5th The morning foggy, with small rain. Cleared up about 12 o'clock & continued fine. Wind NW but scarcely perceptible.
At Olafsvig.

Therm. at 9 AM 51°   Barom. at 9 AM 29.82
   at 10 PM 52°   Therm. – 59°
at midnight   48°   By an observation which I made this night, the sun was 2h 35m under the horizon. It rose 58° East of North by the Compass.

6th The day fine, though not perfectly clear. Scarcely any wind.
From Olafsvig to Grönnefiord.

| Therm. at 9½ AM 60° | Barom. at 9 AM 29.92 |
| at 10 PM 51° | Therm^r at 9 AM 63° |

July 7. A clear & fine day. Wind North   (Observations at Reikiaviik)
From Gronnefiord to Stikkesholm   Barom. at 9 AM 29.9
Therm. at 8 AM 55°   Therm^r   50°
   at 2 PM 61°

8th A fine clear day – Wind North
At Stikkesholm
Therm. at 10 AM 50°   Barom. at 9 AM 29.84
   8 PM 49°   Therm. at 9 AM 63°

9th A fine day upon the whole, though not perfectly clear.
Wind went round from N to SE.

From Stikkesholm to Narfeyre
Therm. at 9 AM 50°
     9 PM 49°

Barom. at 9 AM 29.84
Therm^r 58°

10th A very cold day, but clear –
Wind from NE, & blowing
fresh.
From Narfeyre to Snoksdalr
Therm. at 6 AM 45°
     9 PM 38½°

Barom. at 9 AM 29.80
Therm^r 59°

11th A continuance of the cold
wind from North East. The
morning clear. The afternoon
cloudy, & in the evening
some rain.
At Snoksdalr
Therm. at 10 AM 42°
     7 PM 41°

Barom. at 9 AM 29.65

12th A clear, fine day, but with the
continuance of a cold wind
from NNE.
From Snoksdalr to Hvam
Therm. at 4 AM 42°
     1 PM 58° in the
     shade
     8 PM 40°

Barom. at 9 AM 29.62

13th A cold, cloudy day, with
occasional showers of rain –
Wind NNE
From Hvam to Hvanneiri
Therm. at 5 AM 41°
     10 PM 42°

Barom. at 9 AM 29.71

14th A fine day, though not
perfectly cloudless. Wind
Northerly.

Therm. at 8 AM 45°   Barom. at 9 AM 29.68
6 PM 45°
From Hvanneiri to Reikolt & back

15th   The morning cloudy. The
remainder of the day fine &
clear. Wind North, but
scarcely perceptible.
Hvanneiri to Reikiaviik
Therm. at 8 AM 52°   Barom. at 9 AM 29.72
9 PM 48°

16th   A fine, clear day. Wind N.
Westerly.
At Reikiaviik.
Therm. at 10 AM 60   Barom. at 9 AM 29.75
at 9 PM 53

17th   A calm & fine day – though
not perfectly clear – Wind
Westerly.
Therm. at 9 AM 59°   Barom. at 9 AM 29.91
10 PM 52°

18th   A remarkably fine, & clear
day. The weather very sultry.
Wind Westerly.
Therm. at 8 AM 60°   Barom. at 9 AM 30.015
in the sun at 1 PM 80°
in the shade at 1 PM 68°
at 10 PM 55°

19th   The early part of the day
clear and fine. Cloudy in the
afternoon, but without rain.
Wind Westerly.
Therm. at 9 AM 58°   Barom. at 9 AM 30.26
11 PM 54°

20th A clear & fine day, with a
continuance of the Westerly
wind.
Therm. at 9 AM 57°   Barom. at 9 AM 30.22
9 PM 58°

21st The early part of the day fine,
with NW wind – In the
afternoon the wind went
round to the East. In the
evening heavy rain came on.
Therm. at 9 AM 61°   Barom. at 9 AM 30.18
9 PM 56°

22^d Some rain in the morning –
— occasionally during the
day. Wind W and SW.
Therm. at 9 AM 60°   Barom. at 9 AM 29.77
10 PM 52°

Observations at Reikiaviik

July 23^d The day fine, though not
clear. No rain – Wind from
the West in the morning. In
the ev^g went round to E.
Therm. at 9 AM 54°   Barom. at 9 AM 29.69
9 PM 56°

24th Heavy rain in the morning.
Cloudy with occasional
showers during the
remainder of the day. Wind
East.
Therm. at 8 AM 52°   Barom. at 8 AM 29.34
at 8 PM. 59°   at 11 AM 29.23

25th Cloudy, with heavy showers
of rain during the whole day.
Wind East.
From Reikiaviik to Thingvalla

Therm. at 6 PM 50°   Barom. at 9 AM 29.045
                             Therm^r 54°

26th The morning very fine.
Became cloudy at 3 o'clock
with some rain. Rained again
at night. Wind ESE.
From Thingvalla to Skalholt
Therm. at 6 AM 52°   Barom. at 9 PM 29.13
      at 9 PM 55°   Therm^r 54°

27th The morning rainy. Cleared
up about 11 & continued fine
during the afternoon. The
evening again cloudy, with
some rain.
Wind varying from SE to NE.
Therm. at 9 AM 56°   Barom. at 9 PM 29.2
From Skalholt to the Geysers Therm^r 53½

28th The day tolerably fine,
though not clear. Wind East
At the Geysers
Therm. at 9 AM 55°   Barom. at 9 PM 29.2
        9 PM 56°   Therm^r 52½

29th Showers of rain during the
day. Wind Easterly
Therm. at 9 AM 56°   Barom. at 9 PM 29.72
        9 PM 54°   Therm^r 53
From the Geyers to Skalholt

30th Frequent showers of rain
during the whole morning.
No rain in the afternoon, but
cloudy. Wind SE.
From Skalholt to Kalfholt
Therm. at 9 AM 56°   Barom. at 9 PM 29.91
      at 9 PM 54°   Therm^r 55°

31*st*   The morning fine. The
afternoon cloudy with
frequent showers of rain.
Wind S Easterly
From Kalfholt to Storu-vellir

| Therm. at 10 AM 58° | Barom. at 9 PM 29.94 |
| 9 PM 52° | Therm*r* 54° |

—————————————————————*Observs at Reikiaviik*

August 1*st*   The morning tolerably fine,
though not clear. In the
afternoon very heavy rain.
Wind SSW.
From Kalfholt to the foot of Hecla

| Therm. at 10 AM 57° | Barom*r* at 9 PM 29.93 |
| 7 PM 54° | Therm*r* at   54 |

———————————

2*d*   The morning fine & clear.
About 3 o'clock heavy rain
came on – & continued 2
hours. In the evening cloudy
with small rain. Wind from
SE. to SW.
From Nifurholt to Reikiadalr,
and back today.

| No observations on the | Barom. at 9 PM 29.94 |
| Therm*r* | Therm*r*   60° |

———————————

3*d*   The morning clear & fine.
Afternoon somewhat cloudy,
but without rain. Wind
SWest.
Ascended Mount Hecla.

| Therm. at 10 AM 59° | Barom*r* at 9 PM 29.94 |
| at 9 PM 52° | Therm*r*   50° |

———————————

4*th*   A remarkably fine, clear day.
Wind Southerly.
From Niifurholt to Hlidarende

Therm. at 10 AM 60°   Barom^r at 9 PM 29.91
              12   64   Therm^r   53°
              10 PM 54

5th   A very fine day upon the
       whole, though with some
       rain about 9 PM. Wind
       Southerly.
       From Hlidarende to Odde
       Therm. at 9 AM 58°   Barom at 9 PM 29.84
                      9 PM 57°   Therm^r   50°

6th   A remarkably fine, clear day.
       Wind WNW
       From Odde to Eyarback
       Therm at 8 AM 55°   Barom^r at 9 PM 29.94
                                            Therm.   46°

7th   A remarkably fine day –
       perfectly clear. Wind NW.
       From Eyarback to Reikiaviik
       Therm. at 10 AM 59°   Barom at 9 PM 29.93
              at 1½ in the sun 78°
              at 9 PM 54°

8th   The day cloudy, but without
       rain. Wind S in the morn^g –
       in the ev^g SE
       At Reikiaviik
       Therm. at 9 AM 60°   Barom. at 9 PM 29.71
              at 9 PM 54°

August 9th   The morning rainy, the
       remainder of the day cloudy,
       but without rain. Wind SE
       At Reikiaviik.
       Therm^r at 9 AM 56°   Barom^r at 9 29.61
              at 9 PM 56½°

10th A fine day. Wind NNW.
At Reikiaviik.
Therm^r at 10 AM 62°   Barom. at 9 PM 29.582
    at 9 PM 56°

11th The morning tolerably fine.
At 2 o'clock heavy rain came
on, & continued during the
remainder of the day. Wind
NWest
Therm^r at 9 AM 62°   Barom. at 9 AM 29.61
    at 9 PM 52°

12th A fine day, though not
properly clear. Wind North.
Therm^r at 10 AM 61°   Barom. at 9 AM 29.723
    9 PM 56°

13th A very fine, clear day. Wind
North.
Therm. at 9 PM 58°   Barom. at 9 PM. 29.86

14th A fine day, though not
perfectly clear. Wind NW.
Therm. at 9 AM 57°   Barom^r at 9 PM 30.18
    9 PM 56°

15th A fine day. Wind S & SE.
Therm. at 10. AM 59½°   Barom^r at 9 AM 30.12
    at 8 PM 56°

16th In the morning a high wind
from SE. About 11, it went
down with heavy rain,
continuing for some hours. In
the ev^g wind NW.
Therm. at 9 AM 55°   Barom. at 9 AM 29.798
    at 9 PM 55½°

August 17th	During the whole day, a high gale of wind from SE with much rain. In the ev[g] the wind went down.

Therm. at 9 AM 55½°   Barom. at 2 PM 29.06

NB A remarkably high tide to   at 7 PM 28.78

day

18th	At an early hour this morning, the wind round to the West. Blew a strong gale from this quarter the whole day. No rain. In the ev[g] wind NW

Therm. at 9 AM 50°   Barom. at 9 AM 29.08

at 8 PM 46°   at 8 PM 29.44

APPENDIX B[HH]

[*The parishes of Iceland*]

Results collected from a Table given us by Bishop Vidalin, enumerating the Parishes in Iceland, the names of the Ministers & the number of People in each parish, & the stipends of the respective Ministers.

NB The statement of the population in this Table is according to the enumeration of 1801, which makes the total number of people in the Island 47,207. The stipends of the priests are stated according to the latest regulations which have been made respecting them – viz. the regulation of 1726 in the diocese of Skalholt, & that of 1748 in the diocese of Hoolum.

The Bishopric of Iceland is divided into 19 Districts or *Toparchiæ* corresponding with the *Civil division* into Syssels. One of the ministers in each Præfecture is termed the *Provost* – his office being that of a superintendent of the several churches within his district. The *Toparchiæ* are subdivided into Parishes, some of which contain three or even four churches.

Names of the Toparchiæ	Number of Parishes	Number of Churches	Number of Inhabitants	Remarks
East Skapte fells	5	7	911	The largest specified stipend in this district is 37 Specie dollars. 12 skillings. The smallest, in a parish with 2 churches is 5 Dol. 55sk.
West Skapte fells	7	10	1539	The largest stipend in this district is D43 Sk17–Four between 20 & 30 dollars. The smallest is 10.42, in a parish cont[g] 78 people.
Rangaa-valle & the Westmann Islands	13	26	4187	The largest stipend in this district & indeed in Iceland is that of *Breidibolstadur* – 182.74. The parish contains 376 people. In the parish of Kross in the same district with a population of 527, & 2 churches, the minister's stipend is only 32.85. The stipend at Oddi in this district is 121 dollars.

Names of the Toparchiæ	Number of Parishes	Number of Churches	Number of Inhabitants	Remarks
Aarnes	16	28	4625	No stipend in this Toparchia exceeds 83½ dollars. The greater number are between 15 & 40 dollars. The parish of *Torfastadir*, which includes 5 churches (Skalholt is one of them) & contains 527 people, has a stipend of only 24.46. The smallest in the district is 10.17.
Guldbringe & Kiose	9	17	4015	The largest stipend is that of Reikiavik, with the annexed chapel at Viidoe – 120 dollars. The smallest is 20 dollars in a parish with 3 churches.
Borgar-fiord	6	11	1882	The largest stipend 68.68 – the smallest 15.76.
Myre and Hnappadals	7	14	1478	Largest stipend 102.57 in a parish cont^g only 63 people – smallest is 17.34.
Snæfells-nes	7	16	3541	Three considerable stipends in this district. That of Provost Jonsson at *Staderstad*, 106 dollars. The population of his parish 459. The parish of Ingialdsholl in this district contains 993 people – a greater number than any other in Iceland – 2 churches in this parish – the stipend is only 36.68.
Dale	6	13	1592	The largest salary 67.37.
Bardastrand	8	13	2493	Largest stipend 82.44 – smallest 18.53
W. Isafiord	6	10	1850	Largest stipend 75.12 – smallest 5 dollars
N. Isafiord	7	9	2037	Largest stipend 69^d – stipends of 11.72 – 9 – & 8.
Strande	4	7	982	Largest stipend 39.34 – smallest 10.34.
Hunavatns	15	23	2880	Seven stipends under 20 dollars. Largest 67.35.
Skage-fiord	14	25	3141	Most of the stipends small in this district
Eyafiord	15	23	3453	Largest stipend 68.54. Smallest 8 – 96 people.
Thing-oe or Norder	17	27	3002	The parish of *Greniadarstadr*, with 182 people, & 2 churches, has a stipend of 162 dollars. The other stipends in general small.
Norder Mule	10	12	1762	Largest stipend 61.68. The others in general small. One of only 5 dollars; the parish cont^g 77 people.
Sonder Mule	12	14	1837	Largest stipend 53.89 – smallest 12.85
	184	305	47207	

From the preceding table it appears that there are in Iceland 184 parishes & 305 churches. The average number of inhabitants to each parish is 256 or 257. The average number of people to each church is 155. The largest nominal stipend is 182½ dollars – the smallest, (of which, however there are two or three instances) is 5 dollars. The whole nominal revenue of the Icelandic clergy, (exclusively of the Bishop) amounts according to the table, whence this selection is made, to scarcely 6400 specie dollars, giving an average for each parish in the island of not more than 34 or 35 dollars.

APPENDIX C^{HH}

The Present State of Literature, Education &c in Iceland

Considering the small extent of the public means of education in Iceland, the degree of general information existing among all classes of society in the island, is not a little singular. The only public school is that of Bessasted, situated on the peninsula which forms the northern side of the bay of Havnefiord. At the time of the reformation of religion in Iceland, two schools were instituted – one at Hoolum – the other at Skalholt. These were continued until 1785, when the two were conjoined & transferred to Reikiaviik. At this period the revenues of the two schools, which were derived from landed prosperity & funds bequeathed to the institutions, were appropriated by the King of Denmark, and an annual sum devoted to the support of the school. The amount of this royal donation is .[1]

The school was continued at Reikiaviik until the year 1802, when it was transferred to Bessasted – the building being devoted to the purpose, which previously was the residence of the Governor of Iceland (For a description of this building – the library &c, see Vol. 1. p. 49).[2] The establishment at the present time consists of three masters, & 23 or 24 scholars. A fourth master, however, is about to be added to the number. The head-master, or *Lector*, receives a salary of 600 rix dollars per annum. The other masters, or *adjuncti*, have salaries of 300 dollars each. The office of Lector has of late been filled by Steingrim Jonsson, a man who has obtained much reputation for his learning & acquirements. In the present summer, he has been transferred from this situation to the church of Odde, on the southern coast of the island – one of the most valuable of the Icelandic livings.

The Theological department in the school at Bessasted is confined solely to the Lector, who besides this office, has the charge committed to him of teaching the Hebrew language, & in part the Latin. The 2^d master's office comprehends Latin, History, Geography & Arithmetic. That of the 3^d master the Greek, Danish, & Icelandic languages. It is a

[1] MS omits the figure.   [2] See above pp. 116–19.

singular circumstance connected with the regulations of the school, that each scholar, whether intended for the pastoral office or not, is obliged to study the elements of Hebrew, & to undergo some examination in this language. No exclusion is exercised in the admission of scholars; though a preference is given to the children of ministers. A youth is not admitted until he has been confirmed, which ceremony is usually performed at the age of fourteen. A certificate of his talents, distinctions &c, is given by the minister of the parish in which he has lived. After a certain degree of acquirement has been made in the studies prescribed by the laws of the school, each scholar becomes what is termed a *demissus* – he leaves the school, & pursues his studies at home. No period of time is fixed for a *demission* – this is determined solely by the proficiency of the scholar, which is ascertained by examination. It is part of the office of the Bishop of Iceland to visit the school twice in the course of the year: at the end of May, & about the beginning of October. At the former period, the examinations take place, which continue several days, with a prescribed form of proceeding (See Vol. 1., p. 42).[1] The session or period of study lasts from October to May – the summer is made the period of vacation to accommodate the rural occupations of the Icelanders. To be made a *demissus*, it is required that the student should be able to read & write Latin with accuracy; that he should be familiar with the Danish language; that he should understand the rules for interpreting the Old and New Testament; & that he should have some knowledge of history, geography, & arithmetic. Mathematics are not made a requisite. If a youth has remained 7 years at school, without attaining those qualifications which entitle him to become a demissus, the Lector writes to his friends in the country representing the matter to them; & the young man is not allowed longer to remain at the school.

The examination of the theological students is considered with an attention to the peculiar circumstances of their future vocation. They are questioned as to the doctrines of the Lutheran church – on the Bible History, and on Ecclesiastical History in general. They are likewise made to interpret and explain the more difficult part of the Old & New Testament. When they become *demissi*, an annual examination is still required, which is conducted by the transmission of theological questions from the Bishop, through the medium of the Provost of each Syssel. Answers are returned to these questions in the same way. (See Section on Ecclesiastical State of Iceland).

[1] See above note 1, p. 109; note 1, p. 110.

No other school than that of Bessasted is to be found in Iceland, except a small & very inconsiderable one in the vicinity of the same place, where the children of some farmers receive their education.

Previously to the war, a premium of 10 dollars was proposed every year at Bessasted – to be divided among the three scholars, who appeared, on the examination, to be the most deserving of this reward. Latterly this has been discontinued.

The *stipendia* or *benefices* attached to the ancient school of Skalholt are sufficient for 23 scholars – those at Hoolum for sixteen. They were so far reduced however, when the schools were united, that a maintenance is at present provided for only 24 scholars.

It is not a necessary part of the office of an Icelandic minister, to assist in the education of the children in his parish, nor is this generally done. Nevertheless he has a sort of general superintendence of the different families in it, as regards the attention which is given to the education of the younger members of a family. He is required, previous to giving confirmation, to ascertain that a child is able to read, & to go through the catechism of the country. It is likewise a part of the pastoral office to visit once in the year, each family in his parish – to enquire into the state of their domestic concerns & to ascertain among other things the progress & dispositions of the children of the family, as well as the means which are possessed, in the way of books, &c, for the continuance of their education. For an example of the minute attention which is given by some of the ministers in Iceland to these points, see Vol. 1. p. 84. [Ed. see below, p. 302.]

It is a singular fact connected with the ecclesiastical law of Iceland, that the Bishop has the power of preventing a marriage, if the woman is not able to read – this being deemed indispensable to the proper education of the future children of the family. This law has not infrequently been acted upon – not, however, by the present Bishop. Owing to this and other precautions which are taken to ensure the domestic education of the young, the degree of information existing among the lowest classes in Iceland is greater probably than in any other part of Europe; Scotland alone perhaps excepted.

The high literary character which the Icelanders maintained during a period when the rest of Europe was almost hidden in darkness, gives much interest to a survey of the present state of literature in this remote island. The following is a brief sketch, illustrative of this subject.[1]

[1] No such sketch appears in the MS; see above p. 44.

APPENDIX D^{HH}

[Page from a parish register]

Toparchiæ Saurbæensis in tractu Hvalfjordrstrand numerus Incolarum – inceptus 1st Januar. 1805.

Names of Habitations	Names of People	Situation Occupation &c.	Age	Confirmed	Communicants	Whether able to read	Conduct	General abilities
Storibotn	Gudrin Sigurdardottir	Widow & Owner of the House	57	Yes	Yes	Yes	Clean and industrious	Well informed
	Oddur Jonsson	Widow's son	19	Dᵒ	Dᵒ	Dᵒ	A good boy	Well educated
	Hans Jonsson	Dᵒ	19	Dᵒ	Dᵒ	Dᵒ	Clever at work	Not so good an understanding as his Brother
	Ingibiorg Jonsdottir	Widow's Daughter	18	Dᵒ	Dᵒ	Dᵒ	A hopeful girl	Well-informed
	Gudrin Jonsdottir	Dᵒ	17	Dᵒ	Dᵒ	Dᵒ	Equally good	Above mediocrity in her abilities
	Wigfus Gudmundson	An Orphan kept by the widow	15	No	No	Dᵒ	A tractable boy	Good understanding

The books in the house are the New Psalm Book – Vidalin's Sermons – Thoughts on the Nativity of Christ – Psalms relating to the Passion of Christ – the Conversation of the Soul with Itself – Sermons – Thoughts on the Passion – Diarium – Thordir's Prayers – New Testament – and a few Prayer Books

Names of Habitations	Names of People	Situation Occupation &c.	Age	Confirmed	Communicants	Whether able to read	Conduct	General abilities
Thyrill	Jorundir Gislason	Hreppstiore. Rector Parochiæ or Elder	41	Yes	Yes	Yes	Well disposed & clean	Moderate abilities
	Margaret Thorstens dottir	His Wife	53	Dᵒ	Dᵒ	Dᵒ	Good character	Piously disposed
	Gudrin Eireksdottir	Her daughter	19	Dᵒ	Dᵒ	Dᵒ	A hopeful girl	Well informed
	Gudmundr Grimson	Servant	25	Dᵒ	Dᵒ	Dᵒ	A faithful labourer	He has neglected his improvement & is therefore admonished.
	Thorsdys Sæmnsdottir	Maid servant	42	Dᵒ	Dᵒ	Dᵒ	Neat and faithful	Well informed
	Jarfrudr Stephansdot	Her child	3	—	—	—		—
	Kristin Jonsdottir	An orphan	8	—	—	—	A tractable child	Has finished her Catechism. To be confirmed
	Waldi Steinderson	Dᵒ	6				Tractable & obedient	He is learning the Catechism

The Books in the House are an Old Psalm Book & a New One – Vidalin's Sermons – Vidalin's Doctrines of Religion – Fast Sermons – Seven Sermons – Psalm Books – Sturm's Meditations (translated into Icelandic) – Bible Extracts – Dᵣ Bartholin's Religious Doctrine – A Prayer Book – and a New Testament belonging to the Church.

J. Hjaltalin

Pastor Saurbæensis. die 16 Junii 1810

APPENDIX E^HH

The Commercial State of Iceland

In the measures which have been pursued in relation to the trade of Iceland, the Danish Government has manifested of late years a degree of liberality, if not of judgement, which deserves to be at once known & commended. Previously to the year 1776, the trade of the island was committed to the hands of certain commercial companies in Denmark, who held it by a monopoly, which enabled them occasionally to promote their own interests, at the expence of those of the Icelanders. Nevertheless the trade, when thus vested, was found to be an unprofitable one; & latterly it became difficult to meet with commercial men who were willing to invest their capitals in it. Owing to this circumstance & the other evident evils of such a plan, the commercial system of Iceland underwent a total change in 1776. A project was laid by the Danish Government for rendering the trade of the island perfectly free; and as a preparation for this change, it was determined that during the ensuing 10 years, it should be committed to the hands of the King. This, however, was only nominal. The trade, in fact, was carried upon a fund raised by the Danish Government for this purpose, in the management of which the King was constituted the Director. This fund amounted originally to 4,000,000 dollars. During the 10 years, in which the trade of Iceland was thus invested, the capital decreased by about 600,000 dollars – estimating in this decrease, as well the losses sustained in the trade itself, as also the greatly diminished price, at which the vessels & other stock were sold off at the expiration of the period in question.

At this time, viz. about the commencement of the year 1787, the commerce of Iceland was declared free – the stock of the late trading fund was sold off, as just mentioned, at a very low rate, that encouragement might be given to those now embarking in the trade, & the remaining capital of the fund, about 3,400,000 dollars, appropriated to the support of the system under its present form. Its management is vested in six Commissioners. These are empowered to lend out money from the fund to merchants engaged in the Iceland trade, at an interest of 4 per cent, & for different periods of time, according to different conditions as to the payment of the capital thus advanced. The advantages held out by this fund have not been neglected by the merchants subsequently engaged in the Icelandic trade. The present condition of the fund is not accurately known in Iceland, but it is believed that considerable losses to the capital must of late have been sustained by the events of the war, the difficulty of making remittances &c.

At the time that the trade of Iceland was declared free, a further encouragement was given to its prosecution by an edict, affording an exemption from every tax or duty for a period of 20 years. At the expiration of this term, in 1807, a new edict extended the exemption five years longer, it being considered that this indulgence was necessary to the support of the trade. The present exemption therefore expires in 1812; but it is thought by many intelligent men in Iceland, that the circumstances of the commerce of the island will require a still longer continuance of this freedom from impost. In point of fact, it does not appear that the trade, even under the present system of things, is one of much profit or advantage. This is more especially true at the present time – the war between England & Denmark having interfered in the most material degree with the commerce of the island, by preventing the accustomed intercourse with Norway & Denmark. The most prosperous years altogether for the trade of Iceland were 1797–98 – & 99 During these years, many cargoes of salted & stock fish were exported to different parts in Spain, Italy &c, with much profit to the Icelandic merchant. Mr Thorlacius of Bildudald, in the N. Western part of Iceland, was much engaged in this trade, by which he acquired a considerable fortune. He is at the present time esteemed the wealthiest man in the island.

Previously to the war, from 40 to 50 or 55 vessels were engaged in the Iceland trade – the greater number of these *galliots*, from 100 to 250 tons burthen. Since the war, this number has greatly decreased. During the last year, there were not more than 8 or 10 arrivals in the whole island (this given only as a statement approaching the truth). The effect which the late Order in Council of the English Government may have in relieving this state of things, still remains to be ascertained. The Icelandic merchants themselves do not entertain any very sanguine expectations from this source, alledging as a ground of their opinion, the impossibility of disposing in England of Icelandic produce, particularly fish, to the same advantage as elsewhere; & further, the inconveniences to Danish vessels of entering the ports of Leith or London, obtaining licences &c. These doubts are certainly counte- nanced in some measure by the little effect the Orders in Council have had during the present summer. It is not improbable that many of the licences obtained in England, for the professed purpose of trading to Iceland, have been made the means of carrying on a more lucrative intercourse between Norway & Denmark. The only British House which has taken a part in the Icelandic trade, is that of Phelps & C° of London. The share which this house had in the singular revolution which occurred last summer in Iceland, had interfered much with the success of their mercantile speculation in the island.

The following Tables (from Atastrood Stephansens 18th Century) exhibit the state of the Imports & Exports of Iceland in 1806, the year preceding the commencement of the war. With respect to the accuracy of these Tables, it is probable, from the information I have elsewhere received, that the quantities given in them, are in general below the truth.

It will be seen that the export of tallow, wool & woollen goods is very large from the Reikiaviik district. This is in consequence not so much of the number of sheep kept in this part of the island, as of the quantity of these articles brought down to Reikiaviik by the people from other parts of the island, for the purpose of barter with the merchants.

With respect to the practicability of extending the export trade from Iceland, it may be remarked that *fish* & *oil* are the only articles in the export of which it is probable that any speedy or important extension can take place. The number of sheep is limited by the necessity of providing a certain stock of hay for their winter subsistence; & unless the means of doing this was extended by the improvement of the land &c, it is impossible that the export of tallow, mutton or woollen goods should receive any material increase. The fisheries of Iceland however open an almost unlimited field to speculation, & though now constituting the principal branch of trade, are doubtless capable of very great extension and improvement.

Table of Imports into Iceland in the year 1806

Districts	Rye Meal	Rye	Barley	Oats	Pease	Pearl Barley	Barley Groats	Buck Wheat Groats	Oat Groats	Rice	Wheat flour	Rye bread	Fine Biscuits	Wheat Bread	BRANDY Danish	BRANDY French	BRANDY Grape	Rum	Wine
	Barrels	Barr.	Barrels	Barr.	Barrels	Barrels	Barrels	Barrels	Barrels	Lp. p	Lp. p	Skp. p	Skp. p	Skp. p	Barrels	Barr.	Barr.	Barrels	Hhds
Reikiavik's	3582	2265	27	72	777	531	128	7	8	3.10	66.0	90.15	226.4	47.4	255	43	149	28	60
Eskefiord's	563	575	0	4	310	145	109	0	4	0	0	51.12	21.4	0	59	98	6	4	8
Eyafiord's	978	2965	32	6	866	190	80	5½	4¼	1	28.5	35.14	19.17	0.13	105	52	25¼	12½	6½
Isafiord's	1017	701	26	2	136	161½	56½	2	4	30.13	16.12	53.6	3.5	2.15	150	33½	32	3	12
Total	6140	6506	85	84	2079	1027½	373½	14½	20¼	35.7	111.1	231.7	270.10	50.12	569	226¼	212¼	47½	86½
												Barrels							Pipes
In 1630	4501	—	—	—	17	83	—	—	—	—	—	352	93	—	262	—	--	—	13¾
In 1743	8038	—	—	—	52	135	—	—	—	—	—	1239	684	—	722	14	12½	—	57⅓
In 1779	10665 (with barley mead)	475	1138	98	133	367	—	—	—	—	—	986	422	—	1160	36⅔	--	18	71

	Vinegar	Mead	Beer	Malt	Coffee	Sugar	Treacle	Tobacco	Paper	Soap	Salt	Iron	Tar	Coal Lasts	Hemp Hackled		Fish Lines	Cables	Twine
		Barr.	Barrels	Barr.	Skp. Lp	Skp. Lp	Skp. Lp	Skp. Lp	Reams	Firkins	Barrls	Skp. Lp	Bar.	Barrs.	Skp. Lp	Unhackled	Pieces	Pieces	Skp. Lp.
Reikiavik's	5	24	7	10	13.15	24.17	13.14	96.19	63	46	842	170.13	159	26.4½	27.0	17.6	7117	1122	4.8
Eskefiord's	1	9	0	11	4.10	10.00	4.6	52.5	25	1	325	5.4	31	.9	—	—	817		.3
Eyafiord's	2	17	34½	18	2.7	6.13	5.10	44.3	65	7	549	2.13	13	2.17	.4	1.16	907	—	.1
Isafiord's	2¼	3	11	—	6.6	7.5	1.13	44.13	4	1	862	21.14	116	3	—	.3	3630	23.1	2.0
Total	10¼	53	52½	39	26.18	48.15	25.3	238.0	157	55	2578	200.4	319	32.12½	27.4	19.5	12471*		6.12
In 1630	—	216	—	38	—	—	—	—	—	—	834	181.0	61	—	—	—	34412	—	9.1
In 1743	—	67	—	12	—	—	—	20.10	—	—	1864	272.0	147	—	—	—	--	—	—
In 1779	—	67	—	213	10.7½	27.0	—	256.15	218	lb 2954	2954	310.0	291	22.0	15.0		12890	—	9.5½

* Half this number are probably lines 60 fathoms in length – the remaining half of 40 fathoms.

Tables of Exports from Iceland in the year 1806

Names of Districts	*Salted Fish*	*Dried Fish of different kinds*	*Cod, salted in Barrels*	*Salted Cod in mass*	*Cod*	*OIL Shark*	*Seal*	*Fish Liver*	*Tallow*	*Salted Salmon*	*Salted Beef and Mutton*	*WOOL White*	*WOOL Mixed*	*Woollen Yarn*	*Stockings*
	SkpLp	*SkpLp*	*Barrels*	*SkpLp*	*Barrels*			*Barrels*	*SkpLp*	*Barrels*	*Barrels*	*Skp.Lp.*	*Skp.Lp.*	*Skp.Lp.*	*Pairs*
Reikiavik's	1606.3	1809.2	66	2.8	495½	110	10	12	149.15	28½	20	327.14	58.14	.9	19,567
Eskifiord's	—	—	28	—	36	79½	—	—	151.10	—	1061	92.12	56.4	4.3	26,186
Eyafiord's	30.18	—	36	—	17	561		—	278.6	—	1885	166.17	11.5	24.11	79,900
Isafiord's	364.5	524.16	20	7.13	259	913	14	—	19.8	—	—	92.5	7.18	—	56,023
Total	2001.6	2333.18	150	10.1	807½	1663½	24	12	598.19	28½	2966	679.8	134.1	29.3	181,676
									Barrels						
In 1624	843	5817	444½		930	–	–	—	337	5½	2721½	—	—	—	72,231
1630	207	2823	142		1445¼	–	–	—	133¾	5	1110	—	—	—	21,694
									Skp.Lp.						
1743	392	5380	658		471	–	–	—	475.6	3	5386½	265.	—	—	213,696
1779	3612	4901	1905		1402	–	–	—	609.8	16½	728	23	—	—	111,407

	Frocks or Jackets	*Mittens*	*Wadmal*	*Lamb Skins*	*Salted Sheep Skins*	*Small Shark Skins*	*Fox Skins*	*Swan Skins*	*Goat Skins*	*Eider Down*	*Swan Quills*	*Feathers*	*Iceland Moss*	*Reindeer Horns*
		Pairs	*Pieces*							*Skp.Lp.*		*Skp.Lp.*		
Reikiavik's	130	77,203	3	2442	190	233	63	52	—	1.11	9970	14.12	4	—
Eskifiord's	345	6,737	8	642	23,516	—	32	—	—	.19	—	—	—	—
Eyafiord's	5790	57,798	—	3723	9,091	—	15	—	115	.19	1058	—	—	153
Isafiord's	17	141,338	—	620	6	1335	35	3	—	3.7½	6550	12.1	¼	—
Total	6282	283,076	11	7427	32,803	1568	145	55	115	6.16½	17,578	26.13	4¼	153
			Ells											
In 1624	—	12,232	12,251	—	—	—	—	—	—	—	—	—	—	—
1630	—	13,004	4,042	—	—	—	—	—	—	—	—	—	—	—
1743	1211	110,507	876	—	—	—	—	—	—	—	—	—	—	—
1779	884	186,624	521	20,722	—	—	406	98	—	6⅝	16093	2.9	—	—

Tables of Weights, Measures &c, used in Iceland

MEASURES FOR LIQUIDS

			Gall.
1 *Pibe (Pipe)*	contains 3 *Ame*	or	120
1 *Oxhoved* (hogshead)	contains 2 Bar[rels]	or	60
1 *Ame*	contains 4 Ankers	or	40
1 *Tönde* (Barrel)	cont^s 3 Ankers	or	30
1 *Anker*	cont^s 5 *Kuttinge*	or	10
1 *Kutting*	contains 4 *Kander*	or	2
1 *Kande*	cont^s 2 *Potten*	or	½
1 *Pot* (Quarter of a Gallon)	cont^s 4 *Pæle*	or	2 pints
1 *Pæl* (½ pint)	—	—	—

WEIGHTS

		English Cwt	qr	lbs
1 *Skippund*	contains 20 *Lisepund* or	3	—	22⅖
1 *Lisepund*	contains 16 *Pund*	—	—	17²³⁄₂₅
1 *Pund*	contains 16 *onzes*	—	—	1³⁄₂₅

N.B. 100lb Danish make 112 lb English – The Danish weight is therefore 12 punt [?] heavier.

CLOTH AND LINEN MEASURE

1 Danish y^d contains 24 Niches or ⅔ of an English yard.
N.B. The Danish *Alen* or Yard is divided into 4 quarters.

CORN MEASURE

1 *Tonde* (Barrel) = 8 *Skepper* or 4 English Bushels
1 *Skepper* (½ bushel) contains 18 *potter*, or Quarts

[DISTANCE]

1 Danish mile = 4 English miles
1 Iceland *Thingmannaleid* = 5 Danish
                          20 English

[ABBREVIATIONS]

Tde	Tonde
P^t	Pot
Oxh	Oxhoved
Kutt	Kutting
Skp	Ship-pund
lp	Lise-pund
p	pund
Al	Alen
Skpp	Skeppe

Articles of Dress used by the Women in Iceland

Horn or Cap	Skoit
Chain for the Neck	Hals-Festi
Chain for the Shoulders	Herda-Festi
The Broad Flat Ring, worn at the top of the Jacket	Krage
Jacket or Waistcoat	Troje
Corslet, commonly fastened to the top of the Petticoat	Upphluturs
The ornamented fastenings of the Corslet	Milnur
The Petticoat	Fat
The Petticoat with the Corslet fastened to it	Nærpils
Shift	Skirta
Apron	Svinta
Cloak	Hempa
Stockings	Sockar
Shoes	Skior
The Cloth laid on the bottom of the Shoes	Heppar
Garters	Sockabond

Current prices of Icelandic Produce (1810)

	skil	skil
1 Pair of Woollen Mittens	4	to 6
1 D° of Common Stockings	12	to 18
1 D° Fair Stockings	64	to 1 rix dol.
1 Woollen Waistcoat – ord^y	40	to 64
1 D° – fine	2rd	to 3rd

1 lb (pound) Wool	12	to 20
1 lb Eider Down	2rd48	to 3rd
1 lb Feathers	16	to 20
1 lb Tallow	16	to 22
1 Skippand Stock Fish	12rd	to 20rd
1 D° Salted Fish	15rd	to 30rd
1 Fox Skin	80	to 8rd
100 Swan-quills	2rd48	to 3rd
1 lb of Butter	10	to 28
A Horse	6rd	to 40rd
A Cow	16rd	to 24rd
Ewe with Lamb	2rd	to 2½rd
A Wether	2rd	to 5rd
A Lamb	80	to 1rd32

The circulating Medium in Iceland is the same as that employed in Denmark. Little specie, except of the lowest kind – ([?], *10 skilling, 8 skilling, 4 skilling, 2 skilling, & 1 skilling* pieces) is to be found in the circulation. A considerable number of specie dollars exist in the island – but are seldom seen; it being a practice with the farmers & others in the interior of the country to collect and preserve as many of these as possible. – The paper *rix-dollar* is much used in circulation. When we first arrived in Iceland, the rate of exchange was 6½ rix-dollars for a guinea – Afterwards we received for a guinea 8 and 10 dollars.

In the preceding Tables of Imports and Exports, it will be seen that a division is established of 4 *commercial districts* – viz. *Reikiavik, Eskifiord, Eyafiord* & *Isafiord*; under one or other of which are included all the different ports of the island. Previously to the establishment of the free trade of 1787, there were six of these districts – the Westmann Islands & Eyarback forming one in conjunction, which was called the *Westmann district*; and the several ports on the peninsula of Snæfield's Syssel being connected in another, called the *Grönnefiord district*. The Westmann district in 1787 was included in that of Reikiaviik – & a few years ago, the *district of Grönnefiord* was attached to that of Isafiord. According to present arrangements, the several trading stations in the island are thus distributed:

Reikiavik District	Reikiavik Havnefiord Kieblevik Eyarback Westmann Islands	Eskifiord District	Eskifiord Rutefiord Berufiord Vapnafiord	Eyafiord District	Eyafiord Husavik Siglefiord Hofsos Skagestrand	Isafiord District	Isafiord Patrexfiord Bildudald Olafsvig Grönnefiord Stikkesholm Stappen Buderstad
Southern		Eastern		Northern		Western	

This division is not merely a nominal one; certain regulations being established with respect to the arrival of merchant vessels in each district – A vessel coming from Denmark to the eastern side of the island, for example, visits all the several trading stations included under this district, but is not allowed to go to any of the harbours attached to the other districts – A corresponding division is made with respect to the *Burghership* or *Freedom of Iceland*: No one is permitted to establish himself as a merchant in Iceland, without being a Burgher of the particular district in which he settles – the number, situation & name of the *Burghs* being the same as those of the Commercial districts noticed above – This freedom is obtained without difficulty – generally by favour either of the Governor, or of one of the Sysselmen who officiate as Sherrifs at the different ports – with the expence to the merchant of only a few dollars to pay the expence of writings &c.

From the preceding Tables, it will be seen that the principal articles of export from Iceland are fish, oil, tallow, salted mutton, wool, & woollen goods. It will be observed too that the exportation of fish, salted & dried, is principally, indeed almost entirely, from the *Reikiavik* & *Isafiord* districts – the northern, eastern, & south eastern coasts of the island affording no productive fishery – The quantity of Oil is considerable in the *Eya-fiord* or Northern district, from the *district*, from the excellence both of the cod & shark fisheries on its coasts – Of tallow, salted mutton, wool and woollen goods, the export is most considerable from the northern ports – the pastures in this part of the island keeping a very great number of sheep – These likewise are the principal exports from the eastern or Eskifiord district.

APPENDIX F[HH]

[*The population of Iceland in 1801*]

Names of Districts	Number of farms	Families	Farmers	Hirelings having grass	Hirelings without grass	Priests	Civil Officers	Number of Men	Number of Women	Total
SOUTHERN AMT.										
East Skaptefield's Syssel	58	126	88	29	0	7	2	400	511	911
West Skaptefield's D°	133	248	214	26	1	8	1	678	861	1539
Rangaavalle & the Westmann Islands	374	664	530	104	13	14	4	1876	2311	4187
Arnes Syssel	418	709	495	153	40	21	1	2053	2572	4625
Guldbringe & Kiose Syssels	256	704	302	132	245	13	12	1949	2066	4015
Borger-fiords Syssel	227	285	250	9	11	9	4	854	1028	1882
WESTERN AMT.										
Myre and Hnappadals Syssels	180	235	202	13	9	9	2	694	784	1478
Snæfields Syssel	270	652	337	143	167	10	2	1627	1914	3541
Dale Syssel	181	231	208	10	4	7	3	699	893	1592
Bardæstrands Syssel	203	374	332	12	21	10	2	1161	1332	2493
Western Isafiords	123	261	236	5	13	7	0	884	966	1850
Northern Isafiords	170	305	255	20	22	7	1	961	1076	2037
Strande Syssel	118	150	140	3	0	6	1	438	544	982
NORTHERN & EASTERN AMT.										
Hunevatns Syssel	375	433	405	3	6	20	2	1288	1592	2880
Skagefiords Syssel	412	492	459	9	2	20	3	1385	1756	3141
Oefiords [Ed: Eyjafjarðarsýsla] Syssel	448	535	499	6	1	17	3	1572	1881	3453
Norder Syssel	387	451	420	1	7	23	1	1337	1665	3002
Norder Mule Syssel	217	267	222	32	3	11	1	781	1981[1]	1762
Southern Mule Syssel	211	279	231	25	13	12	0	839	998	1837
	4761	7401	5821[2]	735	590	231	45	21,476	25,731	47,207

[1] Magnús Stephensen, 1808, p. 270 reads 981.

[2] Magnús Stephensen, 1808, p. 270 reads 5825.

The population of Iceland was in

1703	50,444
1770	46,201
1783	47,287
1801	47,207
1804	46,349
1808	48,063

This Table, shewing the Population of Iceland in 1801 is taken from the Register of the Revd Bishop Geir Vidalin. The original table, as published by the Bishop, & afterwards inserted in the Danish Edition of *Atastrood Stephansen's 18th Century*, contains also the detailed statement of the ages of the whole population of the island, of which the following is the general result.

	Males	Females
Below 10 years of age	6231	6300
From 11 to 20	3207	3299
From 21 to 30	3385	4060
From 31 to 40	3190	3901
From 41 to 50	1838	2453
From 51 to 60	1707	2460
From 61 to 70	1162	1842
From 71 to 80	592	1096
From 81 to 90	158	285
From 91 to 100	6	35
Total	21476	25731

From these documents it appears that the excess in the female population of the Island is very considerable; and further that the average longevity of the women is much greater than that of the male population. It will also be seen that the number of people in Iceland has little varied during the last 100 years.

APPENDIX G

Glossary of the principal geological terms used in the Journal

AGATE
    A striped chalcedony. Obsidian was known as Iceland Agate. Chalcedony is not now a formal mineral, but a general term for crypto-crystalline silica.

AMYGDALOIDAL LAVA
    Lava with vesicles (gas bubbles) filled by such minerals as zeolite and calcite.

BARYTES
    Barium sulphate.

BASALT
    Fine grained (sometimes glassy) basic igneous rock. By far the most common igneous rock.

CALC
    Calcite: Calcium carbonate.

CHALCEDONY
    A very fine-grained glassy crypto-crystalline silica. See AGATE.

CONGLOMERATE
    A term used in the early nineteenth century for any mixture of rounded rock materials cemented together. HH's examples are now called agglomerate – accumulations of fragments of volcanic rock of larger size than 2 cm.

FELSPAR
    Now Feldspar. The most important family of the silicate rock-forming minerals.

FLOETZ
    See TRAP.

FRIABLE
    Easy to crumble.

GLANCE
    A term for minerals with high lustre and commonly applied specifically to zinc sulphide (zinc blende or sphalerite).

GNEISS — Coarse-grained banded rocks, of metamorphic origin, commonly of granitic type.

GREENSTONE — A former name for all dark greenish igneous rocks now called diorites, dolerites, etc. The green colour is due to the presence of chlorite, hornblende and epidote.

HÆMATITE — An iron oxide ore.

INDURATED — Hardened.

JASPER — A red chalcedony. The redness is a very fine grained iron oxide disseminated through the chalcedony.

LYDIAN STONE — A fine-grained black silicate.

MICACEOUS SANDSTONE — A sandstone, containing mica, a thin platy silicate mineral giving a strong reflective lustre.

OBSIDIAN — A black, wholly glassy, igneous rock.

OLIVINE — Olive-green silicate minerals of iron and magnesium. A mineral family.

PEARLSTONE — A variety of obsidian.

PITCHSTONE — A glassy and igneous rock, often banded due to partial devitrification.

PORPHYRY — A name given to any igneous rock, containing relatively large crystals of any mineral in a fine-grained matrix.

PUMICE — Vesicular volcanic rock froth, from acidic lavas, with a low density because of its being full of air bubbles.

PYRITES (IRON) — Iron sulphide.

QUARTZ — Hard, fine-grained silica mineral often found in igneous rocks.

SCHISTOSE — Recrystallised, and then foliated. The folia are often folded.

SCORIÆ — Ejected volcanic fragments formed on exposure to air and of higher density than Pumice; these are cooled during initial eruption, but are still sufficiently soft when they fall to flatten and distend before they cool completely.

SLATY A rock that splits readily into thin sheets.

SPAR A term for any lustrous, easily cleaved mineral. Iceland Spar is the varietal name given to crystalline $CaCo_3$.

STEATITE Soap stone; a stone whose major constituent is the soft mineral Talc, from which Talcum powder is made.

TRAP Used in the early nineteenth century as a term for all igneous rocks other than granite. Primitive Trap was stratigraphically distinguished from Floetz Trap. The former was thought to form steep, conical hills, and was characterised by the presence of the black/greenish-black mineral hornblende; the latter, more recently formed, tended to occur at the foot of Primitive mountains. The term Floetz was applied at the same period to a whole range of such older, flat-lying rocks.

TUFF Soft, porous, consolidated volcanic ash.

WHIN-STONE A common term for fine-grained, hard, igneous rocks.

SELECT BIBLIOGRAPHY

A. MANUSCRIPT SOURCES

Bodleian Library, Oxford
 MS Douce d.23
 MSS Icel. e.2, e.3, g.1.
 MSS Junius 36, 120
 MS Marshall 80
 MS Montagu d.7

Bristol Record Office
 Bristol Library Society, Committee Minute Books, 155–6.

Bristol Central Library
 Bristol Library Society, Borrowing Records, MSS B 7473–85.

British Library
 MSS Additional 8100, 33982, 38356
 MSS Egerton 2066–8

British Museum (Natural History), Department of Mineralogy Library
 MSS of 1811–12 mineralogical papers of Richard Bright and Henry Holland.

Cheshire County Record Office
 MS DSA 7/3

David Holland Esq.
 Correspondence of Henry Holland and Maria Edgeworth

Huntington Library, San Marino, California
 MS Larpent LA 1751

John Rylands Library, Manchester
 MS JRL 722

Landsbókasafn Íslands, Reykjavík
 MSS Lbs 30 folio, 342 c folio, 604 folio

MSS Lbs 848 4to, 979 4to, 984 4to, 1150 4to, 3875–6 4to, 4275 4to, 4925 4to.

MSS Lbs 1249 8vo, 1754 8vo
MS Varia VI (þjóðskjalasafn)

National Library of Scotland
MSS 673, 3278, Accession 7515

Royal Botanical Gardens, Kew
Banks Correspondence: MSS B.C. 1: 18–19, 32, 34, 42
MSS B.C. 2: 334–6
Hooker Correspondence: Australian letters, 1834–51 (LXXII)
: New Zealand, Australian and Tasmanian letters, 1835–43 (LXXIII, LXXVI).

Rigsarkivet, Copenhagen
Ges.Ark.London III, Indkomme skrivelser fra Dept. f.u.Anl. 1814–17
Korres. Litr.I: Island og Færøerne 1758–1846.

Sorøe Academisk Bibliotek
Thorkelín correspondence

B. PRINTED SOURCES

Adeane, Jane H.   The early married life of Maria Josepha, Lady Stanley. London, 1900.
Anderson, Johann   Nachrichten von Island, Grönland, und der Strasse Davis. Hamburg, 1746.
Anna Agnarsdóttir   'Ráðagerðir um innlimun Íslands í Bretaveldi á árunum 1785–1815', Saga: tímarit sögufélags, XVII (1979), 5–58.
Arngrímur Jónsson   Brevis commentarius de Islandia (1593) in Hakluyt, 1598–1600, I, 515–50.
A briefe commentarie on Island (1593) in Hakluyt, 1598–1600, I, 550–91.
Bartholinus, Thomas   Antiquitatem Danicarum de causis contemptæ a Danis adhuc gentilibus mortis. Copenhagen, 1689.
Barrow, John   A visit to Iceland by way of Tronyem in the 'Flower of Yarrow' yacht, 1834. London, 1835.
Batten, Charles L.   Pleasurable instruction: form and convention in eighteenth century travel literature. Berkeley, 1978.

Beck, Richard   Jón Þorláksson: Icelandic translator of Pope and
                         Milton. Studia Islandica, XVI (1957).
Benedikz, Benedikt S.   Studia centenalia in honorem memoriæ Benedikt S.
   (ed.)   Þórarinsson. Reykjavík, 1961.
                         Iceland. Amsterdam, 1969 (in The spread of printing,
                         series editor Colin Clair).
                         'Grímur Thorkelín, the University of St
                         Andrews and Codex Scardensis', Scandinavian
                         Studies, XLII (1970), 385–93.
Bennett, J. A. W.   'Hickes's Thesaurus: a study in Oxford book-
                         production', English Studies, New Series 1 (1948),
                         28–45.
Bjarni Jónsson   Íslenzkir Hafnarstúdentar. Akureyri, 1949.
Björn Þorsteinsson   'Henry VIII and Iceland', Saga-Book of the Viking
                         Society, XV (1957–61), 67–101.
                         Enska öldin í sögu Íslendinga. Reykjavík, 1970.
Bogi Benediktsson   Sýslumannaæfir. 5 vols. Reykjavík, 1881–1932.
Briem, Helgi P.   Sjálfstæði Íslands, 1809. Reykjavík, 1936.
                         Byltingin, 1809. Reykjavík, 1936.
Bright, Pamela   Dr. Richard Bright 1789–1858. London, 1983.
Brougham, Henry Lord   The life and times of Henry Lord Brougham. 3 vols.
                         London, 1871.
Browne, Sir Thomas   Works, ed. G. Keynes. Revised edition. 4 vols.
                         London, 1964.
[Campbell, John]   The polite correspondence, or rational amusement.
                         London, [1741]; revised edition, 1754.
Carus-Wilson, E. M.   Medieval merchant venturers. London, 1954; second
                         edition, 1967.
Challinor, John   A dictionary of geology. Cardiff, 1961; sixth edition,
                         1986.
Chitnis, Anand C.   'The University of Edinburgh's natural history
                         museum and the Huttonian–Wernerian debate',
                         Annals of Science, 26 (1970), 85–94.
                         The Scottish enlightenment: a social history. London,
                         1976.
Cottle, Amos   Icelandic poetry; or the Edda of Sæmund, translated
                         into English verse. Bristol, 1797.
Cowan, Edward J.   Icelandic studies in eighteenth and nineteenth century
                         Scotland. Studia Islandica, 31 (1972), 109–51.

Cowper, William Poetic works, ed. H. S. Milford and Norma Russell. Revised fourth edition. Oxford, 1967.

Coxe, William Travels in Poland, Russia, Sweden and Denmark. 3 vols. London, 1784.

Davies, G. L. The earth in decay: a history of British geomorphology 1578–1878. London, 1969.

Dawson, Warren R. The Banks letters: a calendar of the manuscript correspondence. London, 1958.

'Supplementary letters of Sir Joseph Banks', Bulletin of the British Museum (Natural History), Historical series, III (1962–9), 43–93.

Defoe, Daniel The life and strange surprizing adventures of Robinson Crusoe, of York, mariner, ed. J. Donald Crowley. Oxford, 1972.

Downman, Hugh Poems. Second edition. Exeter, 1790.

Dryden, John and Tonson, Jacob The sixth part of poetical miscellanies. 6 vols. London, 1716.

[various editors] Edda Sæmundar hinns fróda. 3 vols. Copenhagen, 1787–1828.

Eldjarn, Kristján 'Myndir af Skálholtsbiskupum', Árbók Hins íslenzka fornleifafélags (1968), 79–107.

'Legsteinn Páls Stígssonar og steinsmiðurinn Hans Maler', Árbók Hins íslenzka fornleifafélags (1978), 83–90.

Eggert Ólafsson and Bjarni Pálsson Reise igiennem Island. 2 vols. Sorøe, 1772.
Travels in Iceland. London, 1805.

Einar Haukur Kristjánsson Lysing Snæfellsnes frá löngufjörum að Ólafsvíkurenni, Ferðafélags Íslands: Árbók (1982).

Elsa E. Guðjónsson 'Fjórar myndir af íslenska vefstaðnum', Árbok Hins íslenzka fornleifafélags (1977), 125–34.

Fairer, David 'Anglo-Saxon studies', in The history of the University of Oxford, Vol. 5 The eighteenth century, eds. L. S. Sutherland and L. G. Mitchell (Oxford, 1986), pp. 807–29.

Fallowes, E. H. [et al.] (eds) English madrigal verse 1588–1632. Third edition. Oxford, 1967.

Farley, Frank E. Scandinavian influence in the English romantic movement. Cambridge, Massachusetts, 1903.

Finnur Jónsson Historia ecclesiastica Islandiæ. 4 vols. Copenhagen, 1772–8.

Finnur Sigmundsson (ed.) — Sendibréf frá íslenskum konum, 1784–1900. Reykjavík, 1952.

(ed.) — Geir biskup góði í vinarbréfum, 1790–1823. Reykjavík, 1966.

Fussell, Paul — The rhetorical world of Augustan humanism. Oxford, 1965.

Galbraith, Georgina (ed.) — The journal of the Rev. William Bagshaw Stevens. Oxford, 1965.

Collected poems of the Reverend William Bagshaw Stevens. London, 1971.

Gilpin, Thomas — Three essays. London, 1792.

Gjerset, Knut — A history of Iceland. London [1923].

Greenway, John L. — The golden horns: mythic imagination and the Nordic past. Athens, Georgia, 1977.

Grimble, Ian — 'Holland's Iceland journal', The Norseman, IX (1951), 163–71.

Guthrie, D. J. — A history of medicine. London, 1945.

Guðmundur Kjartansson — Hekla. Ferðafélags Íslands: Árbók (1945).

Guðmundur Pétursson (ed.) — Víga-Glúms saga. Copenhagen, 1786.

Guðni Jónsson (ed.) — Grettis saga Ásmundarsonar. Íslensk fornrit, VII, Reykjavík, 1936.

Hakluyt, Richard — The principal navigations, voiages, traffiques and discoveries of the English nation. 3 vols. London, 1598–1600.

Halldór Hermannsson — The periodical literature of Iceland down to the year 1874. Islandica, XI (1918).

Sir Joseph Banks and Iceland. Islandica, XVIII (1928).

Hannes Finnsson (ed.) — Kristni saga. Copenhagen, 1773.

Hannes Þorsteinsson — 'Benedikt Jónsson Gröndal: yfirdómari og skald 1760–1825', Skírnir, XCIX (1925), 65–106.

Haraldur Sigurðsson — Kortsaga Íslands. 2 vols. Reykjavík, 1971–8.

Harris, Richard L. — 'William Morris, Eiríkur Magnússon and Iceland: a survey of correspondence', Victorian Poetry, 13 (1975), 119–30.

'George Hickes, White Kennett and the inception of the Thesaurus linguarum septentrionalium', Bodleian Library Record, XI (1983), 169–86.

Henderson, Ebenezer   *Iceland: or the journal of a residence in that island, during the years 1814 and 15.* 2 vols. in 1. Edinburgh, 1818.

Herbert, William   *Works.* 2 vols., London, 1804–6, I.

Hickes, George   *Linguarum veterum septentrionalium thesaurus grammatico-criticus et archæologicus.* 2 vols. Oxford, 1703–5.

Hill, Brian   ' "More fashionable than scientific": Sir Henry Holland Bt., M.D., F.R.C.P., F.R.S.', *The Practitioner,* CCXL (1973), 548–54.

Hill, G. B. and Powell, L. F. (eds)   *Boswell's Life of Johnson.* 6 vols. Oxford, 1934.

Hole, Richard   'The tomb of Gunnar', *Gentleman's Magazine,* LIX (1789), 937.

Holland, Henry   *General view of the agriculture of Cheshire.* London, 1808.

De morbis Islandiæ. Edinburgh, 1811.

Travels in the Ionian Isles, Albania, Thessaly, Macedonia etc. during the years 1812 and 1813. London, 1815.

Chapters on mental physiology. London, 1858.

Essays on scientific and other subjects. London, 1862.

Recollections of past life. London, 1872.

Fragmentary papers. ed. F. J. Holland. London, 1875.

Hooker, William Jackson   *Journal of a tour in Iceland in the summer of 1809.* Yarmouth: privately published, 1811; second edition, 2 vols, 1813.

Horrebow, Niels   *Tilforladelige efterretninger om Island.* [Copenhagen], 1752.

The natural history of Iceland. London, 1758.

Indriði Einarsson   *Síðasti Víkingurinn eða Jörgen Jörgensen.* Reykjavík, 1936.

Jameson, Robert   *Elements of geognesy.* 3 vols. Edinburgh, 1804–8.

Johnson, Samuel   *A journey to the Western Islands of Scotland* (1775), ed. J. D. Fleeman. Oxford, 1985.

Johnson, W. G.   *James Thomson's influence on Swedish literature in the eighteenth century.* Urbana, 1936.

Johnstone, James   *Antiquitates celto-scandicæ.* Copenhagen, 1786.

Jón Árnason   *Íslenzkar þjóðsögur og ævintýri.* 2 vols. Leipzig, 1862–4; revised second edition, 6 vols, Reykjavík, 1954–61.

Jón Espólín	*Íslands árbækur í sögu-formi.* 13 parts in 3 vols. Copenhagen, 1821–55.
Jón Helgason	*Borgarfjarðarsýsla sunnan Skarðsheiðar. Ferðafélag Íslands: Árbók* (1950).
Jón Helgason	*Ritgerðakorn og ræðustúfar.* Reykjavík, 1959.
Jón Þorkelsson	*Saga Jörundar Hundadagakóngs.* Copenhagen, 1892.
Jón Þorláksson	*Tilraun ad snúa á Islendsku Pópes Tilraun um manninn.* Leirárgarðar, 1798.
Kark, Robert M. and Moore, David T.	'The life, work and geological collection of Richard Bright, M.D., 1789–1858', *Archives for Natural History*, X (1981), 119–51.
Klemens Jónsson	*Saga Reykjavíkur.* Reykjavík, 1929.
Kliger, Samuel	'The "Goths" in England: an introduction to the Gothic vogue in eighteenth-century aesthetic discourse', *Modern Philology*, 43 (1945), 107–17.
Landor, Walter Savage	*The complete works,* ed. T. E. Welby and S. Wheeler. 16 vols. London, 1927–36.
Lonsdale, Roger (ed.)	*The poems of Gray, Collins and Goldsmith.* London, 1969.
McKay, Derek	'Great Britain and Iceland in 1809', *Mariner's Mirror*, LIX, 1973, 85–95.
Mackenzie, Sir George S.	*Travels in the island of Iceland, during the summer of the year 1810.* Edinburgh, 1811.
	Second edition, Edinburgh, 1812.
	Revised edition, Edinburgh, 1842.
McKillop, Alan	'A critic of 1741 on early poetry', *Studies in Philology*, 30 (1933), 504–21.
Mackintosh, W. R.	*Glimpses of Kirkwall and its people in the olden times.* Kirkwall, 1887.
Mallet, Paul Henri	*Introduction á l'histoire de Dannemarc.* Copenhagen, 1755.
Manntal á Íslandi 1801	3 vols. Reykjavík, 1978–80.
Marshall, Roderick	*William Morris and his early paradise.* London, 1979.
Marwick, H.	' "A description of Orkney (1773)": an account of an unpublished manuscript of Rev. George Low, Minister of Birsay, 1774–1795', *Proceedings of the Orkney Antiquarian Society*, II (1923–4), 49–58.

Mathias, T. J.   Runic odes imitated from the Norse tongue in the
                        manner of Mr. Gray. London, 1781.
Miles, Pliny   Norðurfari, or rambles in Iceland. London, 1854.
Morgan, Paul   'Bundið fyrir Íslending: Guðbrandsbíblia í
                        Hafnarbandi', Landsbókasafn Íslands: Árbók
                        (1974), pp. 113–17.
Morris, William   Poems by the way. London, [1891].
                        Journals of travel in Iceland 1871, 1873. London,
                        1911.
Nashe, Thomas   Works. Revised edition, ed. Ronald B. McKerrow
                        and F. P. Wilson. 5 vols. Oxford, 1958.
Olavius, Ólafur   Oeconomisk reise igiennem de nordvestlige, nordlige og
                        nordostlige kanter af Island. 2 vols. Copenhagen,
                        1780.
Ólafur Þorvaldsson   'Fornar slóðir milli Krísuvíkur og Hafnarf-
                        jarðar', Árbók Hins íslenzka fornleifafélags (1943–
                        8).
Omberg, Margaret   Scandinavian themes in English poetry 1760–1800.
                        Uppsala, 1976.
Páll Eggert Ólason   Íslenzkar æviskrár. 6 vols. Reykjavík, 1948–76.
Percy, Thomas   Five pieces of runic poetry. London, 1763.
                        Northern antiquities, 2 vols. London, 1770.
                        Revised I. A. Blackwell. London, 1847.
Phelps, Samuel   A treatise on the importance of extending the British
                        fisheries. London, 1817.
Pinkerton, John   A general collection of the best and most interesting
                        voyages and travels in all parts of the world. 17 vols.
                        London, 1804–18. I.
Pjetur Guðmundsson   Annáll nítjándu aldar. 3 vols. Akureyri, 1912–34.
  (ed.)
Polwhele, Richard   Poems, chiefly by gentlemen of Devonshire and
                        Cornwall. Bath, 1792.
Porter, Roy   The making of geology: earth science in Britain 1660–
                        1815. Cambridge, 1977.
Powell, G. E. J. and   Icelandic legends. London, 1864.
  Eiríkur Magnússon
  (trans.)
Price, L. M.   English literature in Germany. University of Califor-
                        nia publications in Modern Philology, 37 (Berkeley,
                        1953).

Rauschenberg, Roy | 'The journals of Sir Joseph Banks's voyage up Great Britain's west coast to Iceland and to the Orkney Isles, July to October, 1772', *Proceedings of the American Philosophical Society*, CXVII (1973), 186–226.

Rodgers, Betsy | *Georgian chronicle: Mrs. Barbauld and her family*. London, 1958.

Rudwick, M. J. S. | 'Hutton and Werner compared: George Greenough's geological tour of Scotland', *British Journal of the History of Science*, 1 (1962–3), 117–35.
'The foundations of the Geological Society of London', *British Journal of the History of Science*, 1 (1962–3), 325–55.

Runólfur Jónsson | *Grammaticæ Islandicæ rudimenta*. Copenhagen, 1651.

Ryan, A. N. | 'The causes of the British attack on Copenhagen in 1807', *English Historical Review*, LXVIII (1953), 37–55.

Sayers, Frank | *Dramatic sketches of Northern mythology*. Norwich, 1790.

Scott, Sir Walter | *Letters*, ed. Sir Herbert Grierson, 12 vols. London, 1932–7.

Seaton, Ethel | *Literary relations of England and Scandinavia in the seventeenth century*. Oxford, 1935.

Seward, Anna | *The poetical works*, ed. Sir Walter Scott, 3 vols. Edinburgh, 1810.

[Shelton, Maurice] (trans.) | *Wotton's short view of G. Hickes's grammatico-critical and archaeological treasure of the ancient northern-languages*. London, 1735.

Sigurður Magnússon | *Northern sphinx: Iceland and the Icelanders from the settlement to the present*. London, 1977.

Sigurdur Thorarinsson | *Hekla: a notorious volcano*, trans. Jóhann Hannesson and Pétur Karlsson. Reykjavík, 1970.

Skagan, Jón | *Saga Hlíðarenda í Fljótshlíð*. Reykjavík, 1973.

Stafford, Barbara M. | *Voyage into substance: art, science and the illustrated travel account 1760–1840*. Cambridge, Mass., 1984.

Stanley, John Thomas | 'An account of the hot springs near Rykum'; 'An account of the hot springs near Haukadal in Iceland', *Transactions of the Royal Society of Edinburgh*, III (1794), 127–37; 138–53.

Stefán Einarsson	*A history of Icelandic literature*. Baltimore, 1957.
Steindór Steindórsson	*Dagbók í Íslandsferð eftir Henry Holland*. Reykjavík, 1960.
	Íslandsleiðangur Stanleys 1789. Reykjavík, 1979.
Stephensen, Magnús	*Kort beskrivelse over den nye vulcans ildsprudning i Vester-Skaptefields-Syssel paa Island i aaret 1783*. Copenhagen, 1785.
	Eptirmæli átjándu aldar. Leirárgarðar, 1806.
	Island i det attende aarhundrede: historisk-politisk skildret. Copenhagen, 1808.
	Instrúx fyrir hreppstjórnar-menn á Islandi. Leirárgarðar, 1810.
	Minning frur stiptamtmannsinnu Sigríðar Magnúsdóttir Stephensen. Leirárgarðar, 1810.
	Hentug handbók fyrir hvörn mann. Leirárgarðar, 1812.
Stephensen, Marta María	*Einfaldt matreiðslu vasa-quer*. Leirárgarðar, 1800.
Sterling, Joseph	*Poems*. Dublin, 1782.
Stevens, William Bagshaw	*Poems, consisting of Indian odes and miscellaneous pieces*. Oxford, 1775.
Sveinbjörn Rafnsson	*Frásögur um fornaldarleifar 1817–23*. 2 vols. Reykjavík, 1983.
Sveinn Níelsson	*Presta tal og prófasta á Íslandi*. Copenhagen, 1869; second edition, Reykjavík, 1949–51.
Temple, William	*Miscellanea: the second part*. London, 1690.
Thompson, J. H.	*Napoleon Bonaparte: his rise and fall*. Oxford, 1952.
Townson, Robert	*The philosophy of mineralogy*. London, 1798.
Torrens, H. S.	'Arthur Aikin's mineralogical survey of Shropshire 1796–1816 and the contemporary audience for geology', *BJHS*, 15–16 (1982–3), 111–53.
Trausti Ólafsson (trans.)	*Íslandskóngur: sjálfsævisaga Jörundar hundadagakonungs*. Reykjavík, 1974.
Tucker, Susie I.	'Scandinavica for the eighteenth-century reader', *Saga-Book of the Viking Society*, XVI (1962–5), 233–47.
Þór Magnússon	'Skyrsla um Þjóðminjarsafn Íslands 1976', *Árbók Hins íslenzka Fornleifafélags* (1977).
Þorkell Grímsson	'Gert við Snorralaug', *Árbók Hins íslenzka fornleifafélags* (1960), 19–45.

Þorkell Jóhannesson	'Magnús Stephensen', *Skírnir*, CVII (1933), 166–93. *Merkir Íslendingar*. 6 vols. Reykjavík, 1947–57.
Verelius, Olaus	*Hervarer saga*. Uppsala, 1672.
von Troil, Uno	*Bref rörande en rese til Island MDCCLXXII*. Uppsala, 1777. *Letters on Iceland*. Dublin, 1780. *Letters on Iceland*. Revised edition in Pinkerton, 1808, I.
Warner, Sir George	*Libelle of Englyshe Polycye* [1436]. Oxford, 1926.
Wawn, Andrew	'John Thomas Stanley and Iceland: the sense and sensibility of an eighteenth-century explorer', *Scandinavian Studies*, 53 (1981), 52–76. *'Gunnlaugs saga ormstungu* and the Theatre Royal, Edinburgh: melodrama, mineralogy and Sir George Mackenzie', *Scandinavica*, 21 (1982), 139–51. 'Hundadagadrottningin. Bréf frá Íslandi: Guðrún Johnsen og Stanleysfjölskyldan frá Cheshire, 1814–16', *Saga: tímarit sögufélags*, 23 (1985), 97–133.
West, John F.	*The journals of the Stanley expedition to the Faroe islands and Iceland in 1789*. 3 vols. Tórshavn, 1970–6.
Whitten, D. G. A. and Brooks, J. R. V.	*The Penguin dictionary of geology*. London, 1972.
Williams, W.	'The Hervarer Saga. A Gothic Ode', *Gentleman's Magazine*, LX (1790), 844.
Worm, Ole	*Antiquitates Danica*. Copenhagen, 1651.
Young, Edward	*Klagen, oder Nachgedanken*. 2 vols. in 4. Brunswick, 1762–9.

INDEX